#71 Attack Fleet One's Call

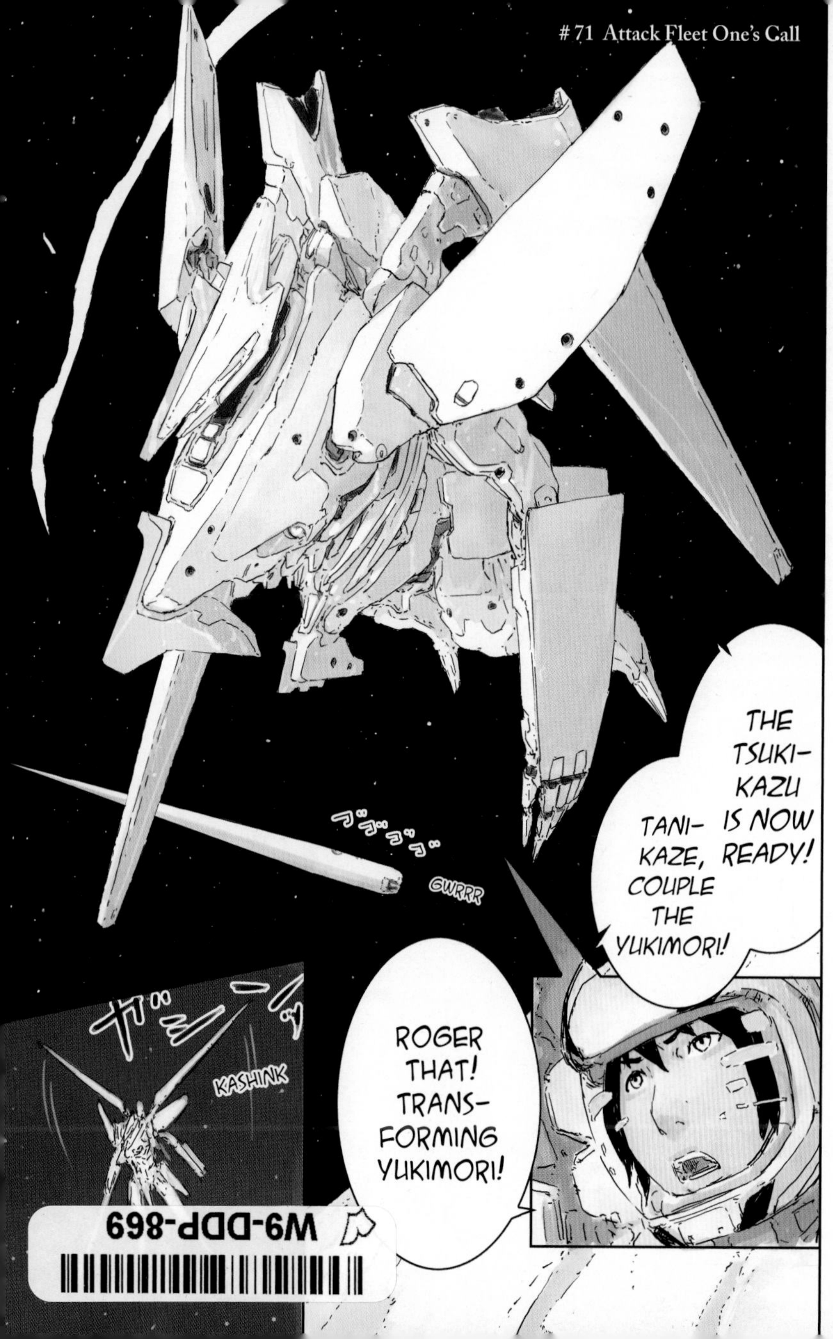
THE TSUKI-KAZU IS NOW READY!
TANI-KAZE, COUPLE THE YUKIMORI!
GWRRR
ROGER THAT! TRANS-FORMING YUKIMORI!
KASHINK

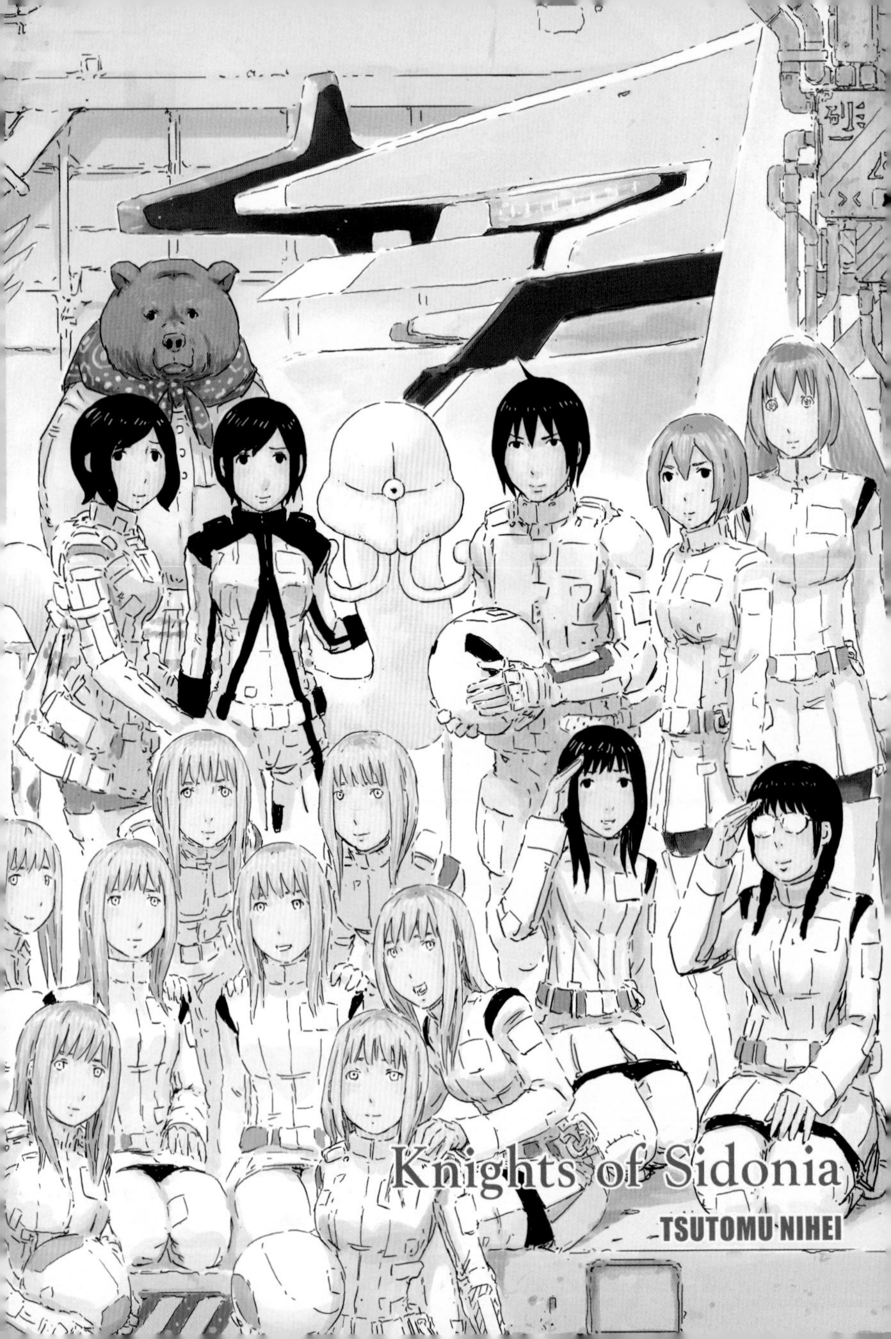
Knights of Sidonia
TSUTOMU NIHEI

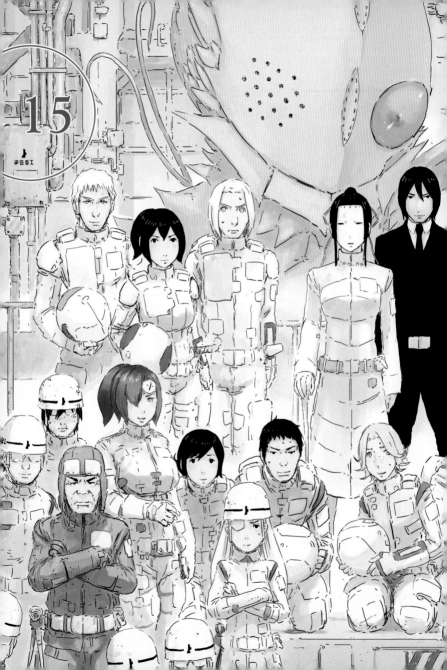

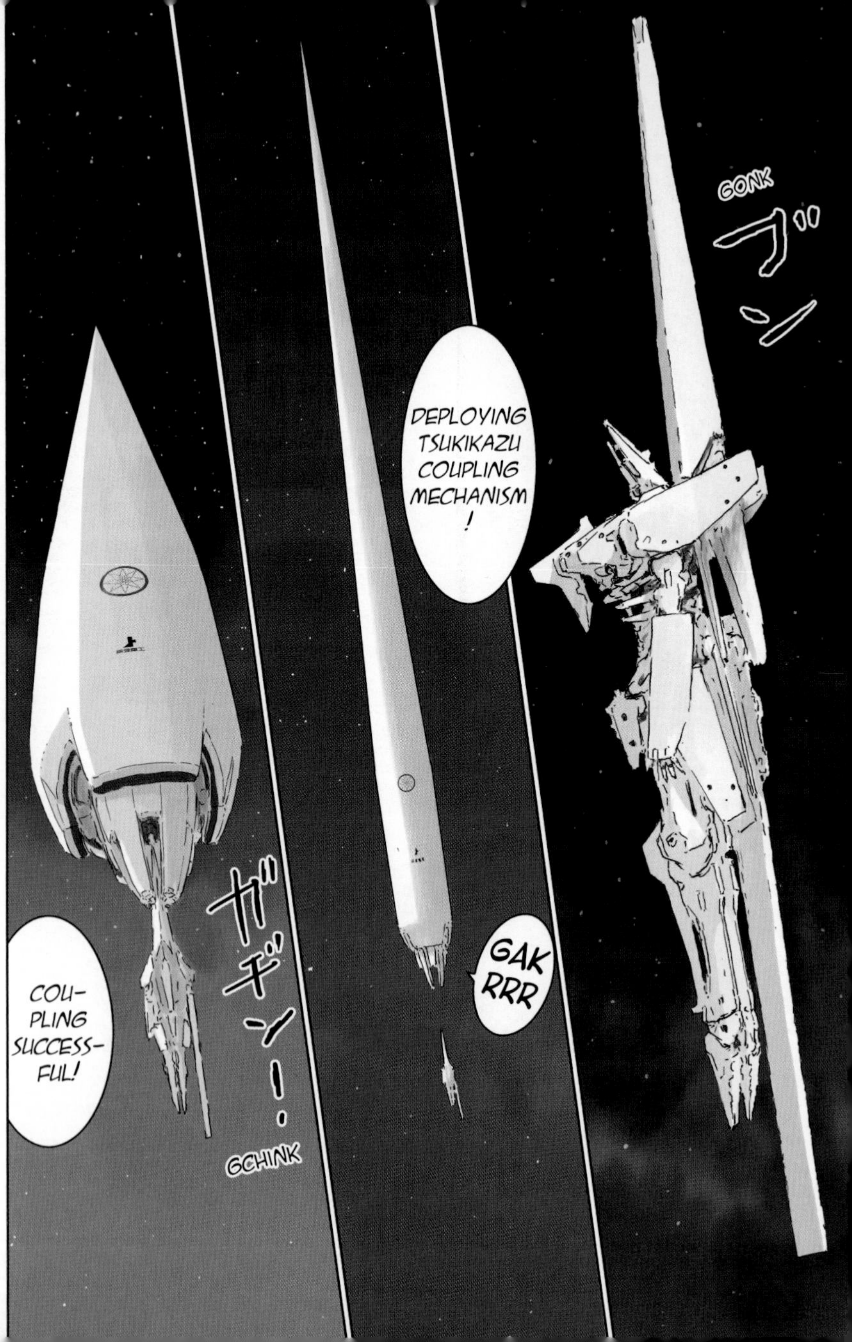
GONK
ブン
DEPLOYING TSUKIKAZU COUPLING MECHANISM!
GAK RRR
ガギンー!
GCHINK
COU-PLING SUCCESS-FUL!

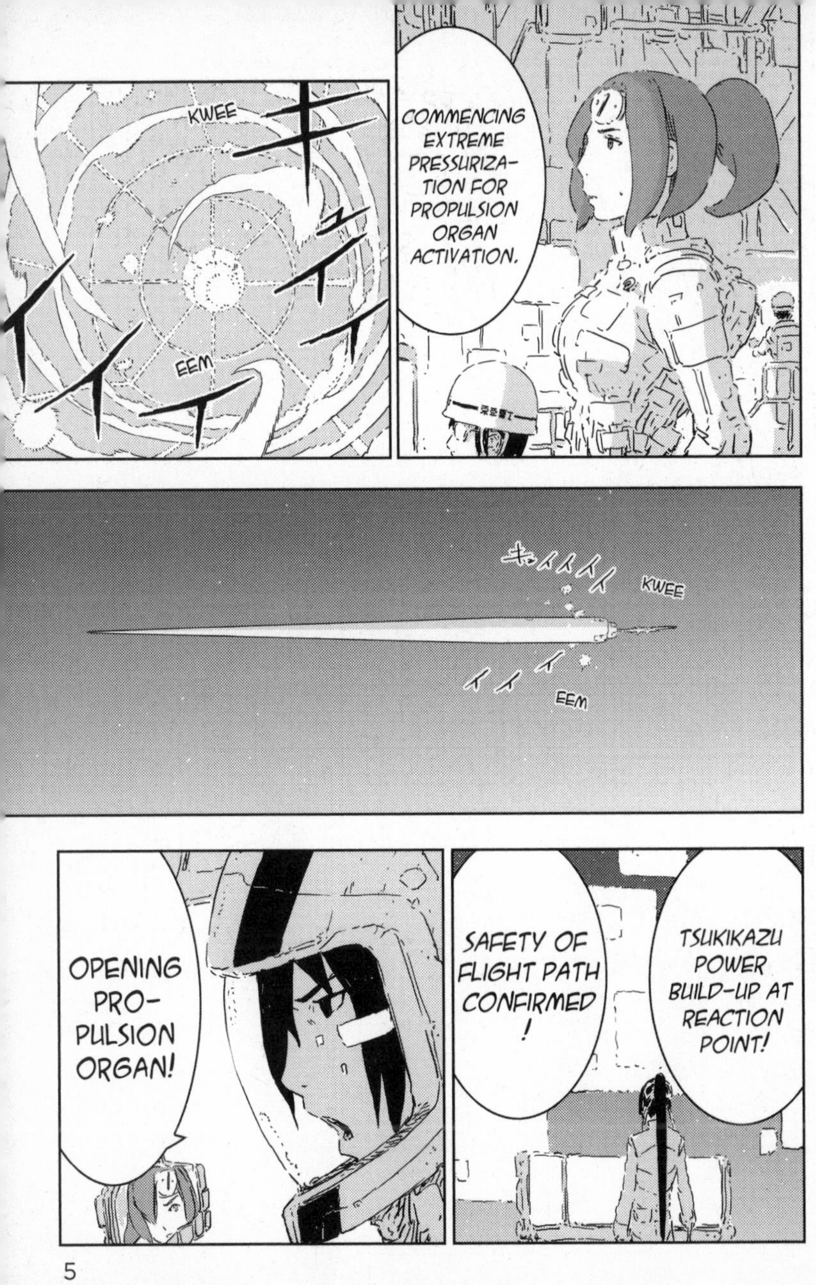
COMMENCING EXTREME PRESSURIZA-TION FOR PROPULSION ORGAN ACTIVATION.
KWEE
EEM
KWEE
EEM
TSUKIKAZU POWER BUILD-UP AT REACTION POINT!
SAFETY OF FLIGHT PATH CONFIRMED!
OPENING PRO-PULSION ORGAN!

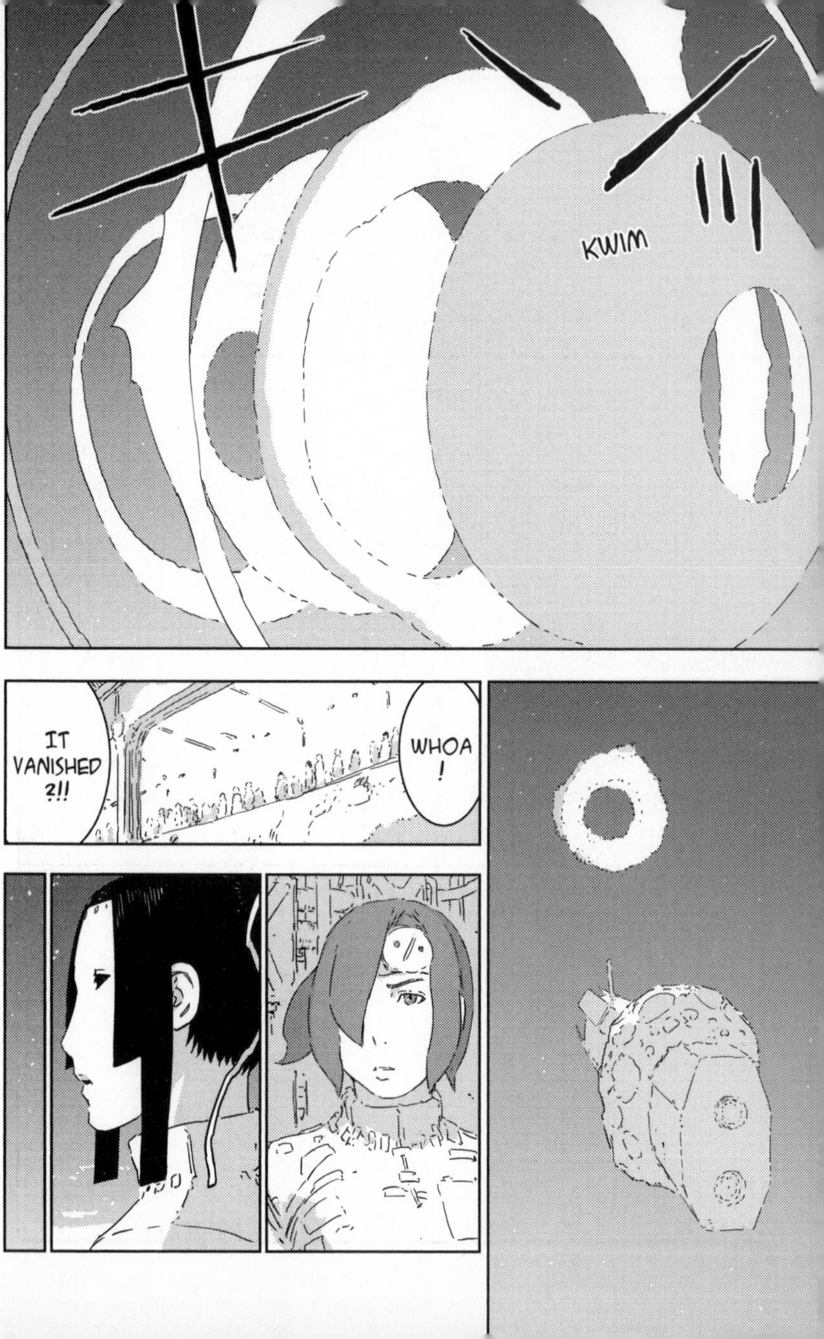
KWIM
WHOA !
IT VANISHED ?!!

ATTACK FLEET ONE, IN THE VICINITY OF THE STAR LEM
ATTACK FLEET ONE
THE CLUSTER SHIP FLEET WILL REACH US IN TEN MINUTES!
ALL SHIPS REPO-SITION QUICKLY!
CAPTAIN MIDORIKAWA, HAVE THEM GET IN LINE WITH THE AXIS OF THE GRAVITON RADIAL EMITTER AS MUCH AS POSSIBLE.
BIP
GRAVITON RADIAL EMITTER: RECONFIGURING
MIZUKI 9

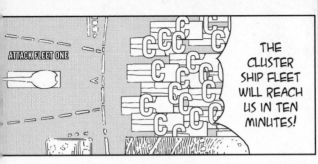

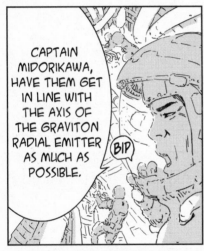

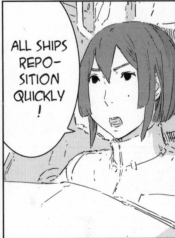

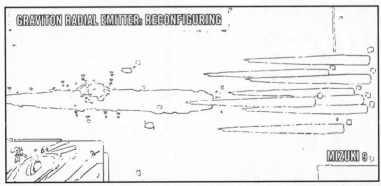

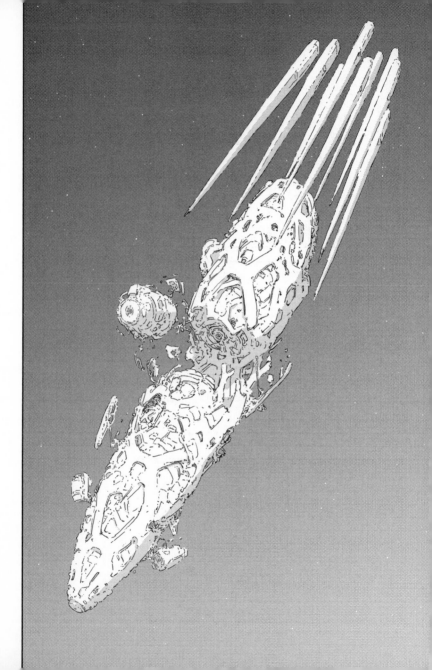

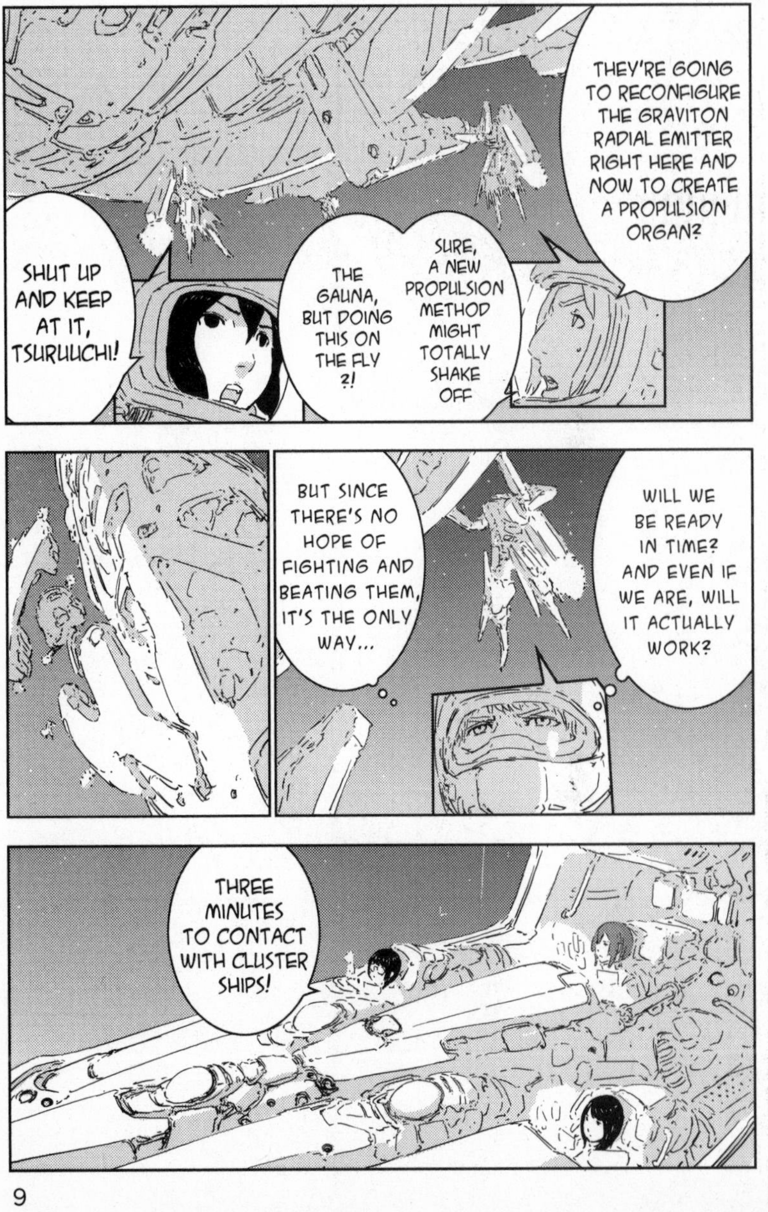
THEY'RE GOING TO RECONFIGURE THE GRAVITON RADIAL EMITTER RIGHT HERE AND NOW TO CREATE A PROPULSION ORGAN?
SURE, A NEW PROPULSION METHOD MIGHT TOTALLY SHAKE OFF
THE GAUNA, BUT DOING THIS ON THE FLY ?!
SHUT UP AND KEEP AT IT, TSURUUCHI!
WILL WE BE READY IN TIME? AND EVEN IF WE ARE, WILL IT ACTUALLY WORK?
BUT SINCE THERE'S NO HOPE OF FIGHTING AND BEATING THEM, IT'S THE ONLY WAY...
THREE MINUTES TO CONTACT WITH CLUSTER SHIPS!

ACTIVATE ORGAN!
MR. TANBA?! HANG ON A MINUTE!!
THE FLOW CHANNEL ISN'T ATTACHED YET!!
THERE'S NO TIME LEFT! WE'LL OPEN THE HIGGS FLOW CHANNEL IN STAGES AS THE WORK PROGRESSES!!
ヴ
VWM
ゴウウウウン
GWOMM
キュイイイ..
KWEEE

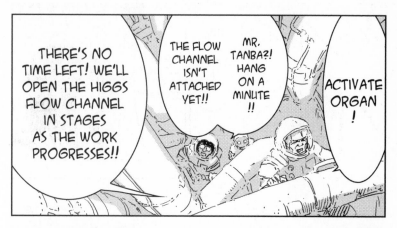

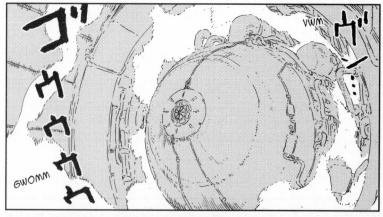

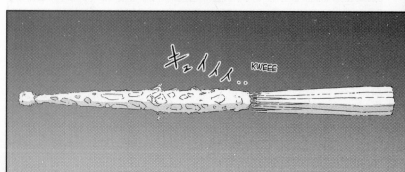

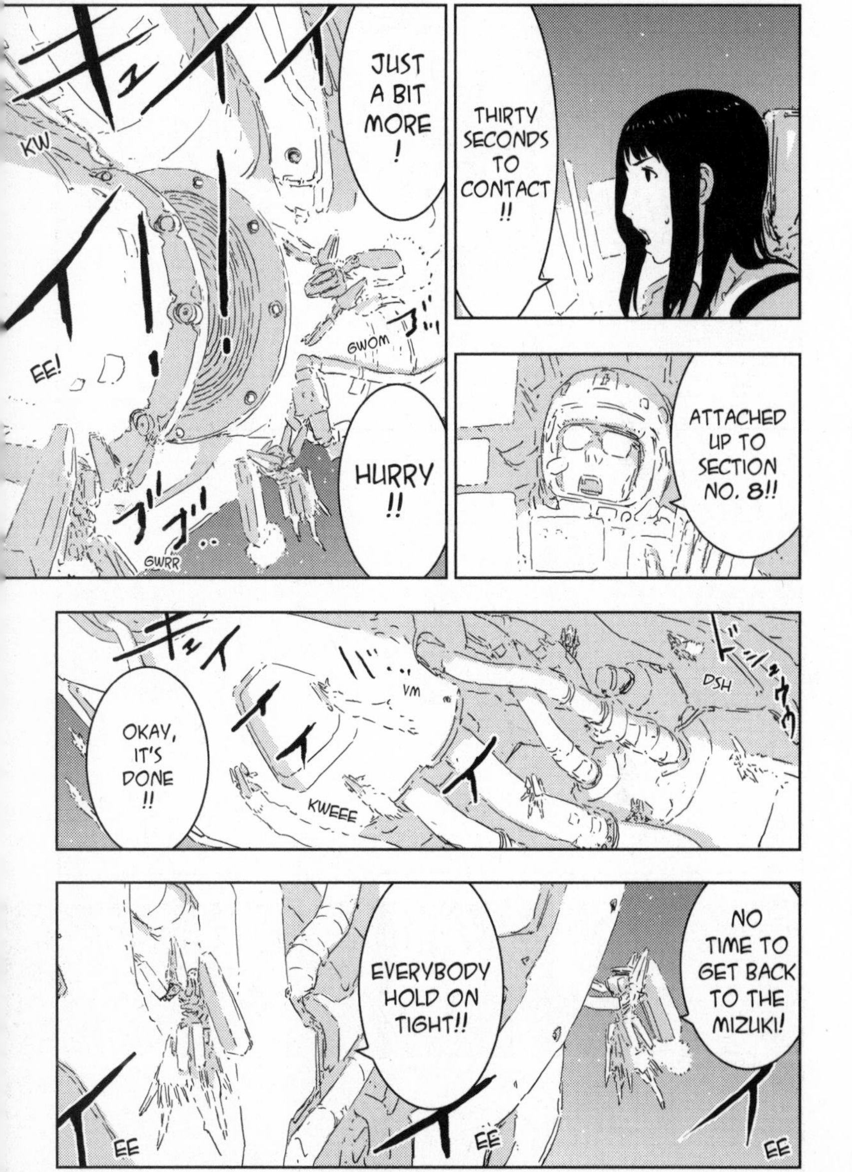
THIRTY SECONDS TO CONTACT!!
ATTACHED UP TO SECTION NO. 8!!
JUST A BIT MORE!
KW
HURRY!!
GWOM
EE!
GWRR
DSH
VM
OKAY, IT'S DONE!!
KWEEE
NO TIME TO GET BACK TO THE MIZUKI!
EE
EVERYBODY HOLD ON TIGHT!!
EE
EE

POWER LEVEL WILL REACH REACTION POINT MOMENTARILY!

!!

AAH

TSURU-UCHI!

EEEEEEEK

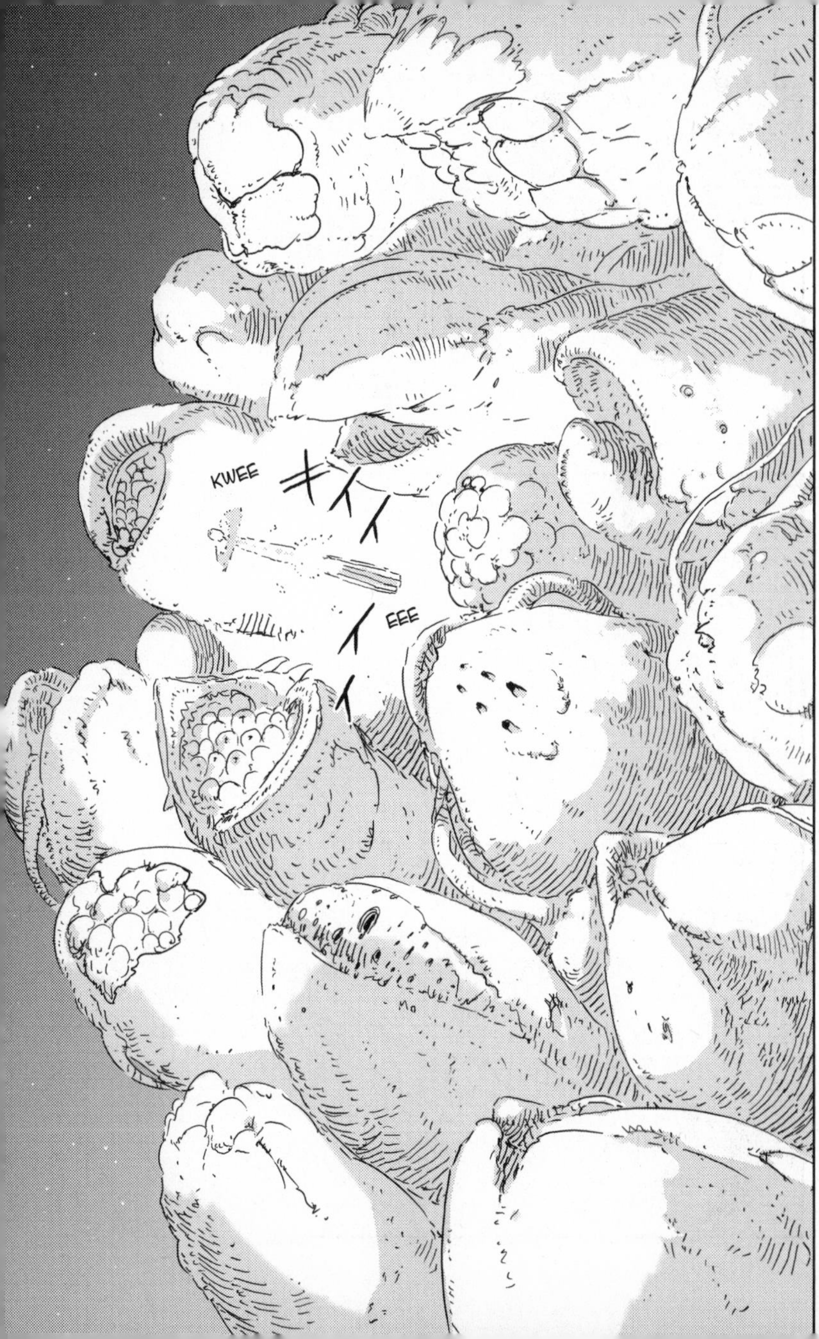
KWEE
EEE

EE
GW
GRAB MY HAND !!
OO
KWIM

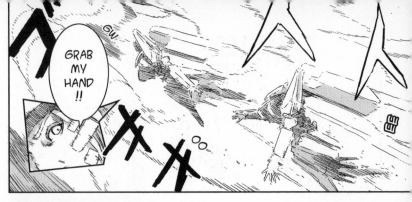

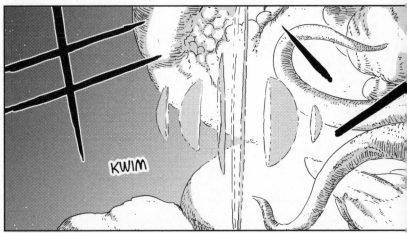

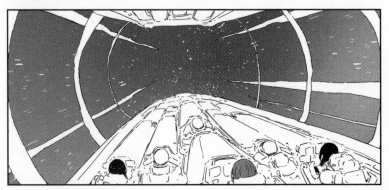

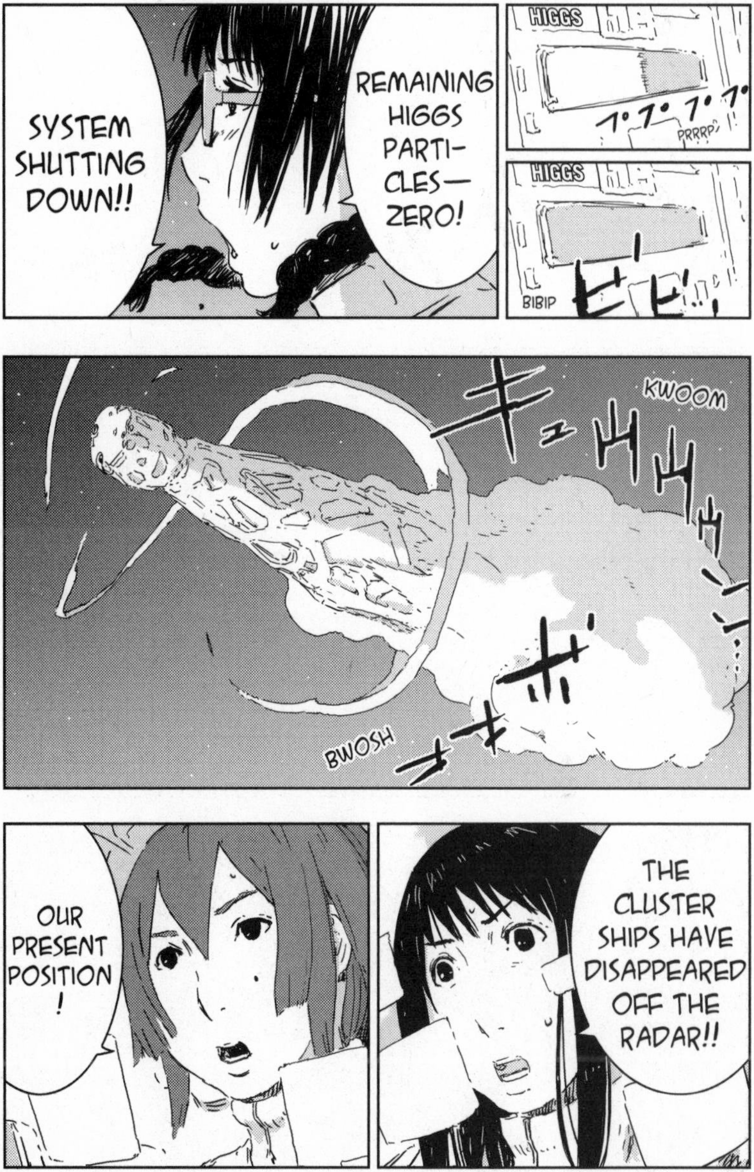
HIGGS
PRRRP
HIGGS
BIBIP
REMAINING HIGGS PARTI- CLES— ZERO!
SYSTEM SHUTTING DOWN!!
KWOOM
BWOSH
THE CLUSTER SHIPS HAVE DISAPPEARED OFF THE RADAR!!
OUR PRESENT POSITION !

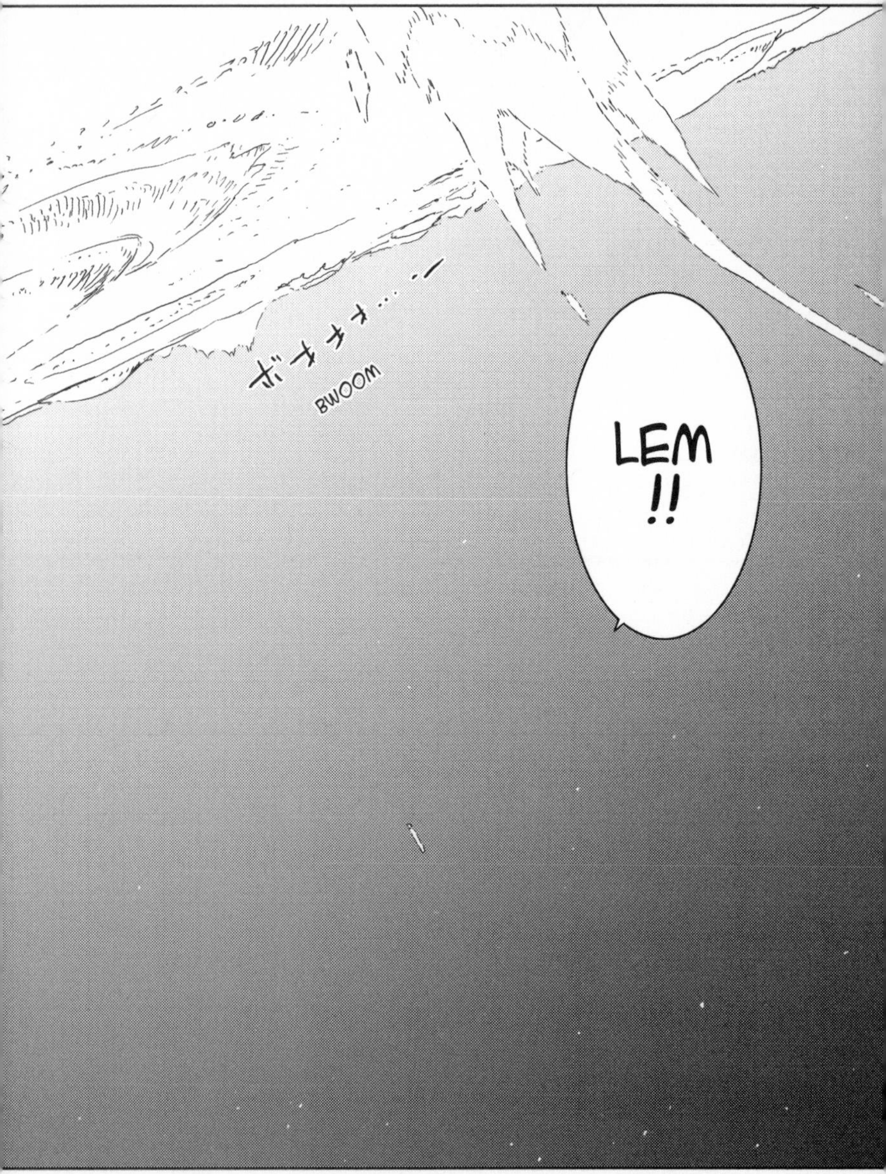
LEM !!
ボォォ…!
BWOOM

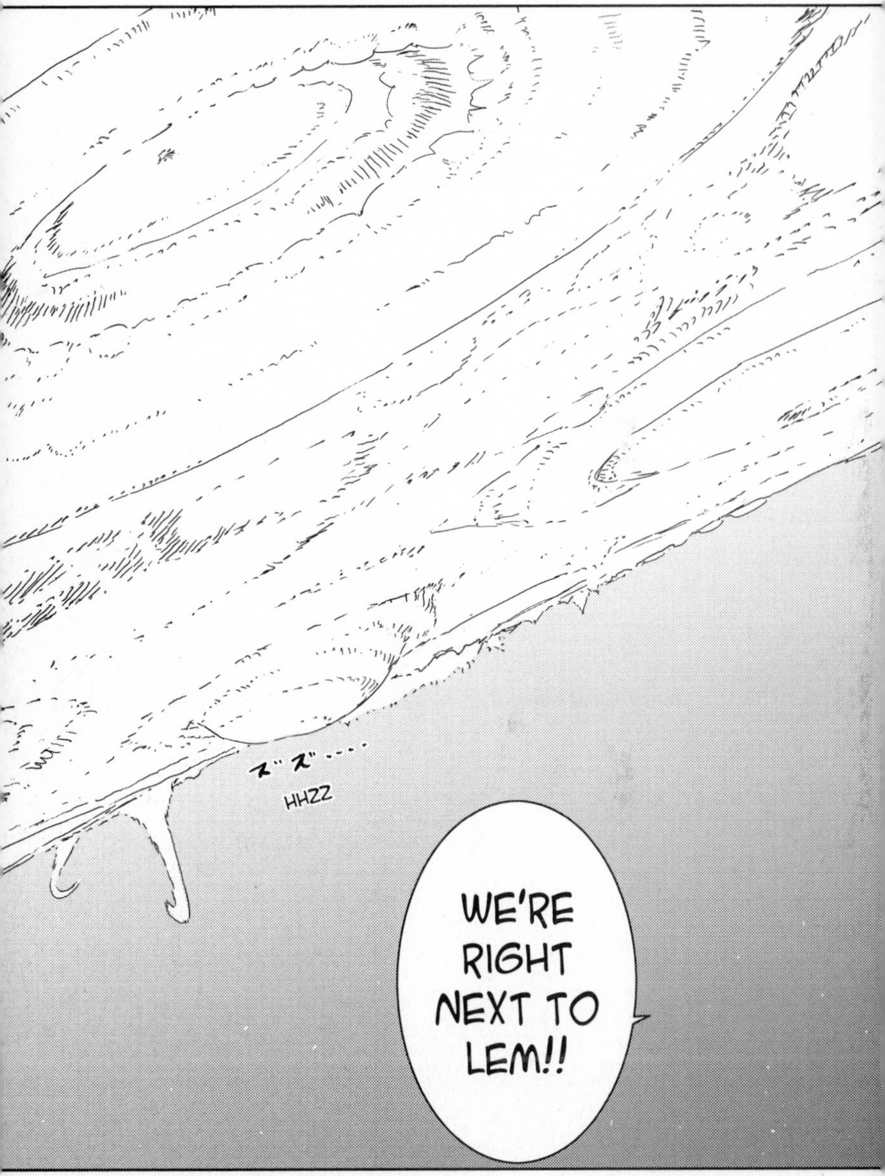
ズ゛ズ゛....
HHZZ
WE'RE RIGHT NEXT TO LEM!!

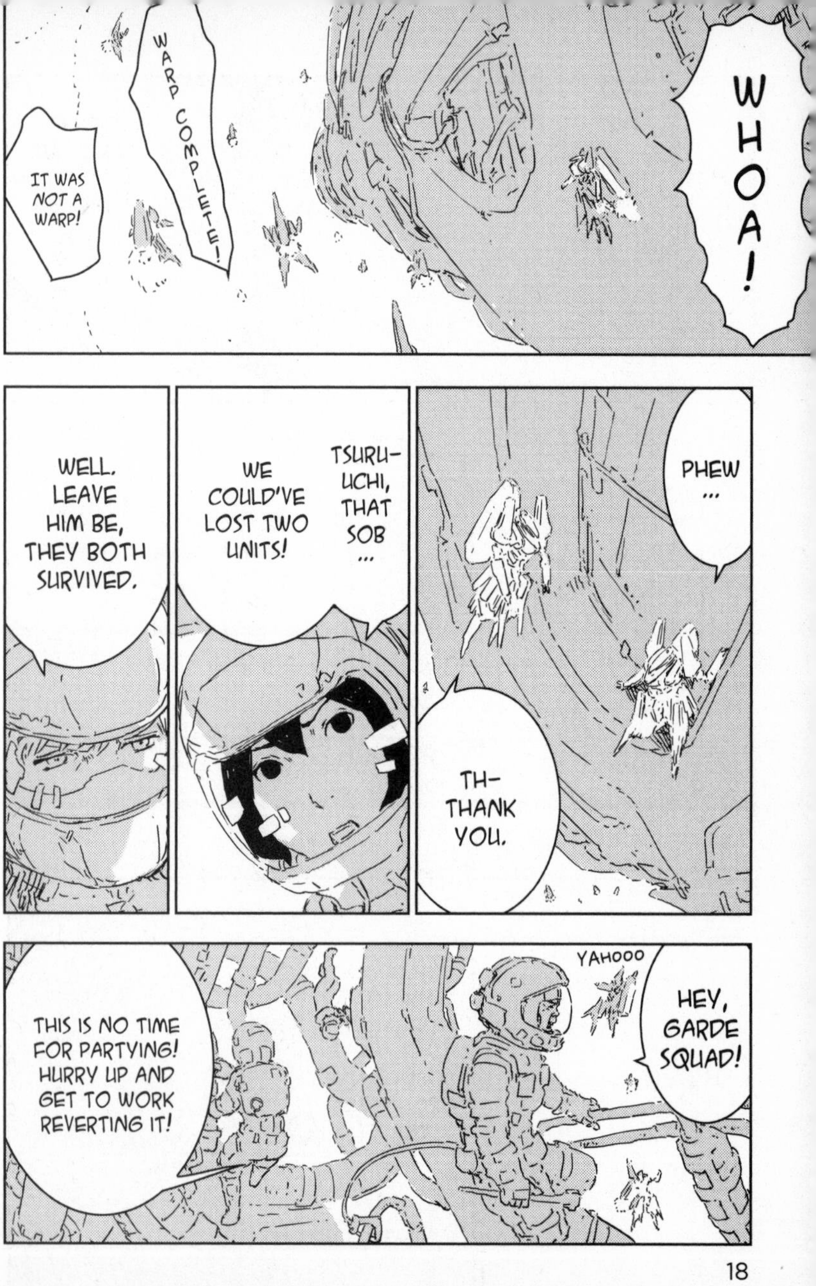
WHOA!
WARP COMPLETE!
IT WAS NOT A WARP!
PHEW...
TH- THANK YOU.
TSURU-UCHI, THAT SOB...
WE COULD'VE LOST TWO UNITS!
WELL. LEAVE HIM BE, THEY BOTH SURVIVED.
YAHOOO
HEY, GARDE SQUAD!
THIS IS NO TIME FOR PARTYING! HURRY UP AND GET TO WORK REVERTING IT!

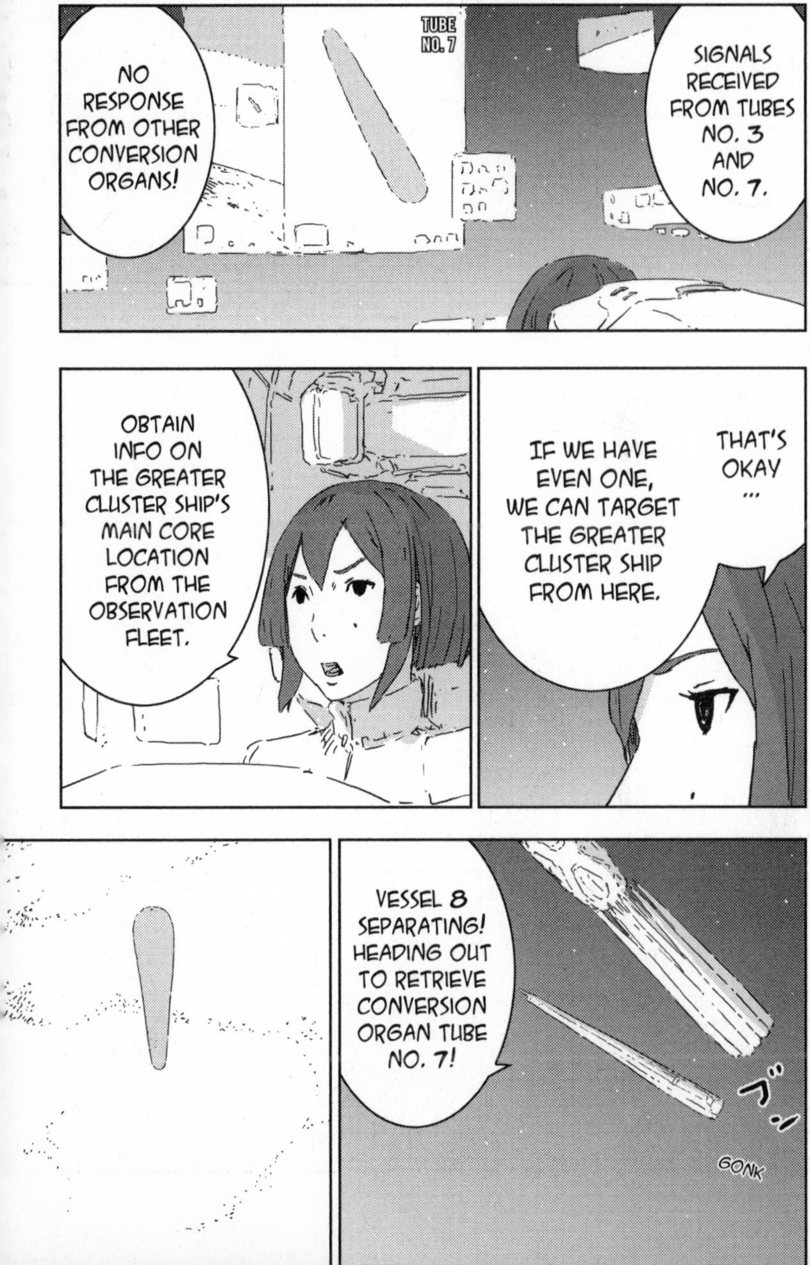
SIGNALS RECEIVED FROM TUBES NO. 3 AND NO. 7.
TUBE NO. 7
NO RESPONSE FROM OTHER CONVERSION ORGANS!
THAT'S OKAY ...
IF WE HAVE EVEN ONE, WE CAN TARGET THE GREATER CLUSTER SHIP FROM HERE.
OBTAIN INFO ON THE GREATER CLUSTER SHIP'S MAIN CORE LOCATION FROM THE OBSERVATION FLEET.
VESSEL 8 SEPARATING! HEADING OUT TO RETRIEVE CONVERSION ORGAN TUBE NO. 7!
ブン
GONK

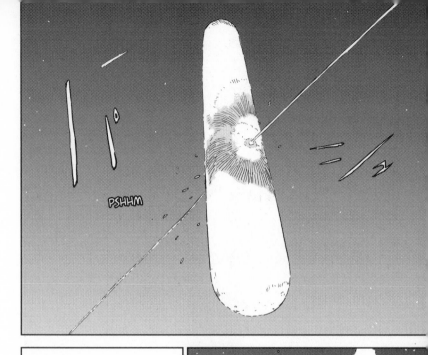

PSHHM

ズズズ‐‐…
HZZ

!!

THE
ORGAN HAS
SUFFERED
MAJOR
DAMAGE
!!

BOM

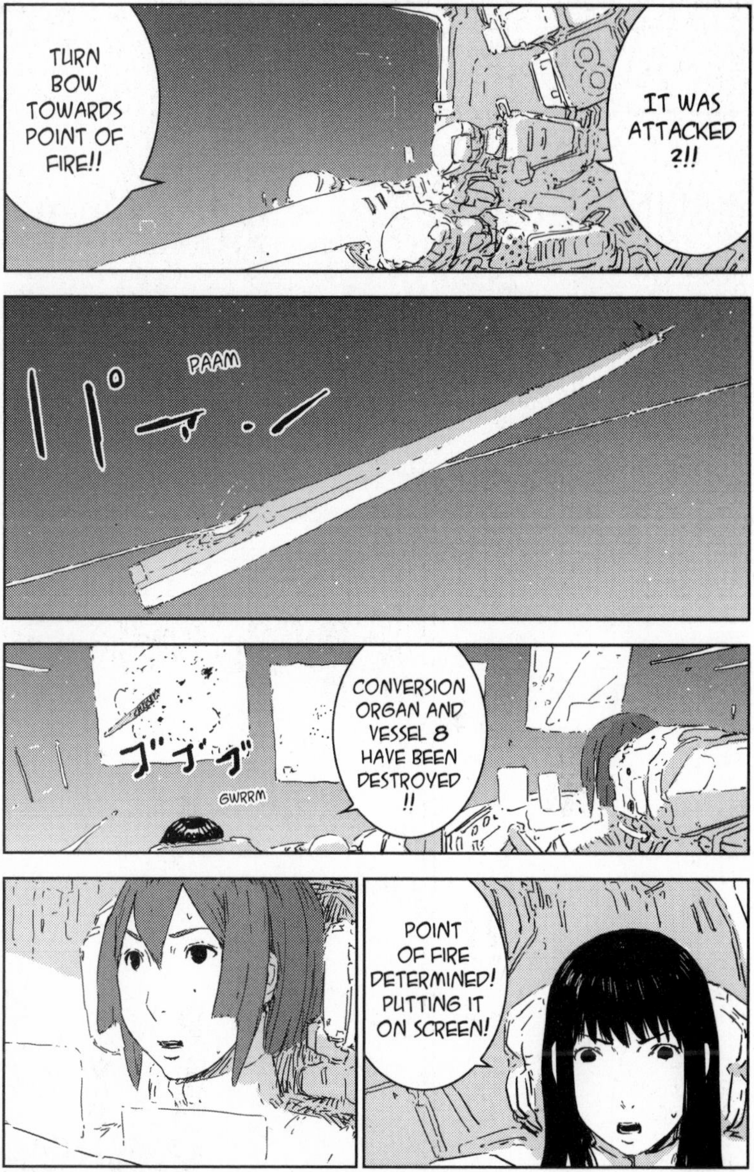

IT WAS ATTACKED ?!!
TURN BOW TOWARDS POINT OF FIRE!!
PAAM
CONVERSION ORGAN AND VESSEL 8 HAVE BEEN DESTROYED !!
ゴゴゴ
GWRRM
POINT OF FIRE DETERMINED! PUTTING IT ON SCREEN!

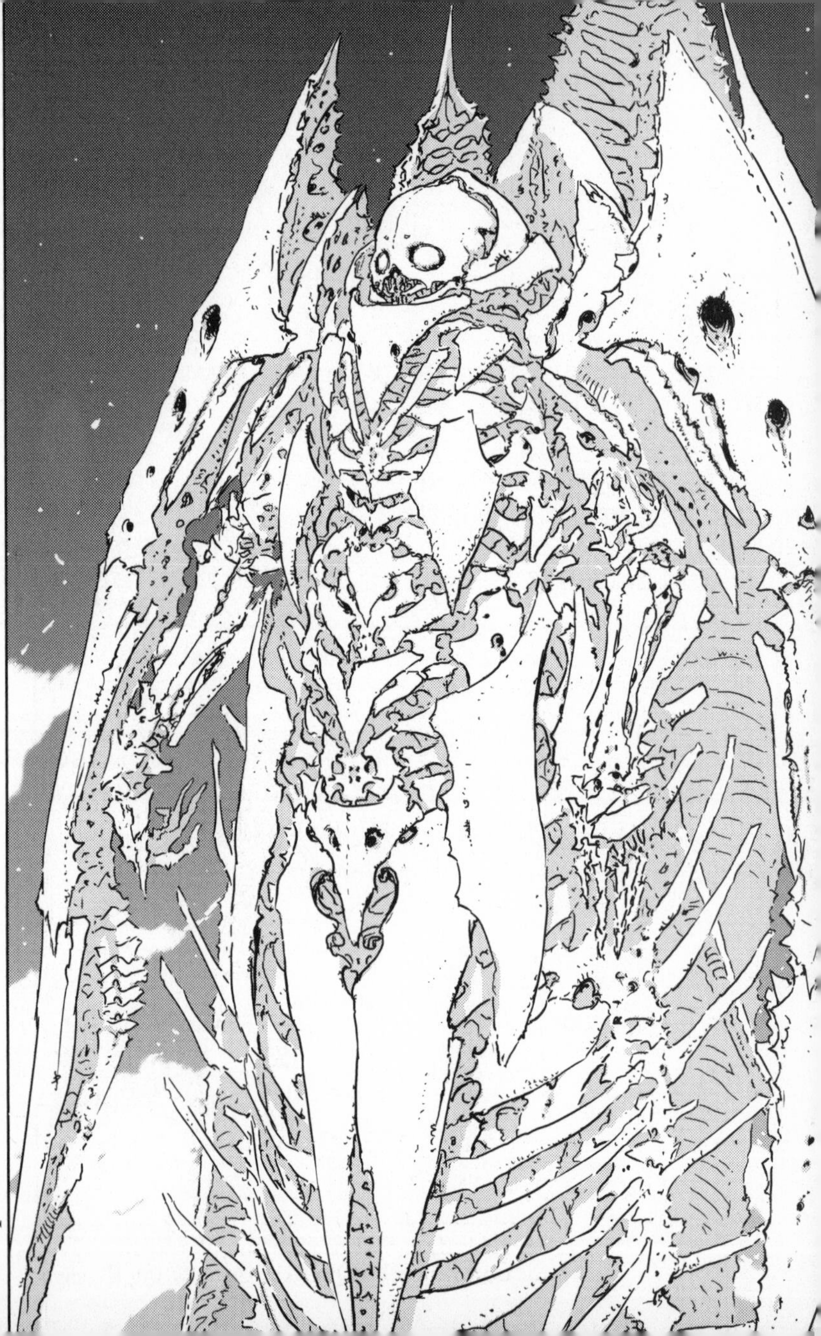

Chapter 71: END

Chapter 72: Tsumugi's Willfulness

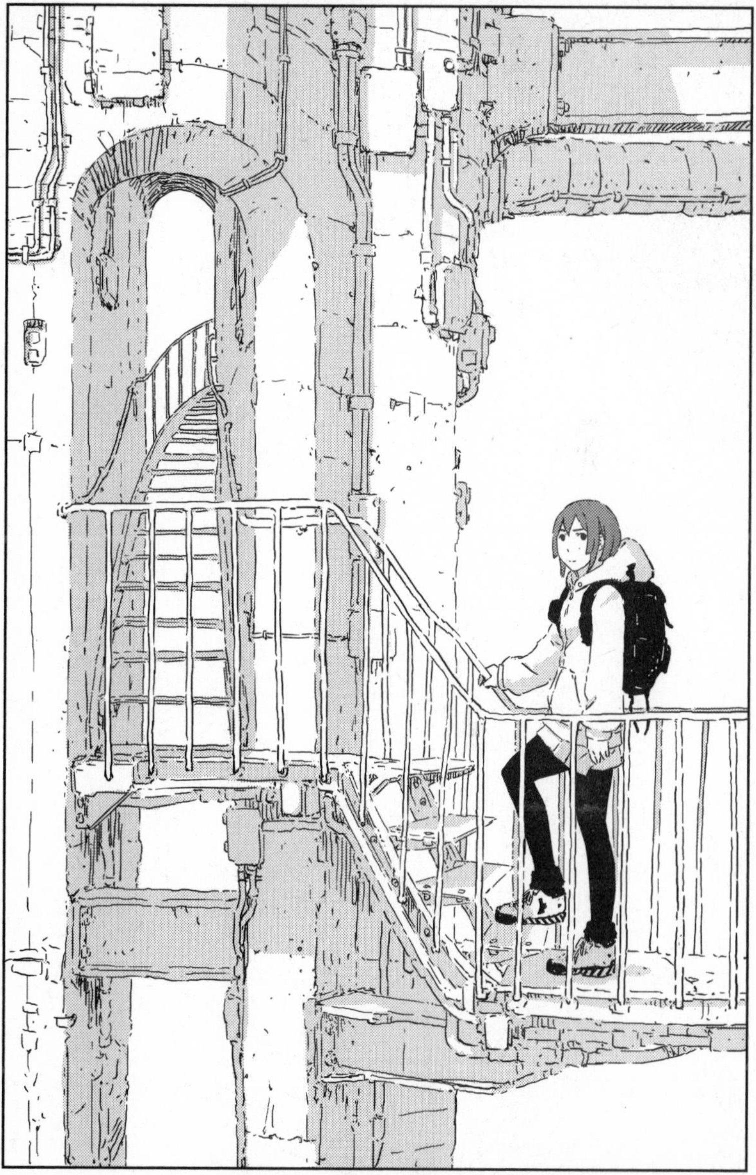

One Hundred Sights of Sidonia Part Fifty-Five:
Vice Commander's Quarters Connecting Passage

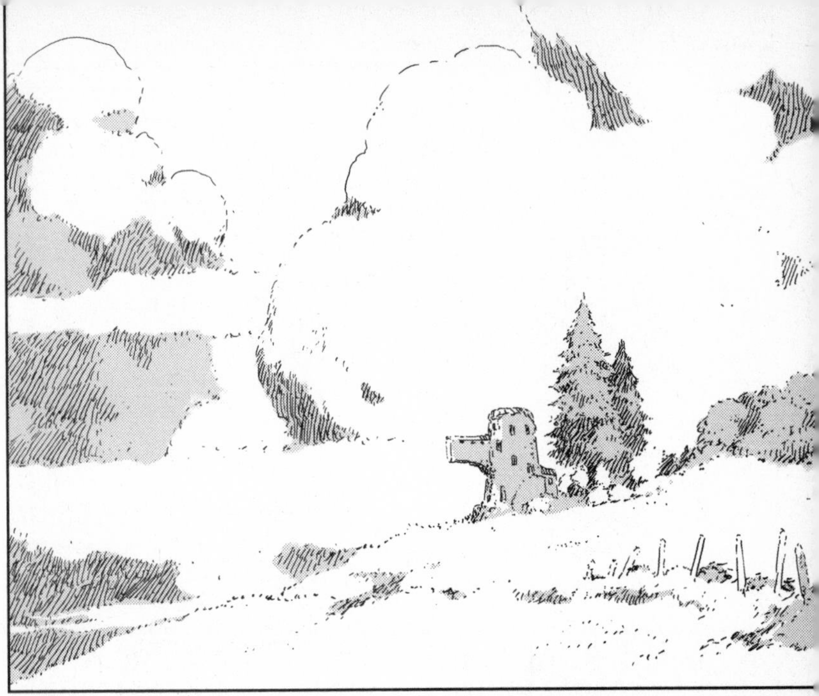
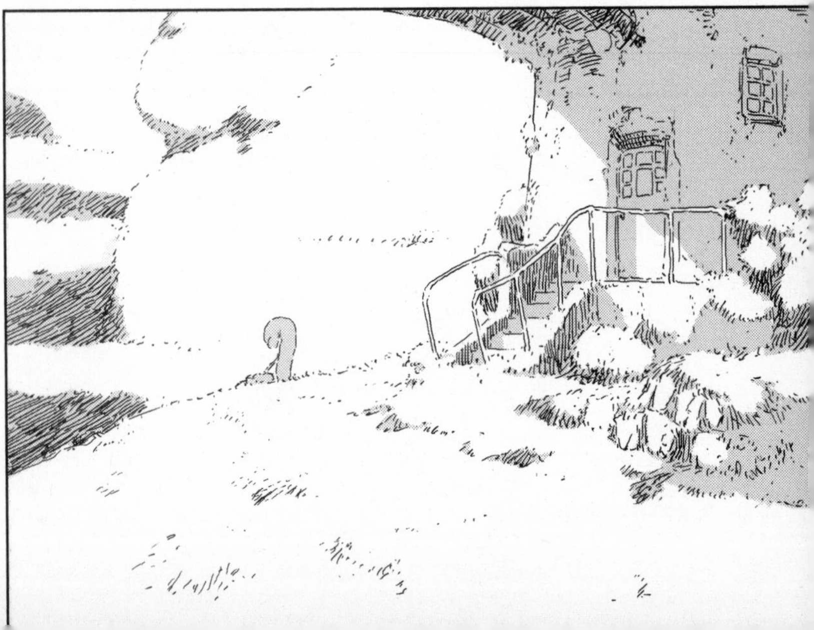

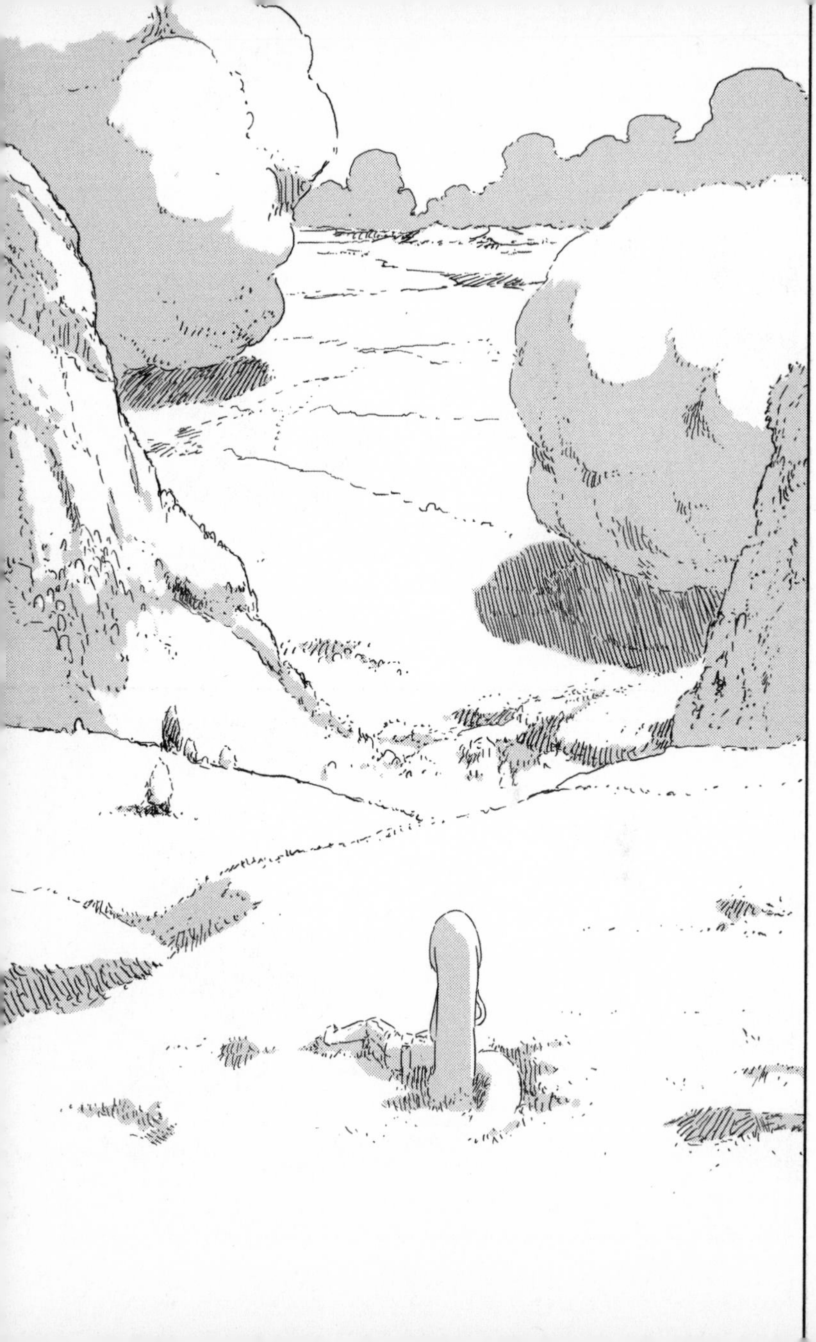

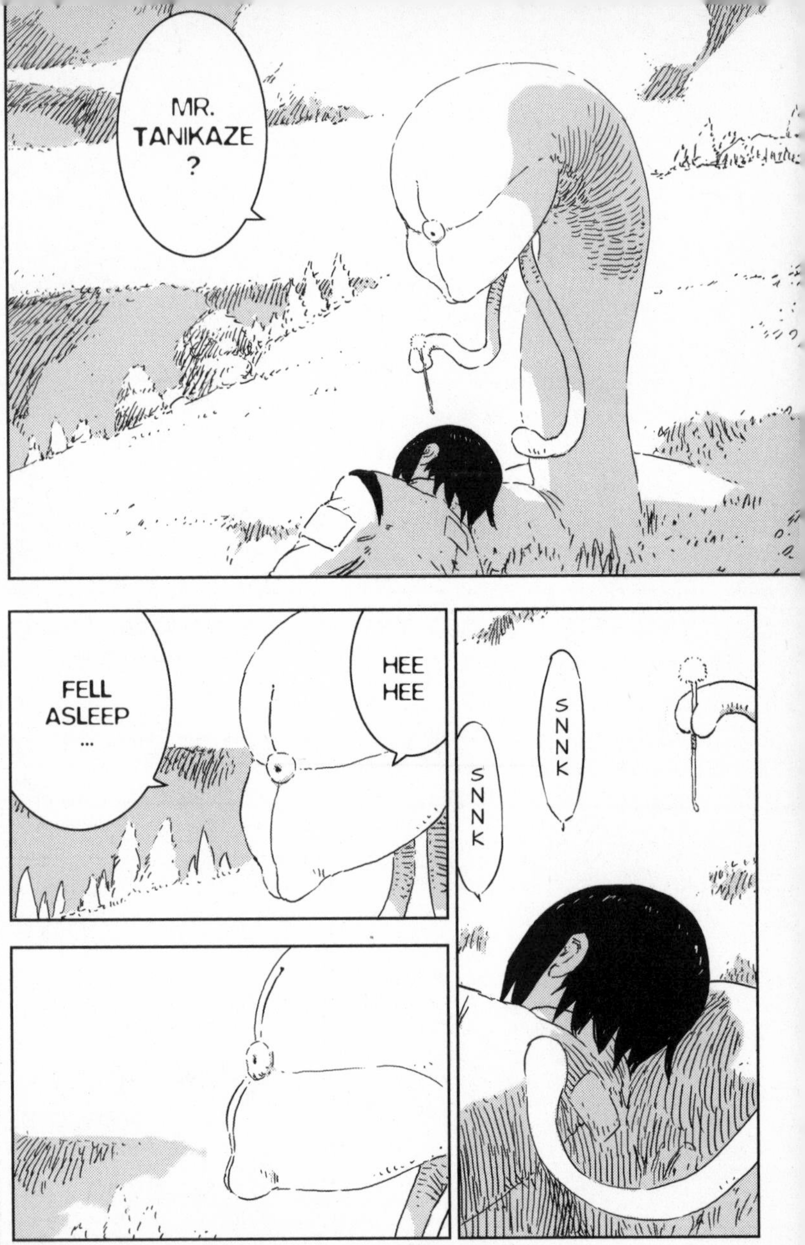
MR. TANIKAZE ?
SNNK
SNNK
HEE HEE
FELL ASLEEP ...

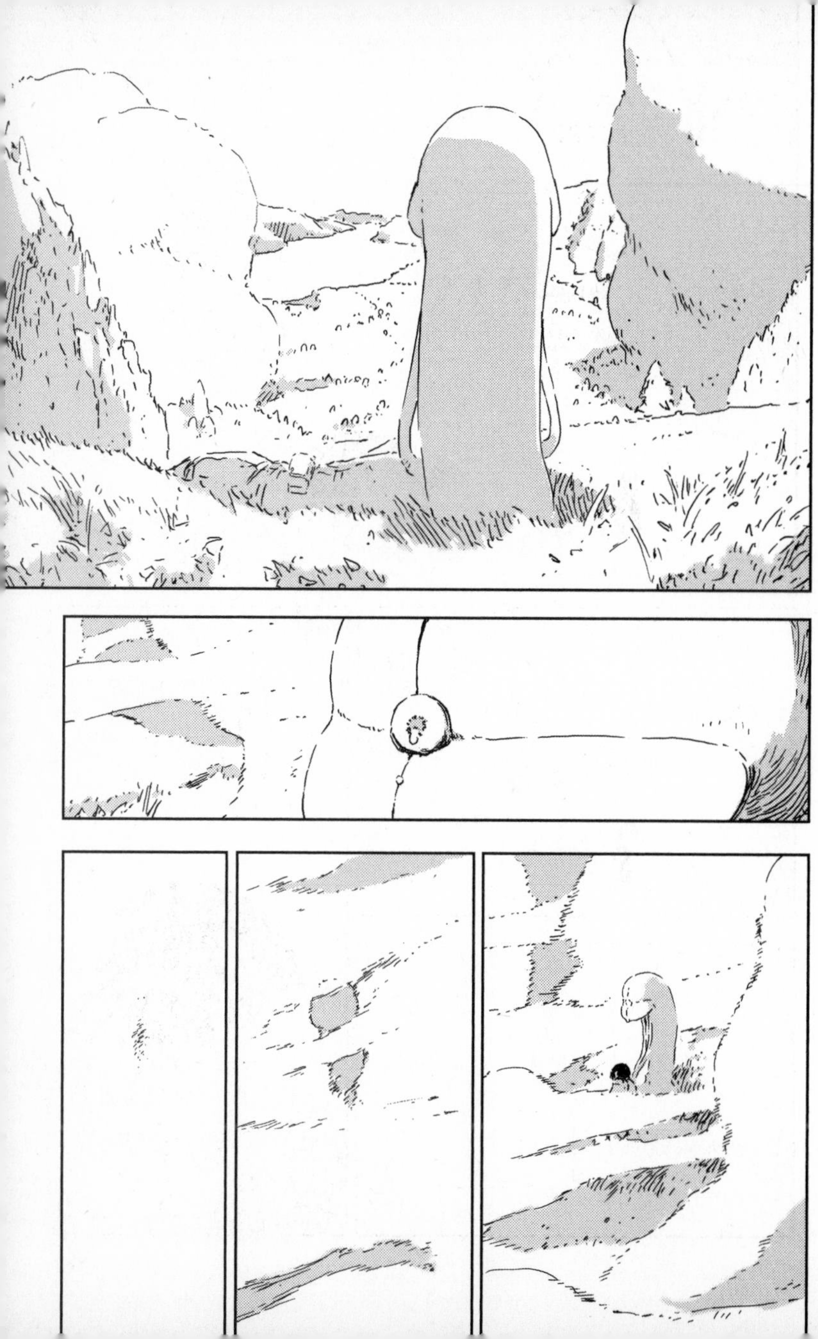

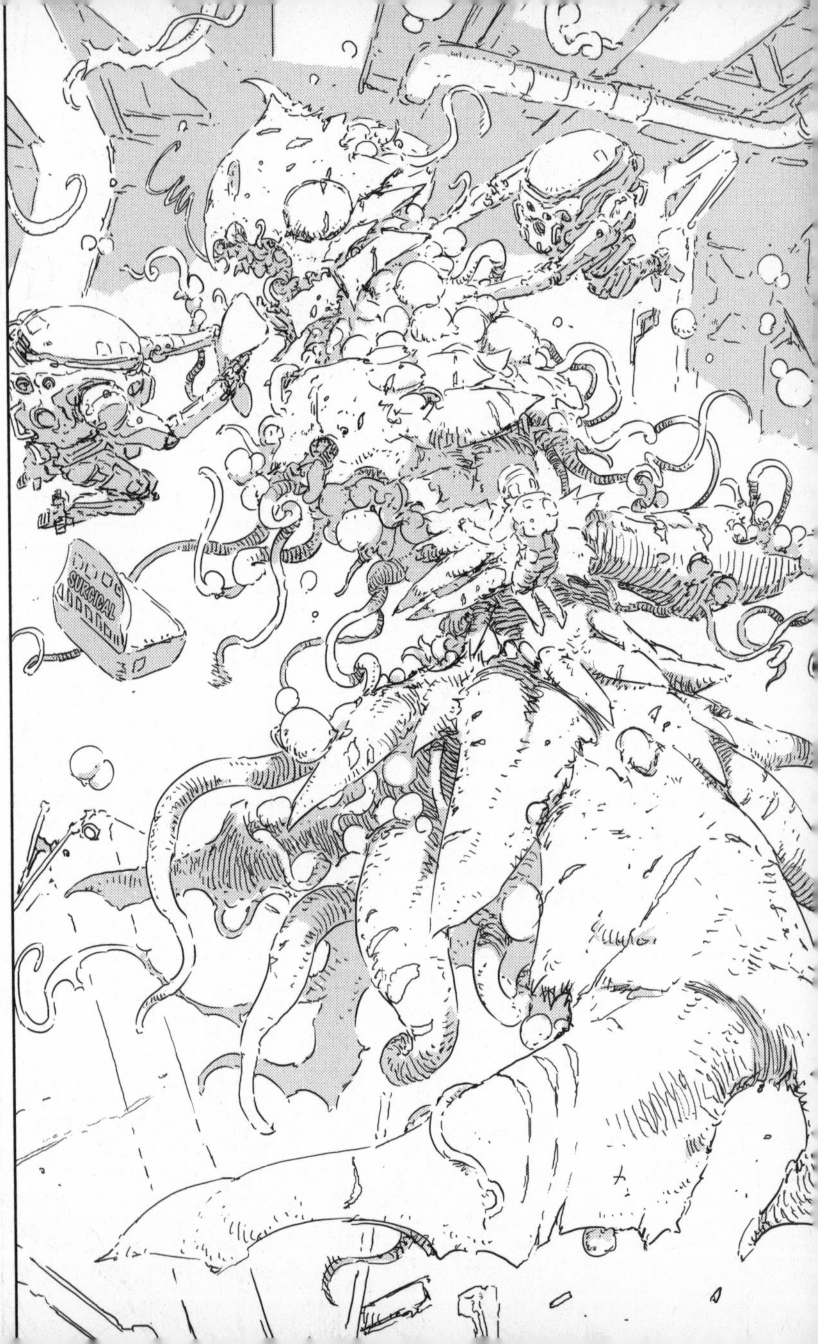
SURGICAL

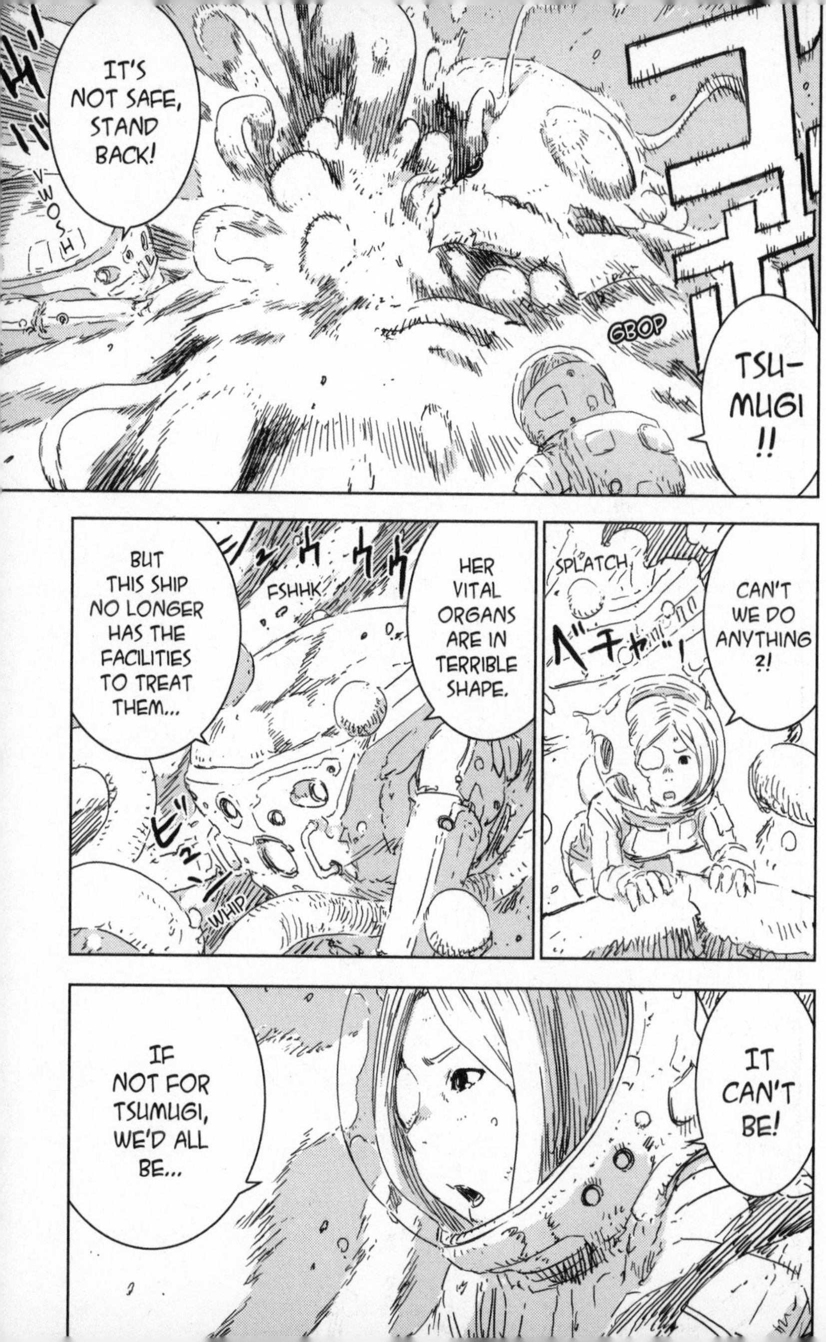
TSU-MUGI!!
GBOP
IT'S NOT SAFE, STAND BACK!
CAN'T WE DO ANYTHING?!
SPLATCH
HER VITAL ORGANS ARE IN TERRIBLE SHAPE.
FSHHK
BUT THIS SHIP NO LONGER HAS THE FACILITIES TO TREAT THEM...
WHIP
IT CAN'T BE!
IF NOT FOR TSUMUGI, WE'D ALL BE...

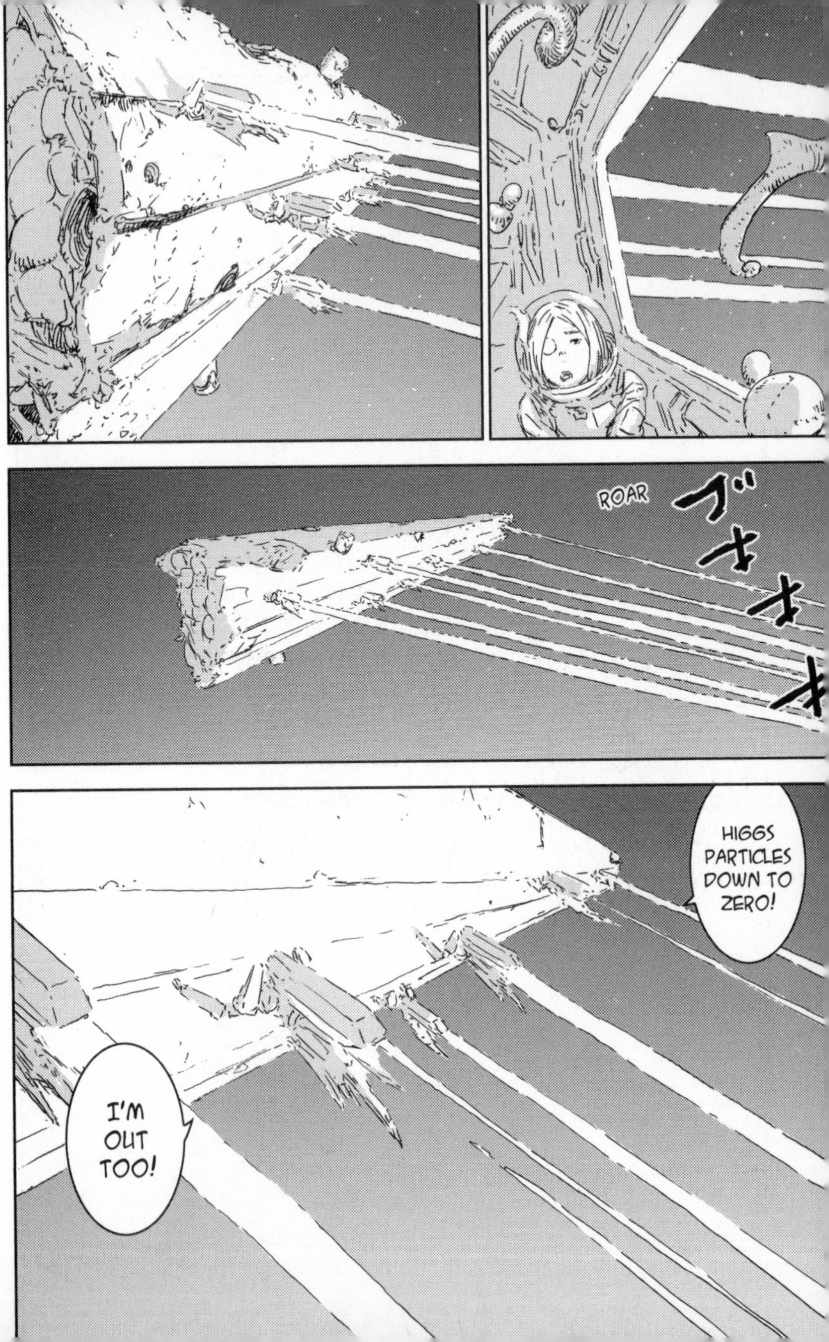
ROAR
HIGGS PARTICLES DOWN TO ZERO!
I'M OUT TOO!

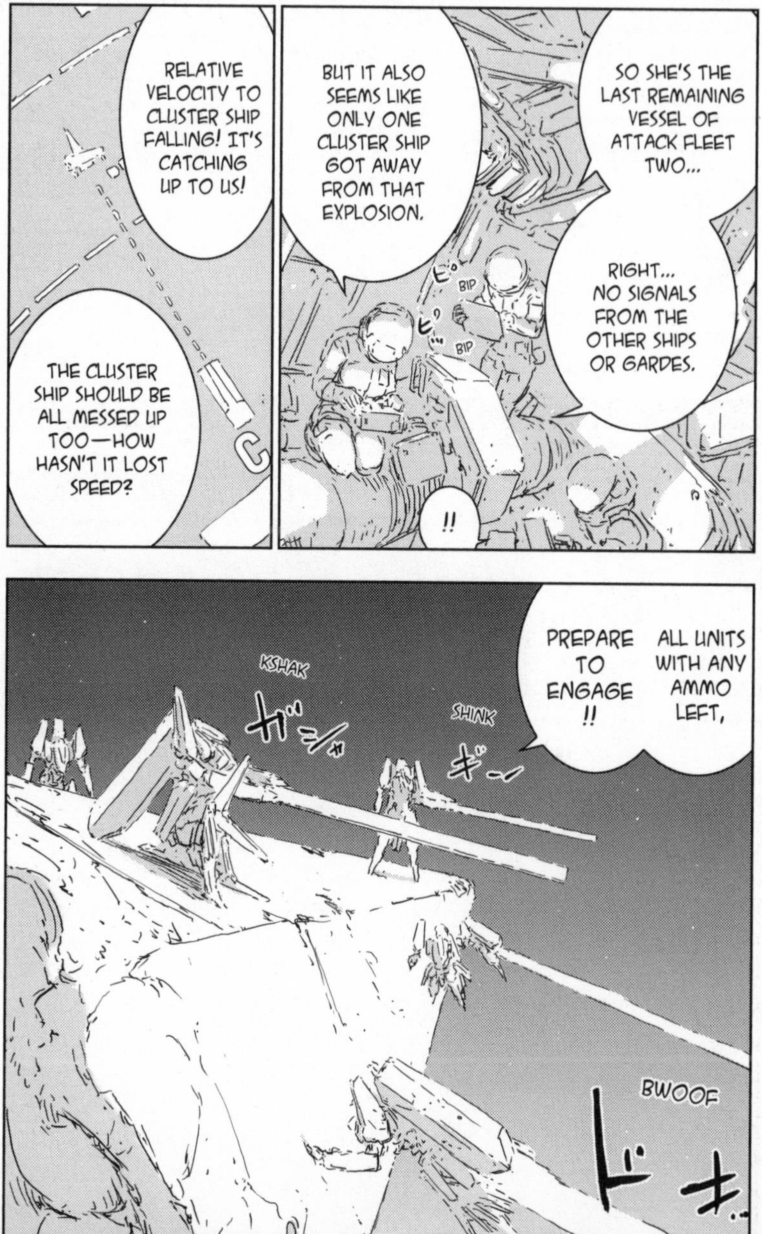
SO SHE'S THE LAST REMAINING VESSEL OF ATTACK FLEET TWO...
BUT IT ALSO SEEMS LIKE ONLY ONE CLUSTER SHIP GOT AWAY FROM THAT EXPLOSION.
RIGHT... NO SIGNALS FROM THE OTHER SHIPS OR GARDES.
BIP
BIP
!!
RELATIVE VELOCITY TO CLUSTER SHIP FALLING! IT'S CATCHING UP TO US!
THE CLUSTER SHIP SHOULD BE ALL MESSED UP TOO—HOW HASN'T IT LOST SPEED?
ALL UNITS WITH ANY AMMO LEFT,
PREPARE TO ENGAGE!!
SHINK
KSHAK
BWOOF

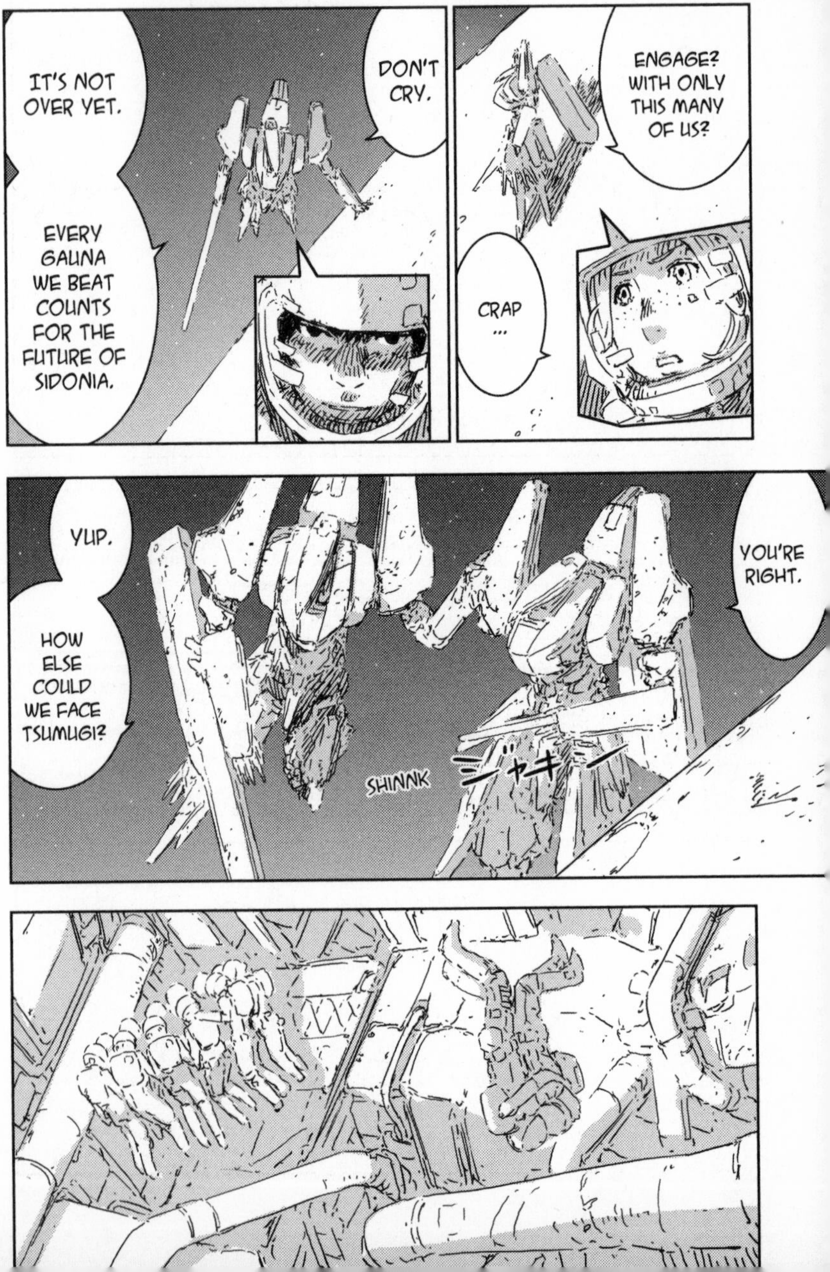
ENGAGE? WITH ONLY THIS MANY OF US?
CRAP ...
DON'T CRY.
IT'S NOT OVER YET.
EVERY GAUNA WE BEAT COUNTS FOR THE FUTURE OF SIDONIA.
YOU'RE RIGHT.
YUP.
HOW ELSE COULD WE FACE TSUMUGI?
ジャキーン
SHINNK

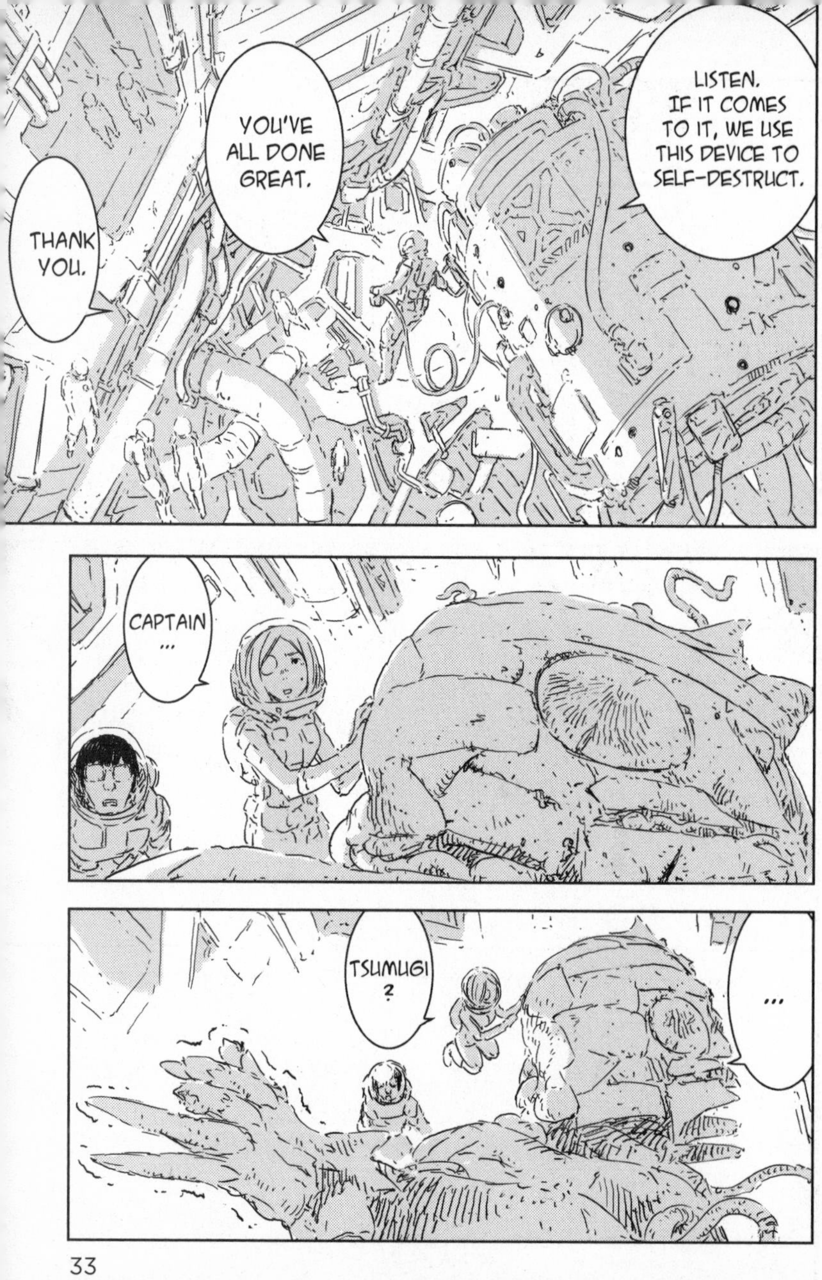
LISTEN. IF IT COMES TO IT, WE USE THIS DEVICE TO SELF-DESTRUCT.
YOU'VE ALL DONE GREAT.
THANK YOU.
CAPTAIN ...
...
TSUMUGI ?

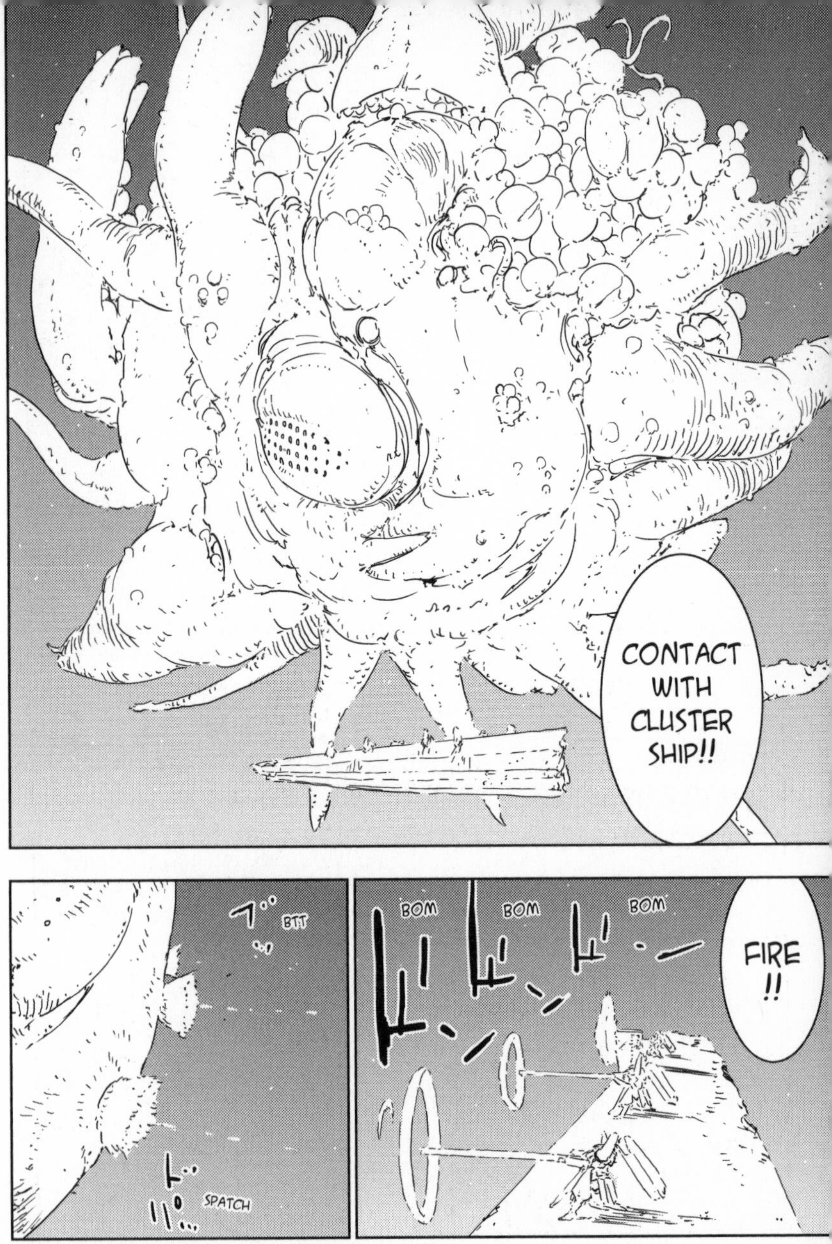
CONTACT WITH CLUSTER SHIP!!
FIRE!!
BOM
BOM
BOM
BTT
SPATCH

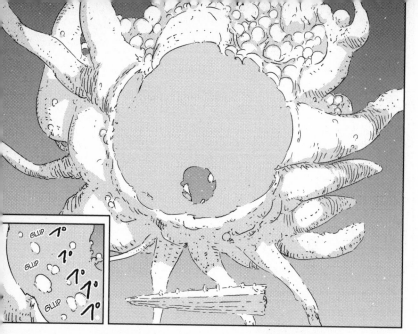

GLIP

GLIP

GLIP

CLUSTER SHIP HAS DISINTEGRATED INTO FOAM STATE!!

?!!

SOMETHING PIERCED THE GREATER CLUSTER SHIP'S MAIN CORE!

!!!

THWOOM

チリ
ZZT
チリ
ZZT
チリリ
GZZT
オオオオ
WOOM
RAM-MING TIP ATTACK SUCCESS-FUL...
ヒュウウウ
WHOOM
TANIKAZE !!
ズズズズ
KKZZ

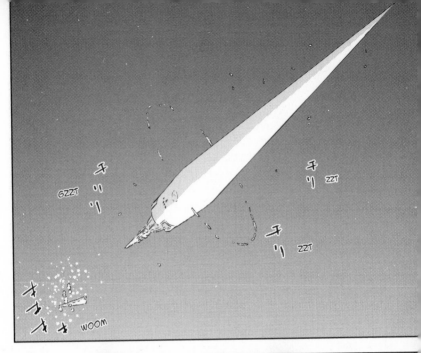

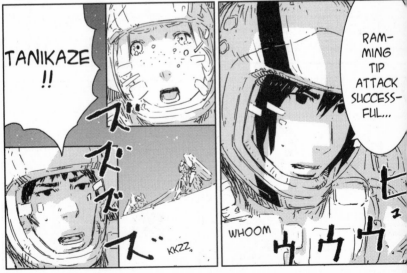

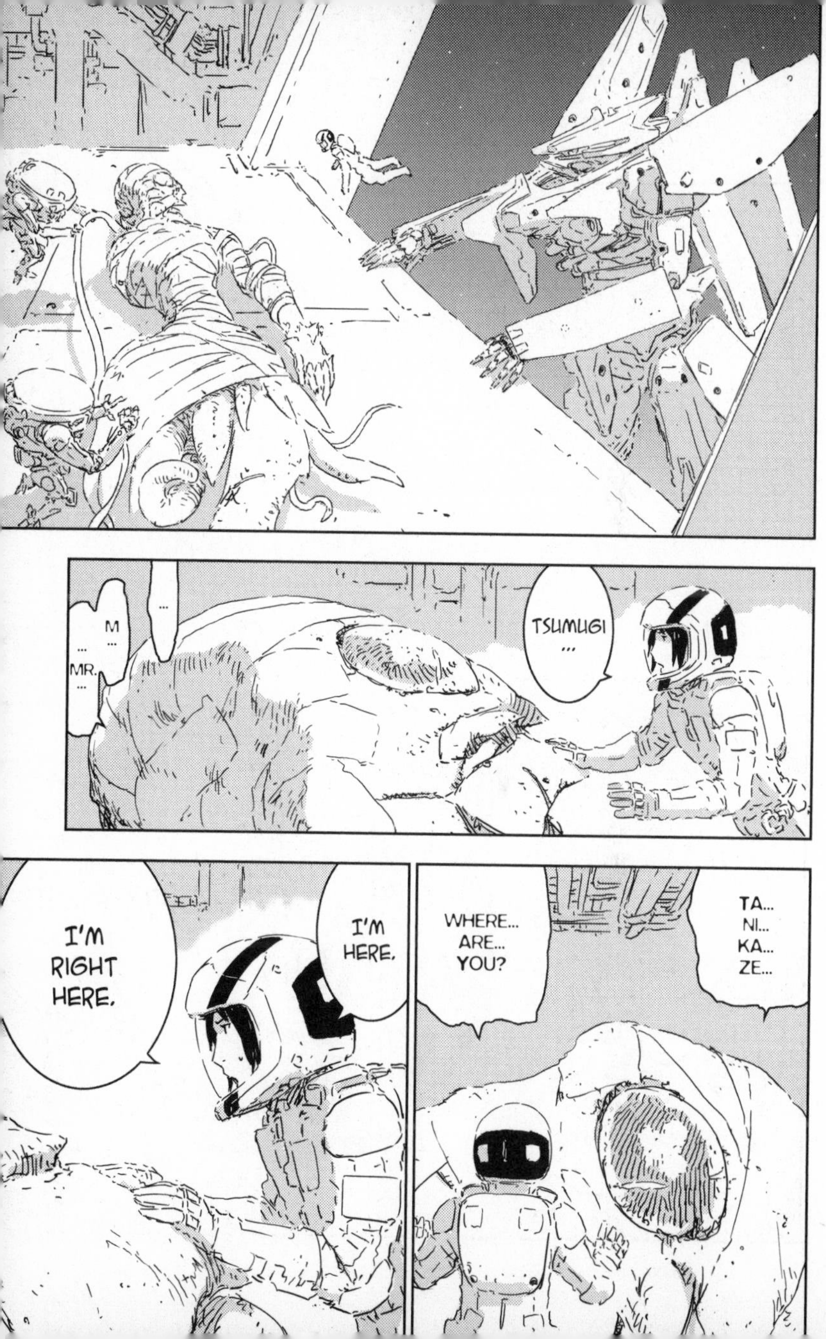
TSUMUGI ...
...
M ... ... MR. ...
TA... NI... KA... ZE...
WHERE... ARE... YOU?
I'M HERE.
I'M RIGHT HERE.

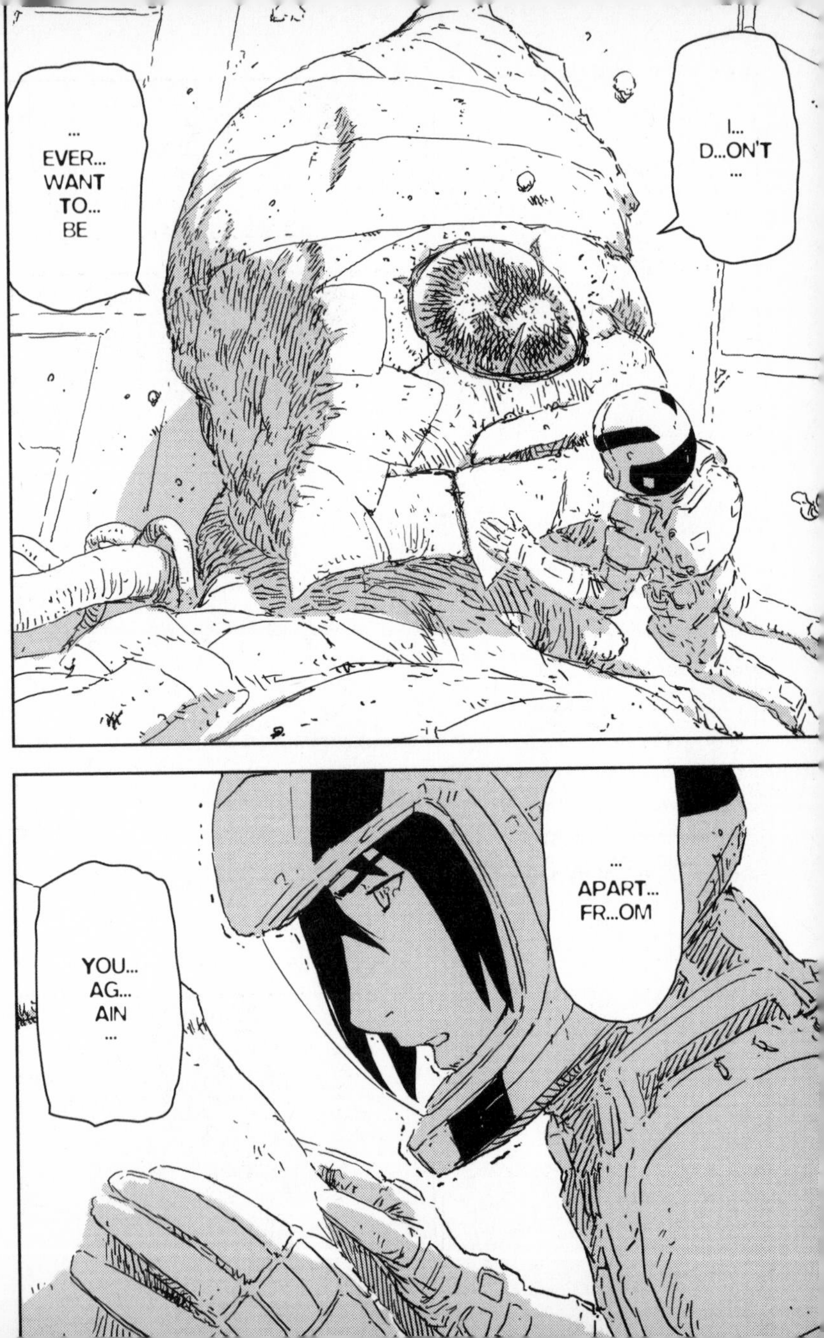
I... D...ON'T ...
... EVER... WANT TO... BE
... APART... FR...OM
YOU... AG... AIN ...

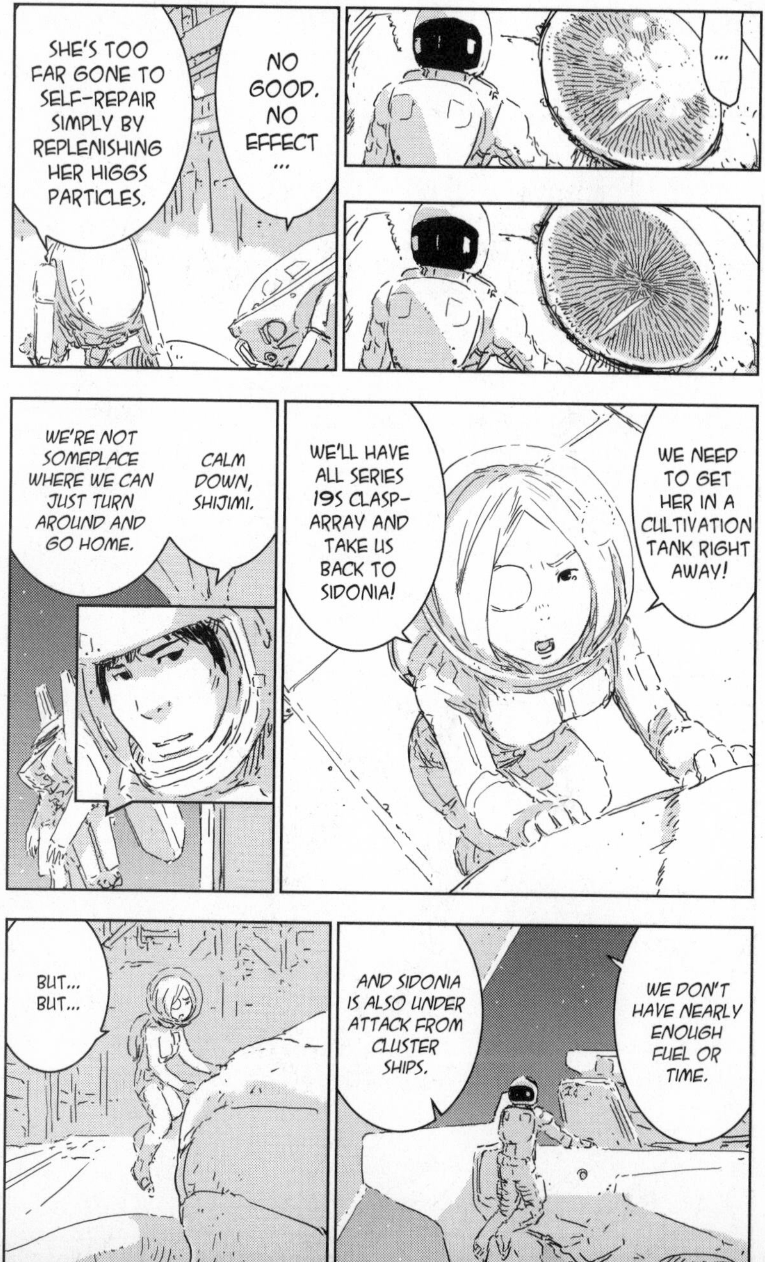
...
NO GOOD. NO EFFECT ...
SHE'S TOO FAR GONE TO SELF-REPAIR SIMPLY BY REPLENISHING HER HIGGS PARTICLES.
WE NEED TO GET HER IN A CULTIVATION TANK RIGHT AWAY!
WE'LL HAVE ALL SERIES 19S CLASP-ARRAY AND TAKE US BACK TO SIDONIA!
CALM DOWN, SHIJIMI.
WE'RE NOT SOMEPLACE WHERE WE CAN JUST TURN AROUND AND GO HOME.
WE DON'T HAVE NEARLY ENOUGH FUEL OR TIME.
AND SIDONIA IS ALSO UNDER ATTACK FROM CLUSTER SHIPS.
BUT... BUT...

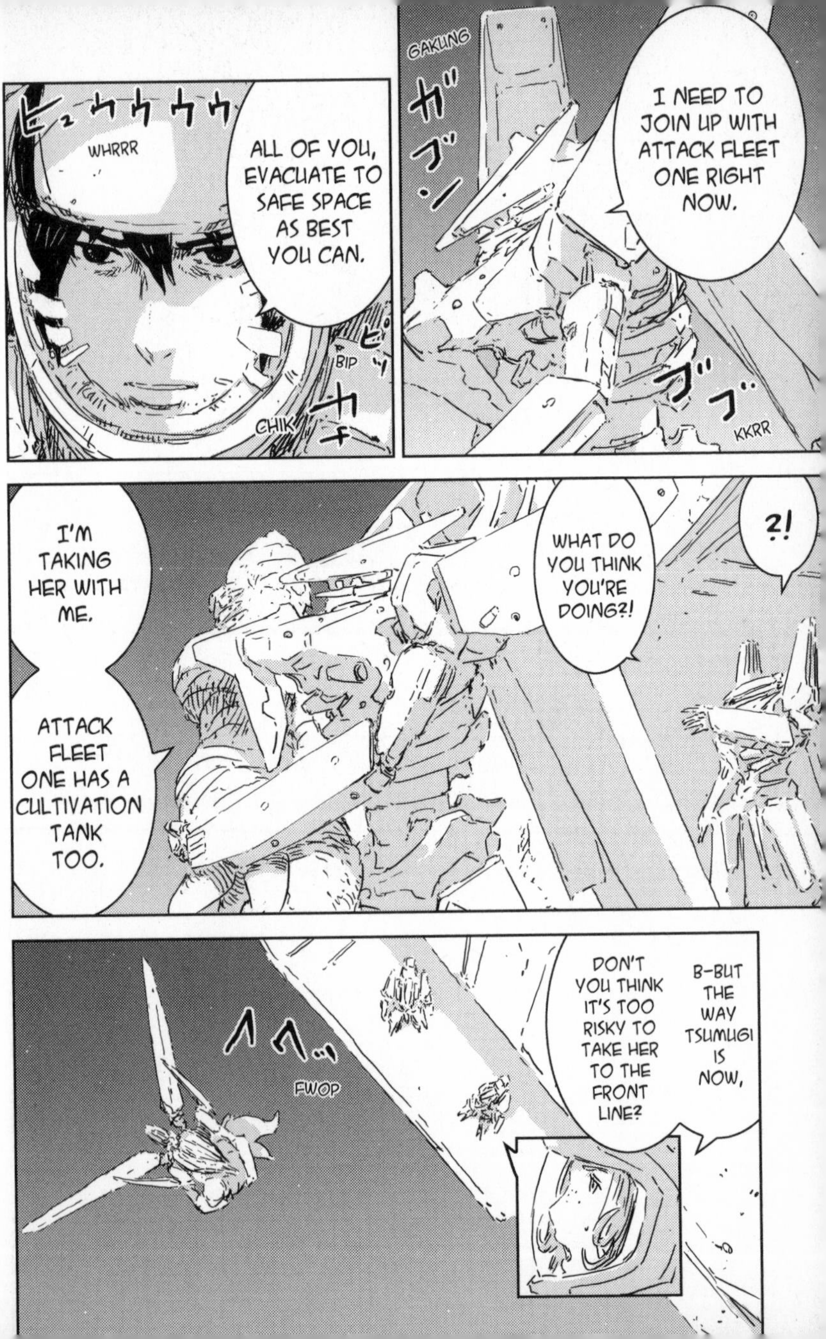
GAKUNG
I NEED TO JOIN UP WITH ATTACK FLEET ONE RIGHT NOW.
KKRR
WHRRR
ALL OF YOU, EVACUATE TO SAFE SPACE AS BEST YOU CAN.
BIP
CHIK
?!
WHAT DO YOU THINK YOU'RE DOING?!
I'M TAKING HER WITH ME.
ATTACK FLEET ONE HAS A CULTIVATION TANK TOO.
B-BUT THE WAY TSUMUGI IS NOW,
DON'T YOU THINK IT'S TOO RISKY TO TAKE HER TO THE FRONT LINE?
FWOP

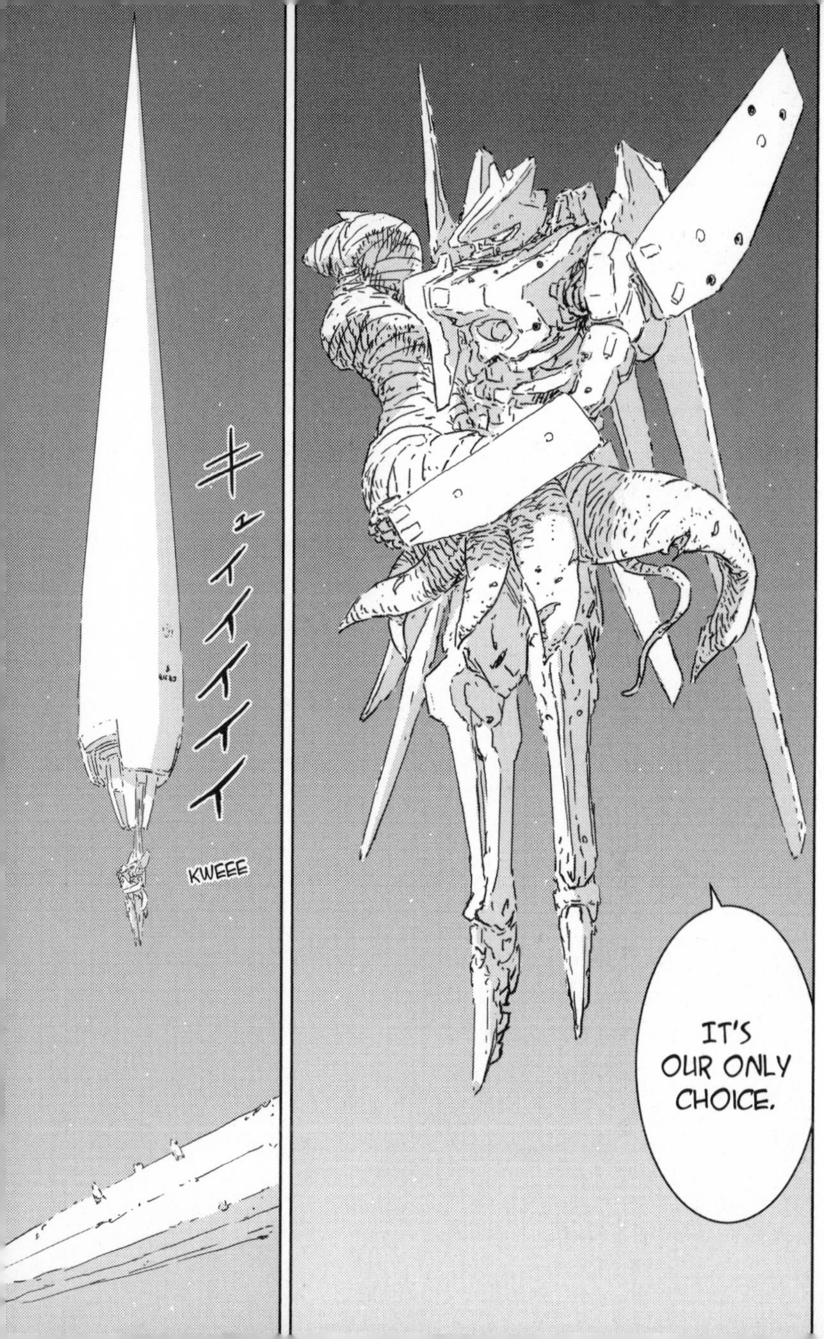
IT'S OUR ONLY CHOICE.
キュイイイイイ
KWEEE

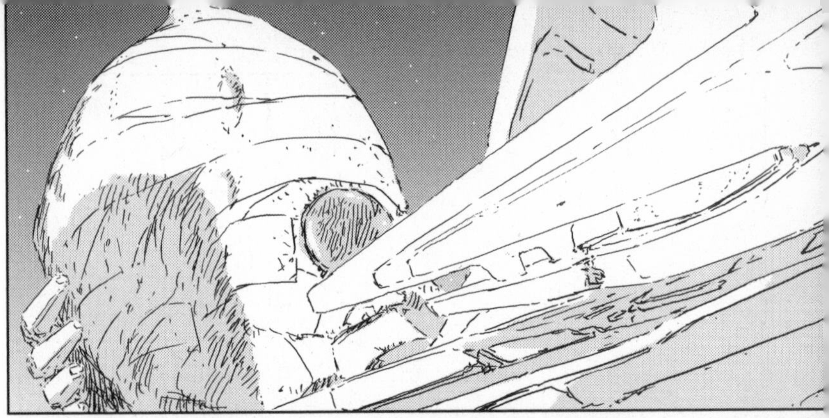

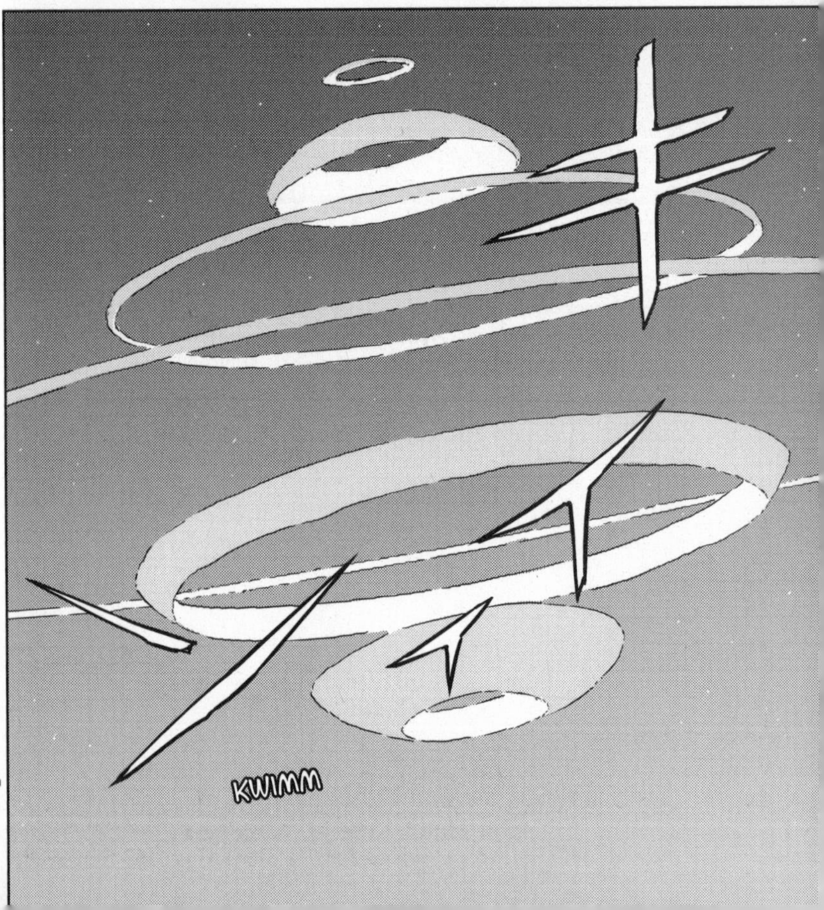
KWIMM

Chapter 72: END

Chapter 73: Attack Fleet One's Interception

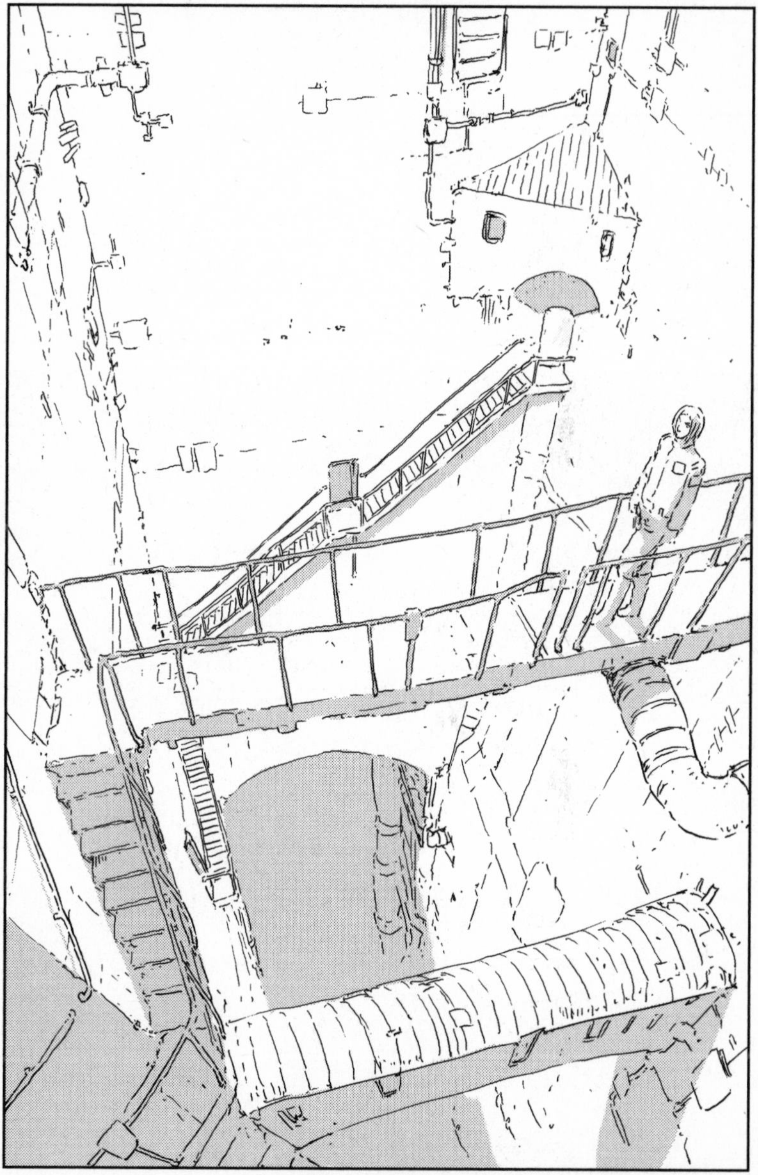

One Hundred Sights of Sidonia Part Fifty-Six:
Residential Block East 463 Stairwell

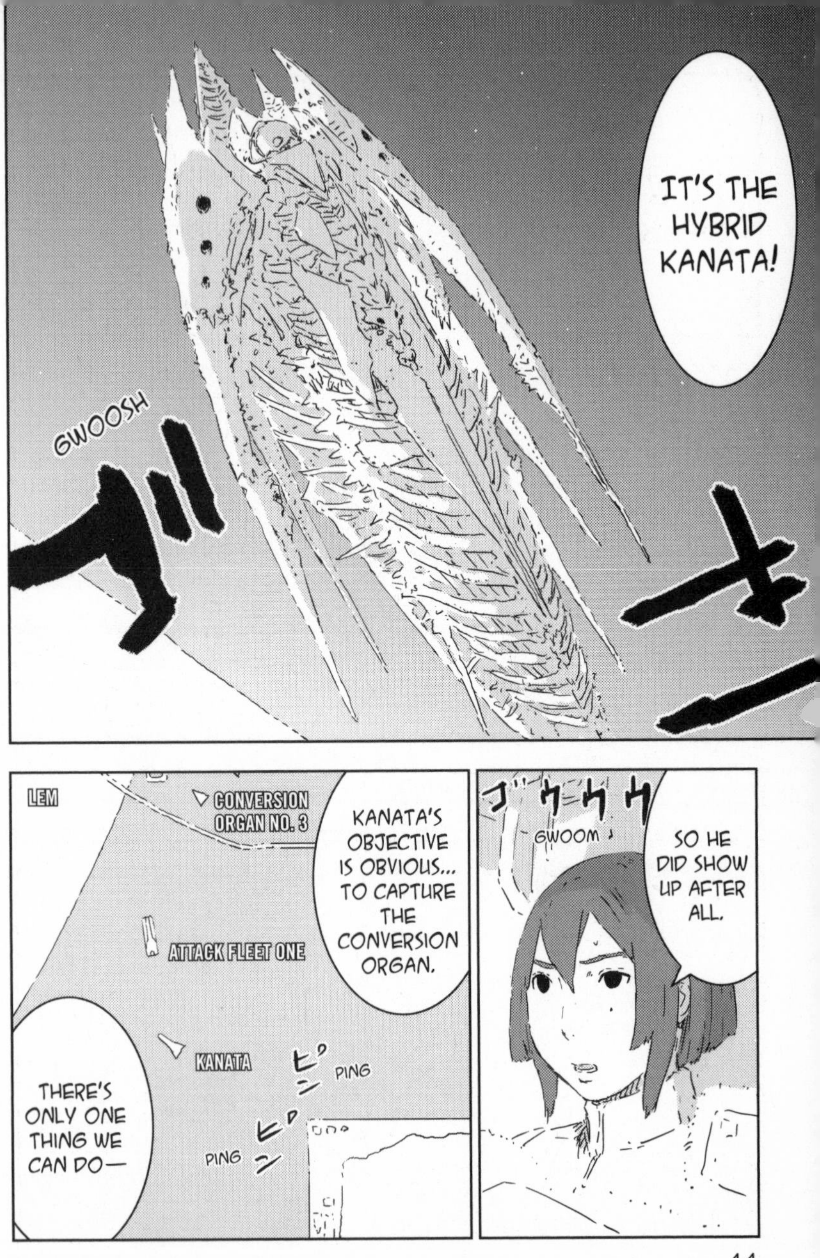
IT'S THE HYBRID KANATA!
GWOOSH
ゴウウウ
GWOOM
SO HE DID SHOW UP AFTER ALL.
LEM
CONVERSION ORGAN NO. 3
KANATA'S OBJECTIVE IS OBVIOUS... TO CAPTURE THE CONVERSION ORGAN.
ATTACK FLEET ONE
KANATA
ピン
PING
ピン
PING
THERE'S ONLY ONE THING WE CAN DO—

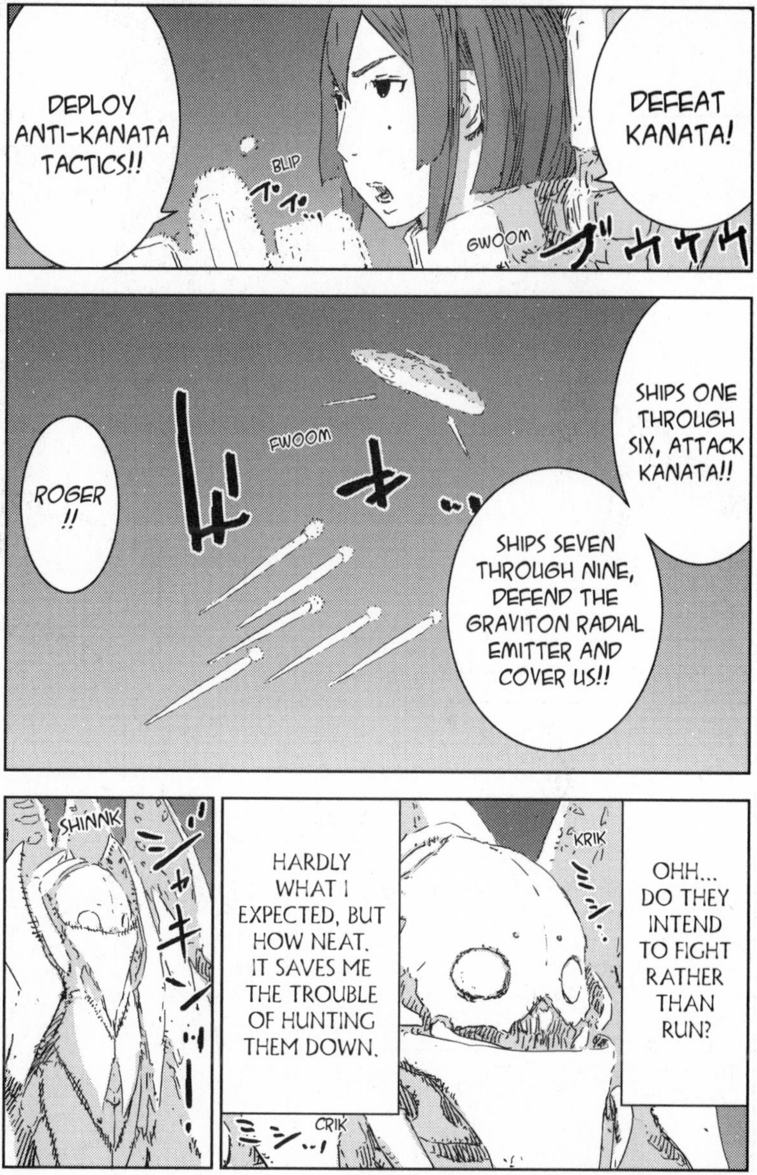
DEFEAT KANATA!
BLIP
DEPLOY ANTI-KANATA TACTICS!!
GWOOM
SHIPS ONE THROUGH SIX, ATTACK KANATA!!
SHIPS SEVEN THROUGH NINE, DEFEND THE GRAVITON RADIAL EMITTER AND COVER US!!
FWOOM
ROGER!!
OHH... DO THEY INTEND TO FIGHT RATHER THAN RUN?
KRIK
HARDLY WHAT I EXPECTED, BUT HOW NEAT. IT SAVES ME THE TROUBLE OF HUNTING THEM DOWN.
CRIK
SHINNK

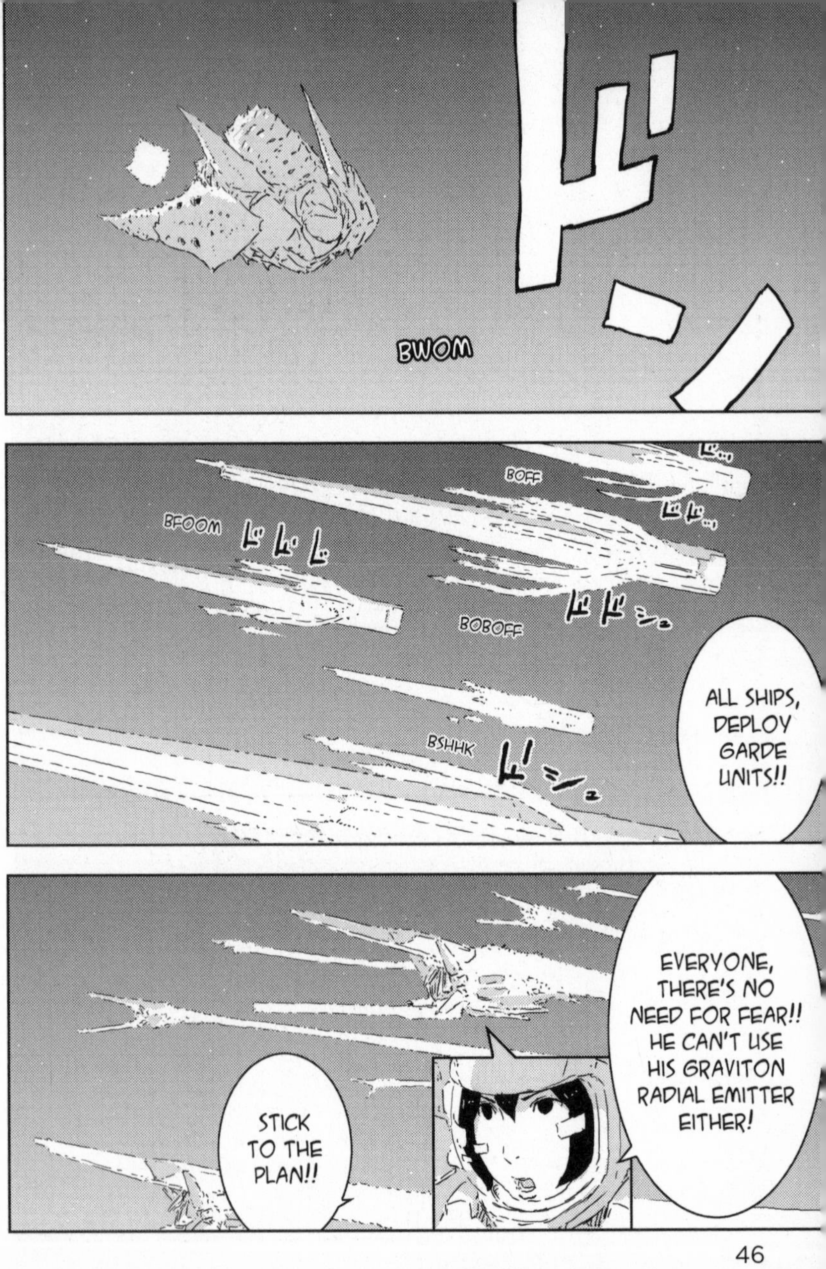

ドン
BWOM
ALL SHIPS, DEPLOY GARDE UNITS!!
BOFF
BFOOM
BOBOFF
BSHHK
EVERYONE, THERE'S NO NEED FOR FEAR!! HE CAN'T USE HIS GRAVITON RADIAL EMITTER EITHER!
STICK TO THE PLAN!!

OCHIAI...
NO MATTER
WHAT YOUR
PHYSICAL FORM,
YOUR INTELLECT
MUST STILL
BE HUMAN.

GWRRRM

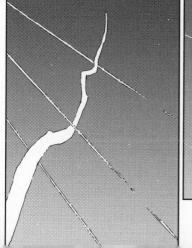

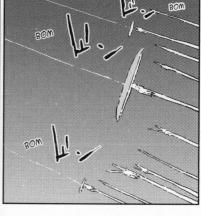

BOM

BOM

BOM

BOM

GKINK

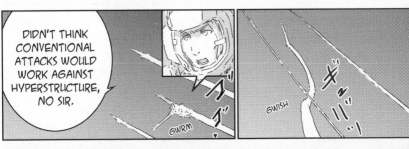

DIDN'T THINK CONVENTIONAL ATTACKS WOULD WORK AGAINST HYPERSTRUCTURE, NO SIR.

GWRM

GWISH

vwwm

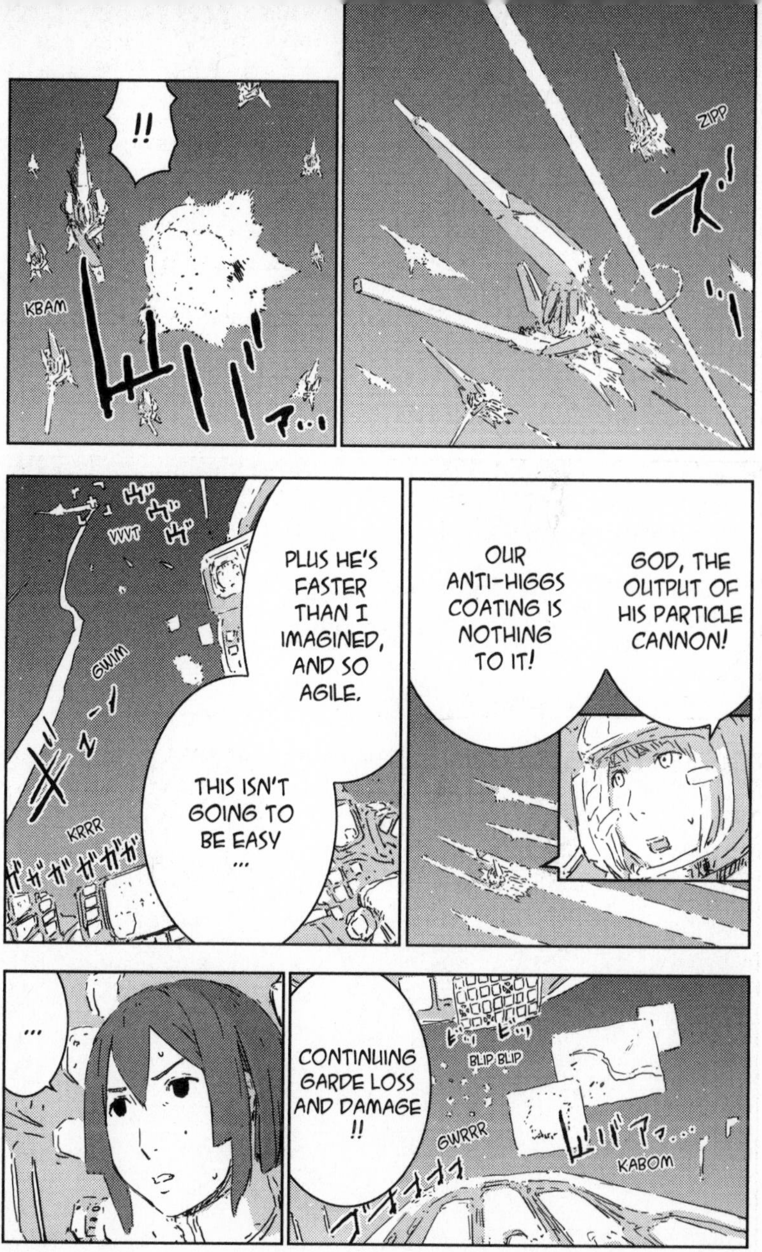
ZIPP
!!
KBAM
GOD, THE OUTPUT OF HIS PARTICLE CANNON!
OUR ANTI-HIGGS COATING IS NOTHING TO IT!
VVVT
PLUS HE'S FASTER THAN I IMAGINED, AND SO AGILE.
GWIM
THIS ISN'T GOING TO BE EASY ...
KRRR
CONTINUING GARDE LOSS AND DAMAGE !!
BLIP BLIP
GWRRR
KABOM
...

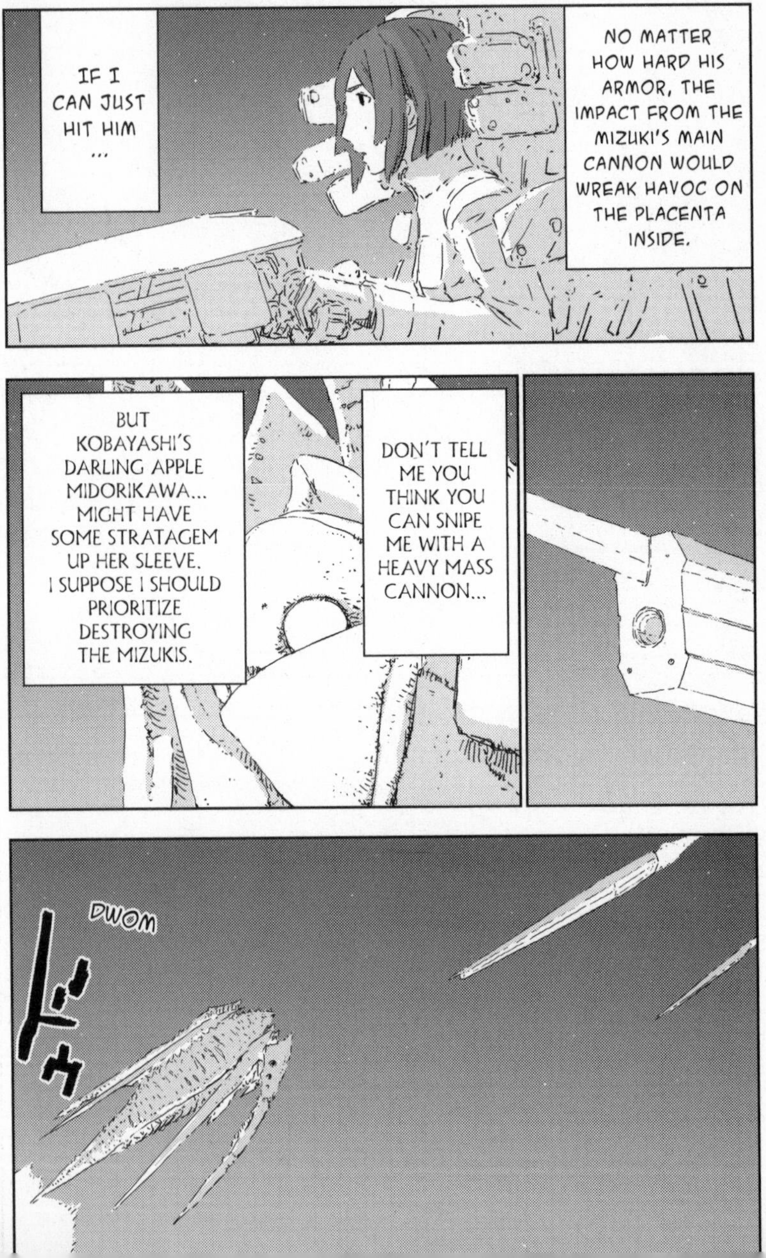
NO MATTER HOW HARD HIS ARMOR, THE IMPACT FROM THE MIZUKI'S MAIN CANNON WOULD WREAK HAVOC ON THE PLACENTA INSIDE.
IF I CAN JUST HIT HIM ...
DON'T TELL ME YOU THINK YOU CAN SNIPE ME WITH A HEAVY MASS CANNON...
BUT KOBAYASHI'S DARLING APPLE MIDORIKAWA... MIGHT HAVE SOME STRATAGEM UP HER SLEEVE. I SUPPOSE I SHOULD PRIORITIZE DESTROYING THE MIZUKIS.
DWOM
ドゥ

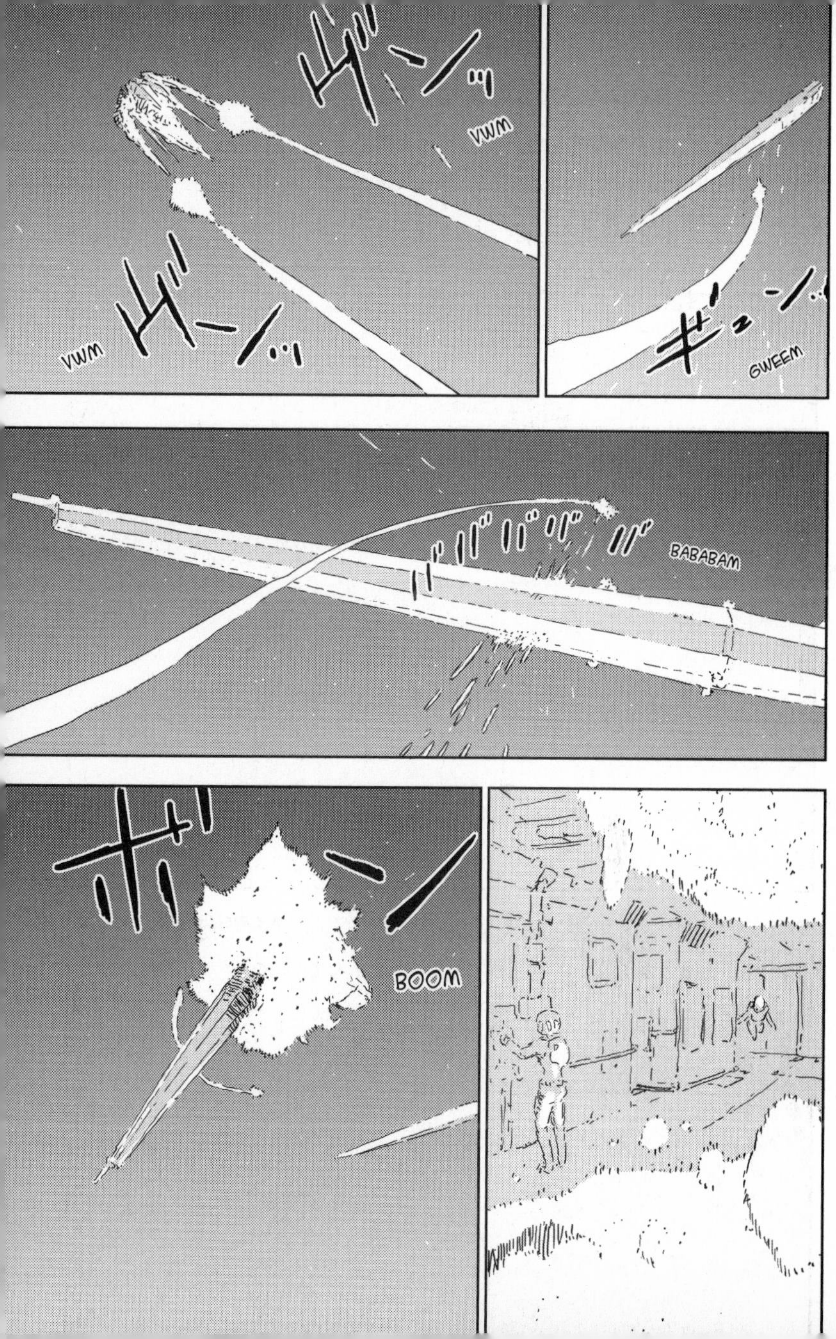
GWEEM
VWM
VWM
BABABAM
BOOM

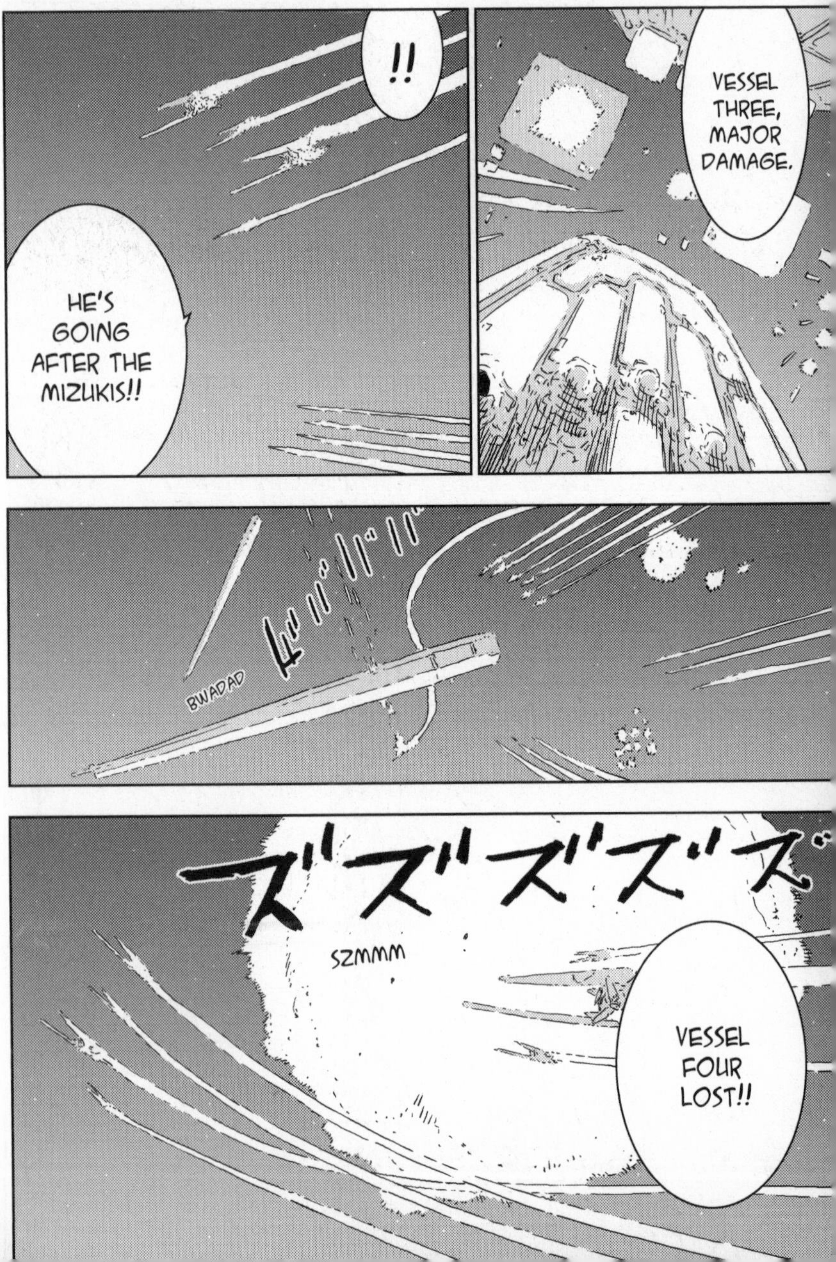

VESSEL THREE, MAJOR DAMAGE.
!!
HE'S GOING AFTER THE MIZUKIS!!
BWADAD
ズズズズズ
SZMMM
VESSEL FOUR LOST!!

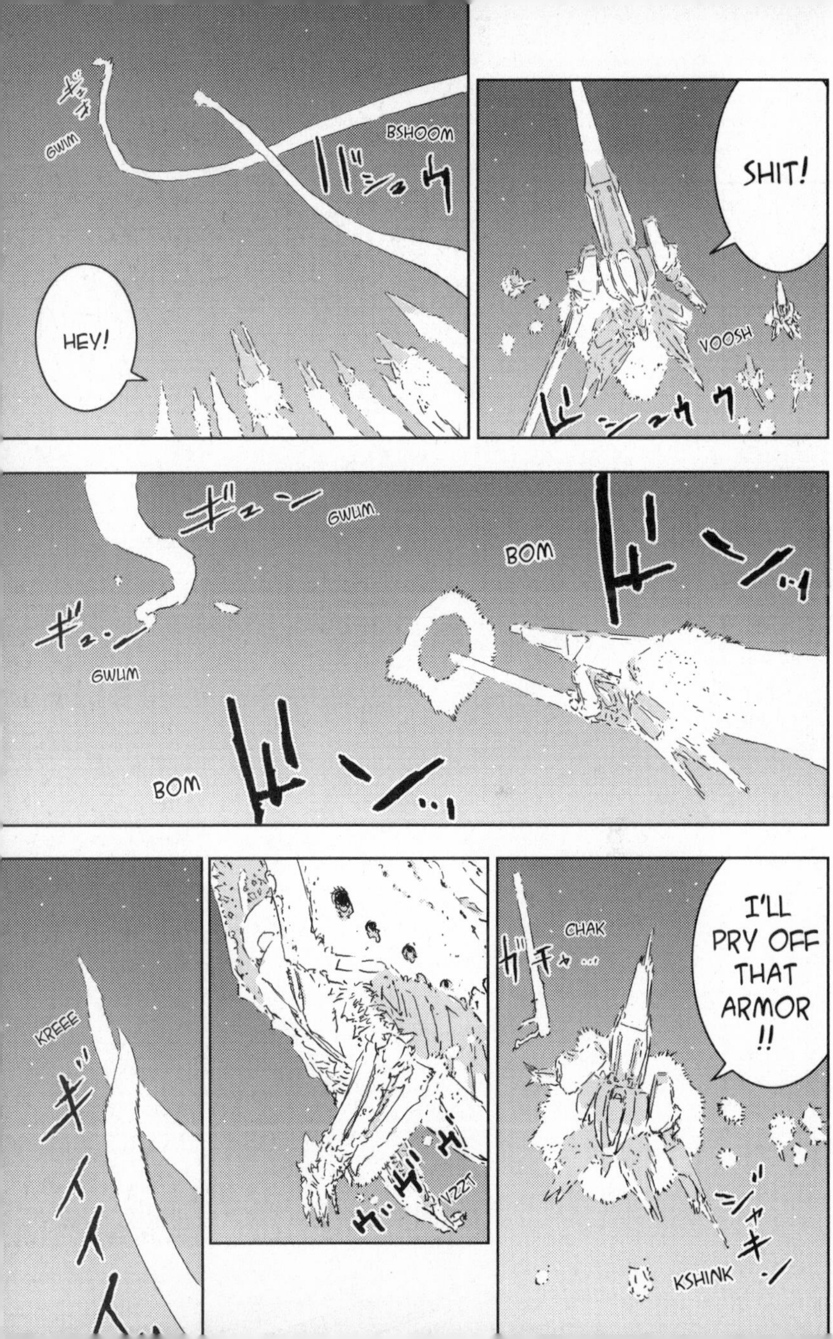
SHIT!
VOOSH
BSHOOM
GWIM
HEY!
BOM
GWUM
GWUM
BOM
I'LL PRY OFF THAT ARMOR !!
CHAK
KSHINK
VZZT
KREEE

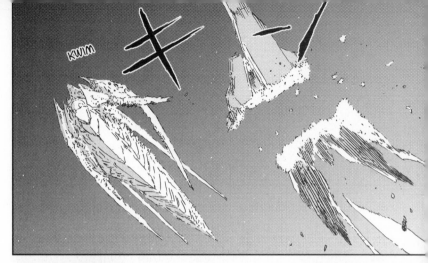

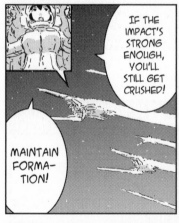

KWIM
KABOMM
MAJOR DAMAGE
UNIT COCKPIT SHELL
MINOR INJURIES
PILOT ALIVE
NOBODY ELSE RUSH IN LIKE AN IDIOT JUST BECAUSE YOU THINK GARDE COCKPIT SHELLS ARE TOUGH!
THRRR
RRRR
IF THE IMPACT'S STRONG ENOUGH, YOU'LL STILL GET CRUSHED!
MAINTAIN FORMA-TION!
BOM
BOM
VVMM
VVMM

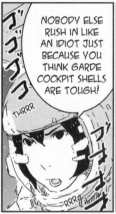

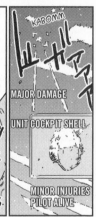

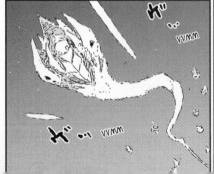

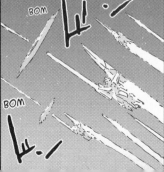

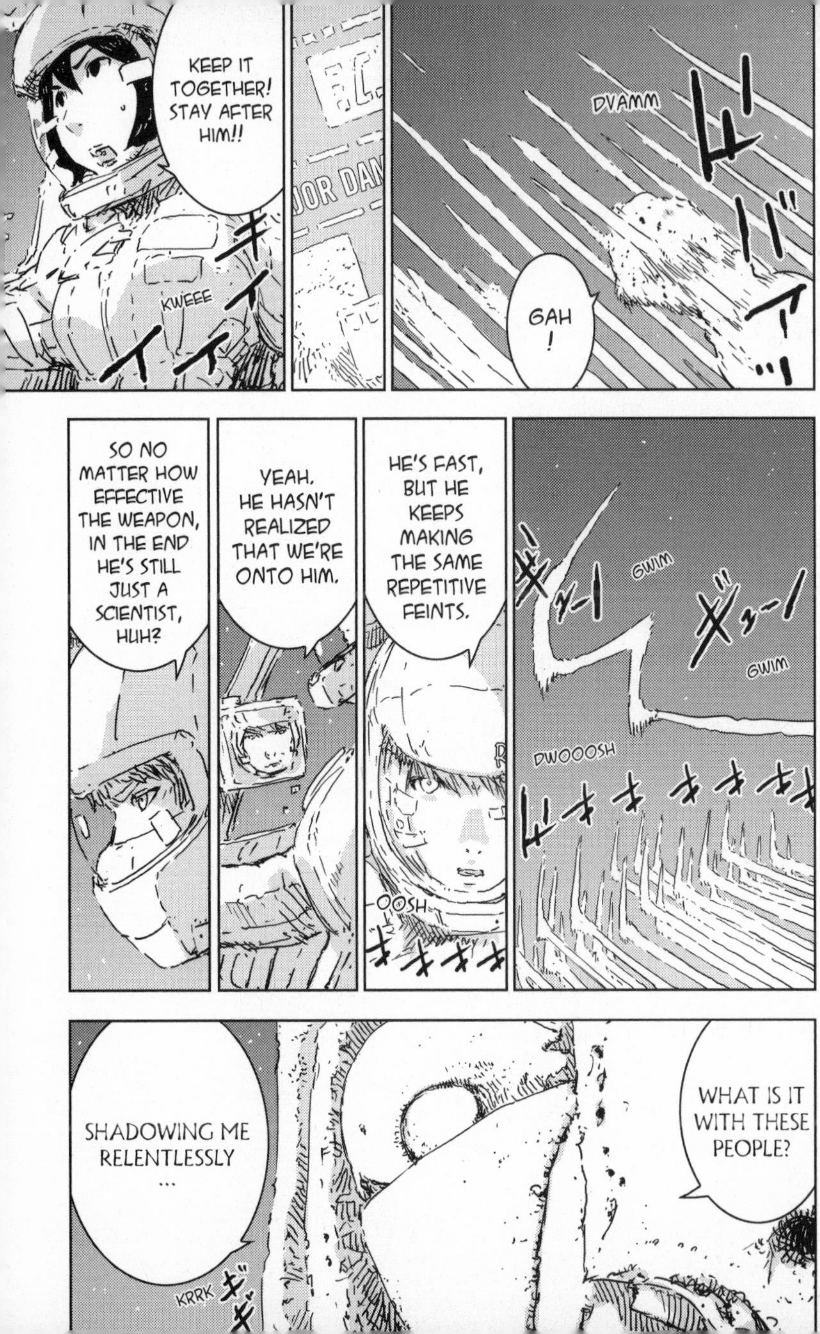
DVAMM
GAH!
KEEP IT TOGETHER! STAY AFTER HIM!!
KWEEE
GWIM
GWIM
DWOOOSH
HE'S FAST, BUT HE KEEPS MAKING THE SAME REPETITIVE FEINTS.
OOSH
YEAH. HE HASN'T REALIZED THAT WE'RE ONTO HIM.
SO NO MATTER HOW EFFECTIVE THE WEAPON, IN THE END HE'S STILL JUST A SCIENTIST, HUH?
WHAT IS IT WITH THESE PEOPLE?
FS
SHADOWING ME RELENTLESSLY ...
KRRK

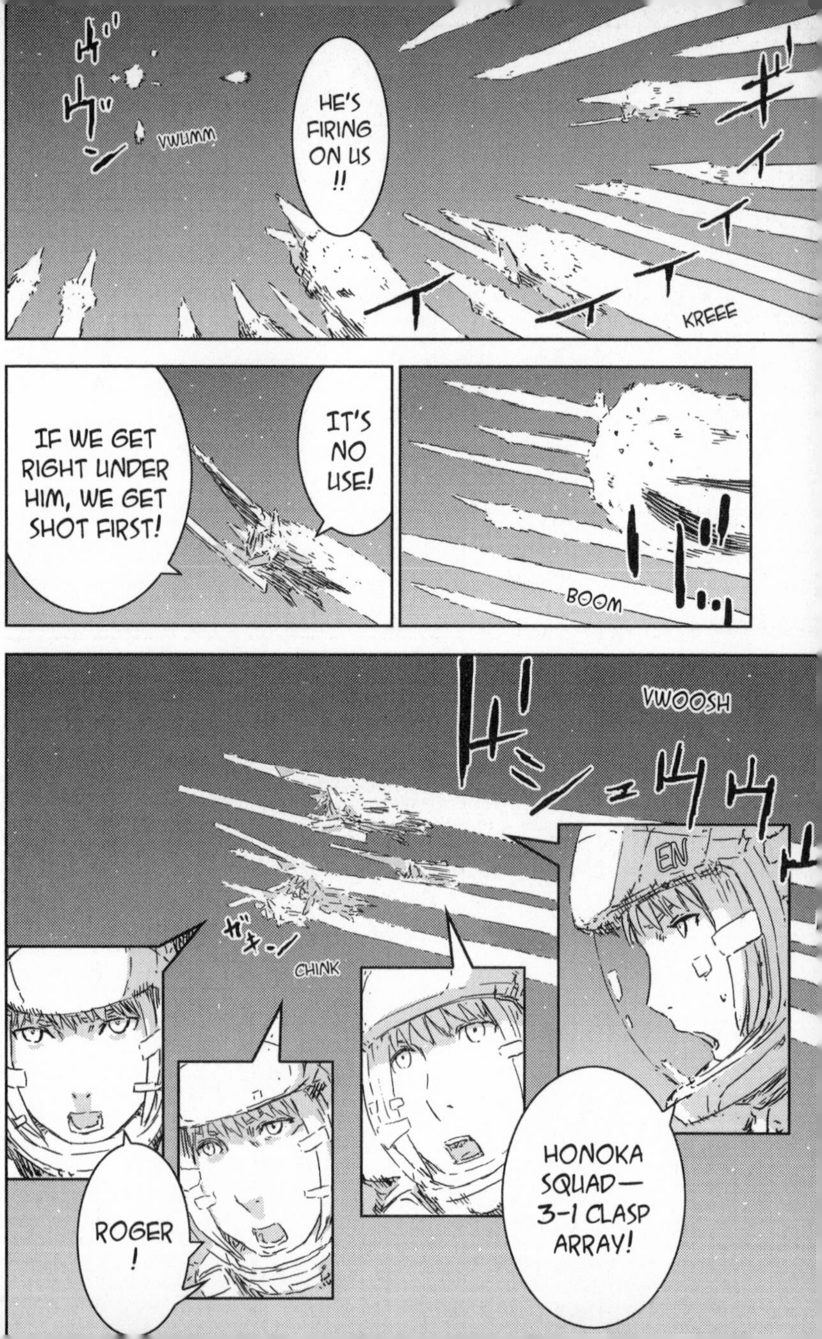

KREEE
HE'S FIRING ON US !!
VWUMM
BOOM
IT'S NO USE!
IF WE GET RIGHT UNDER HIM, WE GET SHOT FIRST!
VWOOSH
HONOKA SQUAD— 3-1 CLASP ARRAY!
CHINK
ROGER !

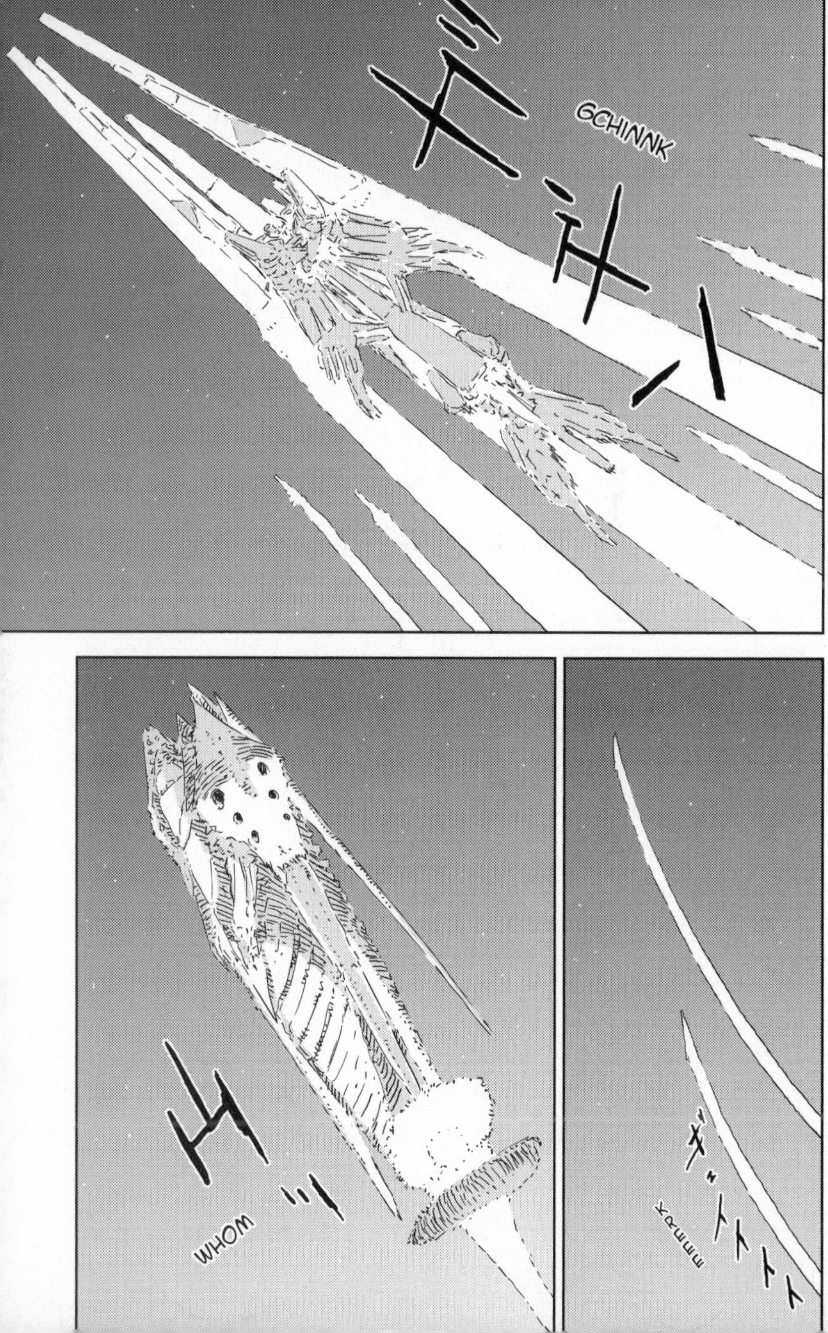
GCHINNK
KREEEE
WHOM

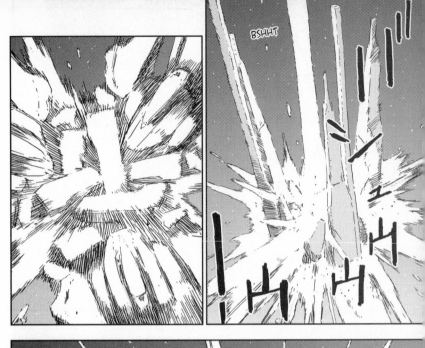

BSHHT

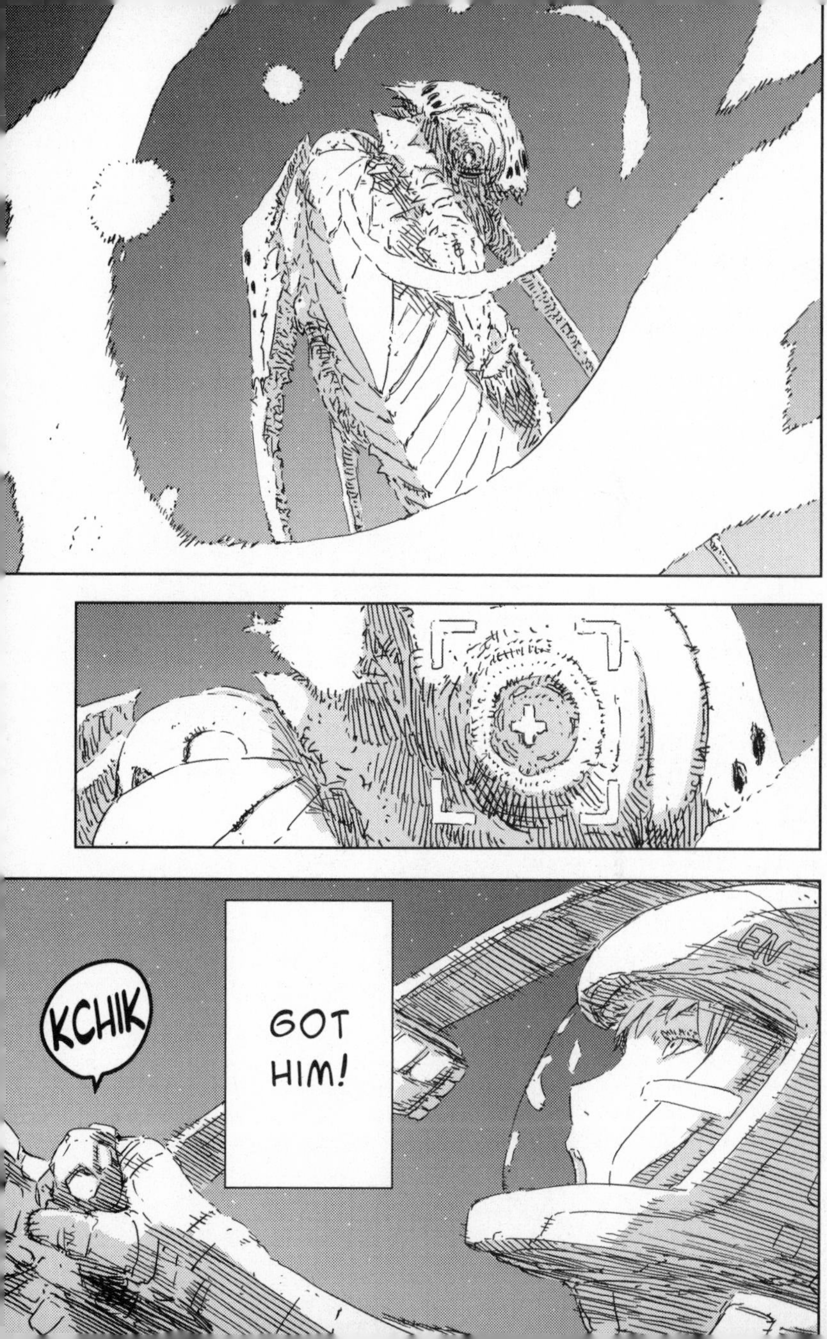
KCHIK
GOT HIM!

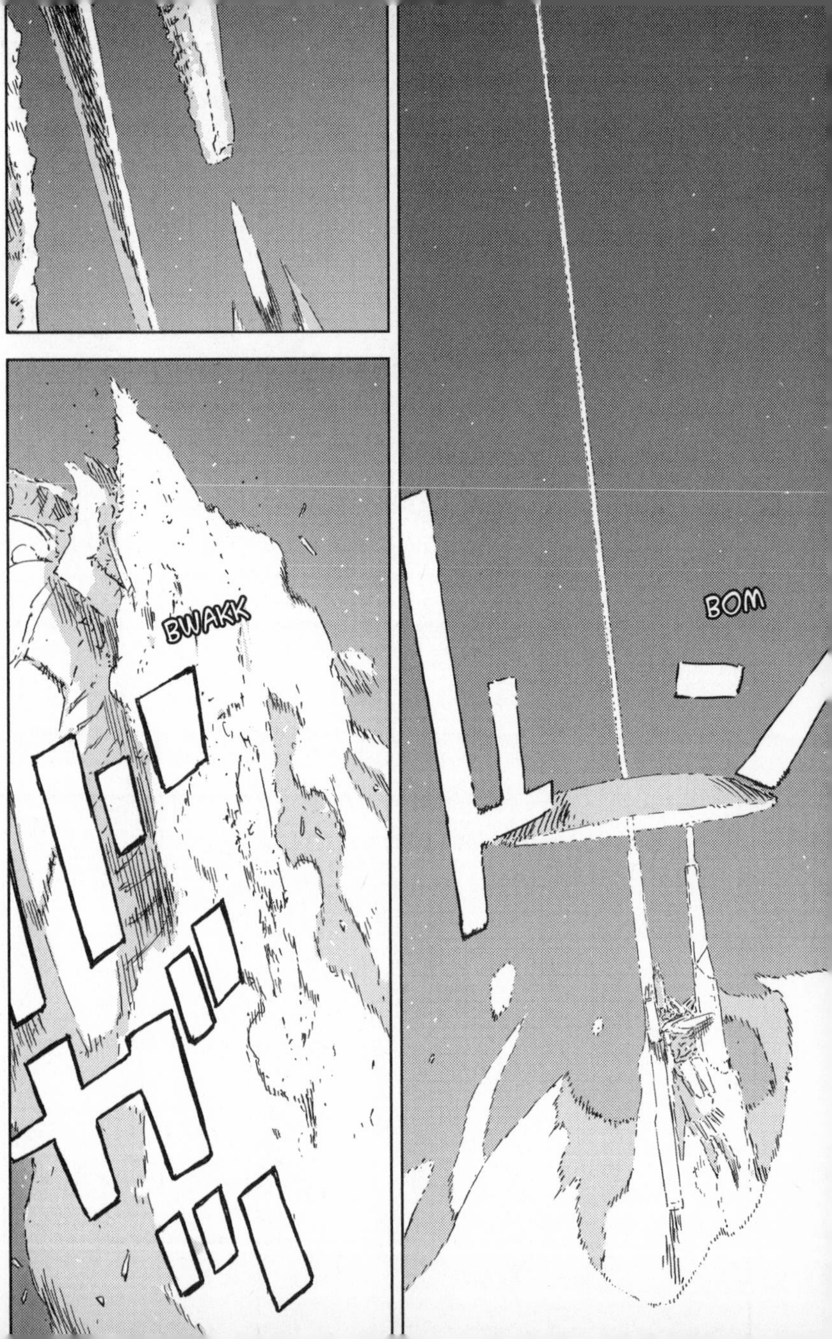
BOM
BWAKK

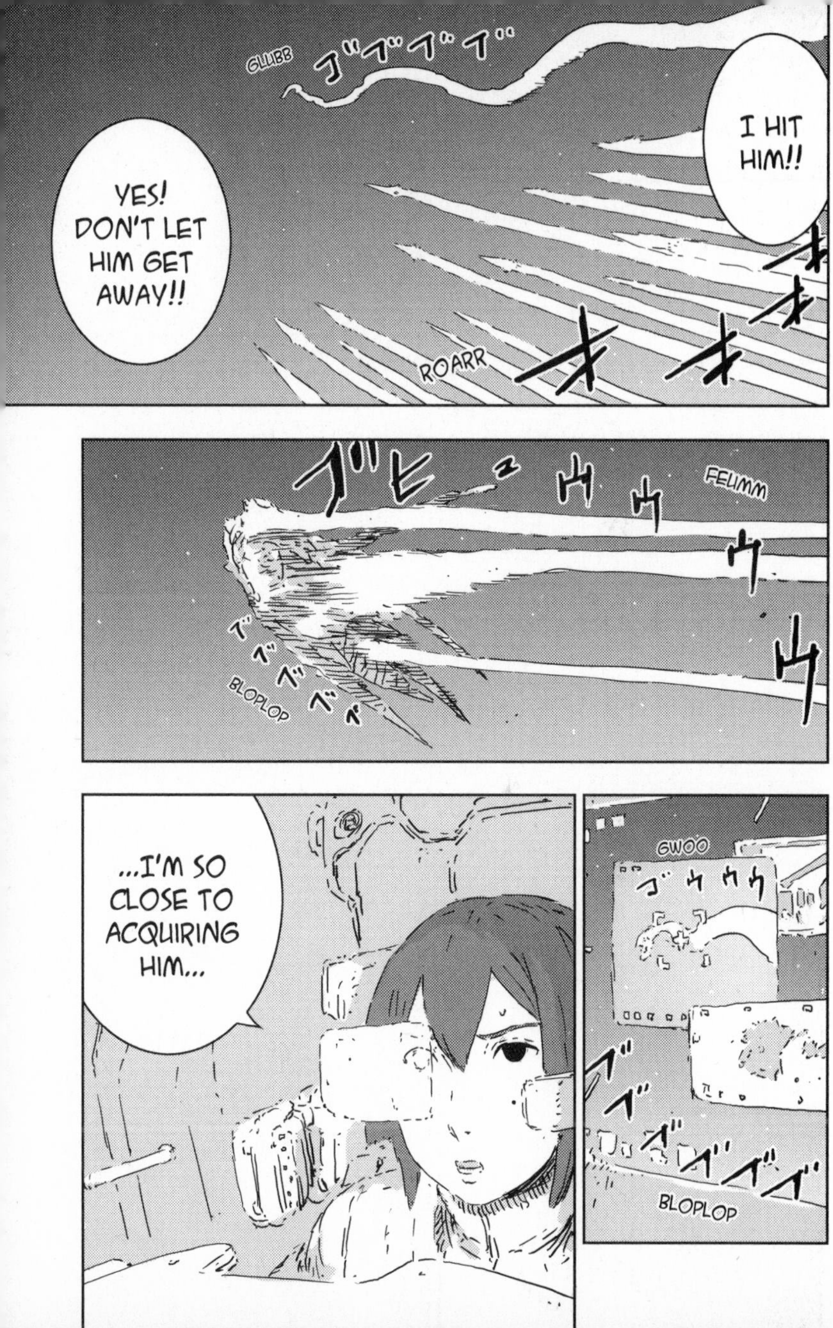
I HIT HIM!!
GLUBB
YES! DON'T LET HIM GET AWAY!!
ROARR
FEUMM
BLOPLOP
GWOO
BLOPLOP
...I'M SO CLOSE TO ACQUIRING HIM...

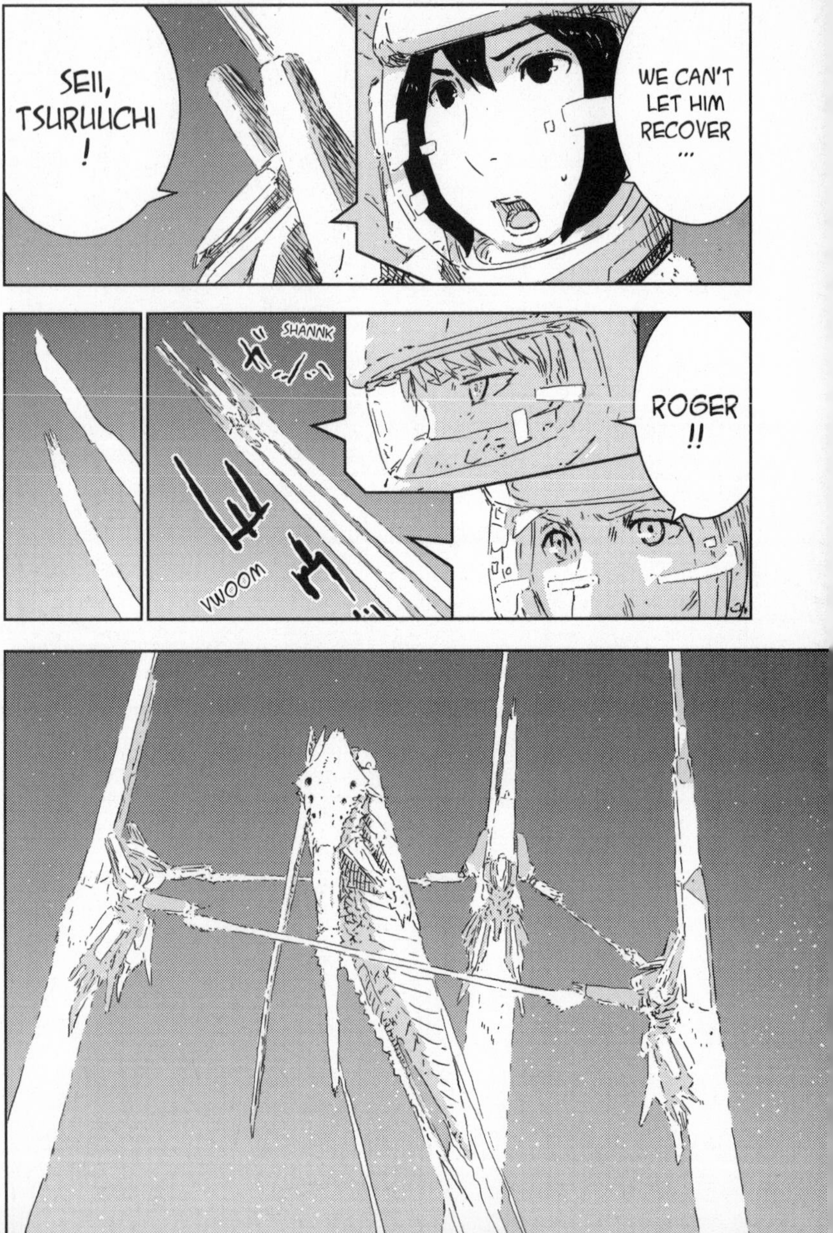
WE CAN'T LET HIM RECOVER ...
SEII, TSURUUCHI !
ROGER !!
SHANNK
VWOOM

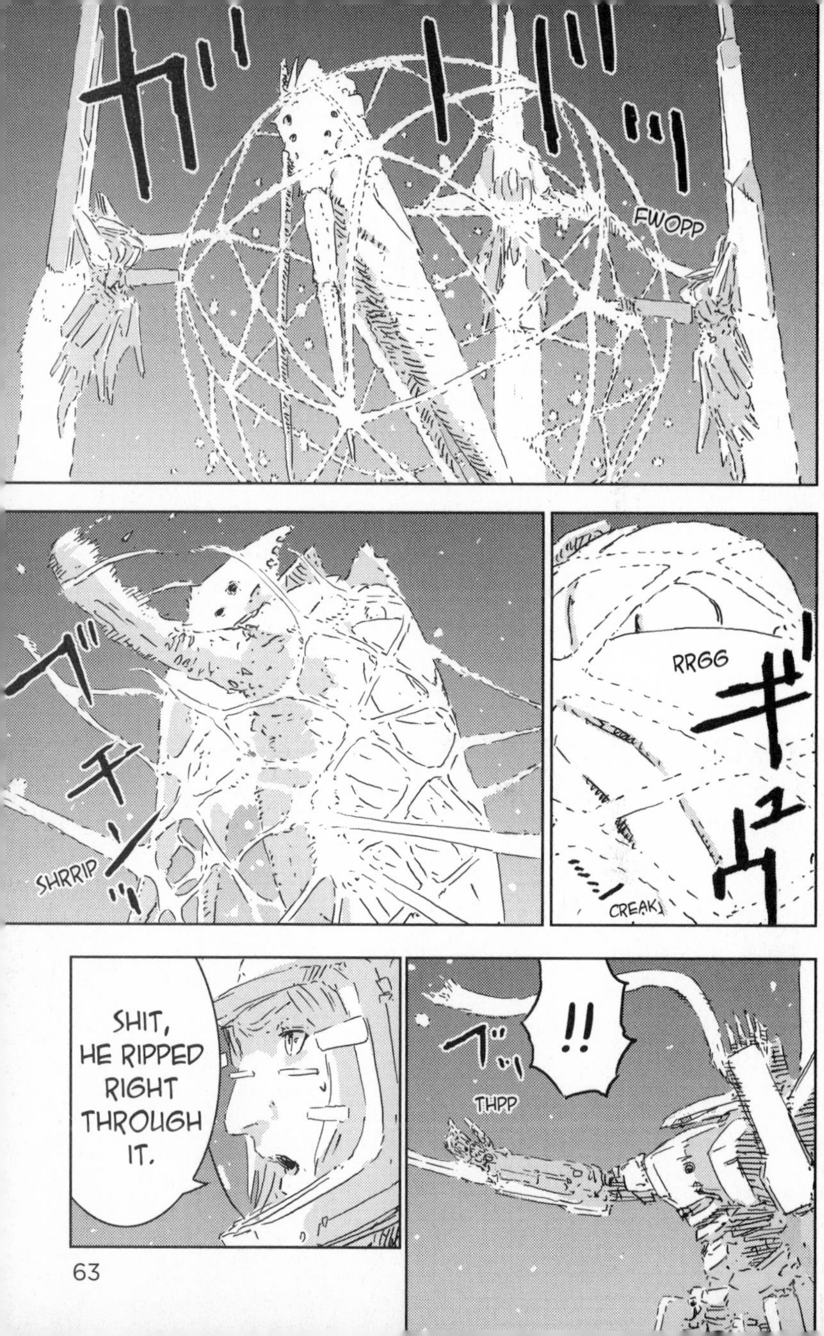
FWOPP
RRGG
CREAK
SHRRIP
!!
THPP
SHIT, HE RIPPED RIGHT THROUGH IT.

THUD

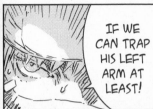

IF WE CAN TRAP HIS LEFT ARM AT LEAST!

PSSHT

BASHT

BCHOOM

WHUNK

GZZZZ

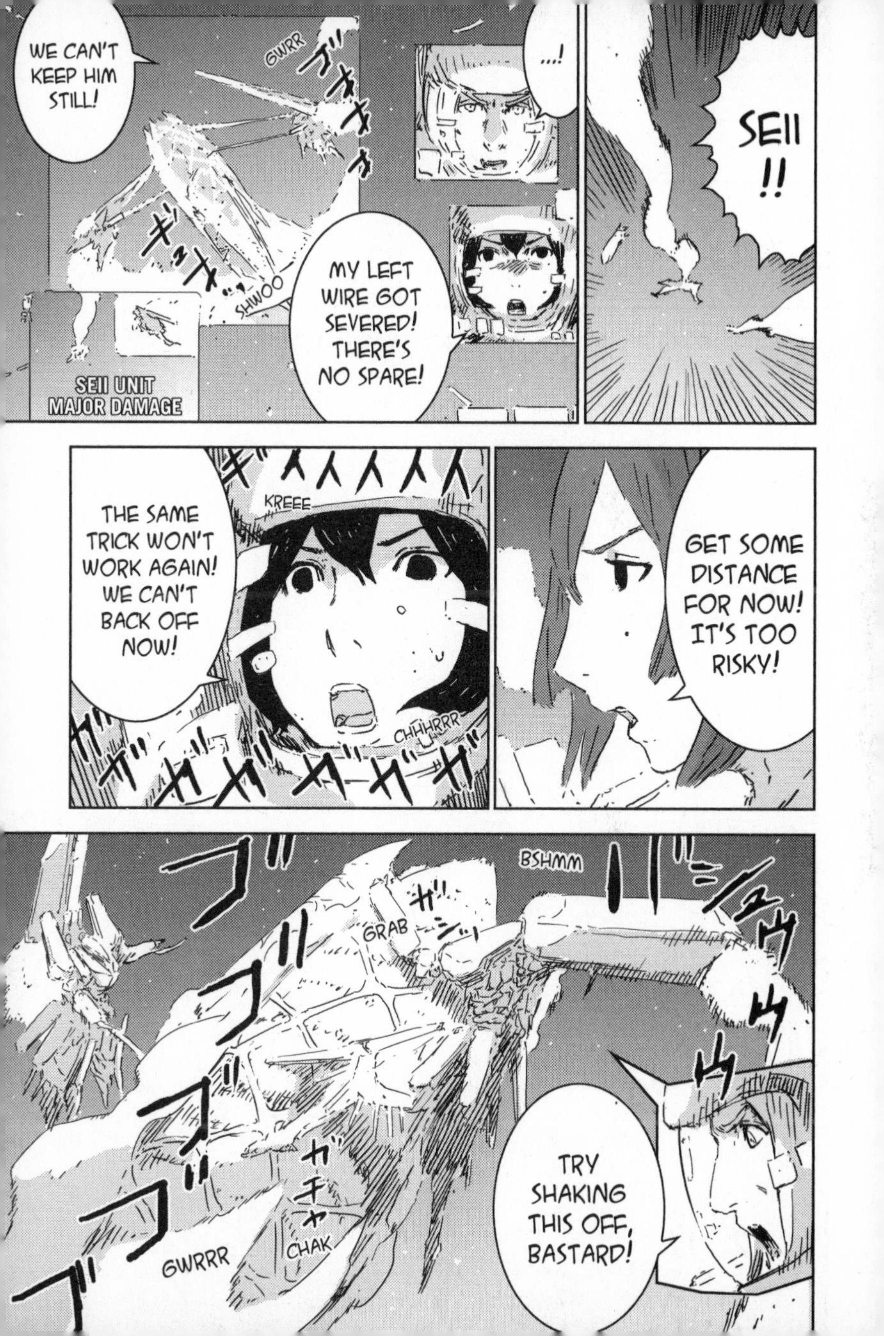
SEII !!
...!
MY LEFT WIRE GOT SEVERED! THERE'S NO SPARE!
WE CAN'T KEEP HIM STILL!
GWRR
SHWOO
SEII UNIT MAJOR DAMAGE
GET SOME DISTANCE FOR NOW! IT'S TOO RISKY!
KREEE
THE SAME TRICK WON'T WORK AGAIN! WE CAN'T BACK OFF NOW!
CHHHRRR
BSHMM
TRY SHAKING THIS OFF, BASTARD!
GRAB
CHAK
GWRRR

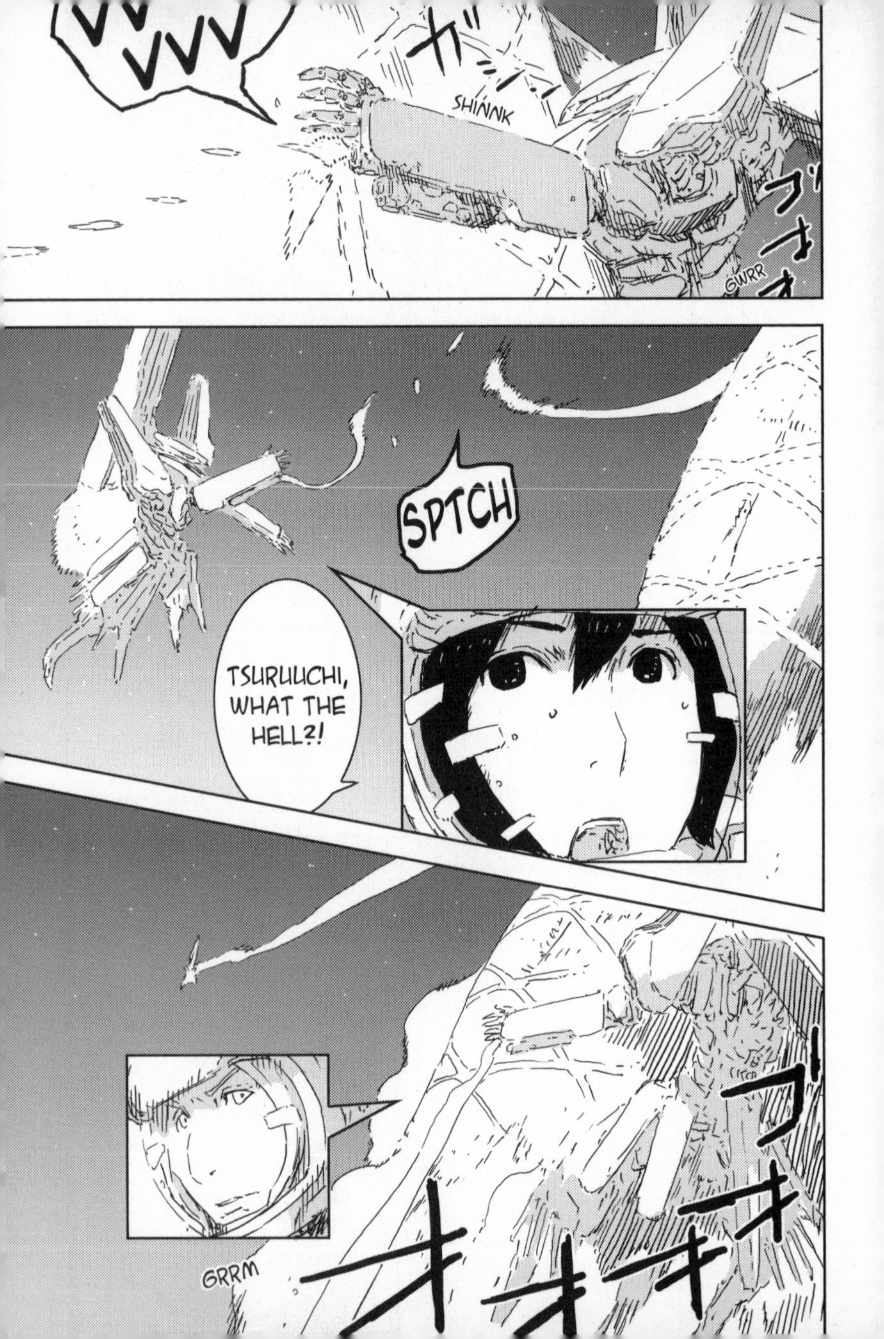
GWRR
SHINNK
SPTCH
TSURUUCHI, WHAT THE HELL?!
GRRM

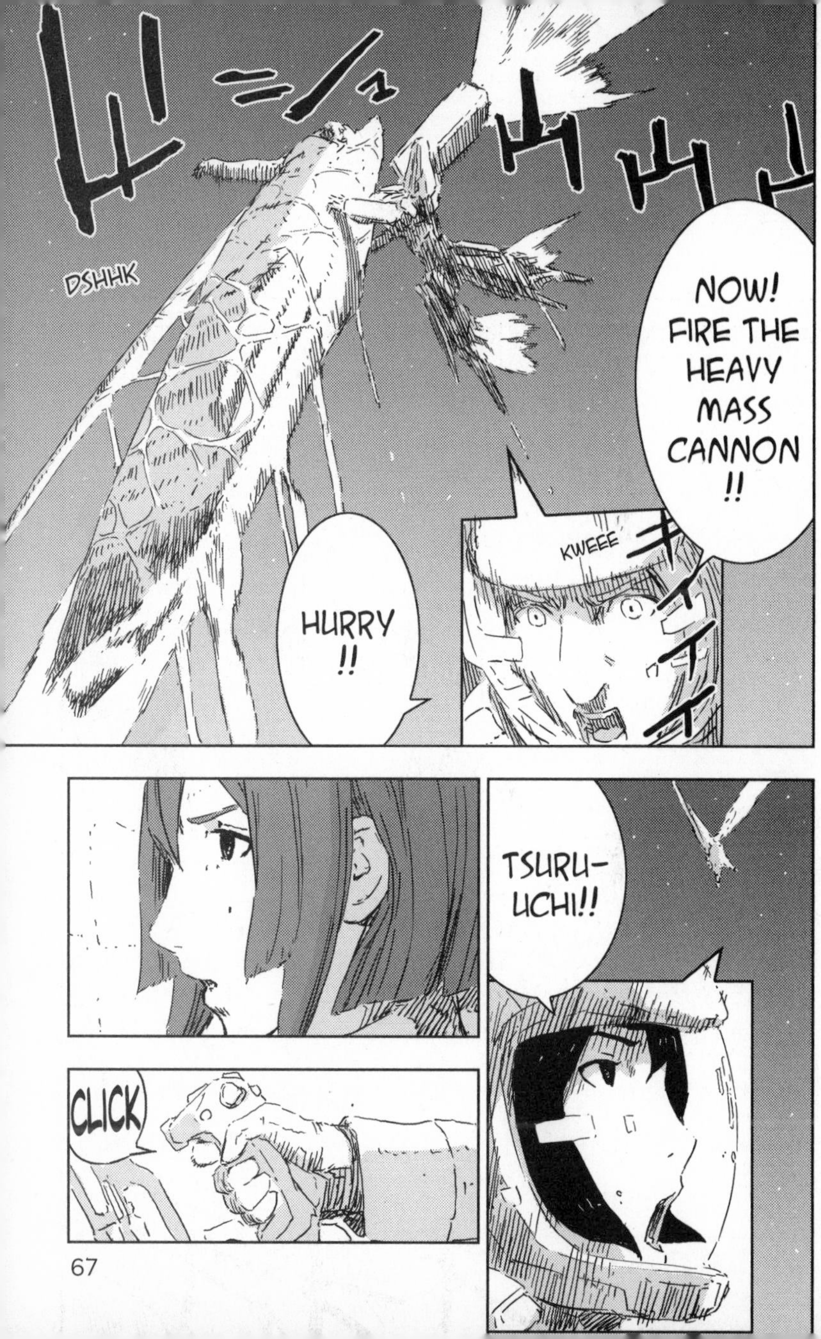
DSHHK
NOW! FIRE THE HEAVY MASS CANNON !!
KWEEE
HURRY !!
TSURU-UCHI!!
CLICK

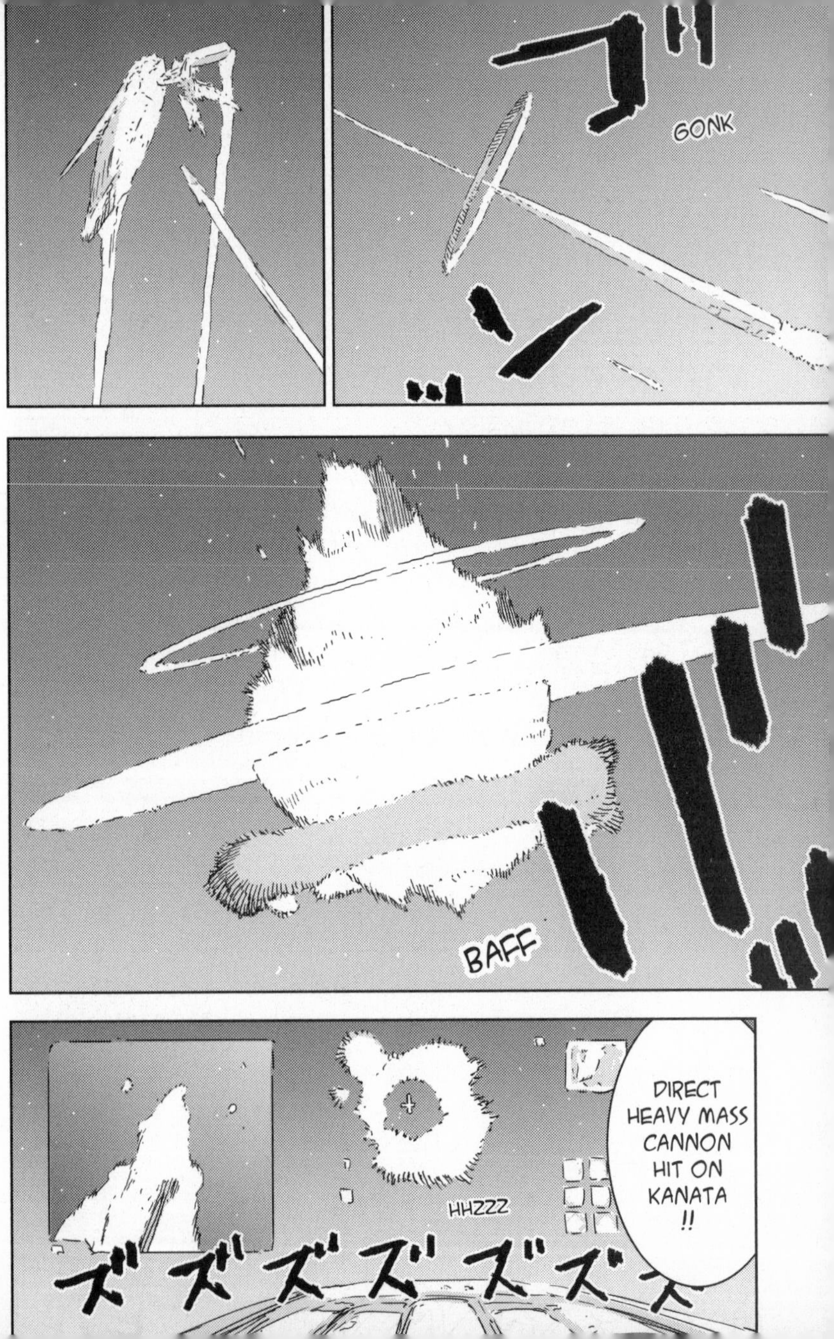
GONK
BAFF
DIRECT HEAVY MASS CANNON HIT ON KANATA !!
HHZZZ

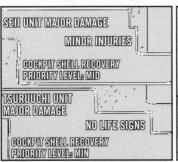

SEII UNIT MAJOR DAMAGE

MINOR INJURIES

COCKPIT SHELL RECOVERY
PRIORITY LEVEL: MID

TSURUUCHI UNIT
MAJOR DAMAGE

NO LIFE SIGNS

COCKPIT SHELL RECOVERY
PRIORITY LEVEL: MIN

AFTER HIM!!

DSHOO

DESTROY THE CORE BEFORE THE PLACENTA REGENERATES!!

TSURU-UCHI...

OOM

ROGER!!

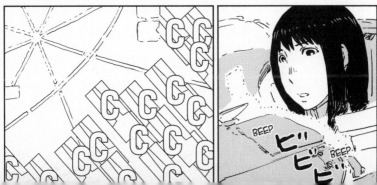

BEEP

ビ゛ビ゛

BEEP

ビ

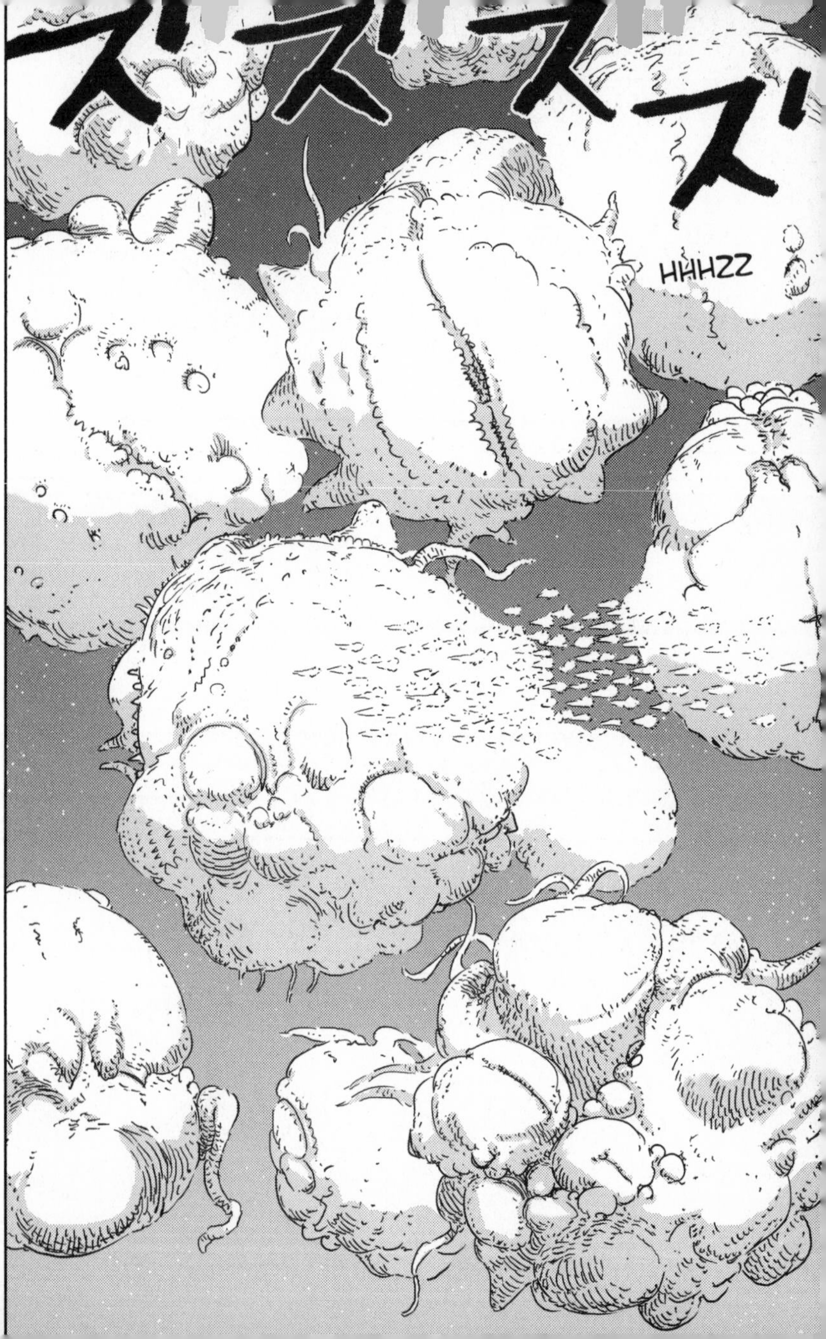
ズズズズ
HHHZZ

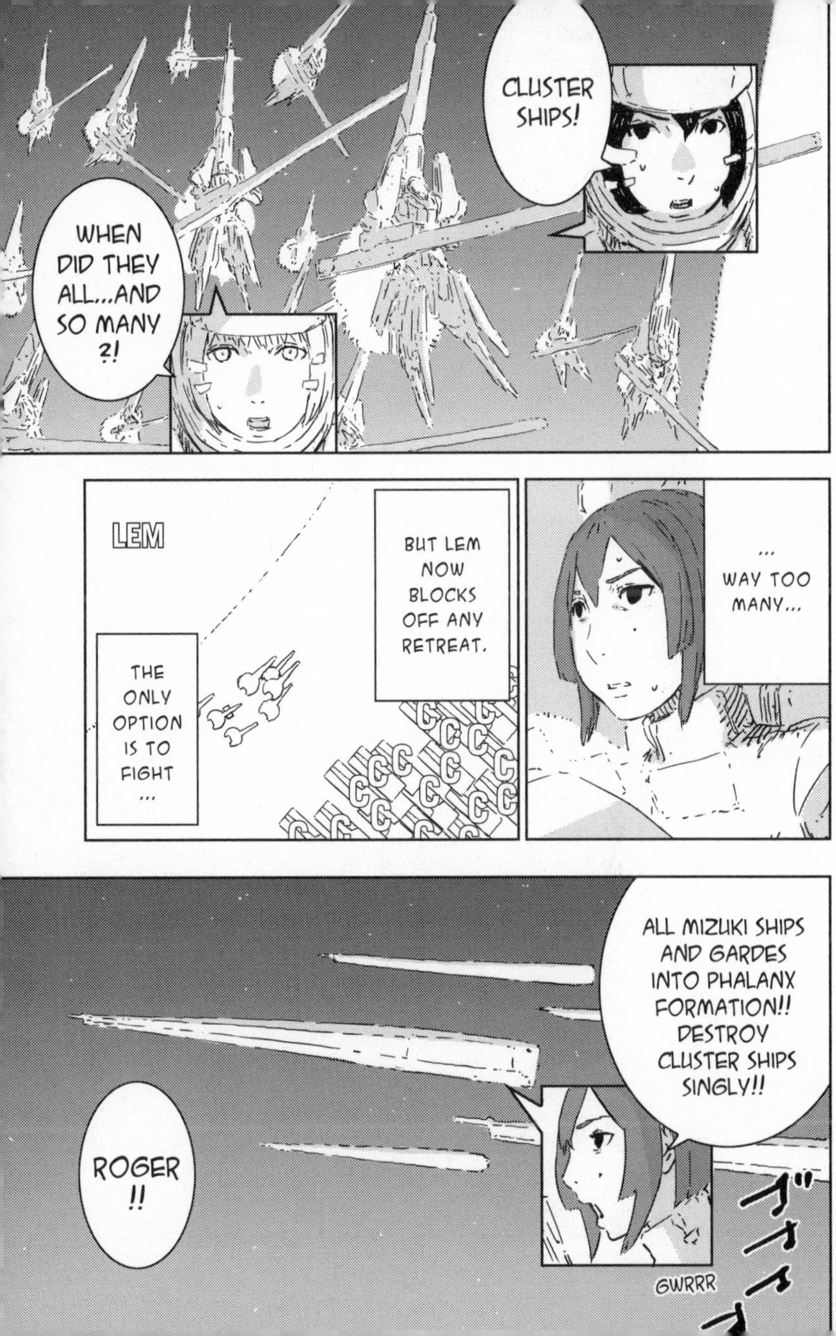
CLUSTER SHIPS!
WHEN DID THEY ALL...AND SO MANY ?!
... WAY TOO MANY...
BUT LEM NOW BLOCKS OFF ANY RETREAT.
LEM
THE ONLY OPTION IS TO FIGHT ...
ALL MIZUKI SHIPS AND GARDES INTO PHALANX FORMATION!! DESTROY CLUSTER SHIPS SINGLY!!
GWRRR
ROGER !!

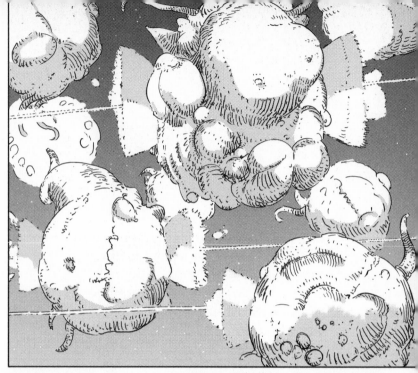

THREE CLUSTER SHIPS HAVE DISINTEGRATED INTO FOAM STATE!!

THWOOM

?!

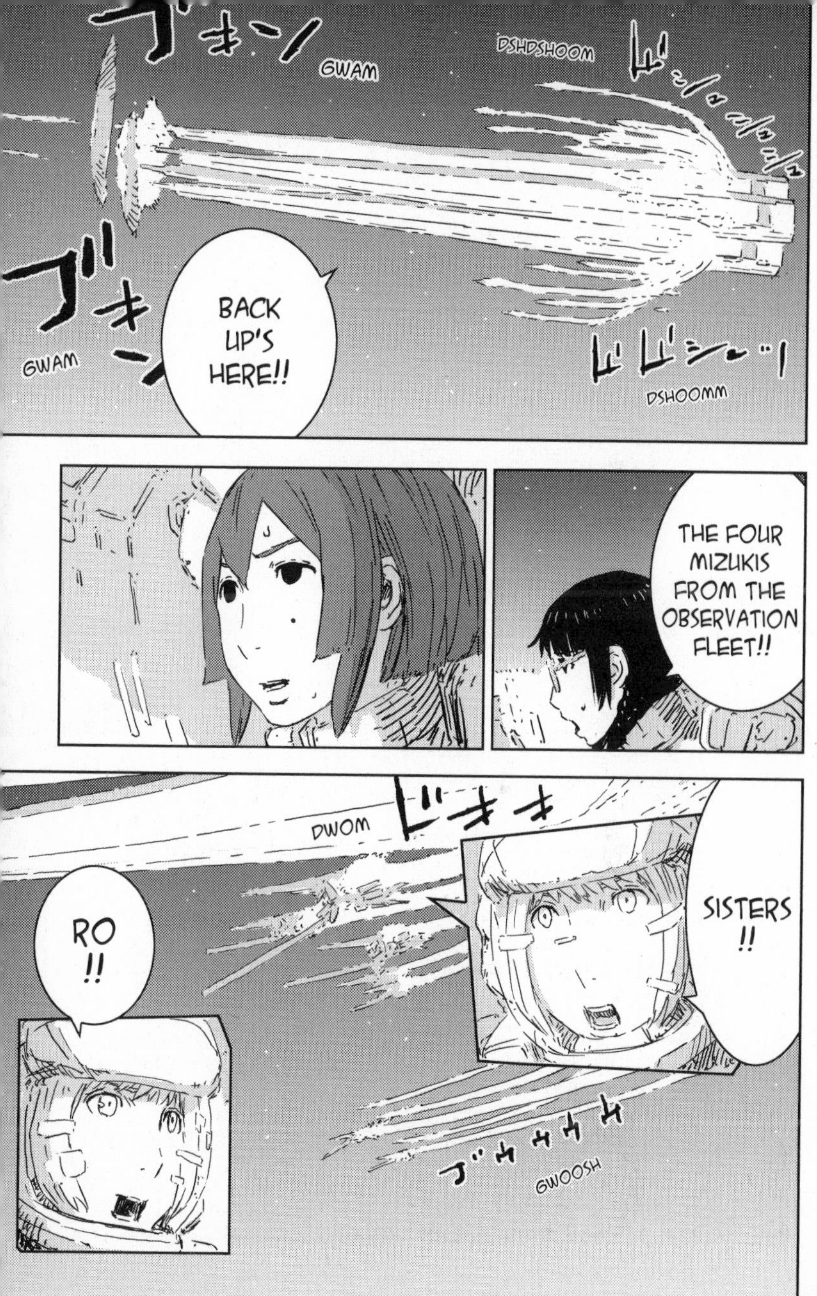
DSHDSHOOM
GWAM
DSHOOMM
BACK UP'S HERE!!
GWAM
THE FOUR MIZUKIS FROM THE OBSERVATION FLEET!!
DWOM
SISTERS!!
RO!!
GWOOSH

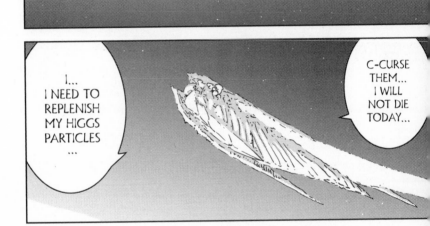

C-CURSE THEM... I WILL NOT DIE TODAY...
I... I NEED TO REPLENISH MY HIGGS PARTICLES ...
THE CONVERSION ORGAN... QUICK...
!!! ...

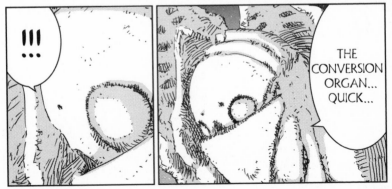

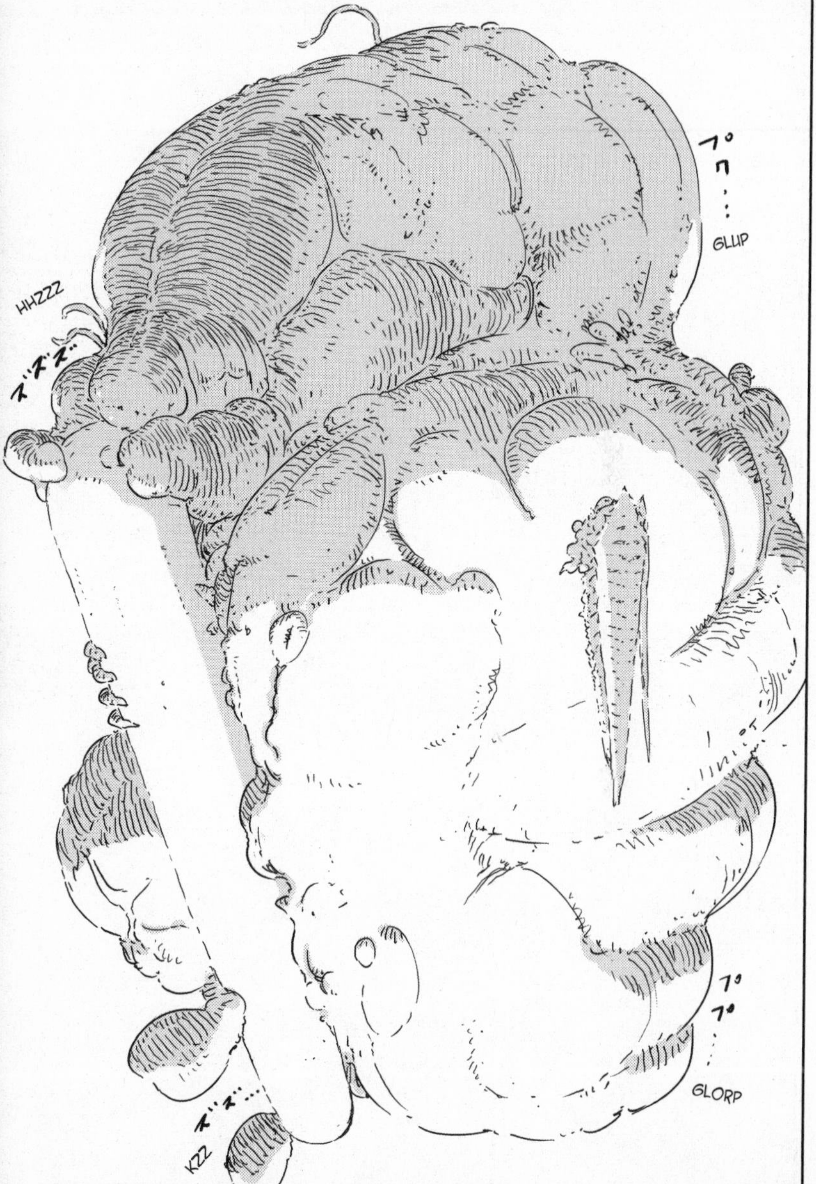

プク…
GLUP
ズズズ…
HHZZZ
ププ…
GLORP
ズズ…
KZZ

Chapter 73: END

シドニアの騎士
KNIGHTS OF SIDONIA

Chapter 74: Captain Kobayashi's Determination

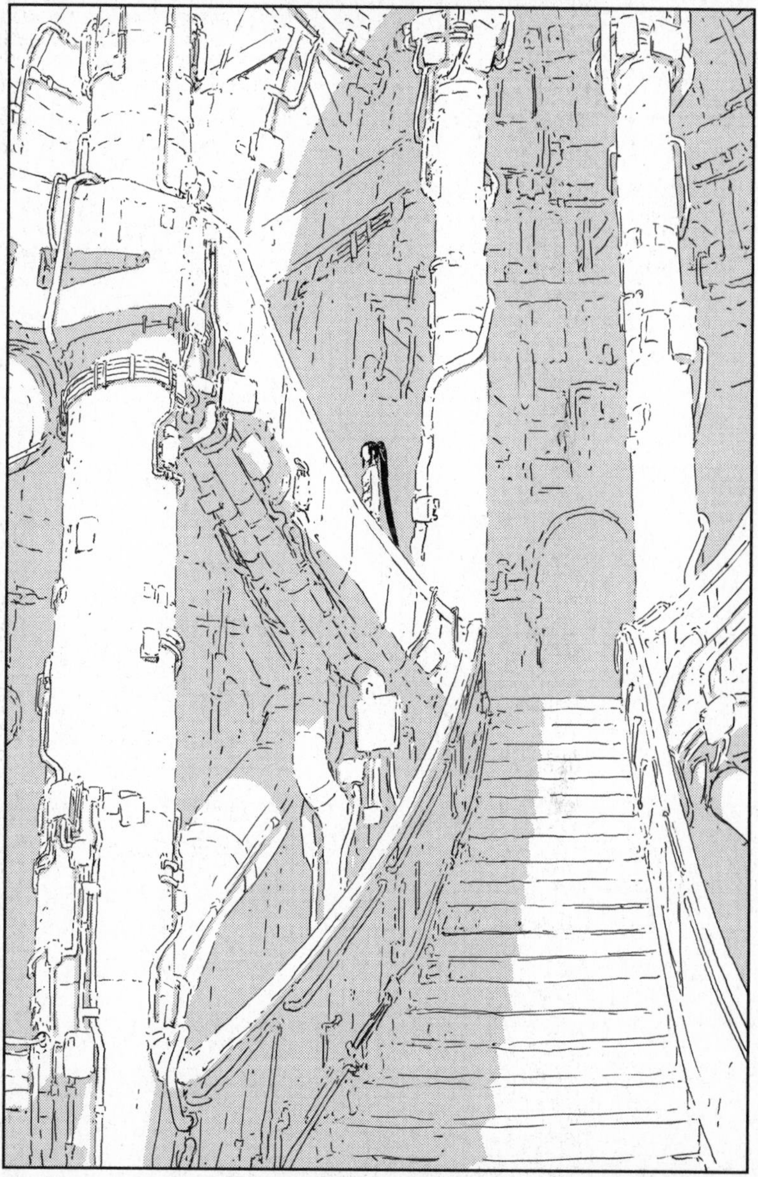

One Hundred Sights of Sidonia Part Fifty-Seven: Captain's Official Residence

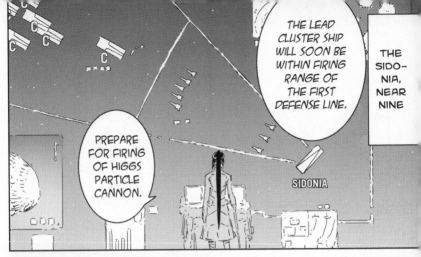

THE SIDO-NIA, NEAR NINE
THE LEAD CLUSTER SHIP WILL SOON BE WITHIN FIRING RANGE OF THE FIRST DEFENSE LINE.
PREPARE FOR FIRING OF HIGGS PARTICLE CANNON.
SIDONIA
VVVVTT
VWUMM

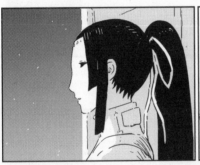

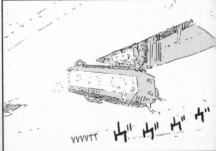

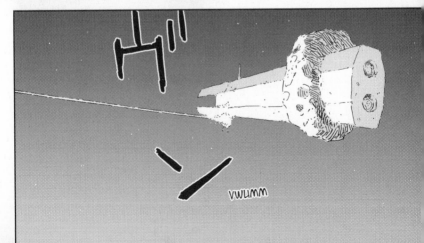

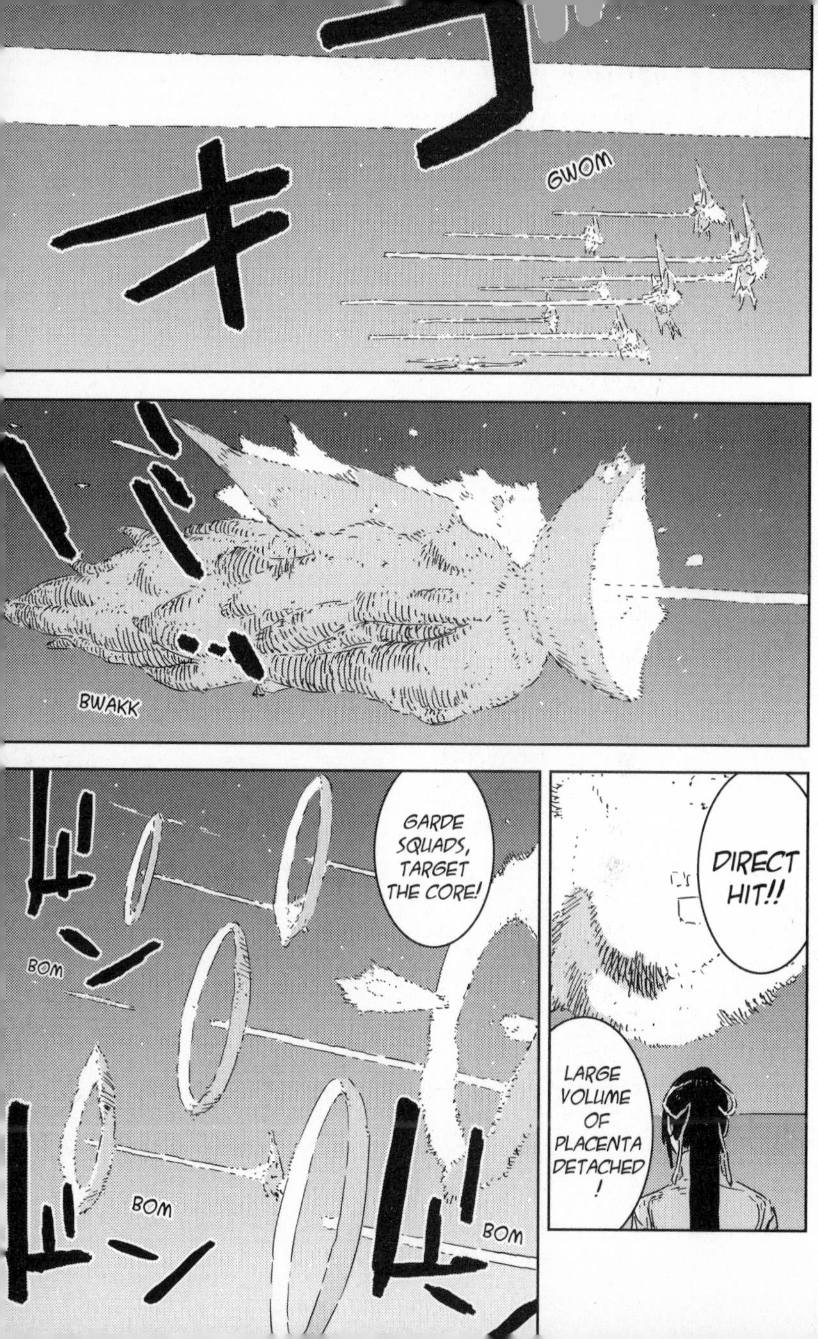
GWOM
BWAKK
DIRECT HIT!!
LARGE VOLUME OF PLACENTA DETACHED!
GARDE SQUADS, TARGET THE CORE!
BOM
BOM
BOM

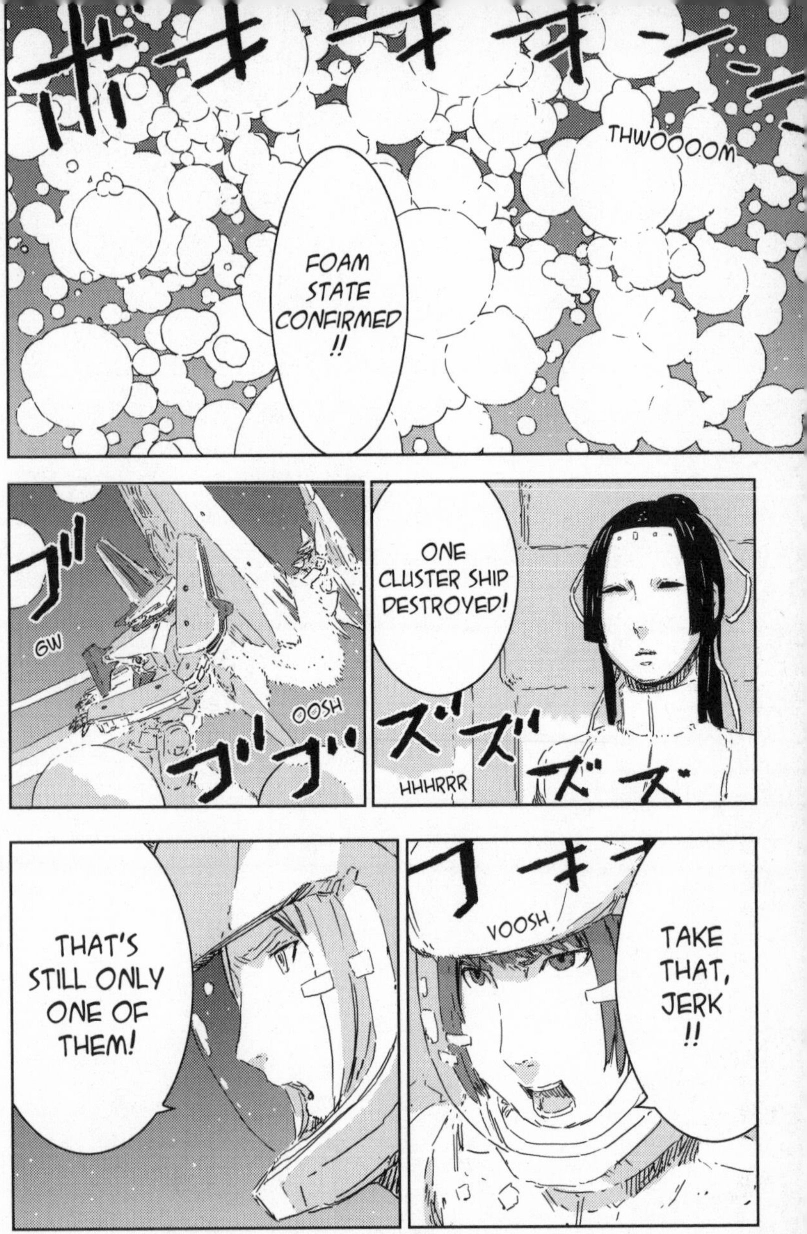
THWOOOOM
FOAM STATE CONFIRMED!!
ONE CLUSTER SHIP DESTROYED!
HHHRRR
GW
OOSH
VOOSH
TAKE THAT, JERK!!
THAT'S STILL ONLY ONE OF THEM!

?!
THE CLUSTER SHIPS ARE AMASSING !!
ズズ…
SHZZ
KRRK
ズズ…
HHZZ
KRIK
ギギ
GLLSH

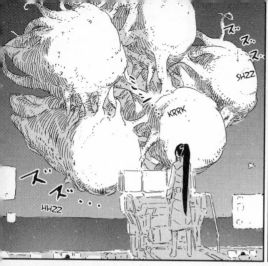

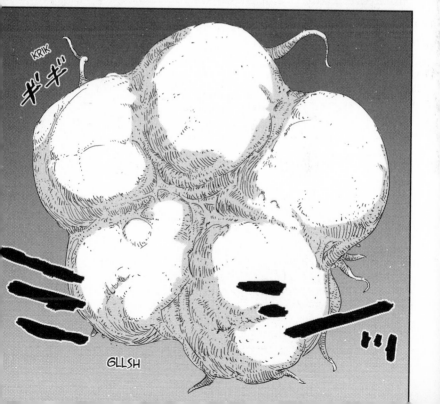

THEY'VE LINKED UP!!
SUITS ME, IT MEANS WE ONLY HAVE TO DESTROY THE ONE MAIN CORE!!
BOM
BOM
BOFF
BUP
BWUF
WE'RE NOT DOING ANY-THING!!
RIPPLES?!
THE FIRST WE'VE EVER SEEN!
THE PLACENTA HAS A HIGHER VISCOSITY THAN USUAL!!
MAIN CORE
PLACENTA
EVEN IF WE EXHAUSTED ALL OF SIDONIA'S HEAVY MASS CANNONS, WE'D NEVER BE ABLE TO PEEL IT OFF!
VWMM
BWOSH

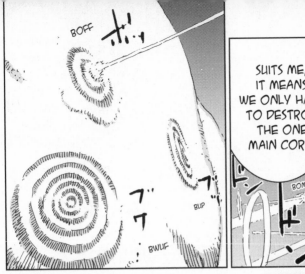

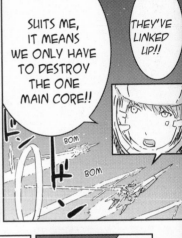

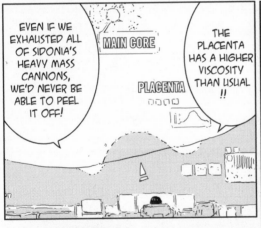

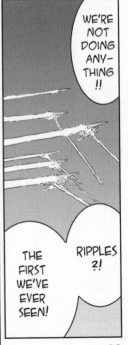

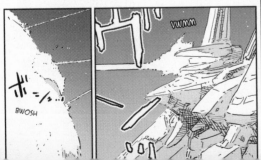

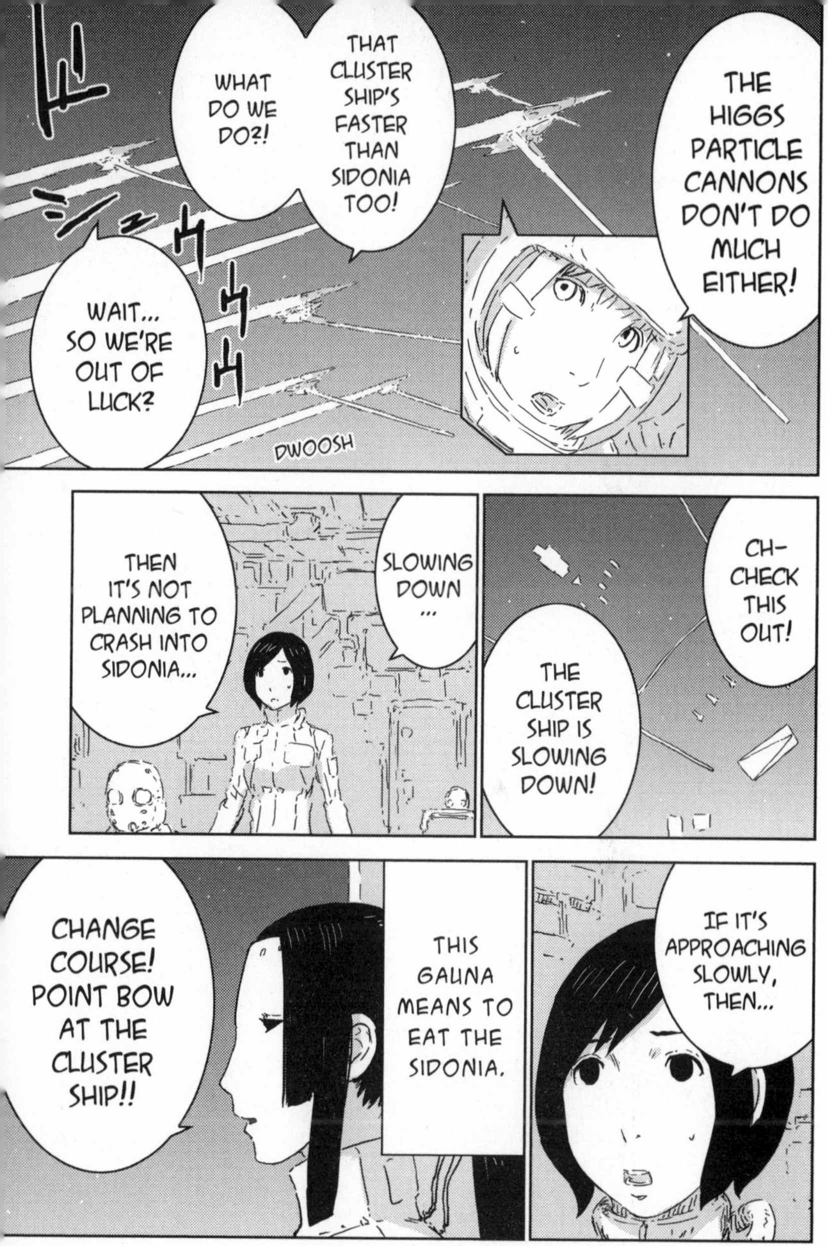
THE HIGGS PARTICLE CANNONS DON'T DO MUCH EITHER!
THAT CLUSTER SHIP'S FASTER THAN SIDONIA TOO!
WHAT DO WE DO?!
WAIT... SO WE'RE OUT OF LUCK?
DWOOSH
CH-CHECK THIS OUT!
THE CLUSTER SHIP IS SLOWING DOWN!
SLOWING DOWN ...
THEN IT'S NOT PLANNING TO CRASH INTO SIDONIA...
IF IT'S APPROACHING SLOWLY, THEN...
THIS GAUNA MEANS TO EAT THE SIDONIA.
CHANGE COURSE! POINT BOW AT THE CLUSTER SHIP!!

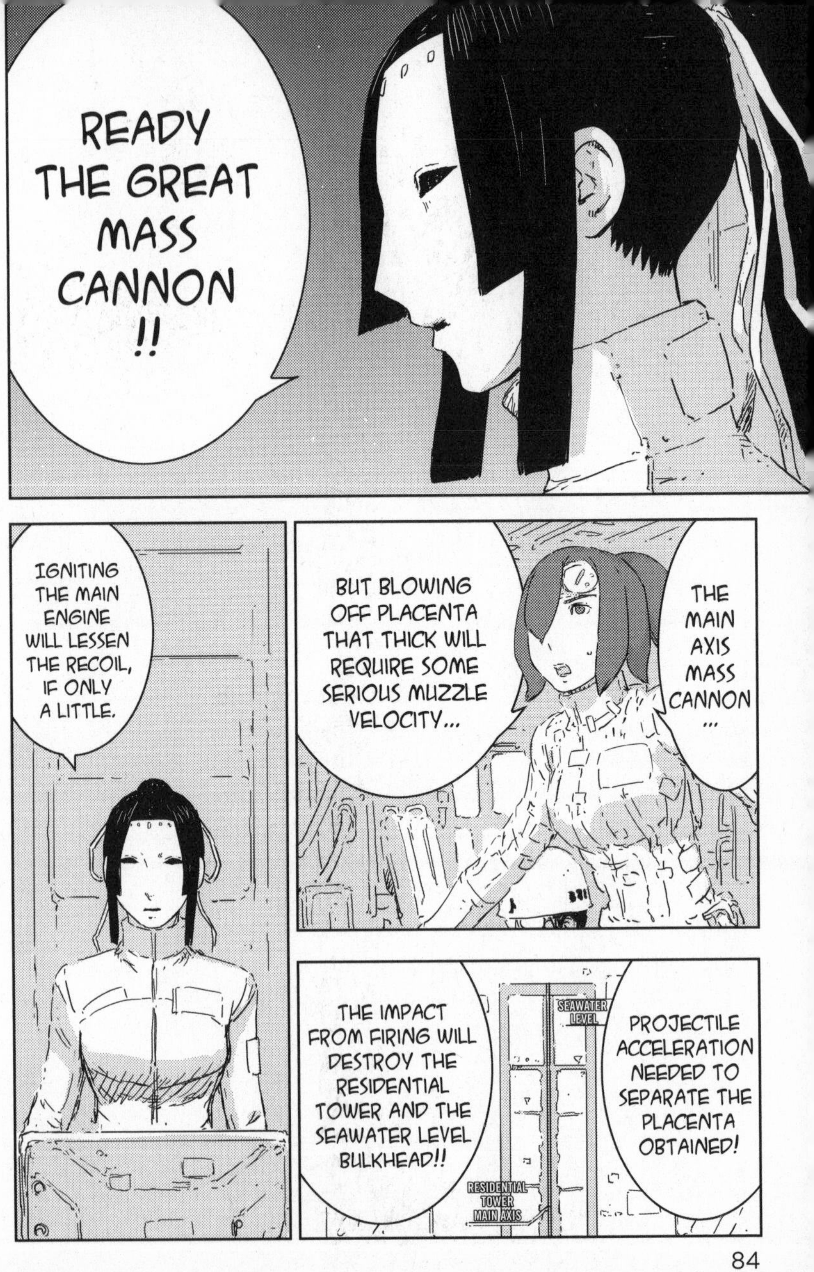
READY THE GREAT MASS CANNON !!
THE MAIN AXIS MASS CANNON ...
BUT BLOWING OFF PLACENTA THAT THICK WILL REQUIRE SOME SERIOUS MUZZLE VELOCITY...
PROJECTILE ACCELERATION NEEDED TO SEPARATE THE PLACENTA OBTAINED!
SEAWATER LEVEL
THE IMPACT FROM FIRING WILL DESTROY THE RESIDENTIAL TOWER AND THE SEAWATER LEVEL BULKHEAD!!
RESIDENTIAL TOWER MAIN AXIS
IGNITING THE MAIN ENGINE WILL LESSEN THE RECOIL, IF ONLY A LITTLE.

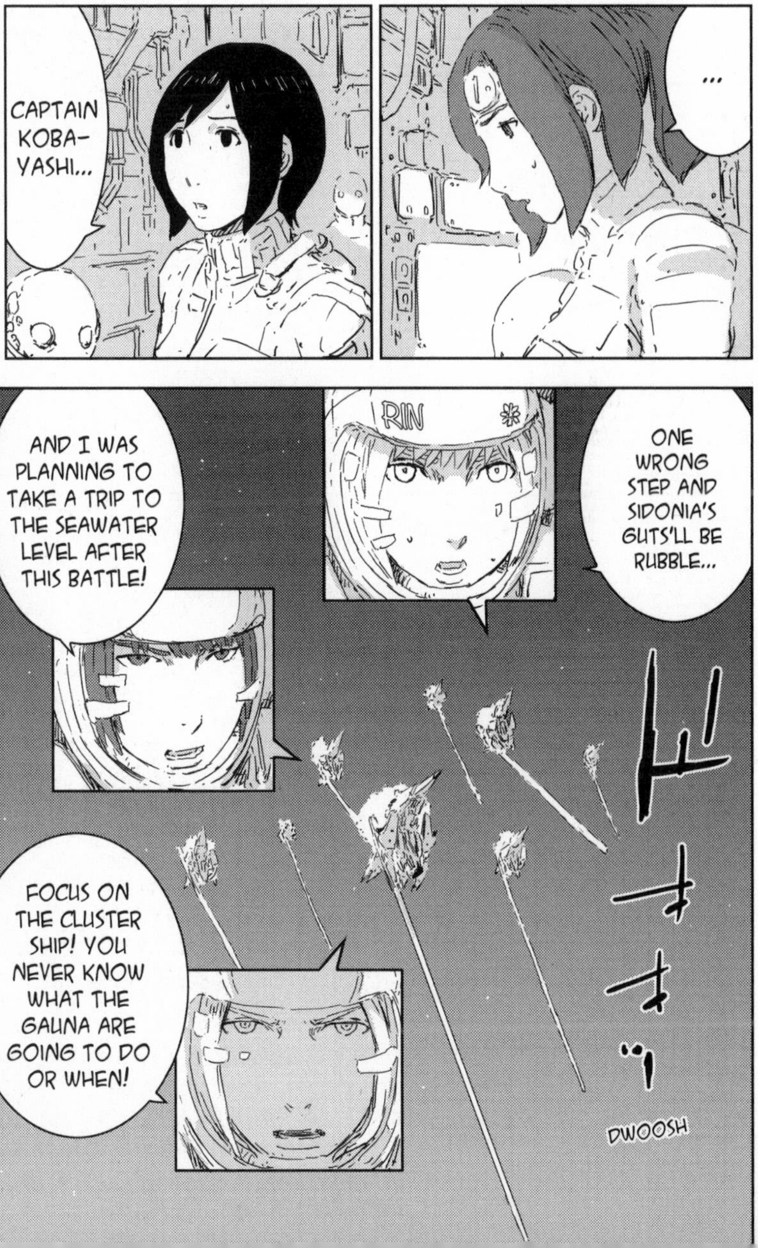
...
CAPTAIN KOBA-YASHI...
ONE WRONG STEP AND SIDONIA'S GUTS'LL BE RUBBLE...
AND I WAS PLANNING TO TAKE A TRIP TO THE SEAWATER LEVEL AFTER THIS BATTLE!
DWOOSH
FOCUS ON THE CLUSTER SHIP! YOU NEVER KNOW WHAT THE GAUNA ARE GOING TO DO OR WHEN!

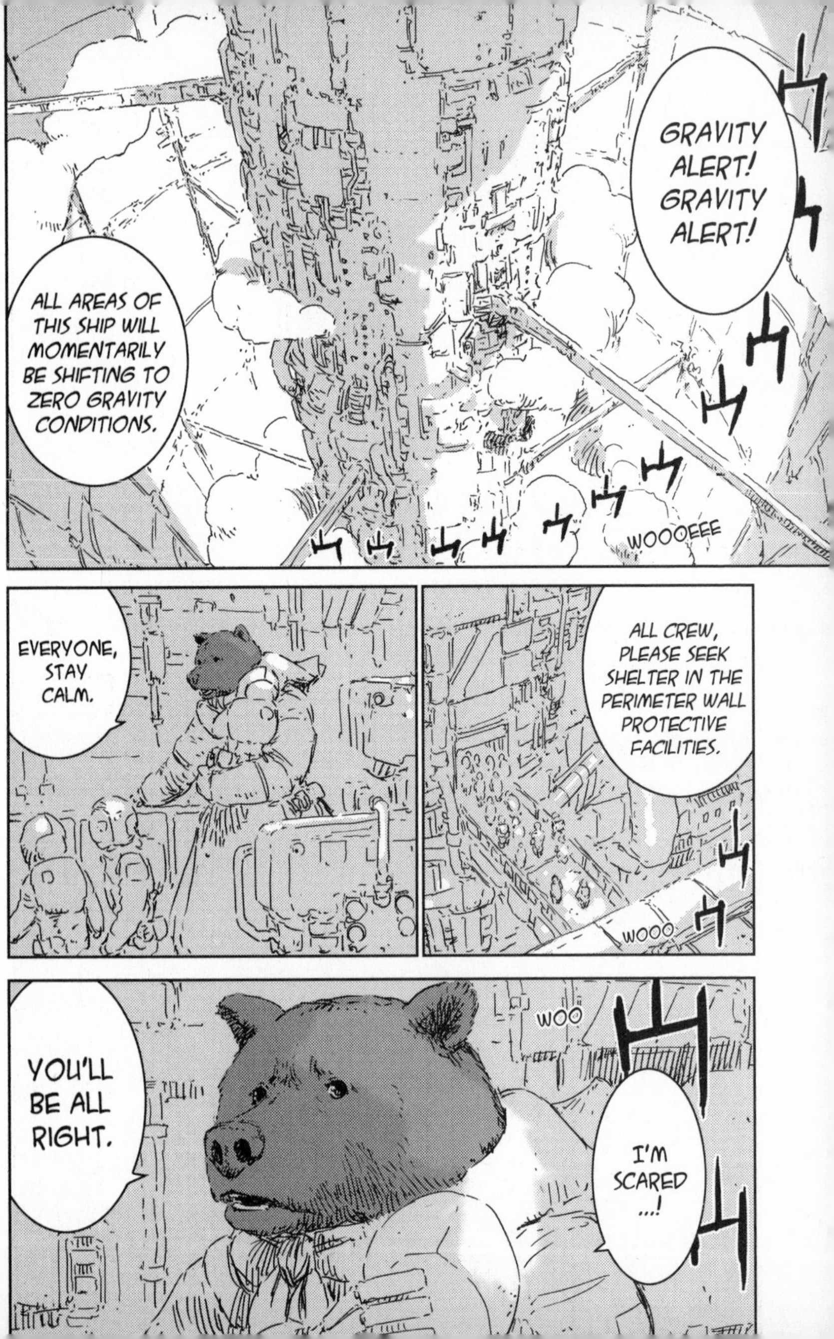
GRAVITY ALERT! GRAVITY ALERT!
ALL AREAS OF THIS SHIP WILL MOMENTARILY BE SHIFTING TO ZERO GRAVITY CONDITIONS.
WOOOEEE
ALL CREW, PLEASE SEEK SHELTER IN THE PERIMETER WALL PROTECTIVE FACILITIES.
WOOO
EVERYONE, STAY CALM.
WOO
I'M SCARED ...!
YOU'LL BE ALL RIGHT.

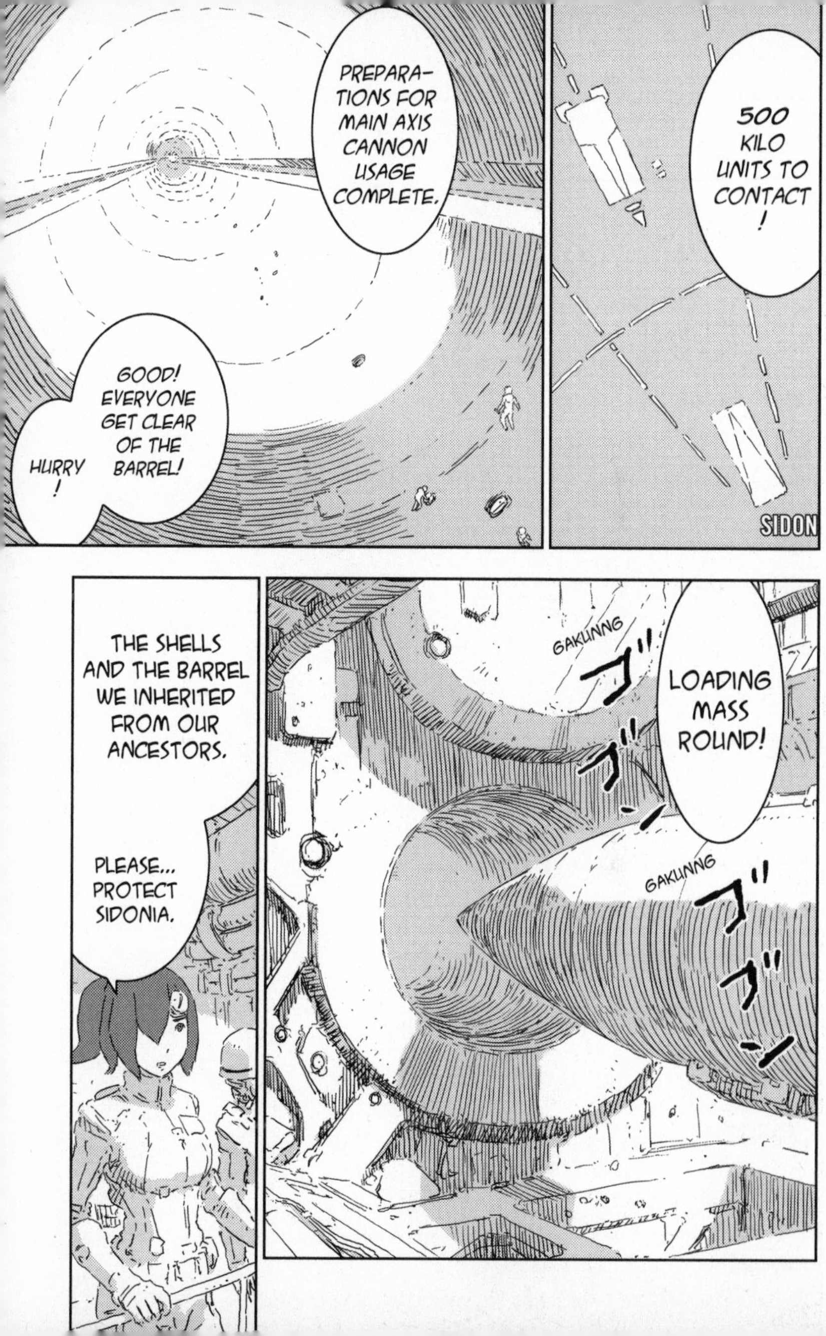
500 KILO UNITS TO CONTACT!
SIDON
PREPARATIONS FOR MAIN AXIS CANNON USAGE COMPLETE.
GOOD! EVERYONE GET CLEAR OF THE BARREL!
HURRY!
LOADING MASS ROUND!
GAKUNNG
ゴゴン
GAKUNNG
ゴゴン
THE SHELLS AND THE BARREL WE INHERITED FROM OUR ANCESTORS.
PLEASE... PROTECT SIDONIA.

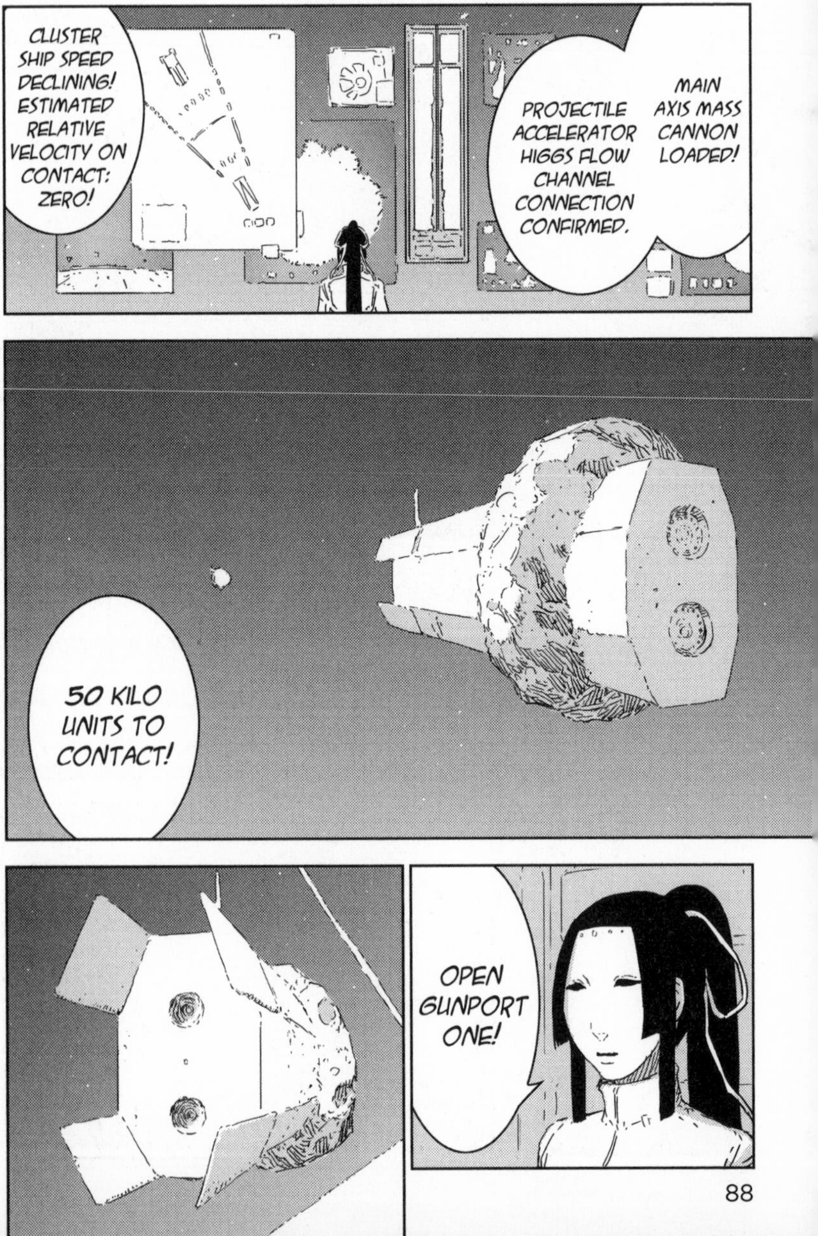
MAIN AXIS MASS CANNON LOADED!
PROJECTILE ACCELERATOR HIGGS FLOW CHANNEL CONNECTION CONFIRMED.
CLUSTER SHIP SPEED DECLINING! ESTIMATED RELATIVE VELOCITY ON CONTACT: ZERO!
50 KILO UNITS TO CONTACT!
OPEN GUNPORT ONE!

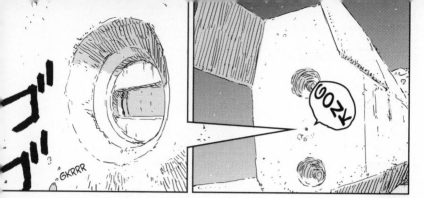

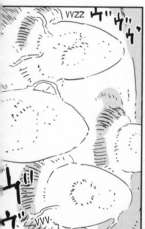

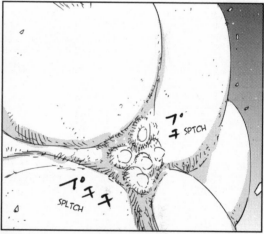

GOZK
ゴゴ
GKRRR
プチ
SPTCH
プチチ
SPLTCH
ヴヴヴ
VVZZ
ヴヴ
VVV
THE CLUSTER SHIP'S FORMING HIGGS PARTICLE CANNONS ON ITS NOSE!!
DESTROY THEM!! ALL UNITS, ATTACK!!
HIGH HIGGS ACTIVITY IN CLUSTER SHIP!!

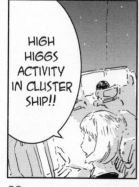

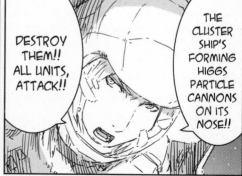

BOM
BOM
BOM
BGOM
BAM
VVRR
IT'S FIRING !!
CLOSE GUNPORT !!

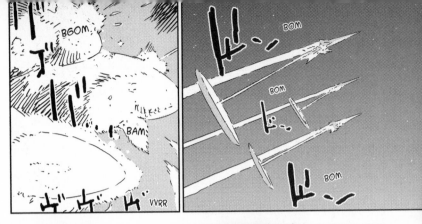

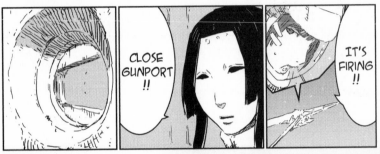

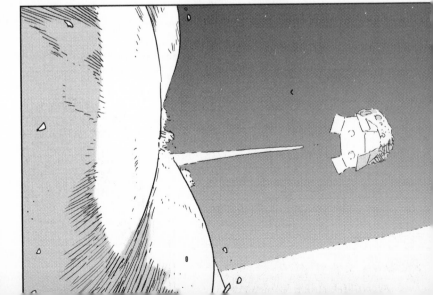

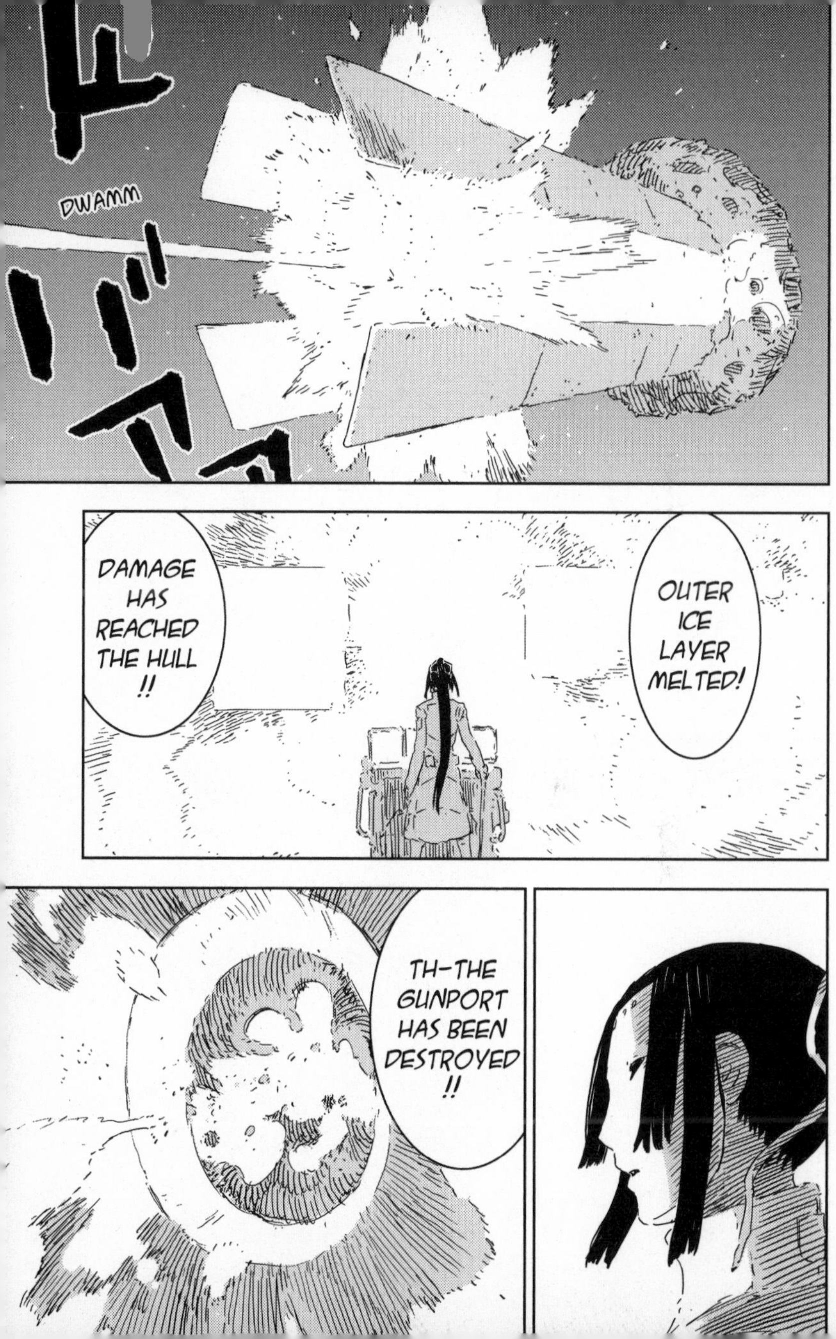
DWAMM
OUTER ICE LAYER MELTED!
DAMAGE HAS REACHED THE HULL !!
TH-THE GUNPORT HAS BEEN DESTROYED !!

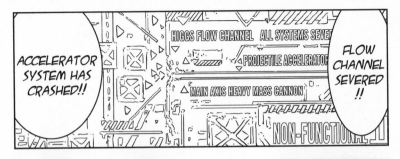

FLOW CHANNEL SEVERED !!
HIGGS FLOW CHANNEL
ALL SYSTEMS SEVER
PROJECTILE ACCELERATOR
MAIN AXIS HEAVY MASS CANNON
NON-FUNCTIONAL
ACCELERATOR SYSTEM HAS CRASHED!!
CONTACT WITH CLUSTER SHIP!!!
VVT
VVT

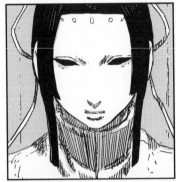

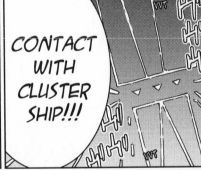

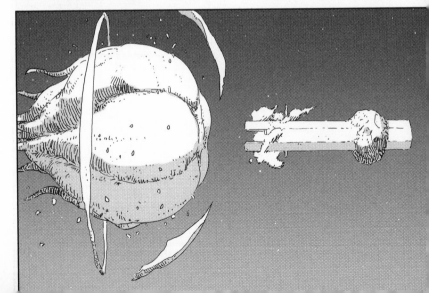

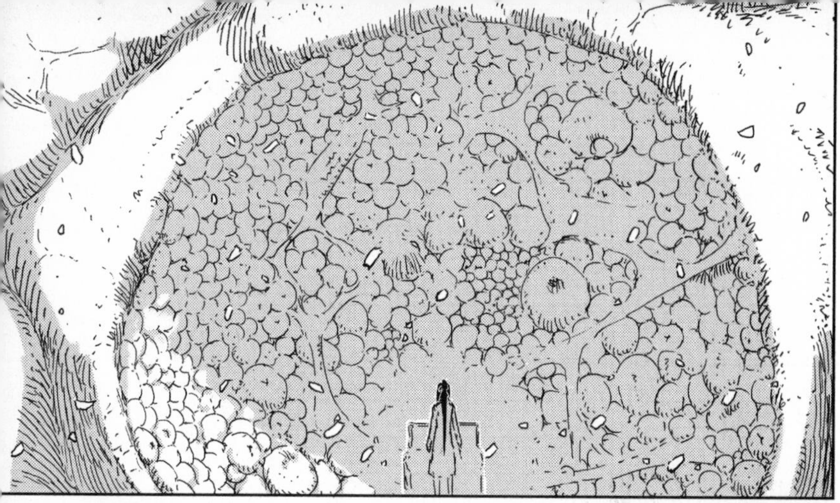
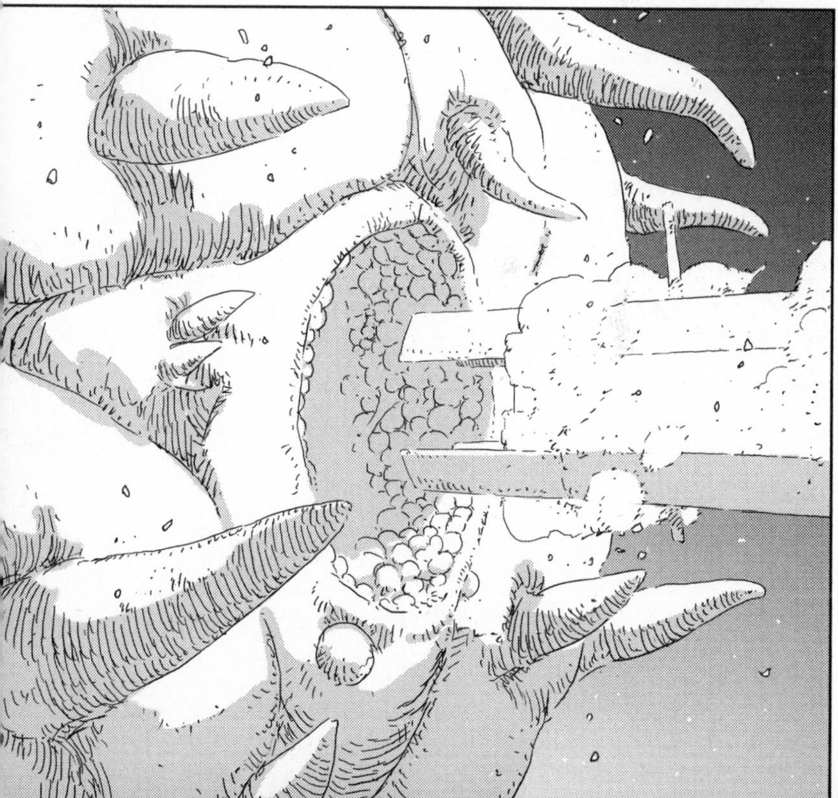

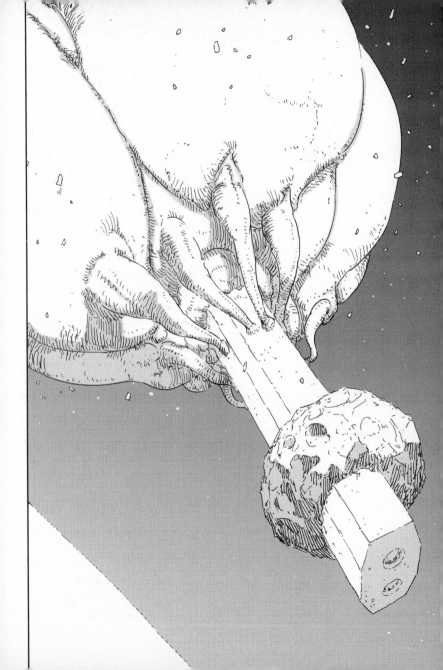

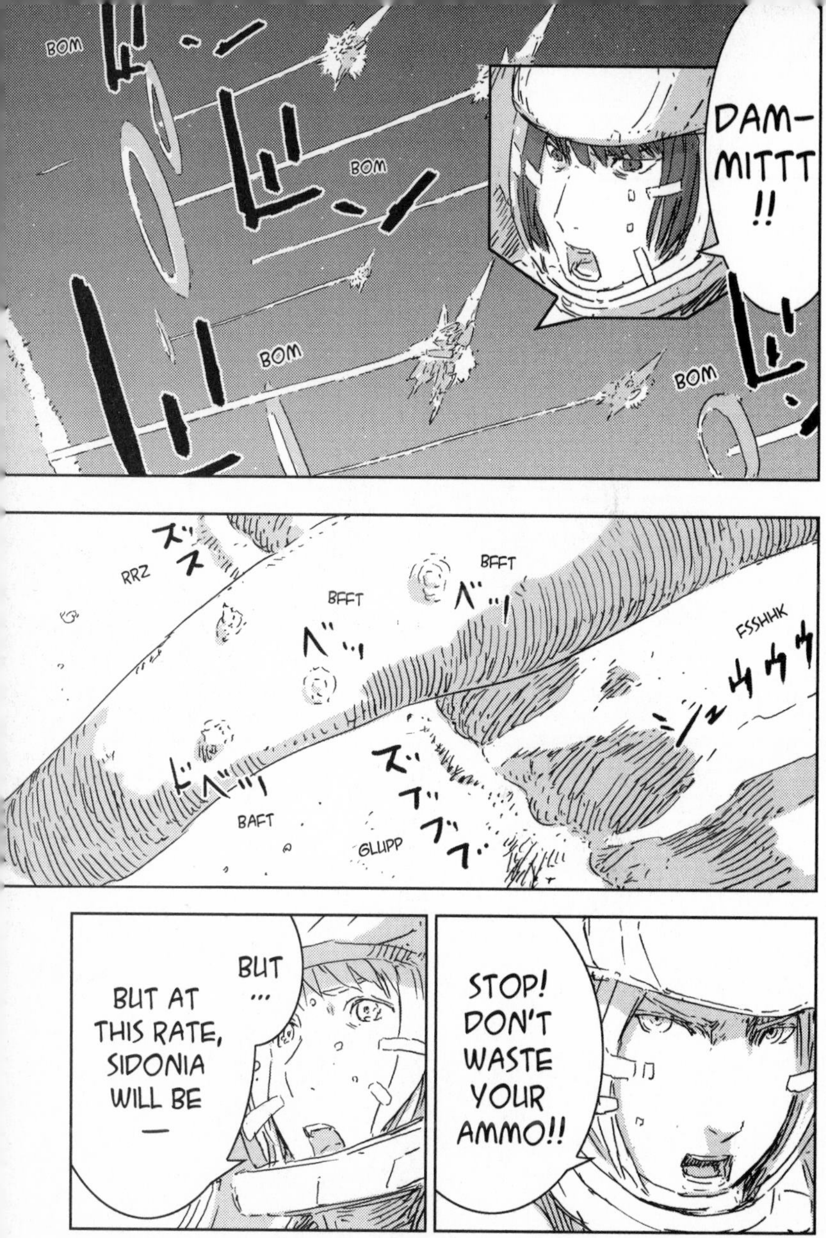
DAM-MITTT!!
BOM
BOM
BOM
BOM
FSSHHK
BFFT
BFFT
RRZ
GLUPP
BAFT
STOP! DON'T WASTE YOUR AMMO!!
BUT ...
BUT AT THIS RATE, SIDONIA WILL BE —

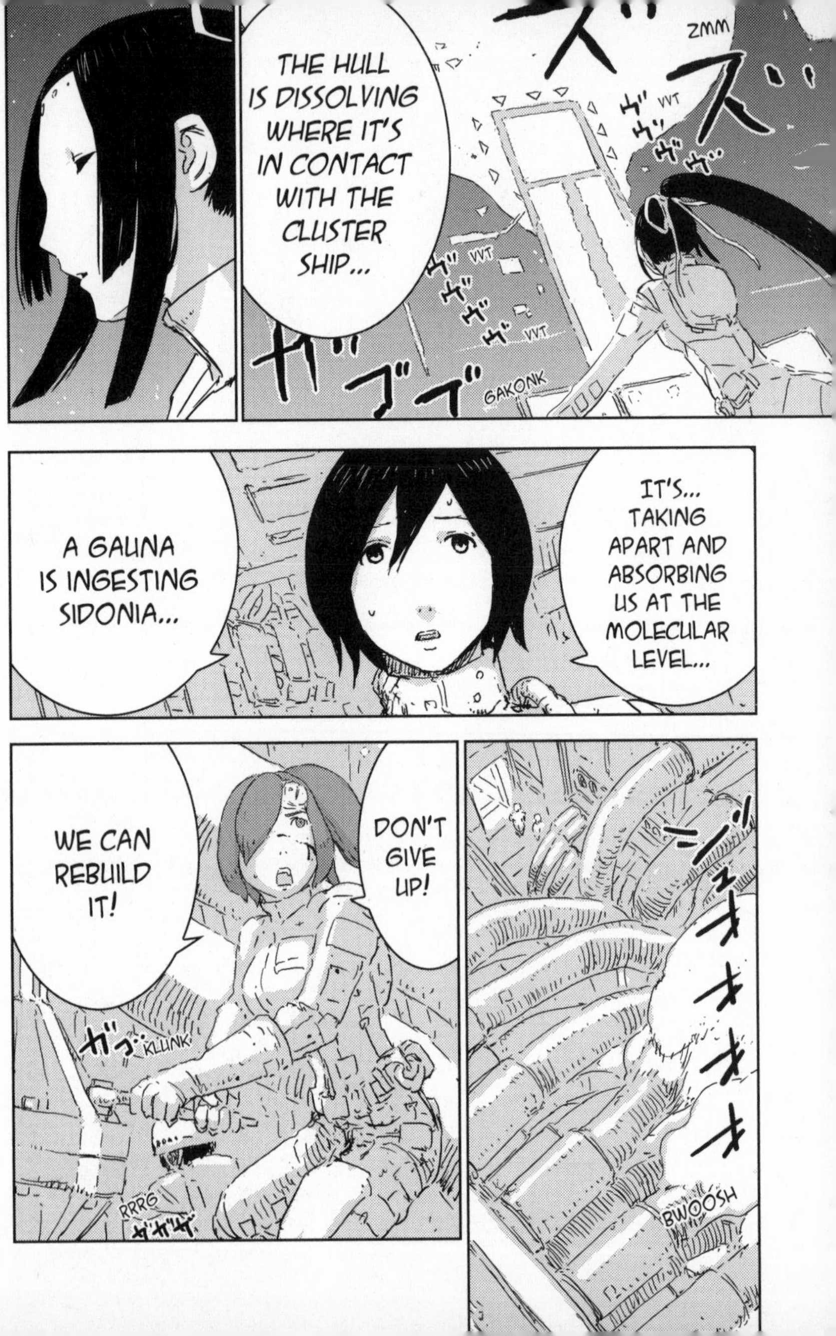
ZMM
VVT
THE HULL IS DISSOLVING WHERE IT'S IN CONTACT WITH THE CLUSTER SHIP...
VVT
VVT
GAKONK
IT'S... TAKING APART AND ABSORBING US AT THE MOLECULAR LEVEL...
A GAUNA IS INGESTING SIDONIA...
BWOOSH
DON'T GIVE UP!
WE CAN REBUILD IT!
KLUNK
RRRG

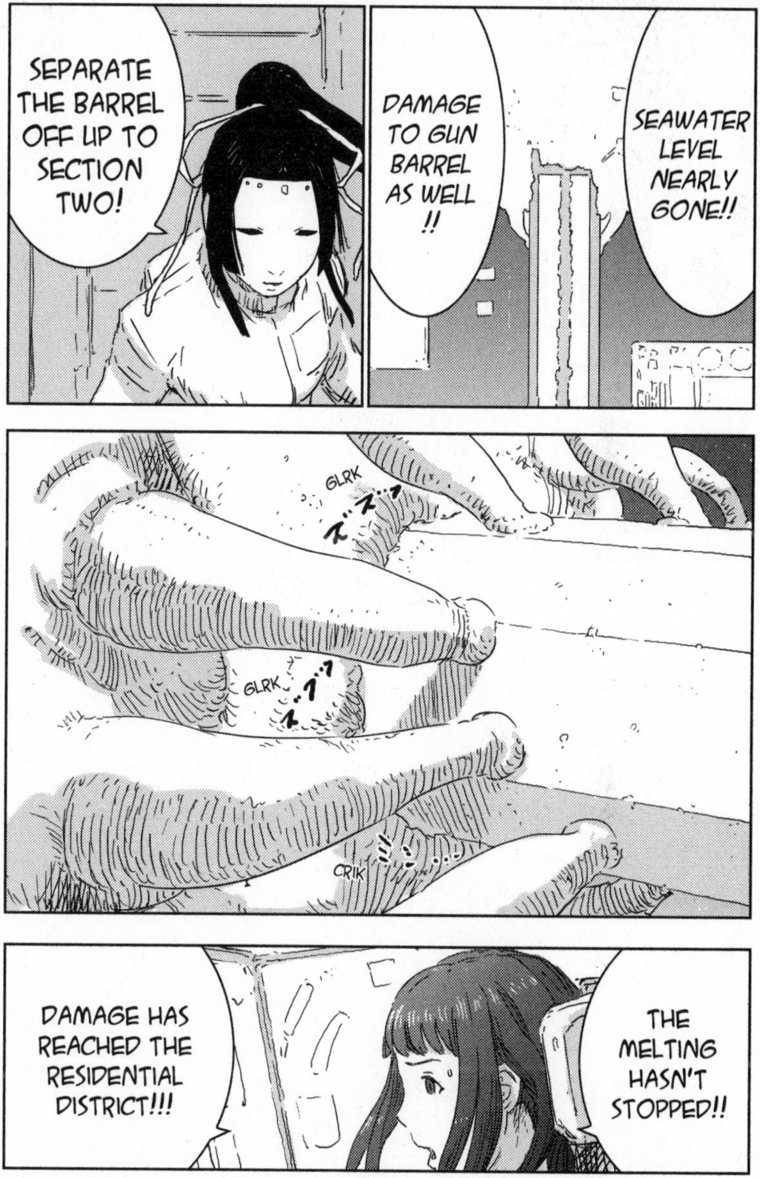
SEAWATER LEVEL NEARLY GONE!!
DAMAGE TO GUN BARREL AS WELL!!
SEPARATE THE BARREL OFF UP TO SECTION TWO!
GLRK
GLRK
CRIK
THE MELTING HASN'T STOPPED!!
DAMAGE HAS REACHED THE RESIDENTIAL DISTRICT!!!

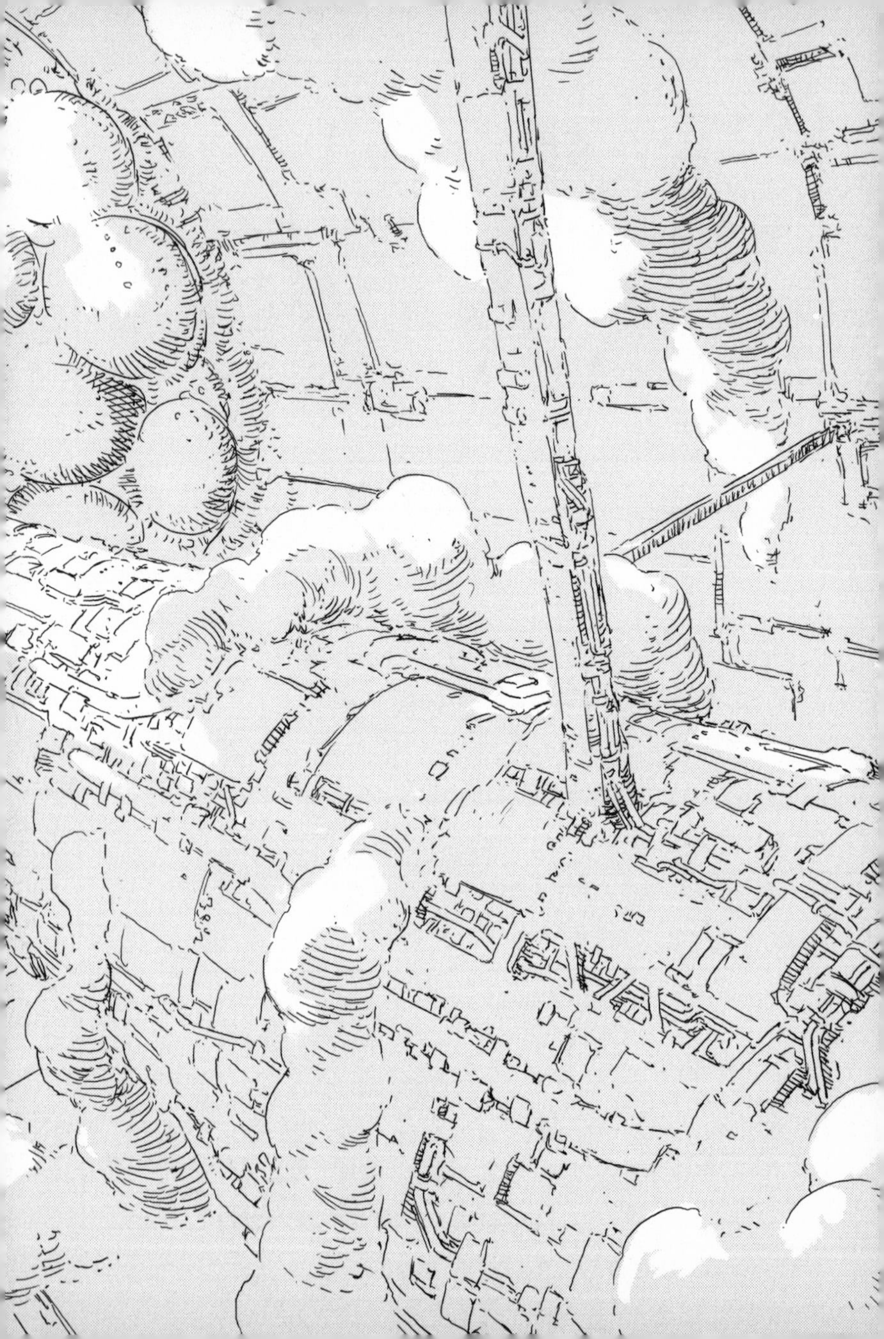

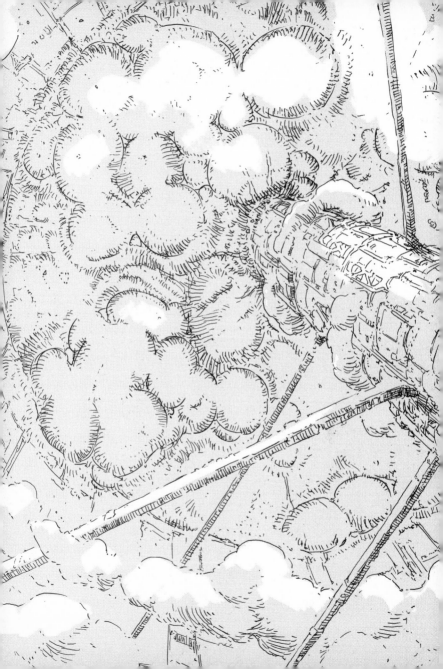

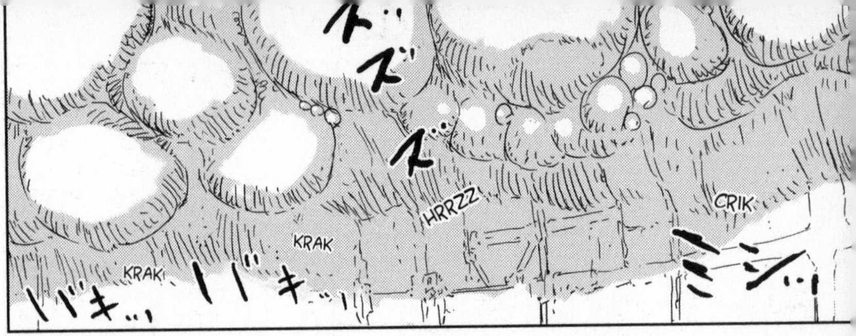
ミシッ
CRIK
ズズズ
HRRZZ
バキッ
KRAK
バキッ
KRAK

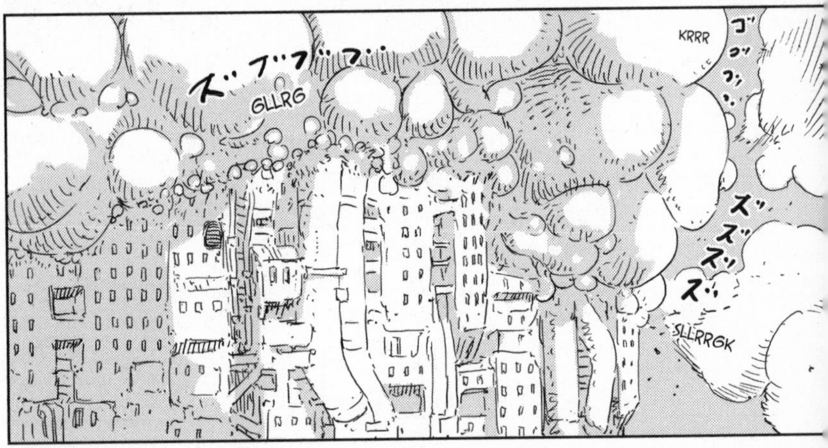
ゴゴゴゴ
KRRR
ズズズズ
SLLRRGK
ズブブブ
GLLRG

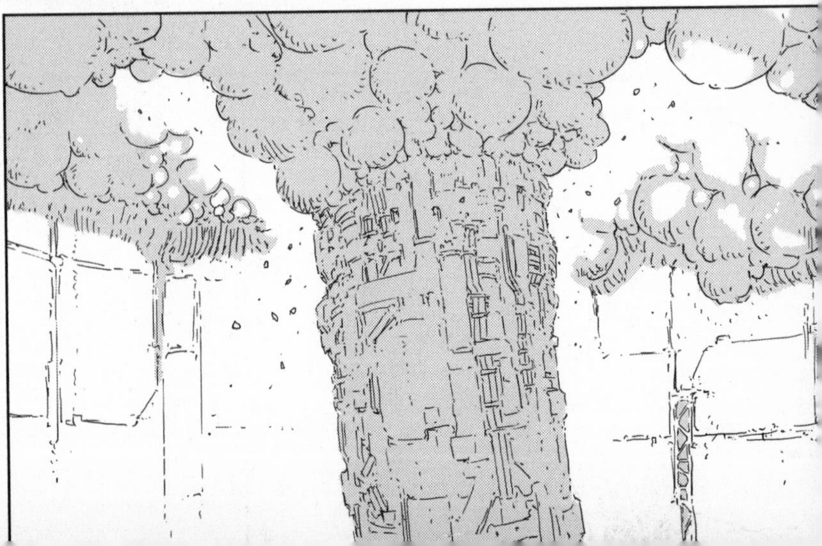

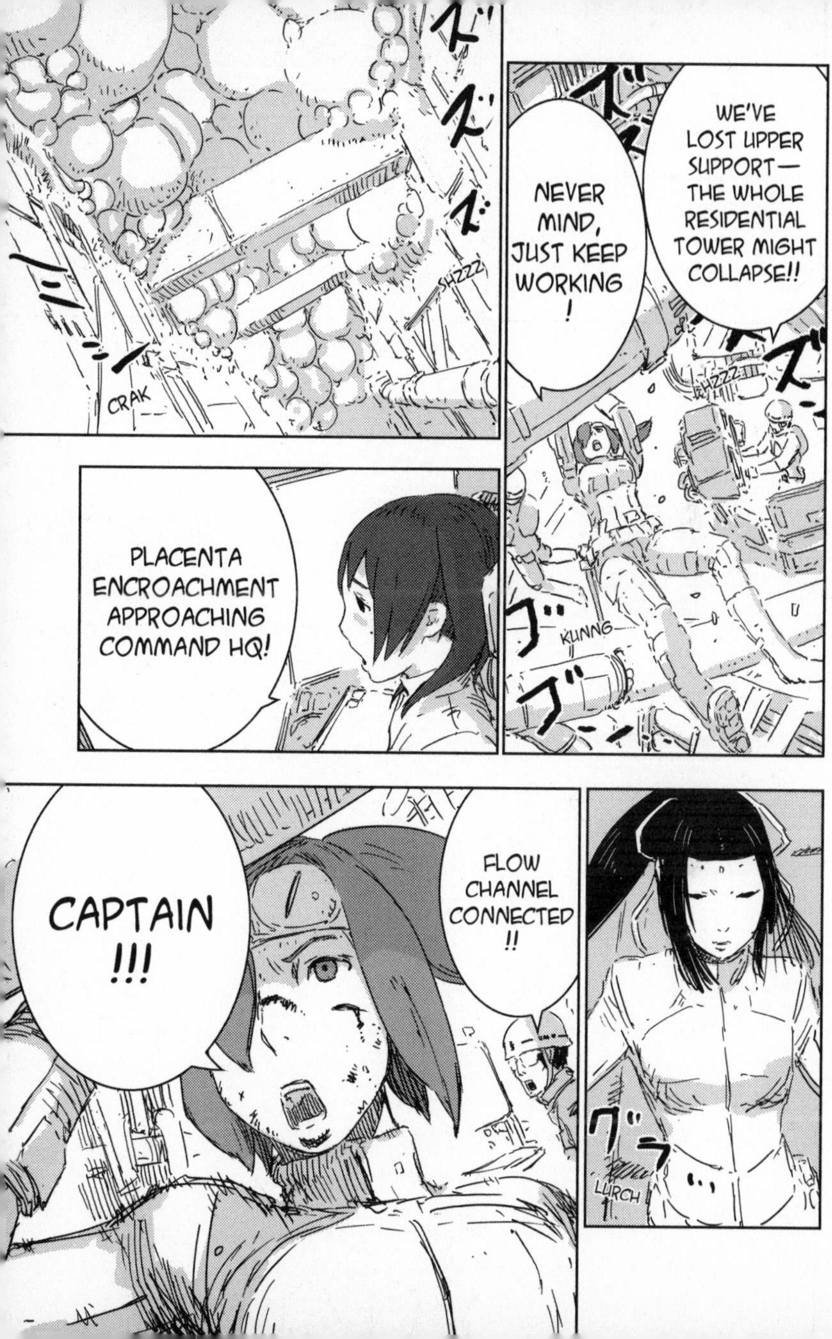
WE'VE LOST UPPER SUPPORT— THE WHOLE RESIDENTIAL TOWER MIGHT COLLAPSE!!
NEVER MIND, JUST KEEP WORKING!
SHZZZ
KUNNG
SHZZZ
CRAK
PLACENTA ENCROACHMENT APPROACHING COMMAND HQ!
LURCH
FLOW CHANNEL CONNECTED!!
CAPTAIN!!!

FIRE

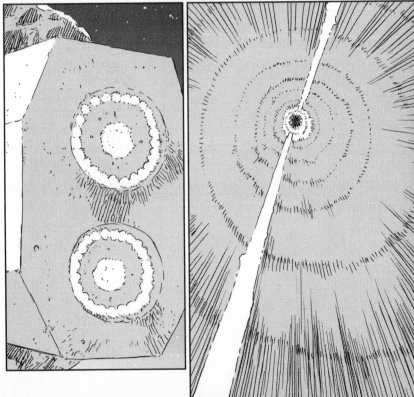

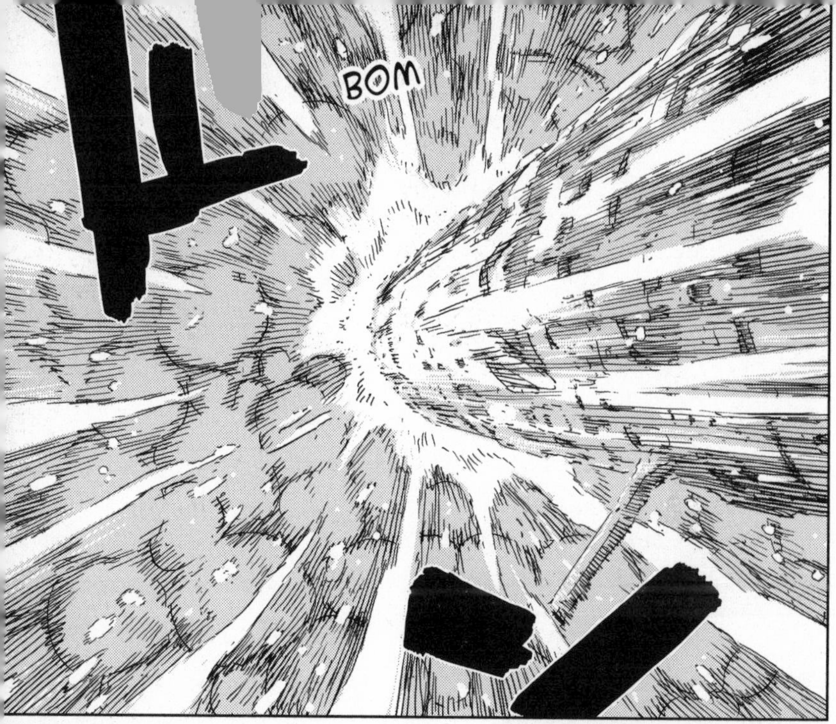
BOM
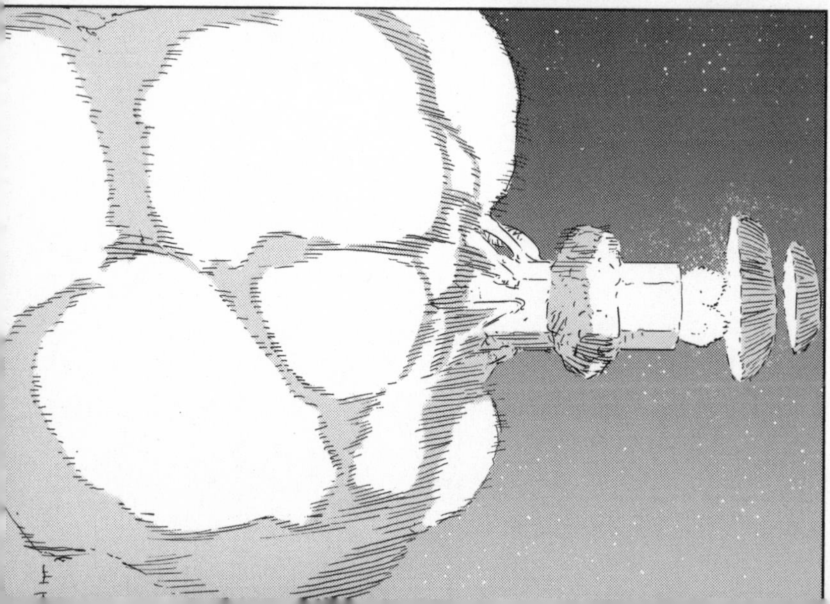

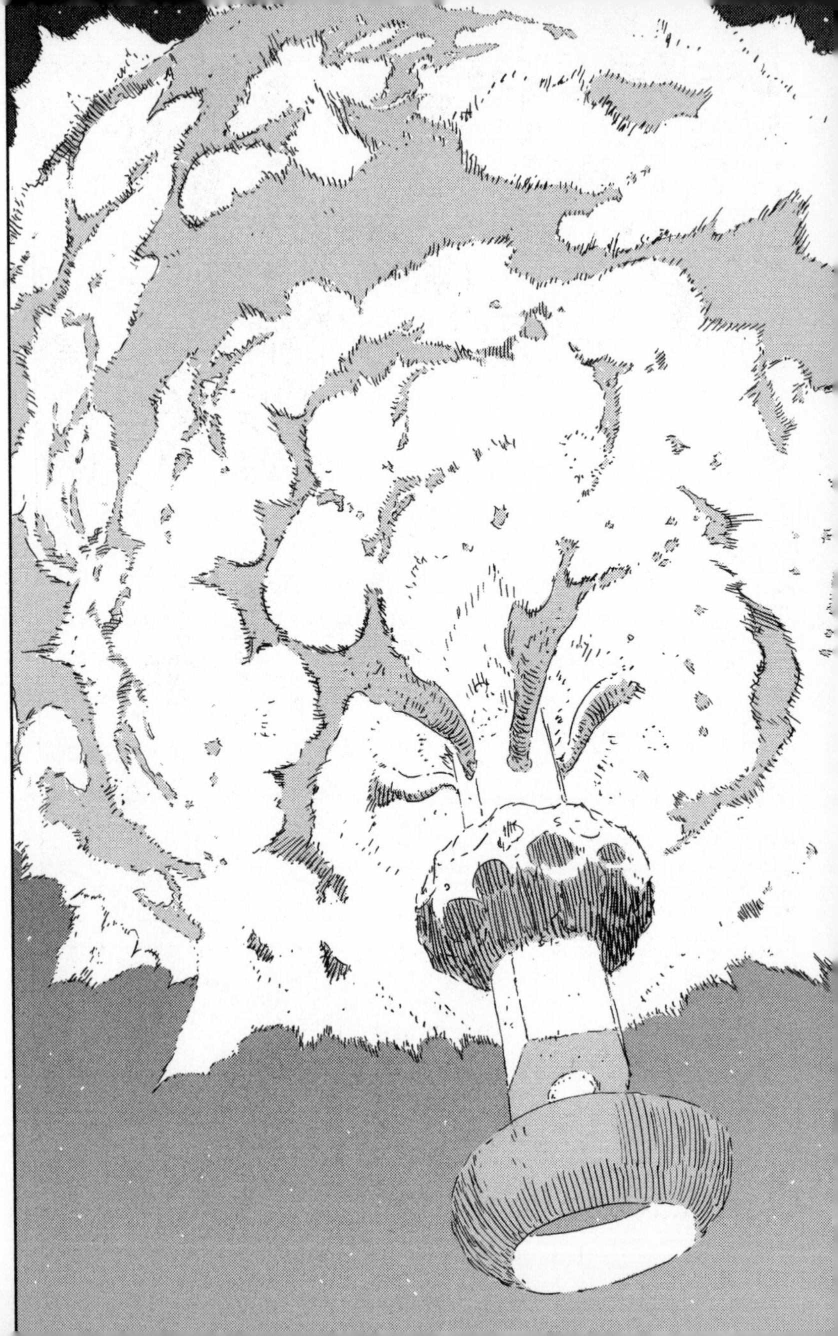

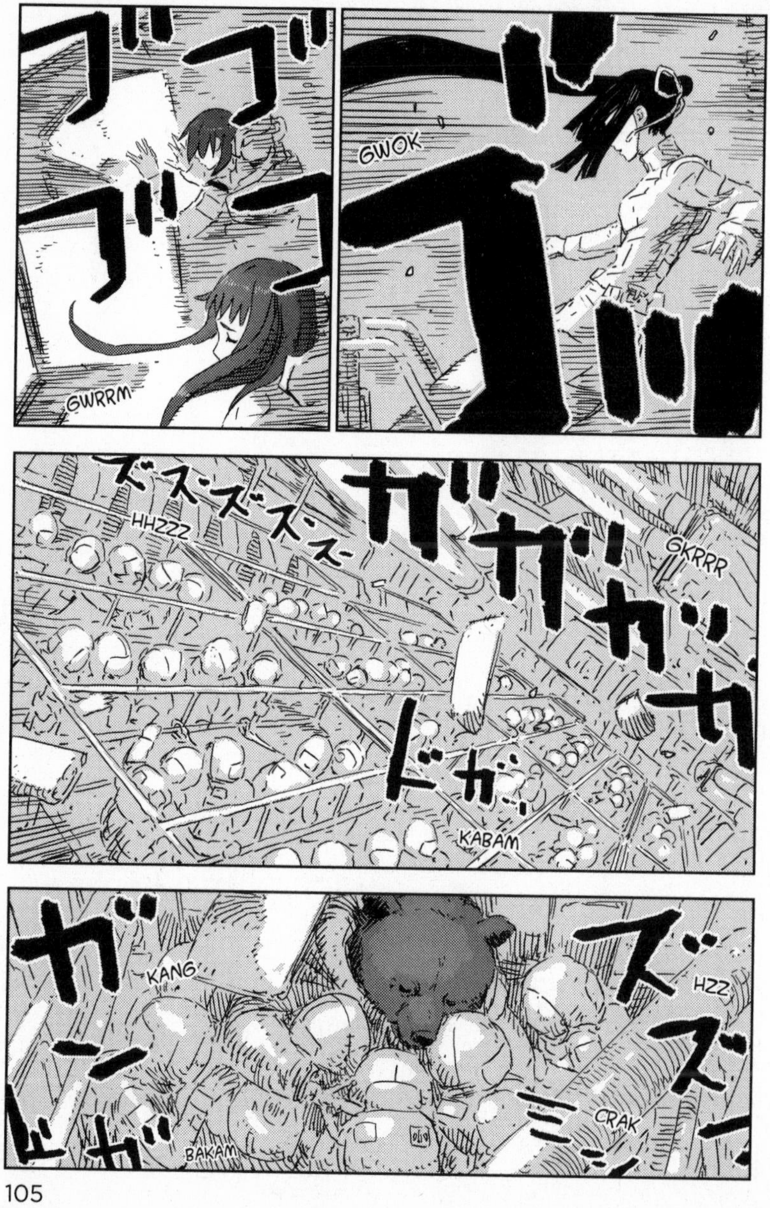
GWOK
GWRRM
GKRRR
HHZZZ
KABAM
HZZ
KANG
CRAK
BAKAM

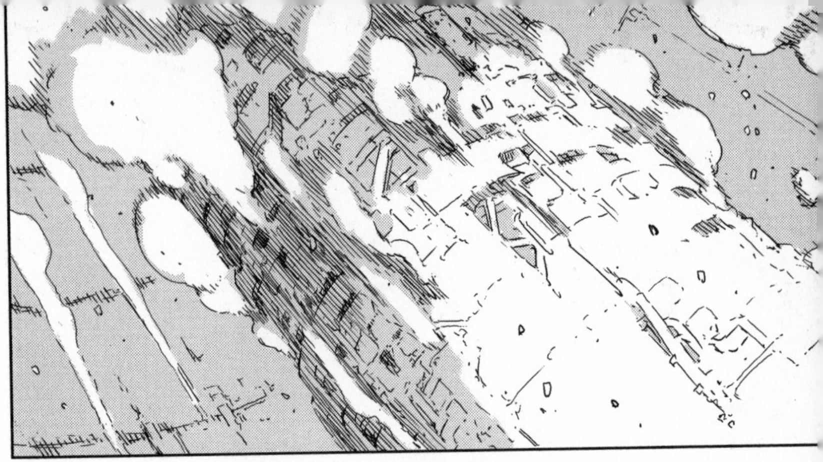
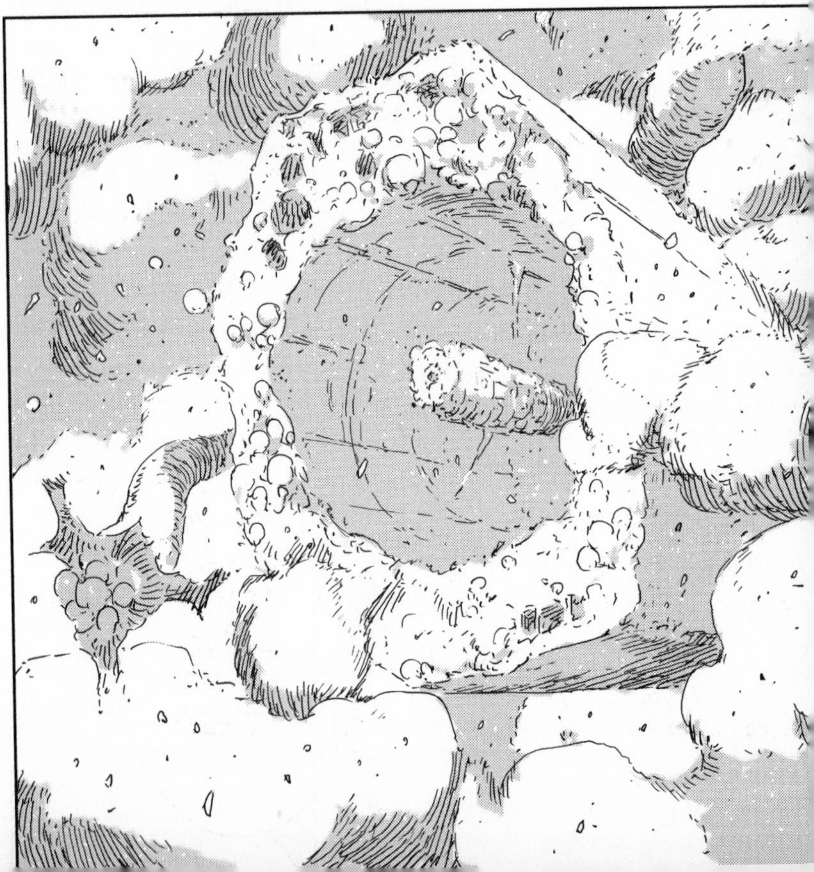

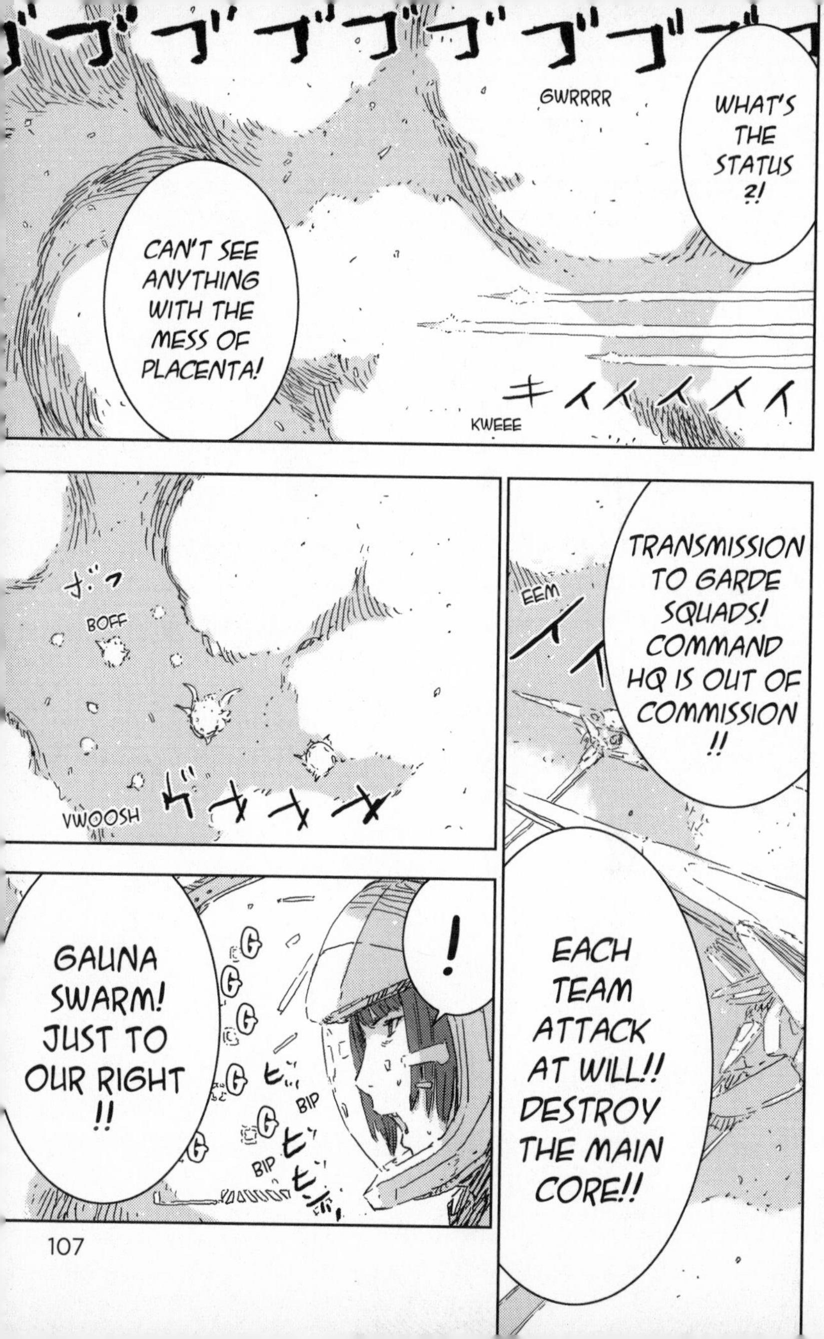
GWRRRR
WHAT'S THE STATUS ?!
CAN'T SEE ANYTHING WITH THE MESS OF PLACENTA!
キイイイイイ
KWEEE
TRANSMISSION TO GARDE SQUADS! COMMAND HQ IS OUT OF COMMISSION !!
EEM
EACH TEAM ATTACK AT WILL!! DESTROY THE MAIN CORE!!
BOFF
VWOOSH
!
GAUNA SWARM! JUST TO OUR RIGHT !!
BIP
BIP

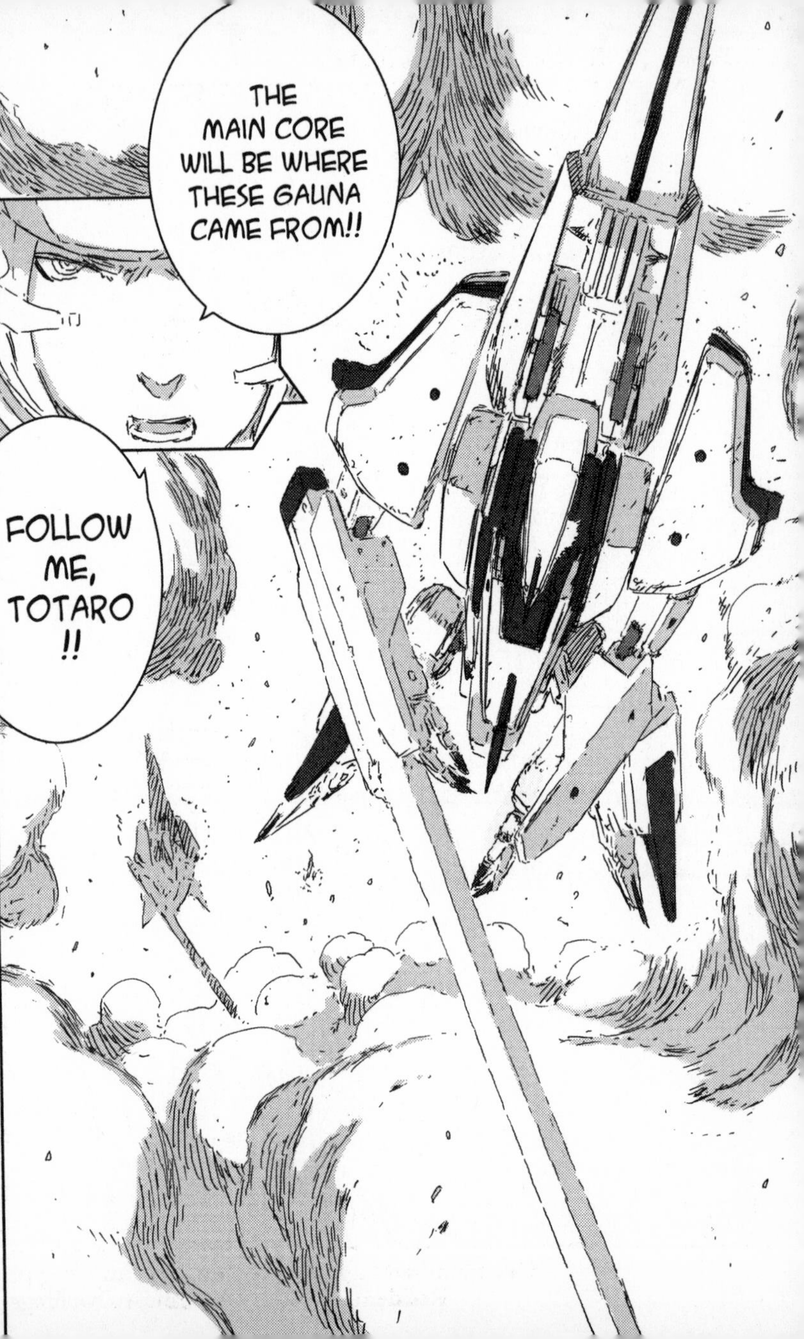
THE MAIN CORE WILL BE WHERE THESE GAUNA CAME FROM!!
FOLLOW ME, TOTARO!!

Chapter 74: END

Chapter 75: The Kunato Team's Fight

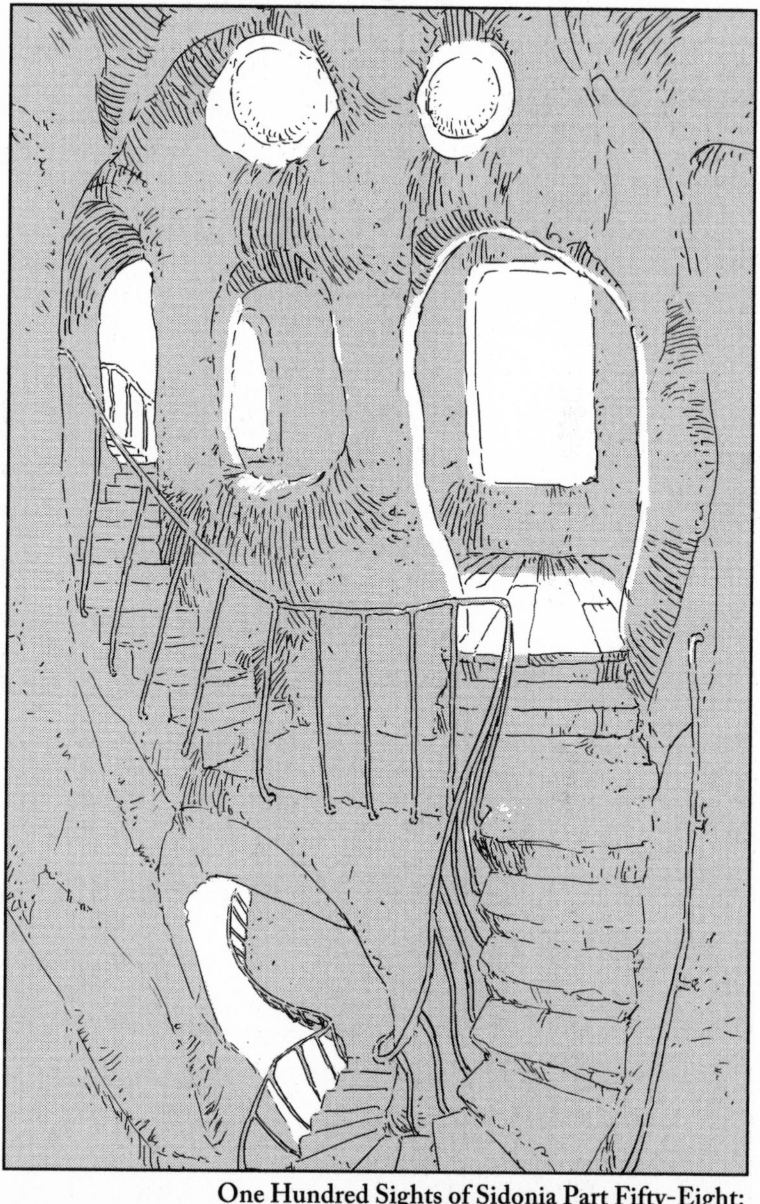

One Hundred Sights of Sidonia Part Fifty-Eight:
Residential Tower Uppermost Dwellings

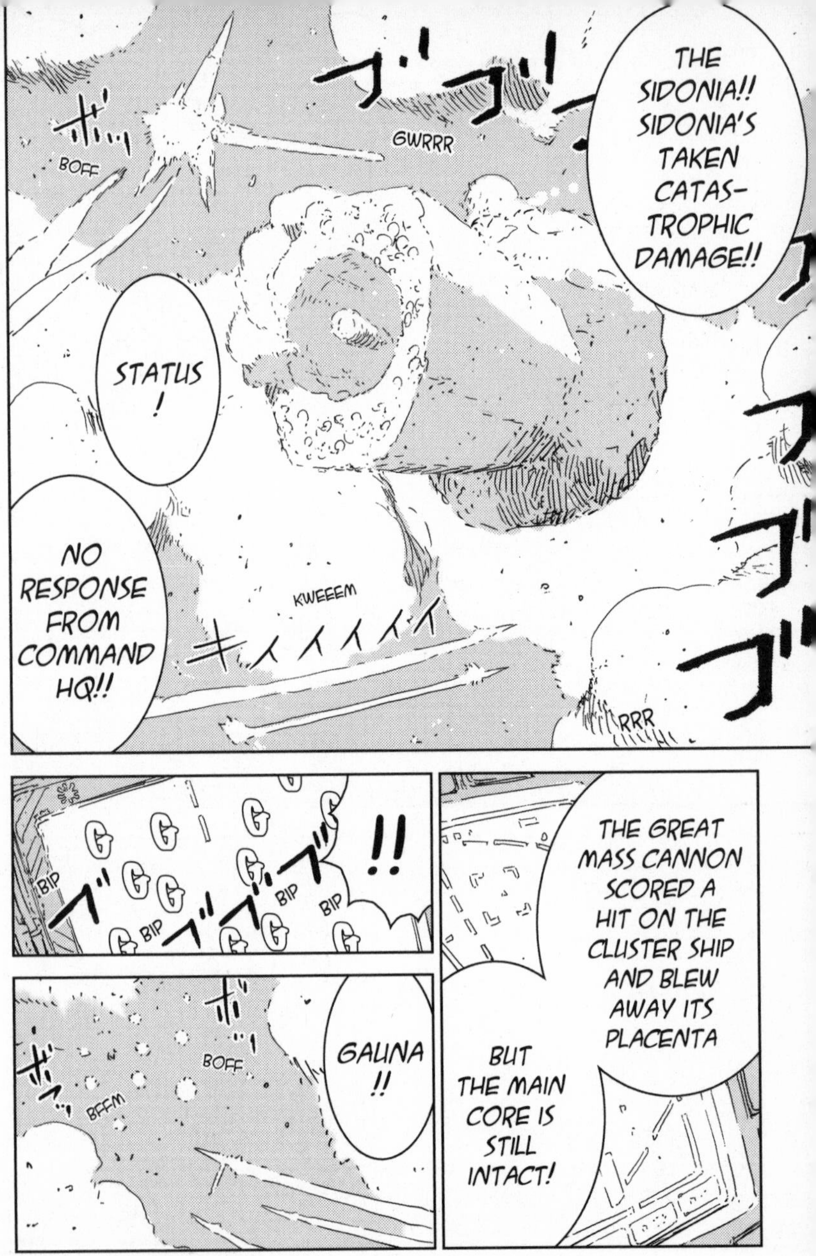
THE SIDONIA!! SIDONIA'S TAKEN CATAS-TROPHIC DAMAGE!!
GWRRR
BOFF
STATUS!
NO RESPONSE FROM COMMAND HQ!!
KWEEEM
RRR
THE GREAT MASS CANNON SCORED A HIT ON THE CLUSTER SHIP AND BLEW AWAY ITS PLACENTA
BUT THE MAIN CORE IS STILL INTACT!
BIP
BIP
BIP
BIP
GAUNA!!
BOFF
BFFM

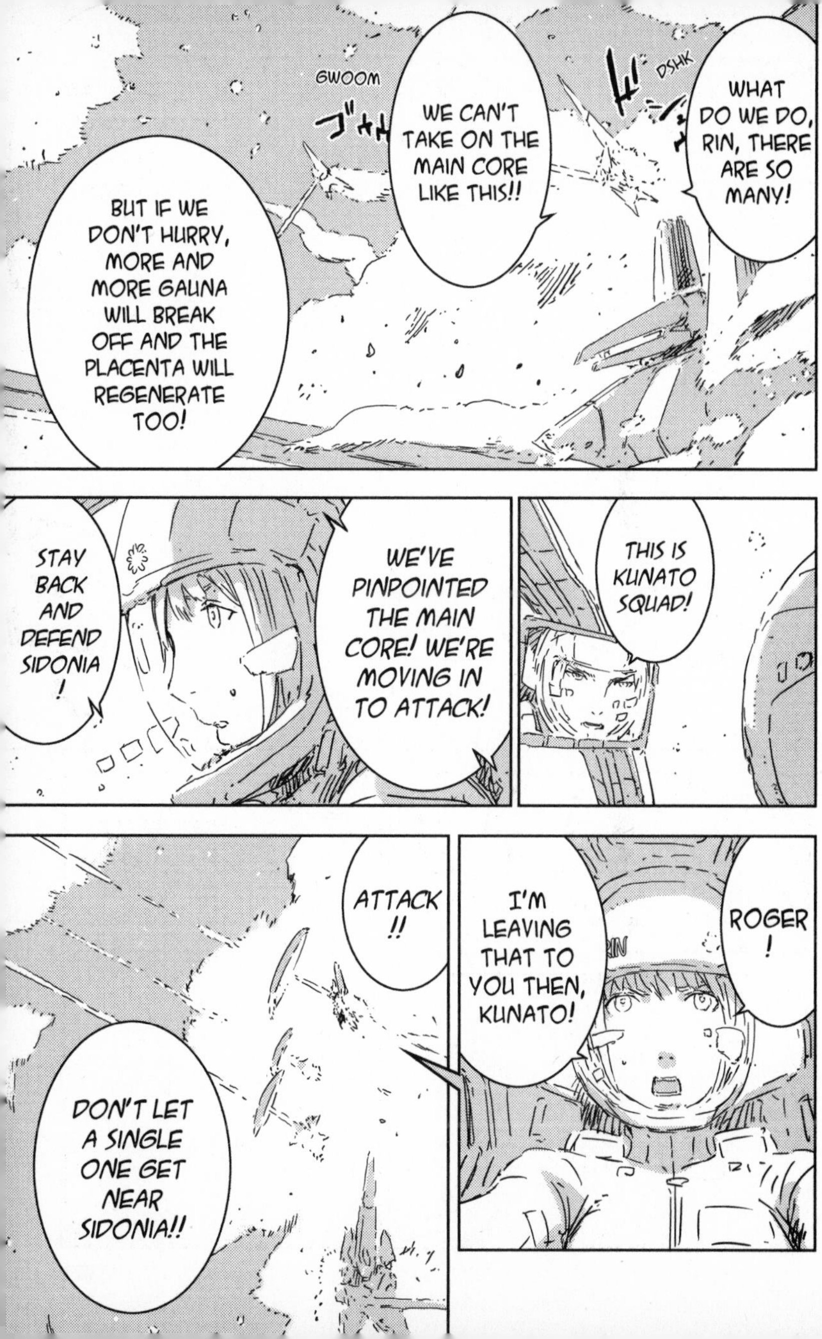
WHAT DO WE DO, RIN, THERE ARE SO MANY!
DSHK
WE CAN'T TAKE ON THE MAIN CORE LIKE THIS!!
GWOOM
BUT IF WE DON'T HURRY, MORE AND MORE GAUNA WILL BREAK OFF AND THE PLACENTA WILL REGENERATE TOO!
THIS IS KUNATO SQUAD!
WE'VE PINPOINTED THE MAIN CORE! WE'RE MOVING IN TO ATTACK!
STAY BACK AND DEFEND SIDONIA!
ROGER!
I'M LEAVING THAT TO YOU THEN, KUNATO!
ATTACK!!
DON'T LET A SINGLE ONE GET NEAR SIDONIA!!

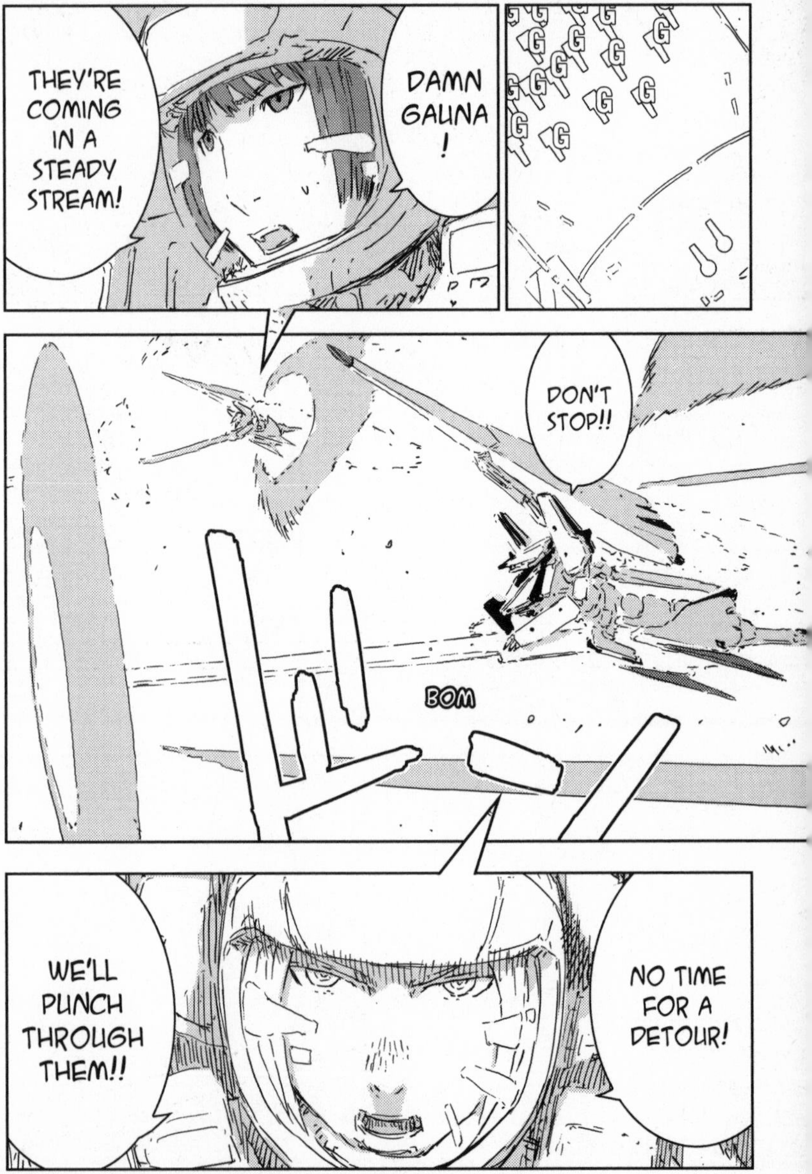
DAMN GAUNA!
THEY'RE COMING IN A STEADY STREAM!
DON'T STOP!!
BOM
NO TIME FOR A DETOUR!
WE'LL PUNCH THROUGH THEM!!

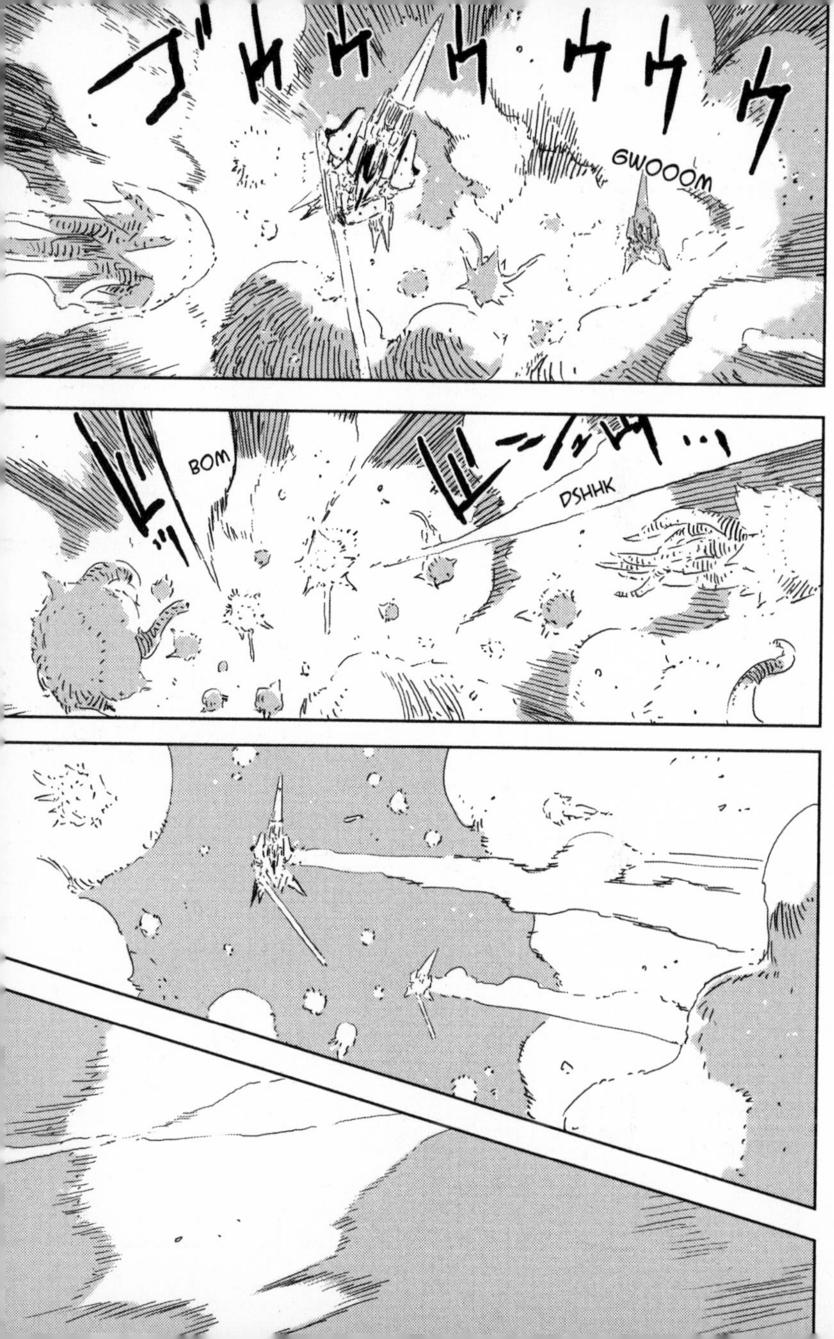
GWOOOM
DSHHK
BOM

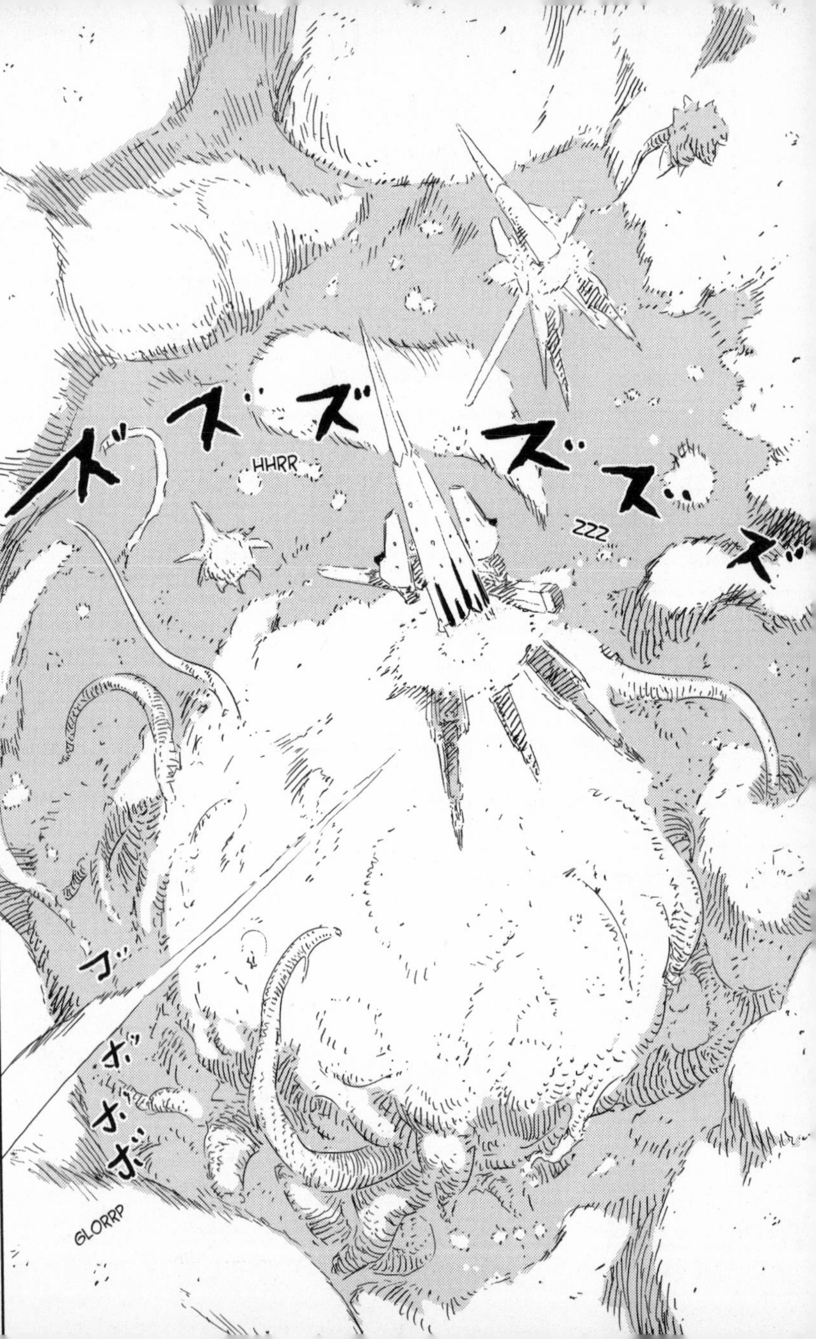
ズズズ
ズズズ
ZZZ
HHRR
ゴッ
ざざざ
GLORRP

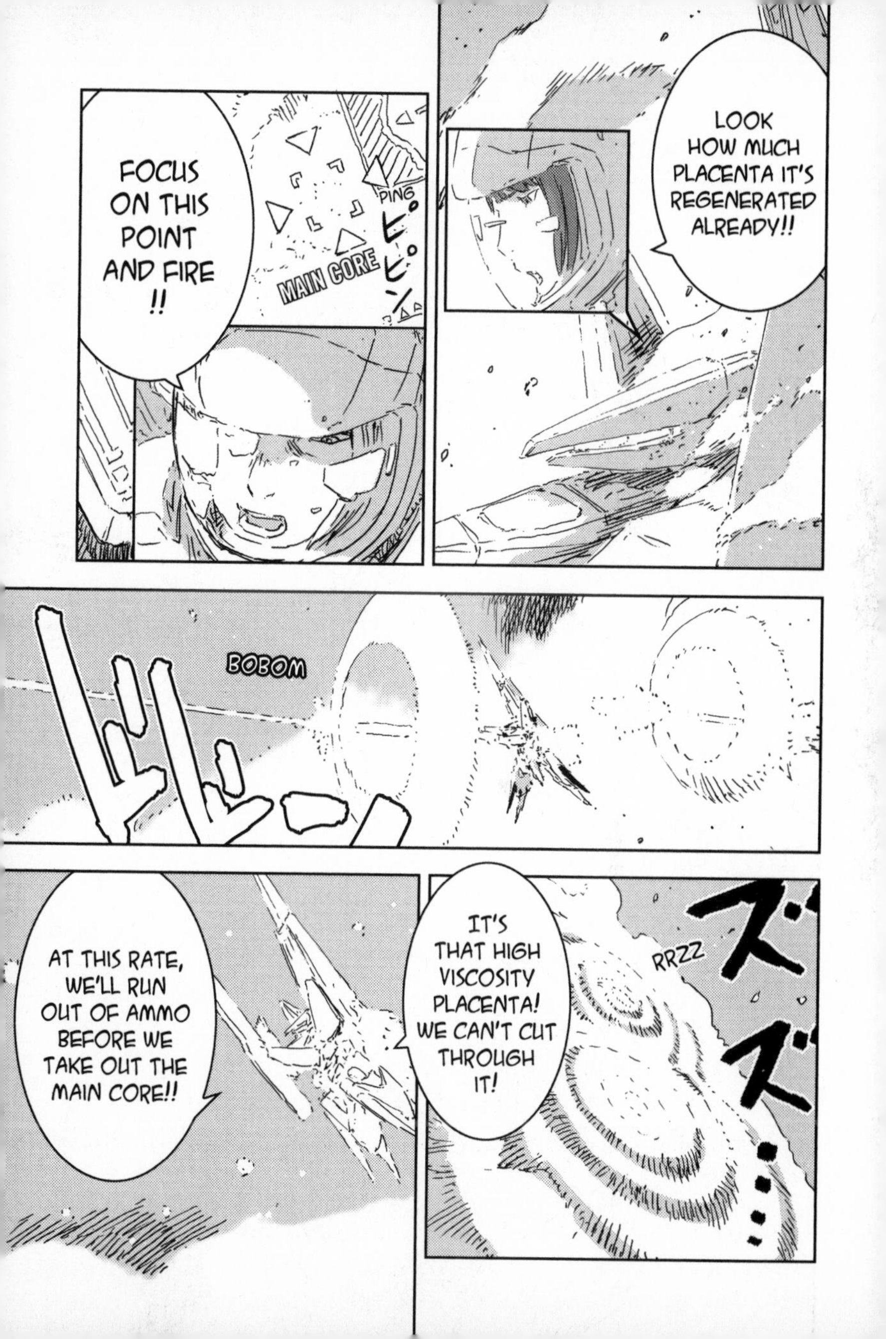
LOOK HOW MUCH PLACENTA IT'S REGENERATED ALREADY!!
FOCUS ON THIS POINT AND FIRE!!
PING
MAIN CORE
BOBOM
RRZZ
IT'S THAT HIGH VISCOSITY PLACENTA! WE CAN'T CUT THROUGH IT!
AT THIS RATE, WE'LL RUN OUT OF AMMO BEFORE WE TAKE OUT THE MAIN CORE!!

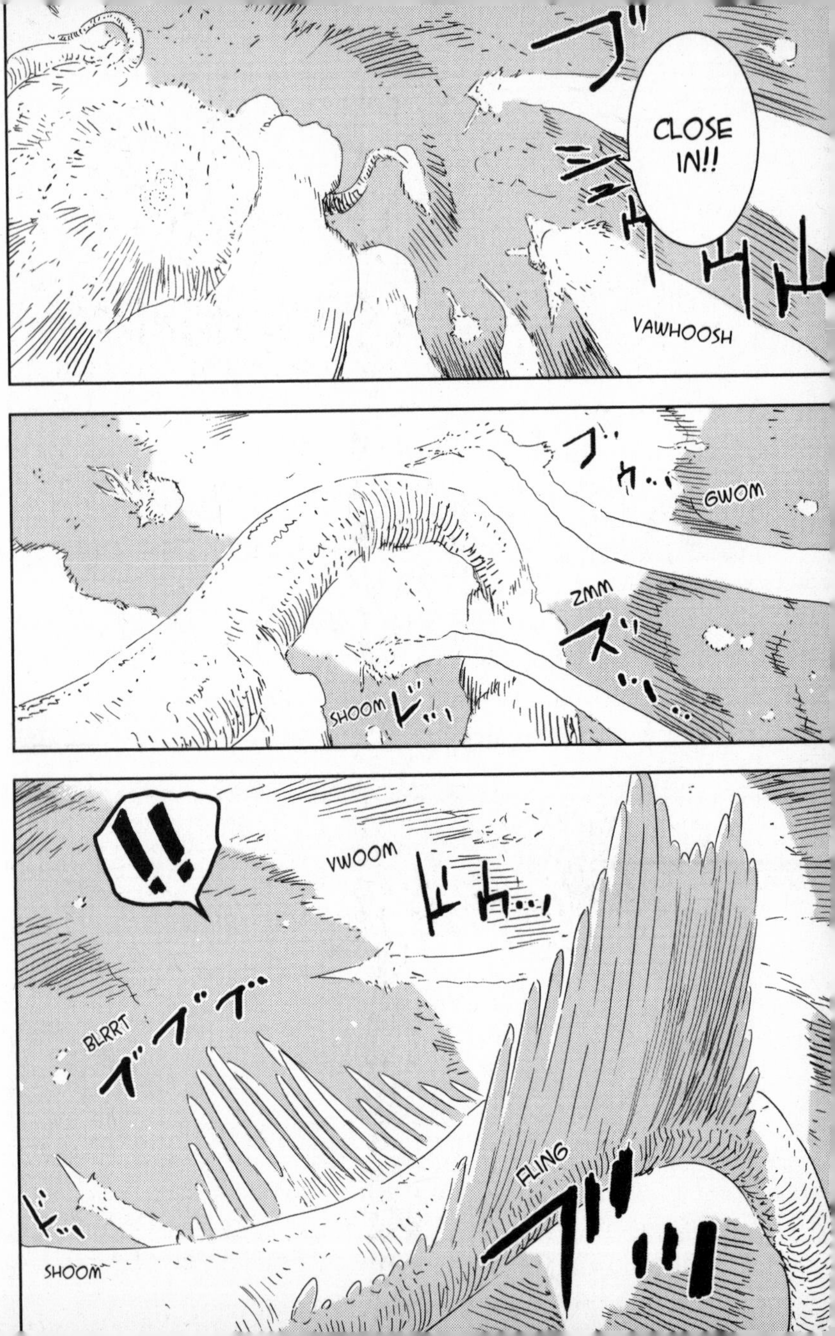
CLOSE IN!!
VAWHOOSH
GWOM
ZMM
SHOOM
VWOOM
!!
FLING
BLRRT
SHOOM

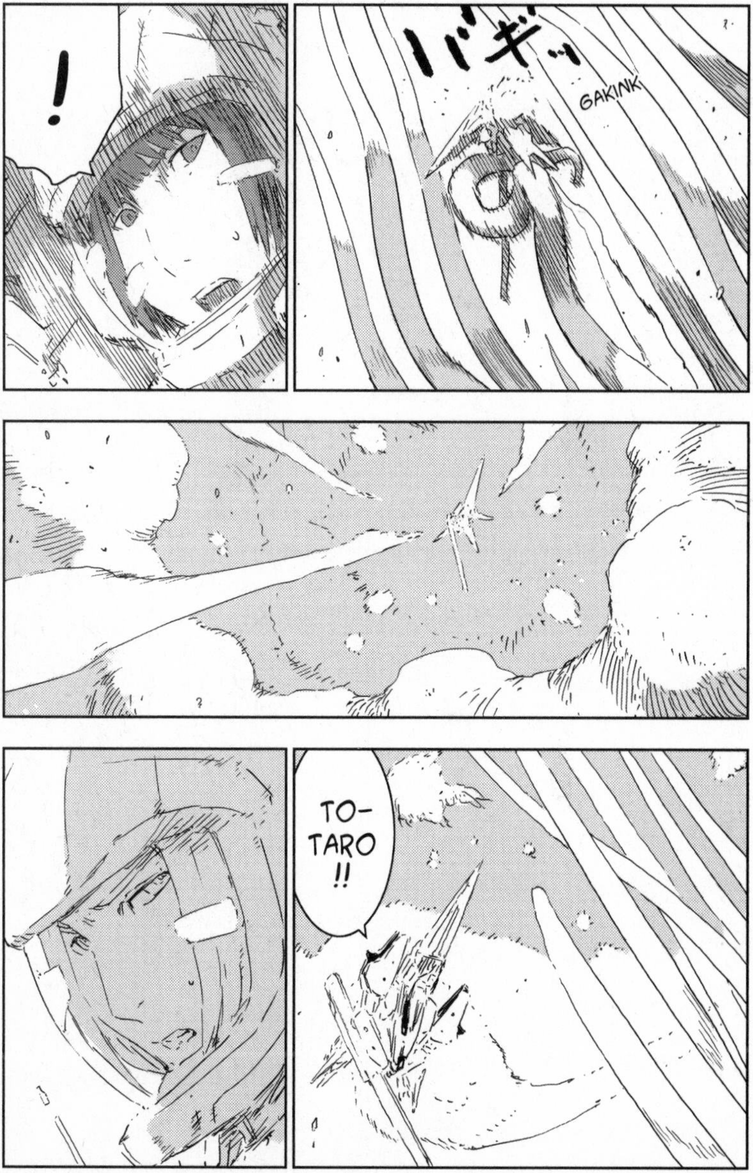
バギッ
GAKINK
!
TO-TARO!!

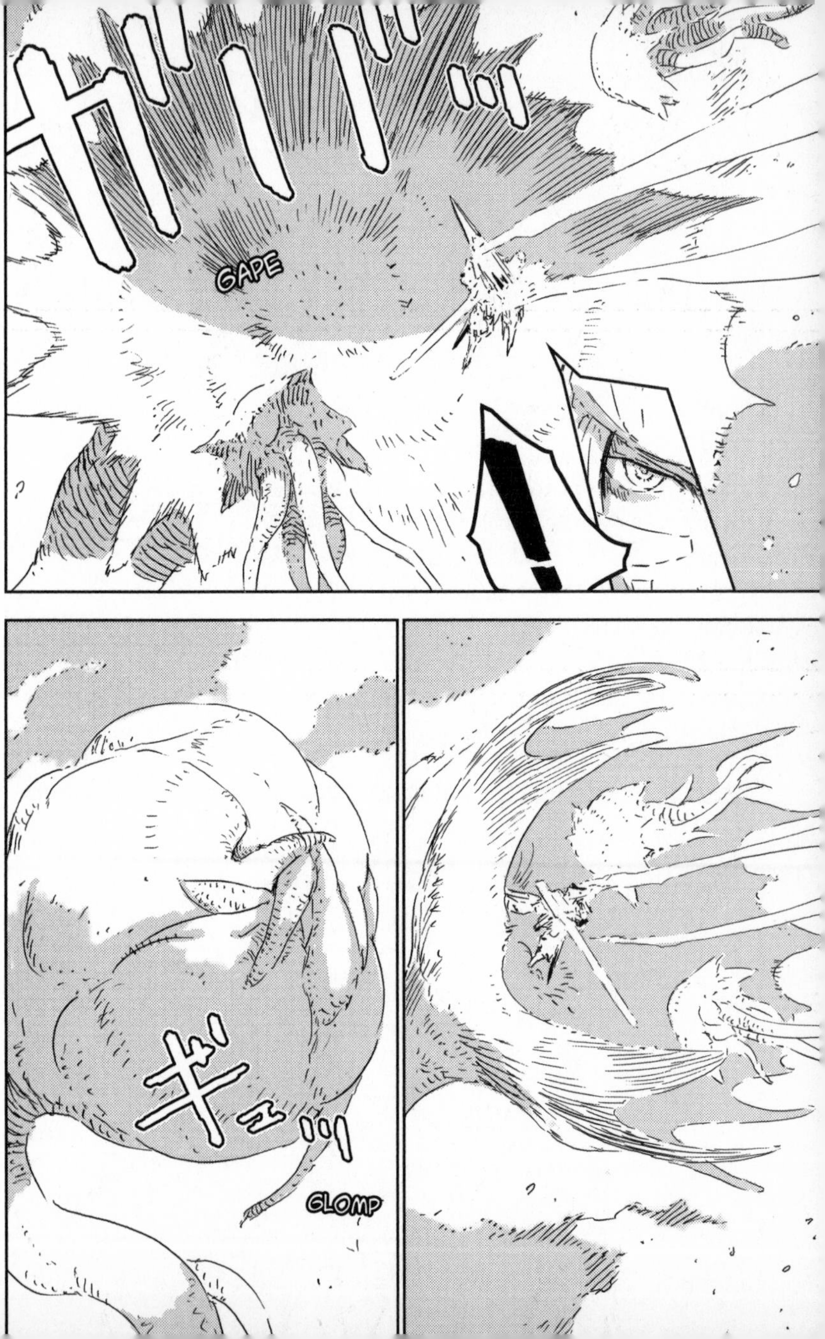
GAPE
GLOMP

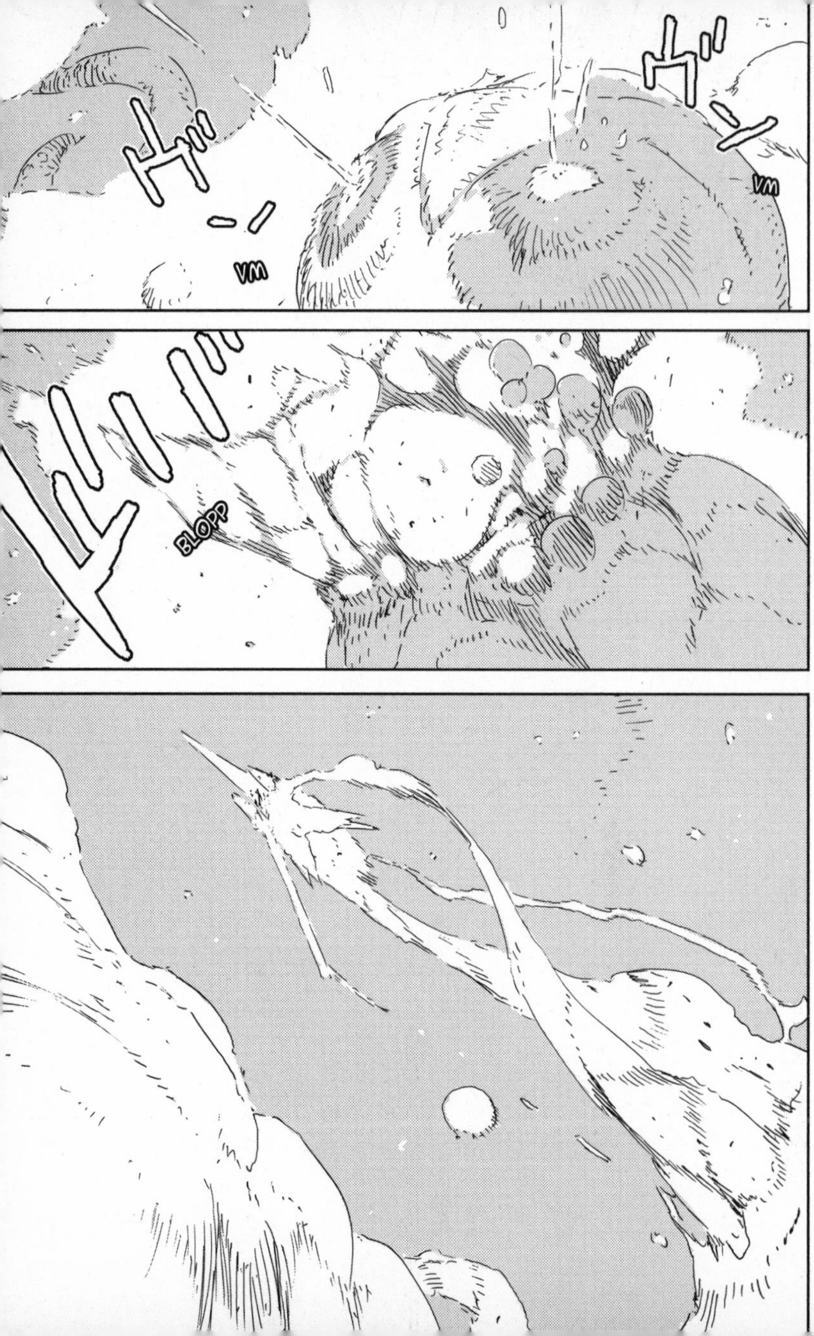
VM
VM
BLOPP

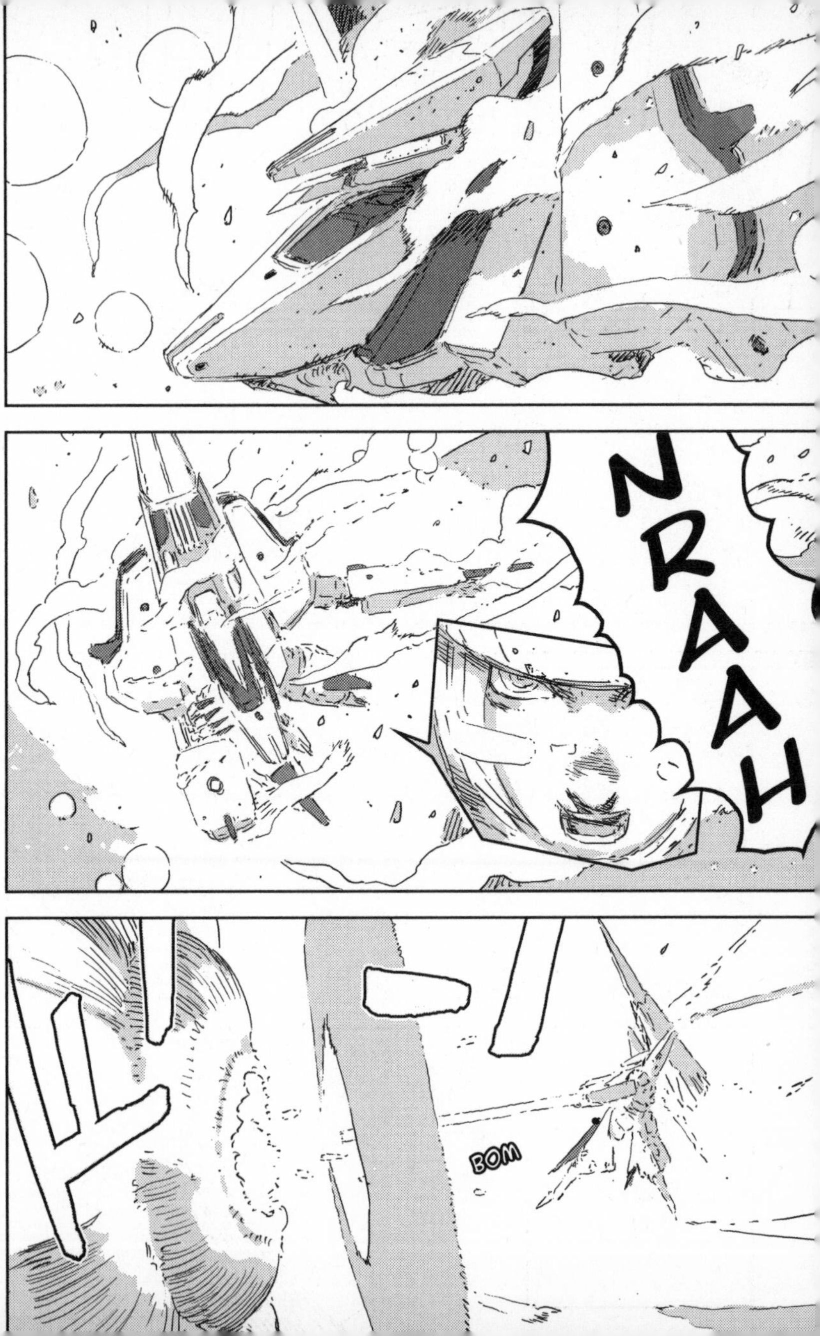
NRAAH
BOM

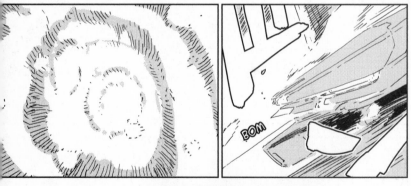

JUST
A BIT
MORE
!!

IT'S
WORKING
!!

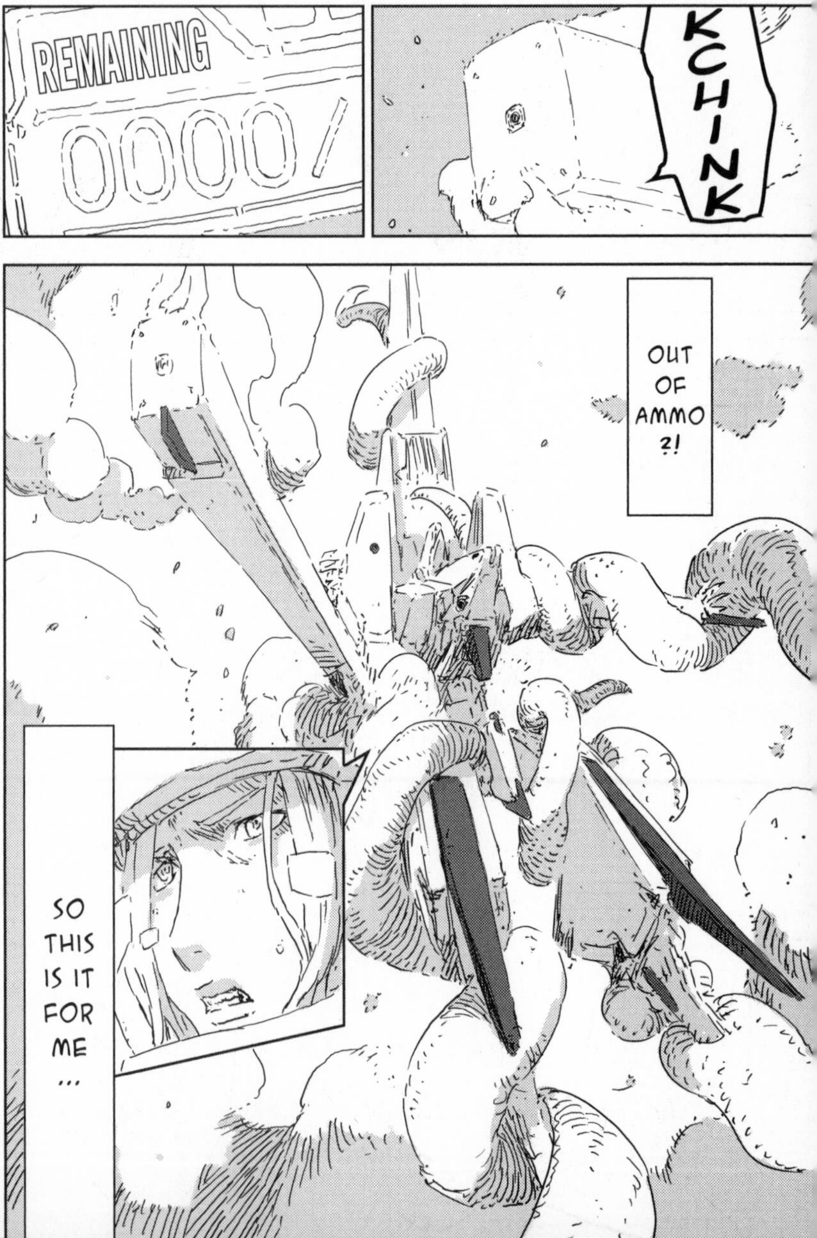
REMAINING
0000/
KCHINK
OUT OF AMMO ?!
SO THIS IS IT FOR ME ...

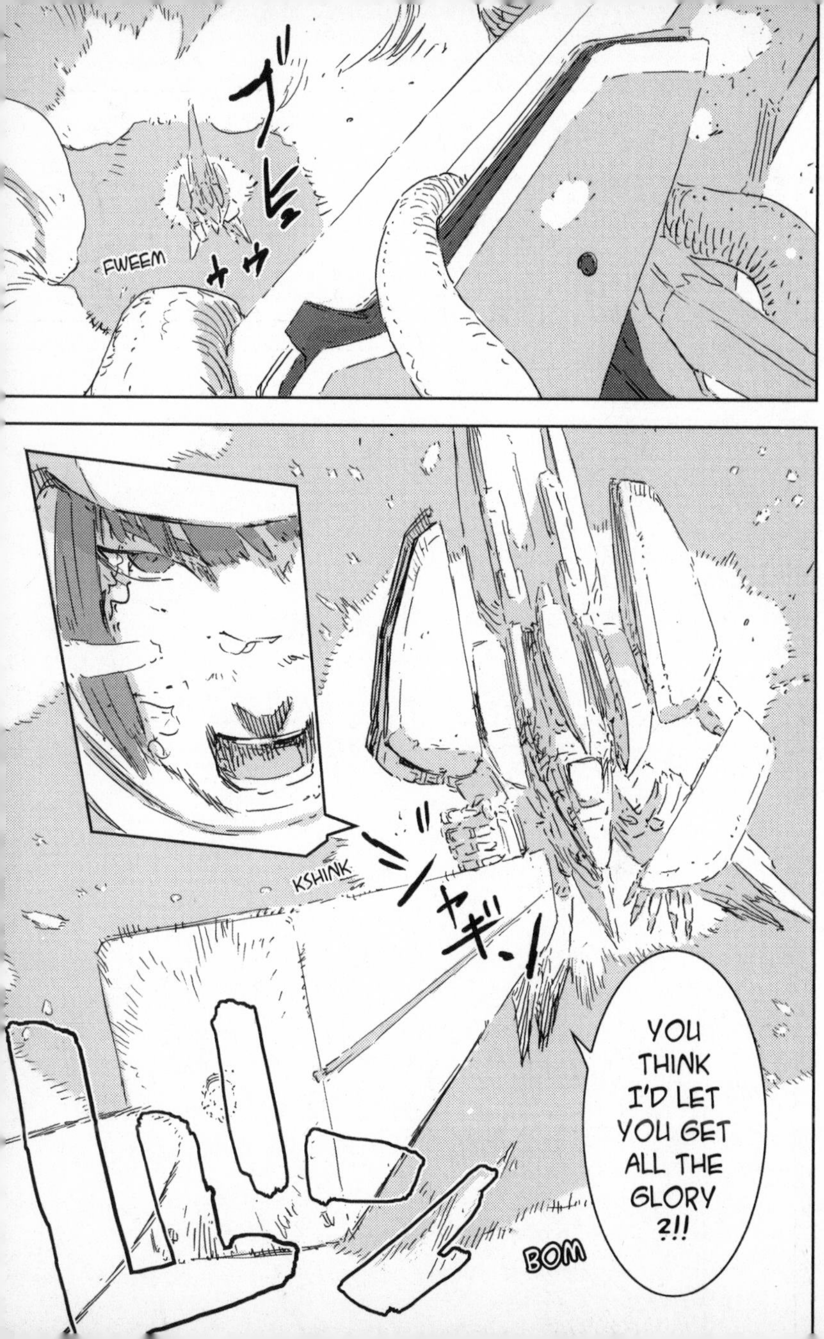
FWEEM
YOU THINK I'D LET YOU GET ALL THE GLORY ?!!
KSHINK
BOM

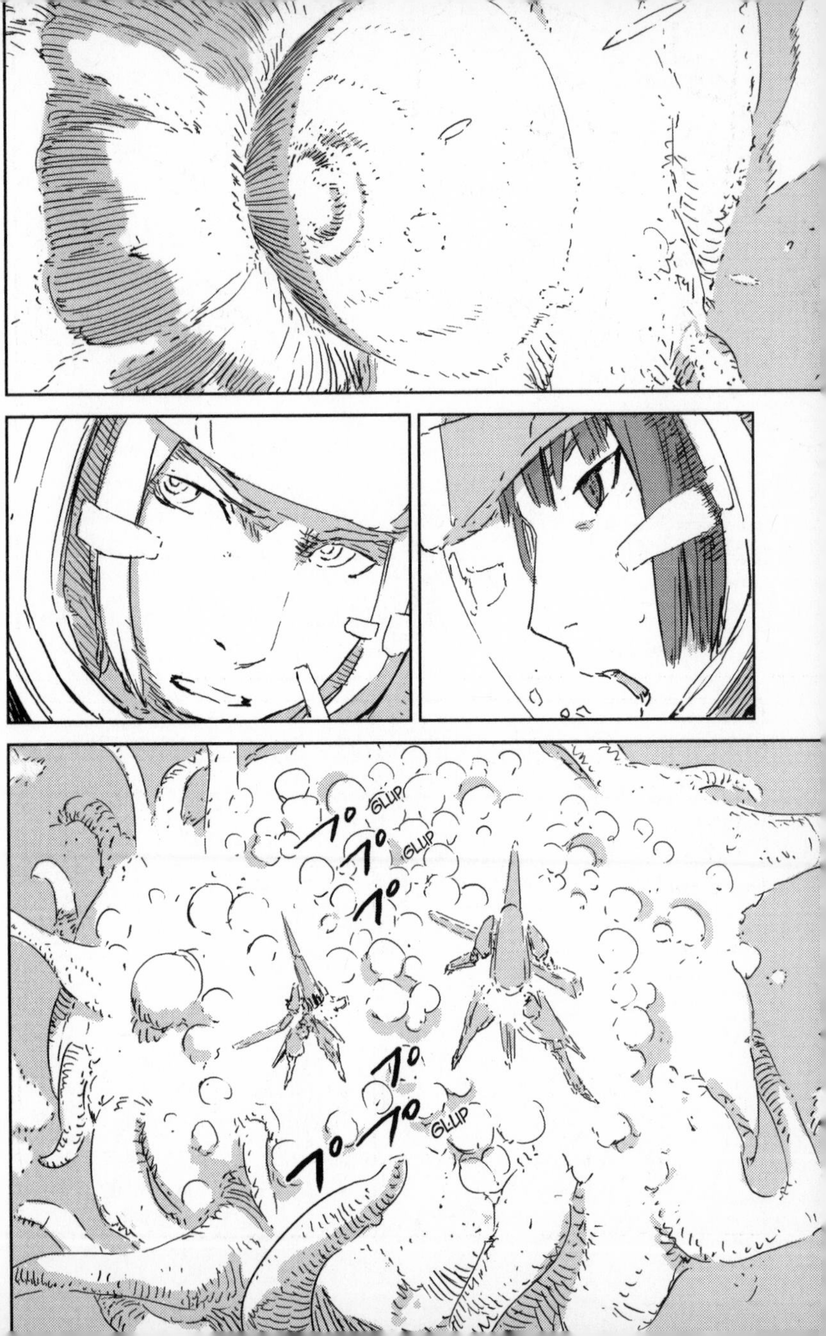
GLUP
GLUP
GLUP

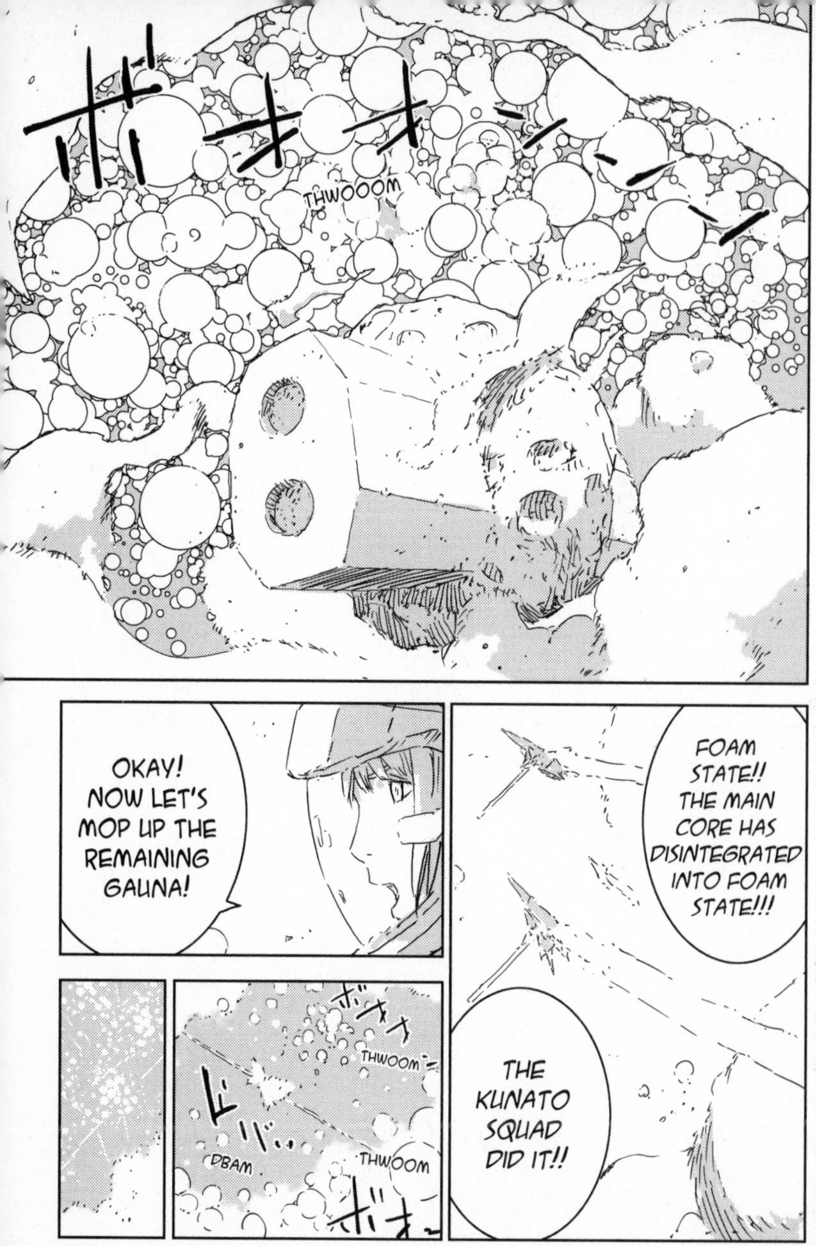
THWOOOM
FOAM STATE!! THE MAIN CORE HAS DISINTEGRATED INTO FOAM STATE!!!
THE KUNATO SQUAD DID IT!!
OKAY! NOW LET'S MOP UP THE REMAINING GAUNA!
THWOOM
DBAM
THWOOM

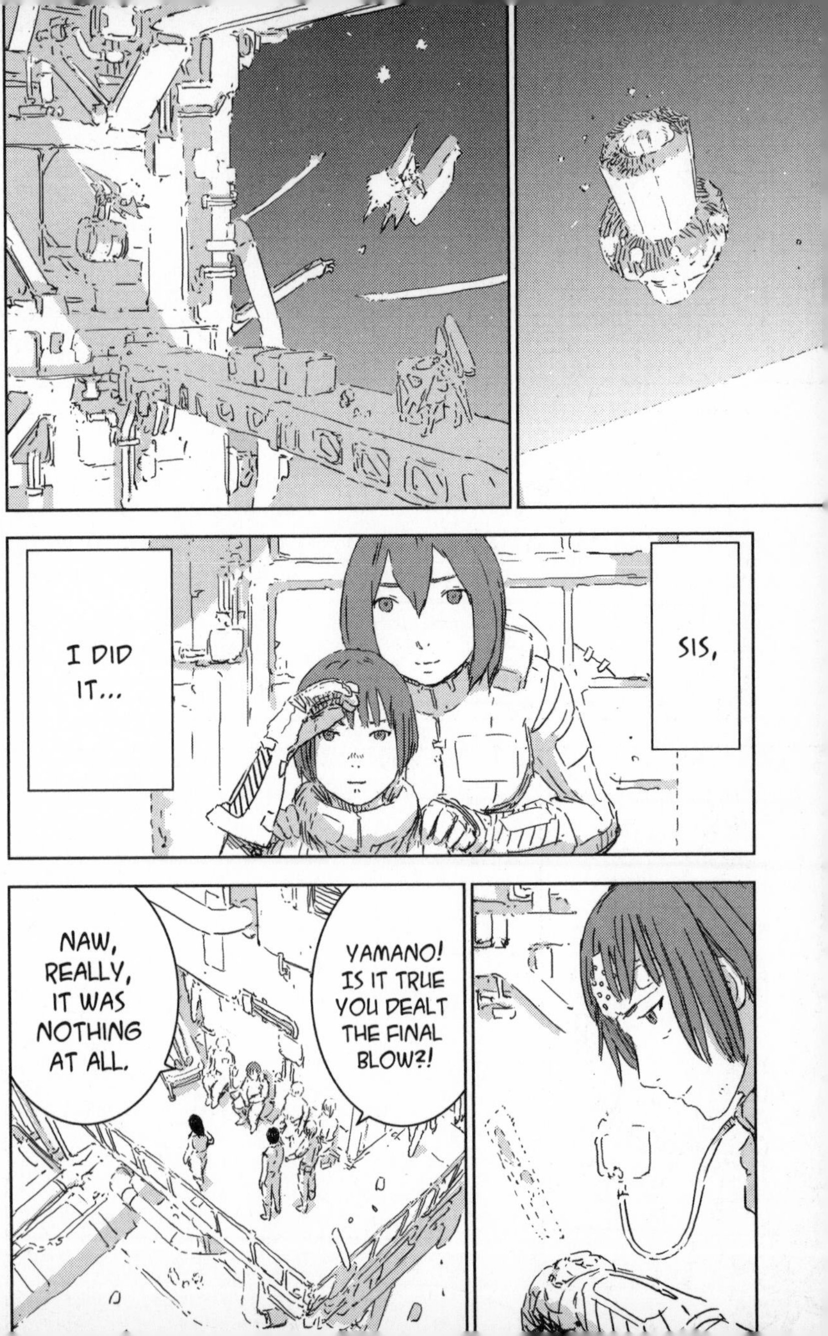
SIS,
I DID IT...
YAMANO! IS IT TRUE YOU DEALT THE FINAL BLOW?!
NAW, REALLY, IT WAS NOTHING AT ALL.

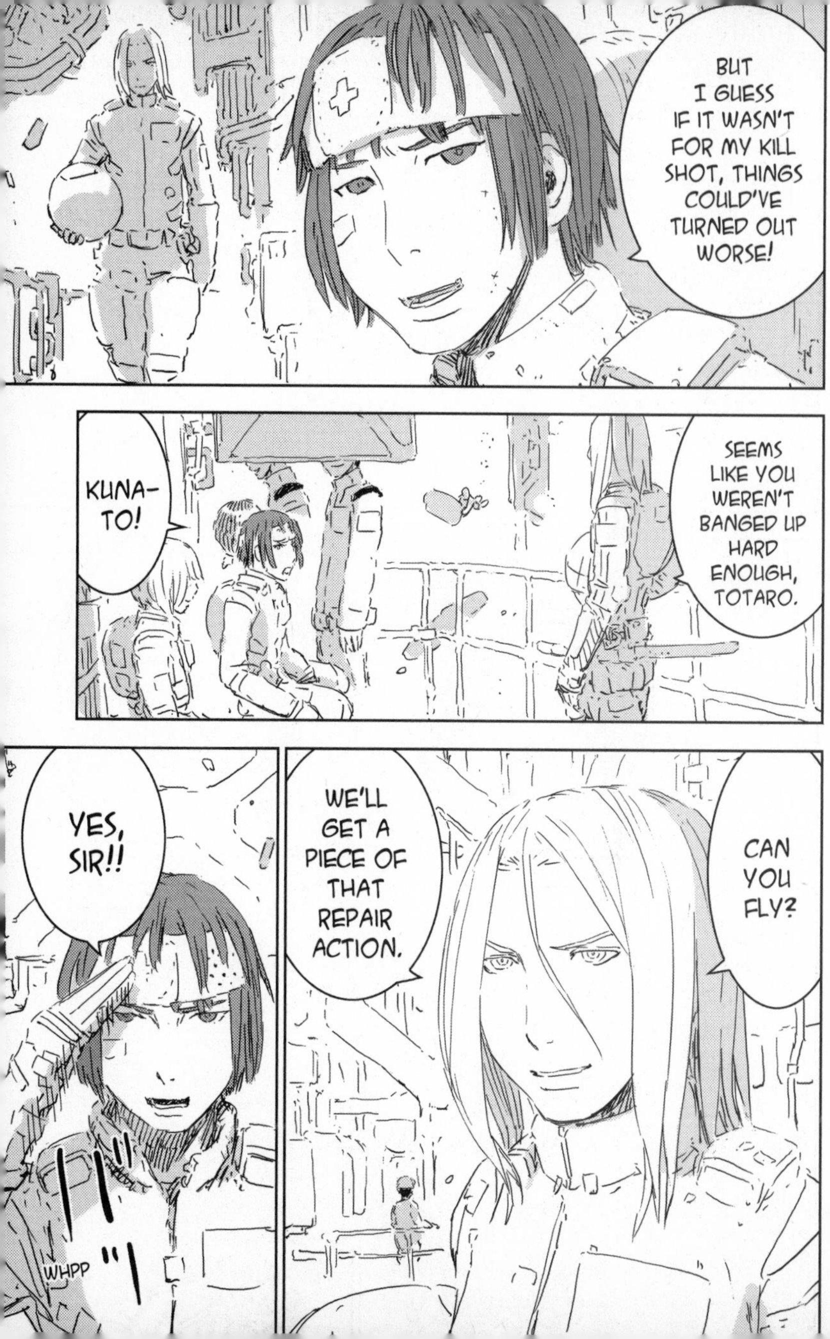
BUT I GUESS IF IT WASN'T FOR MY KILL SHOT, THINGS COULD'VE TURNED OUT WORSE!
SEEMS LIKE YOU WEREN'T BANGED UP HARD ENOUGH, TOTARO.
KUNA-TO!
CAN YOU FLY?
WE'LL GET A PIECE OF THAT REPAIR ACTION.
YES, SIR!!
WHPP

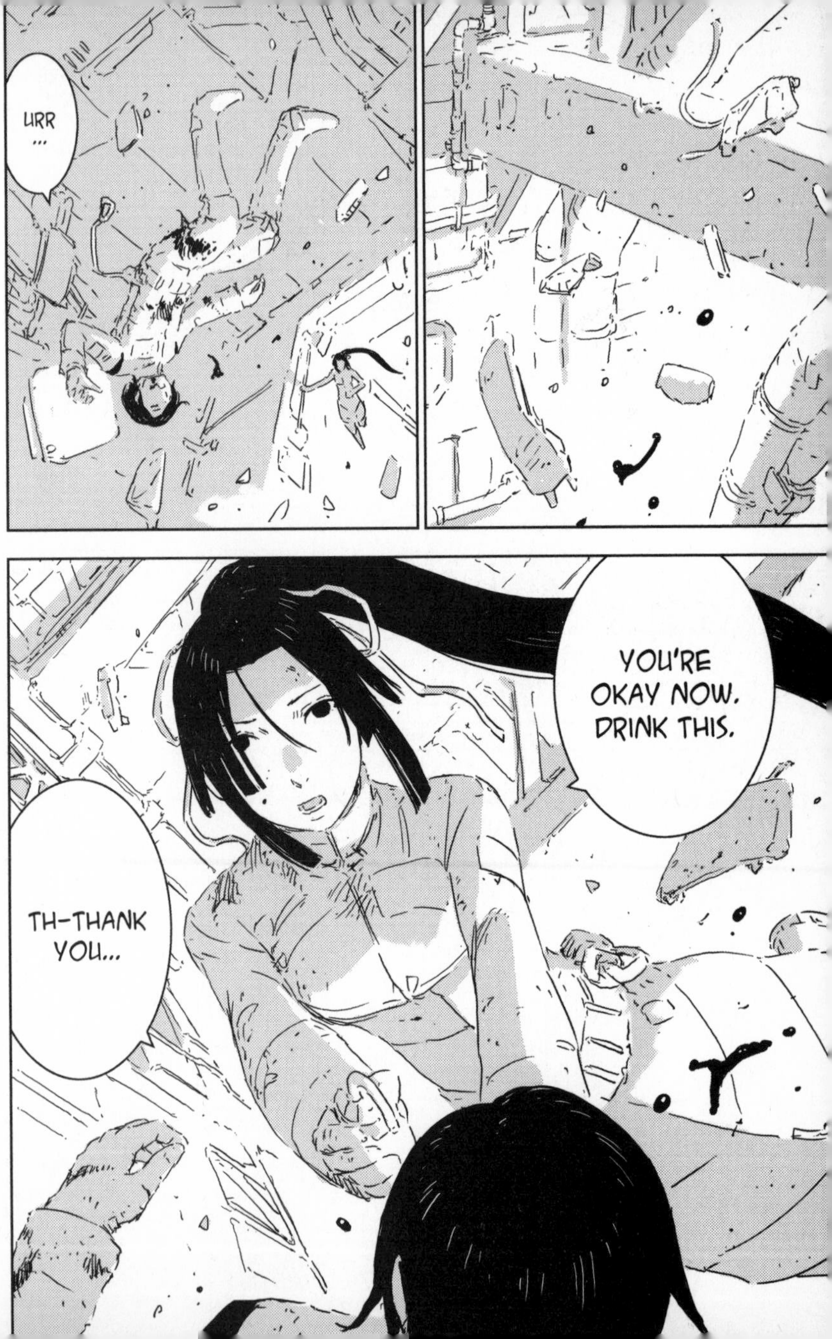
URR ...
YOU'RE OKAY NOW. DRINK THIS.
TH-THANK YOU...

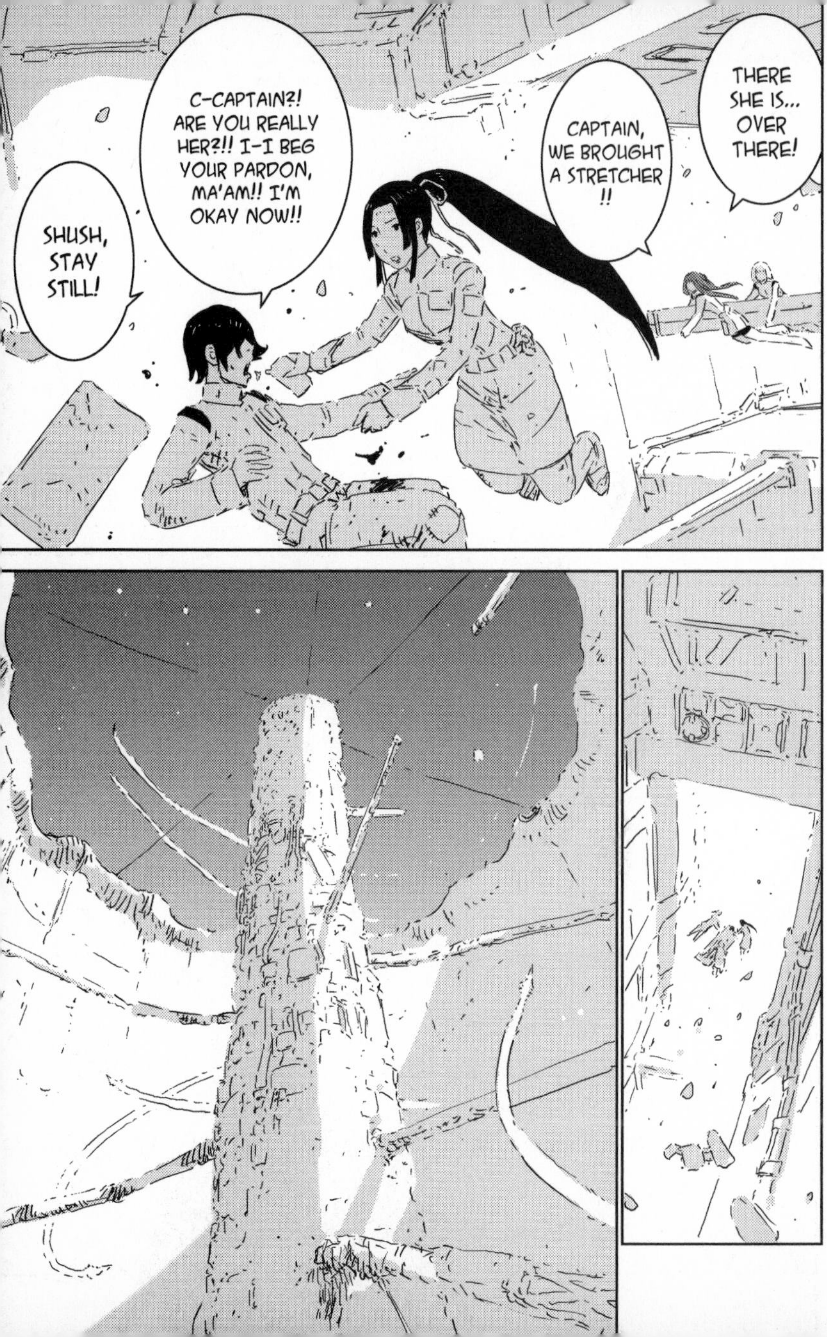
THERE SHE IS... OVER THERE!
CAPTAIN, WE BROUGHT A STRETCHER !!
C-CAPTAIN?! ARE YOU REALLY HER?!! I-I BEG YOUR PARDON, MA'AM!! I'M OKAY NOW!!
SHUSH, STAY STILL!

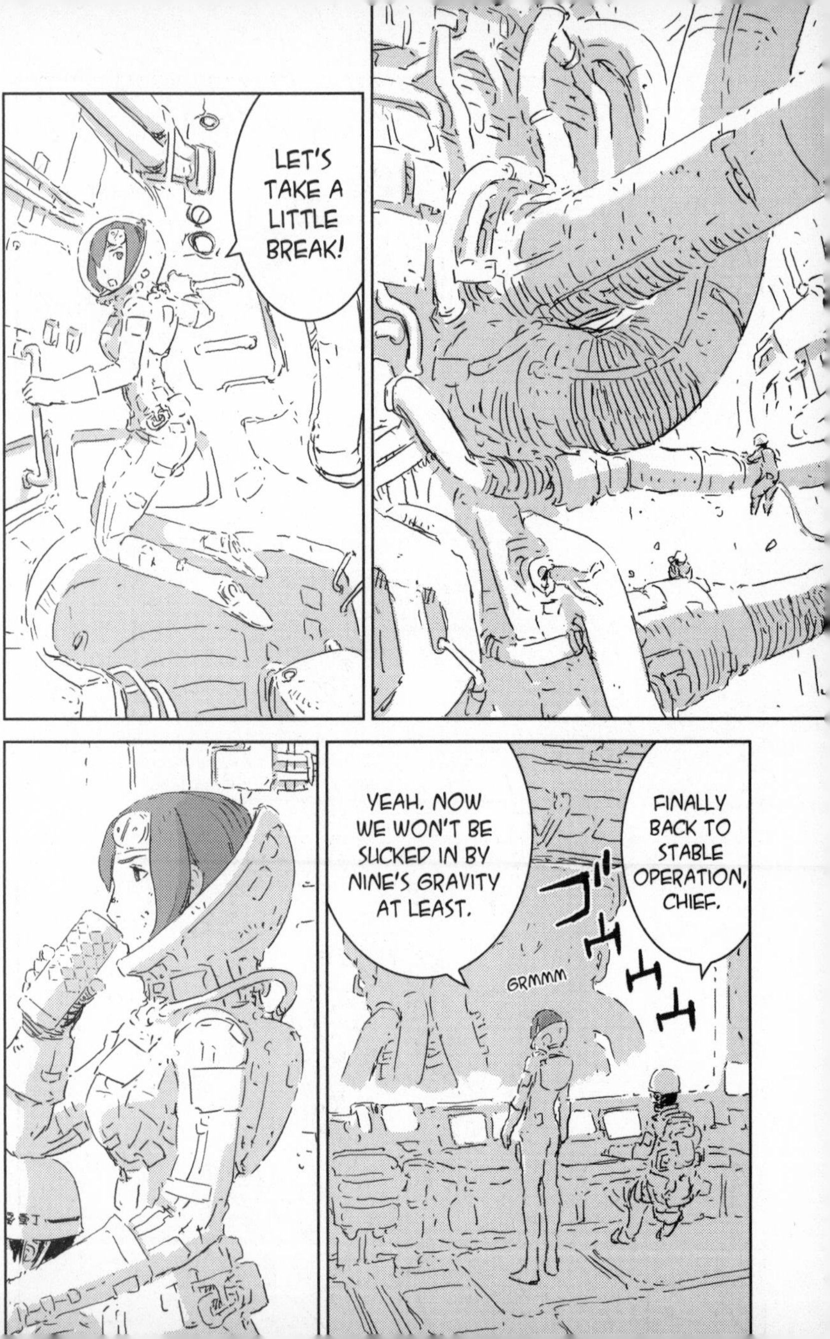
LET'S TAKE A LITTLE BREAK!
FINALLY BACK TO STABLE OPERATION, CHIEF.
ゴォォォ
YEAH. NOW WE WON'T BE SUCKED IN BY NINE'S GRAVITY AT LEAST.
GRMMM

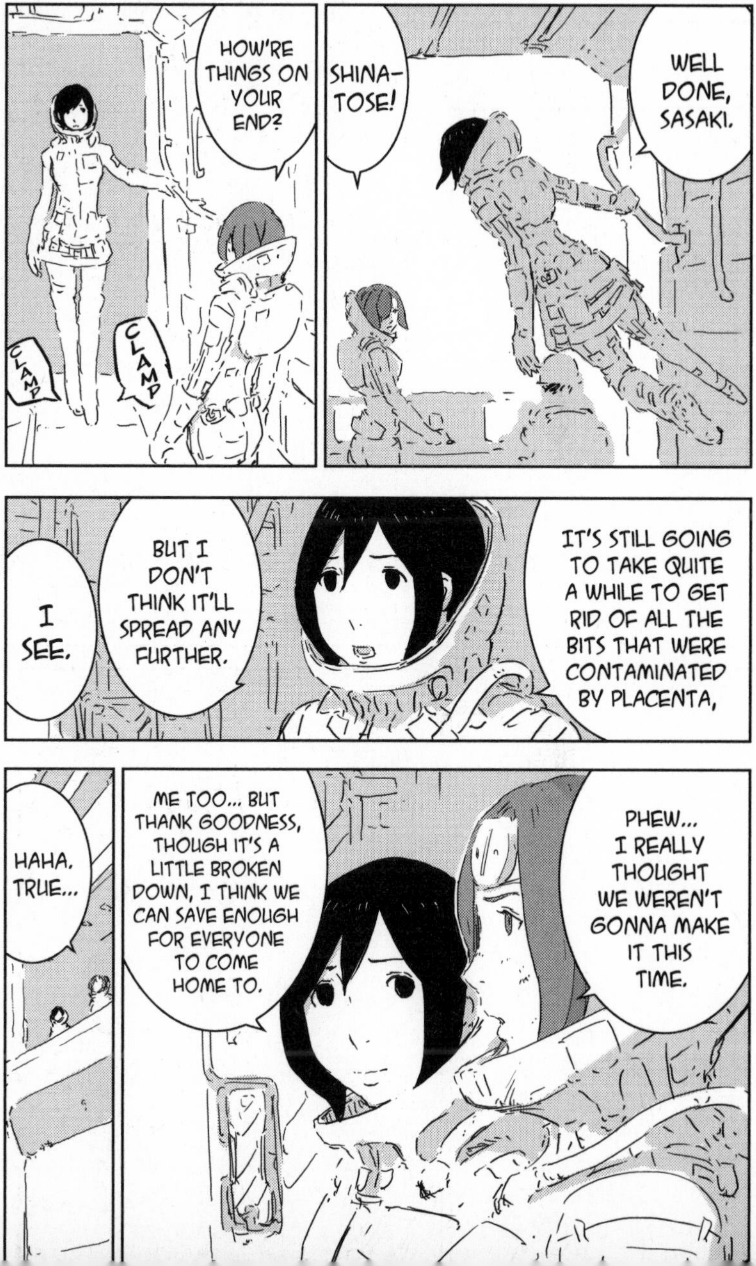
WELL DONE, SASAKI.
SHINA-TOSE!
HOW'RE THINGS ON YOUR END?
CLAMP
CLAMP
IT'S STILL GOING TO TAKE QUITE A WHILE TO GET RID OF ALL THE BITS THAT WERE CONTAMINATED BY PLACENTA,
BUT I DON'T THINK IT'LL SPREAD ANY FURTHER.
I SEE.
PHEW... I REALLY THOUGHT WE WEREN'T GONNA MAKE IT THIS TIME.
ME TOO... BUT THANK GOODNESS, THOUGH IT'S A LITTLE BROKEN DOWN, I THINK WE CAN SAVE ENOUGH FOR EVERYONE TO COME HOME TO.
HAHA. TRUE...

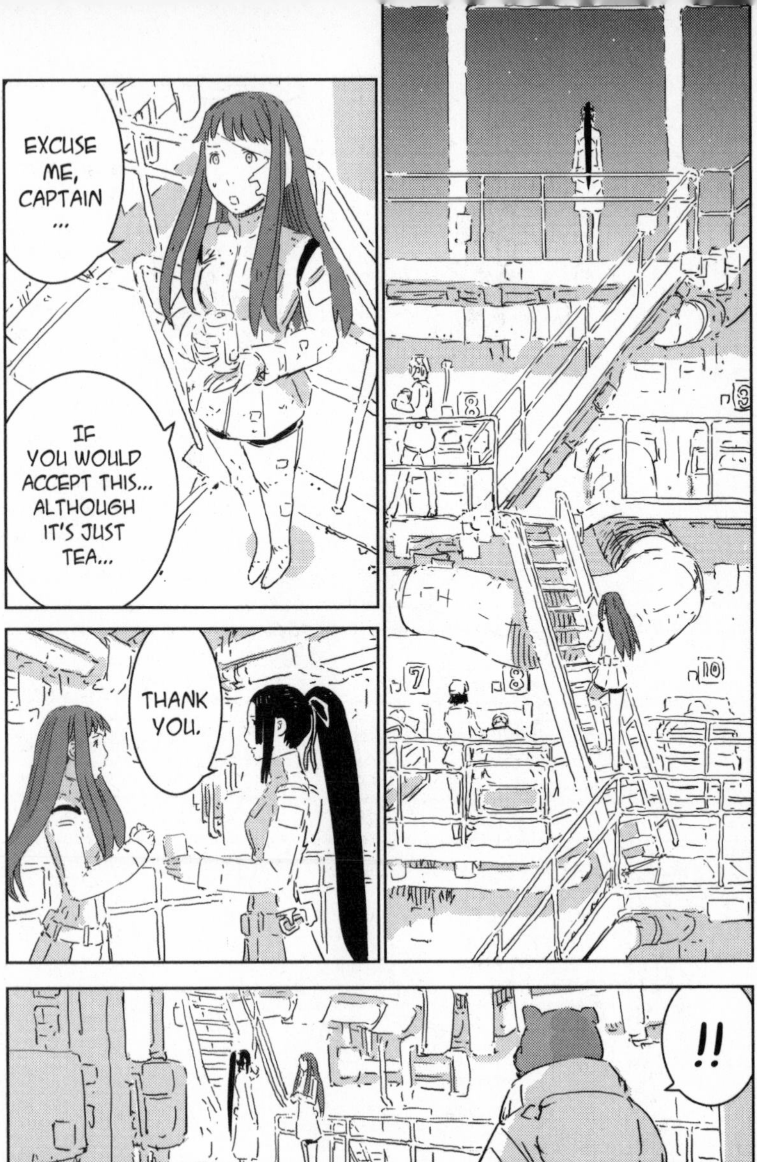
EXCUSE ME, CAPTAIN ...
IF YOU WOULD ACCEPT THIS... ALTHOUGH IT'S JUST TEA...
THANK YOU.
!!

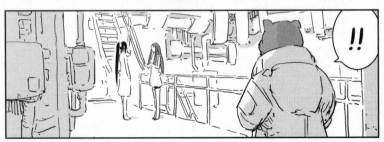

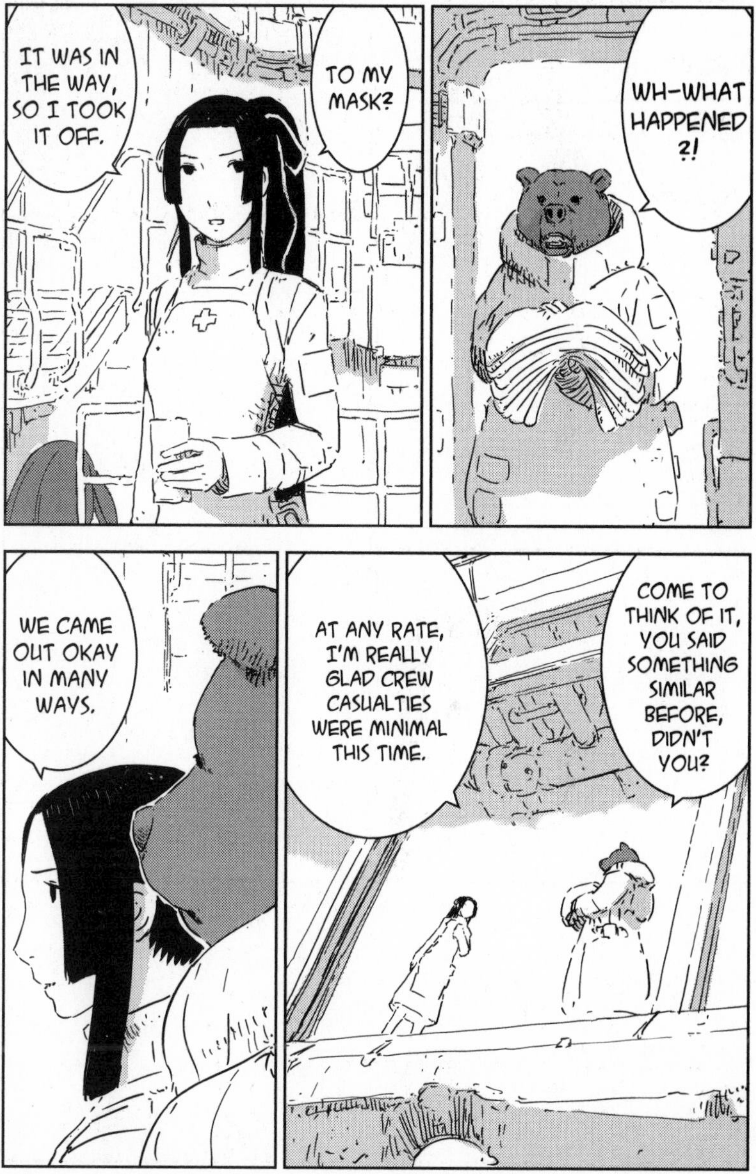
WH-WHAT HAPPENED ?!
TO MY MASK?
IT WAS IN THE WAY, SO I TOOK IT OFF.
COME TO THINK OF IT, YOU SAID SOMETHING SIMILAR BEFORE, DIDN'T YOU?
AT ANY RATE, I'M REALLY GLAD CREW CASUALTIES WERE MINIMAL THIS TIME.
WE CAME OUT OKAY IN MANY WAYS.

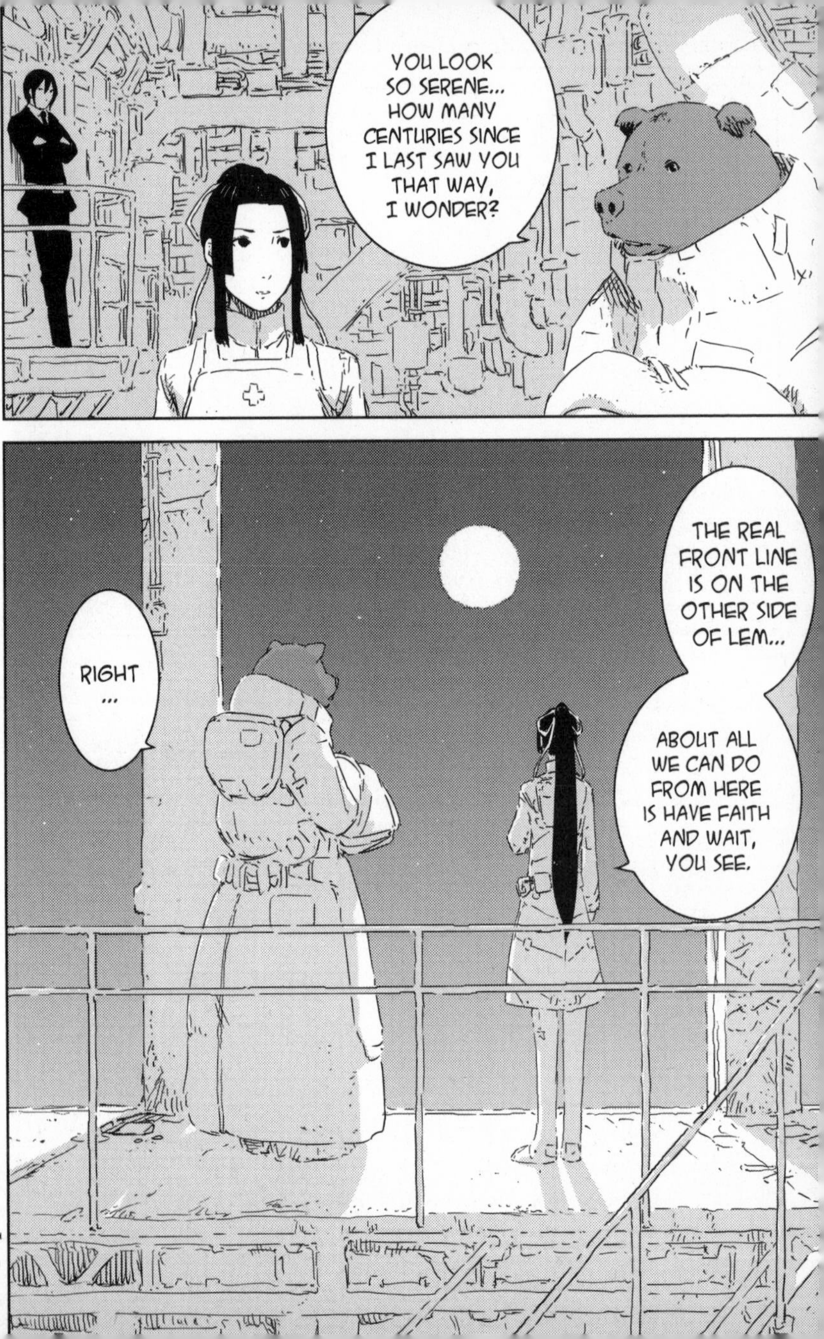
YOU LOOK SO SERENE... HOW MANY CENTURIES SINCE I LAST SAW YOU THAT WAY, I WONDER?
THE REAL FRONT LINE IS ON THE OTHER SIDE OF LEM...
ABOUT ALL WE CAN DO FROM HERE IS HAVE FAITH AND WAIT, YOU SEE.
RIGHT ...

Chapter 75: END

Chapter 76: The Cluster Ship Fleet's Counterattack

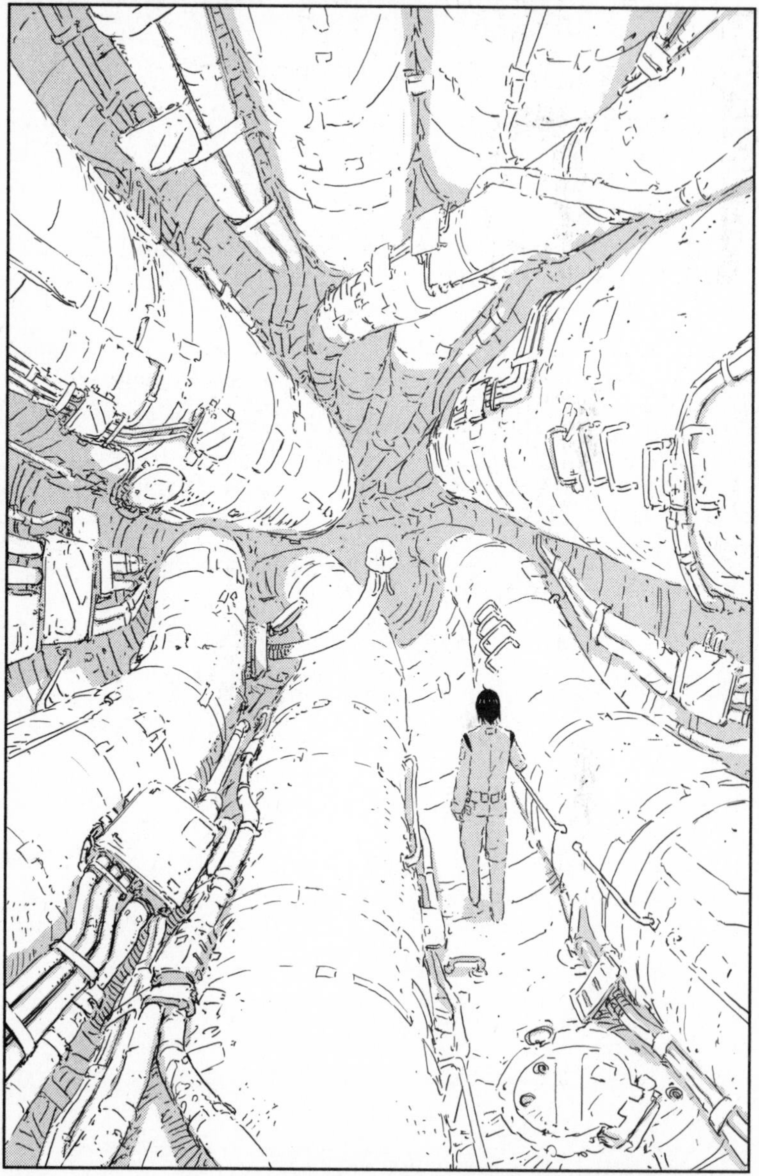

One Hundred Sights of Sidonia Part Fifty-Nine:
Shared Tubes Interior

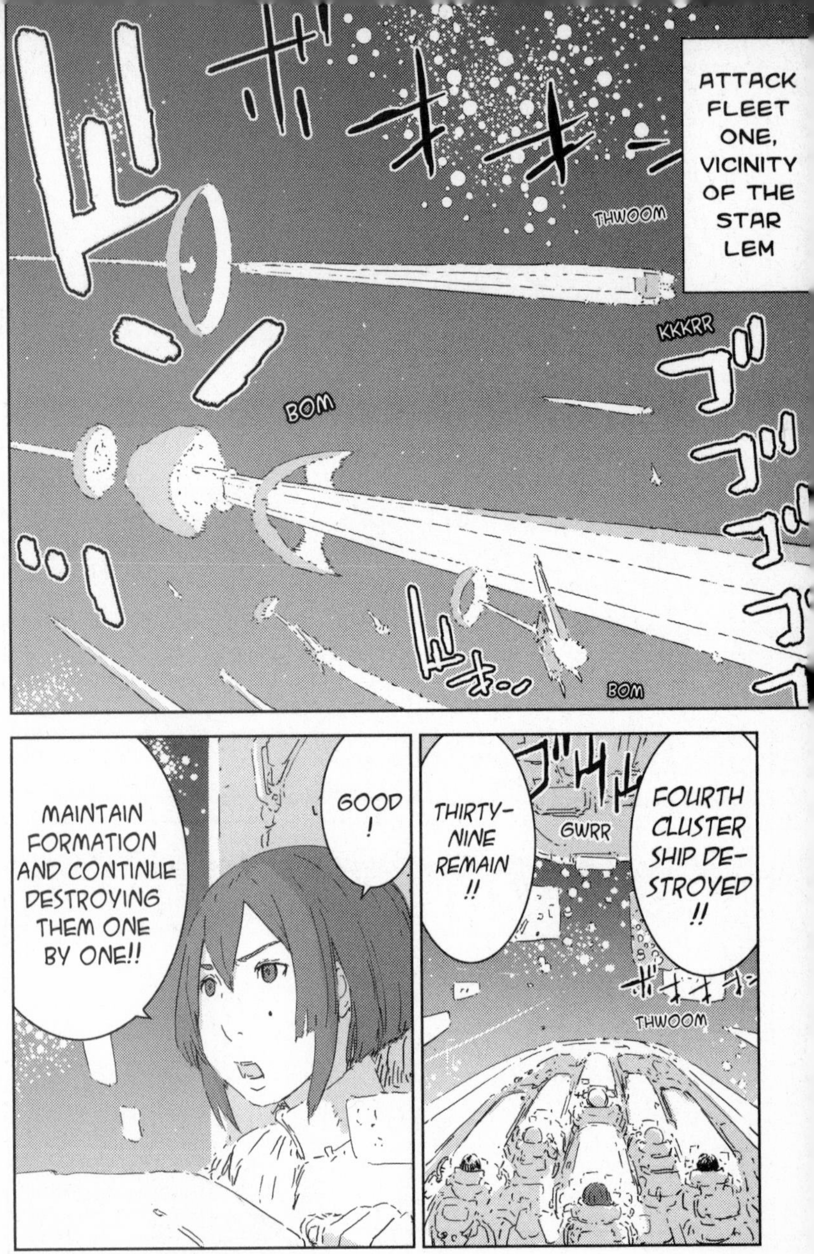
ATTACK FLEET ONE, VICINITY OF THE STAR LEM
THWOOM
KKKRR
BOM
BOM
FOURTH CLUSTER SHIP DE-STROYED !!
THIRTY-NINE REMAIN !!
GWRR
THWOOM
GOOD !
MAINTAIN FORMATION AND CONTINUE DESTROYING THEM ONE BY ONE!!

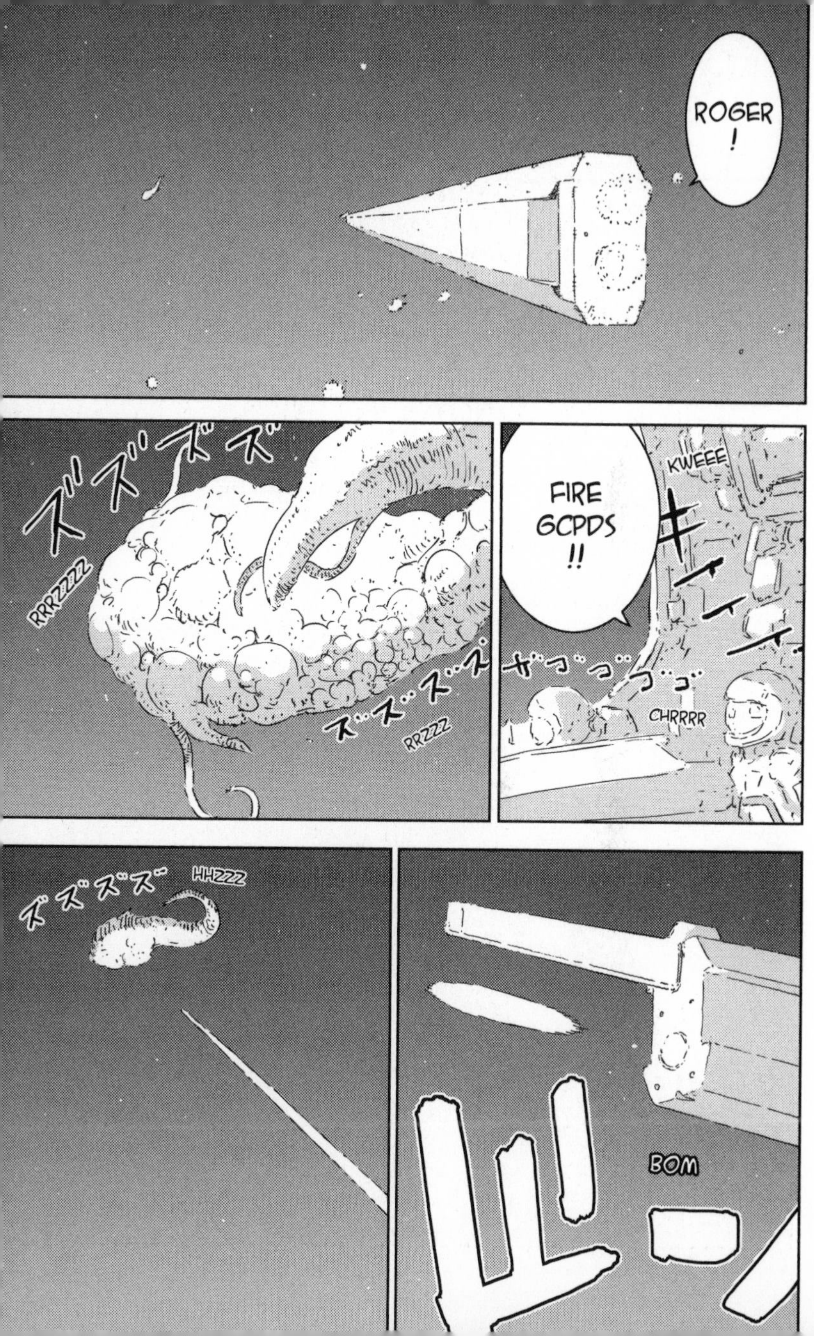
ROGER !
FIRE GCPDS !!
KWEEE
CHRRRR
RRRZZZZ
RRZZZ
BOM
HHZZZ

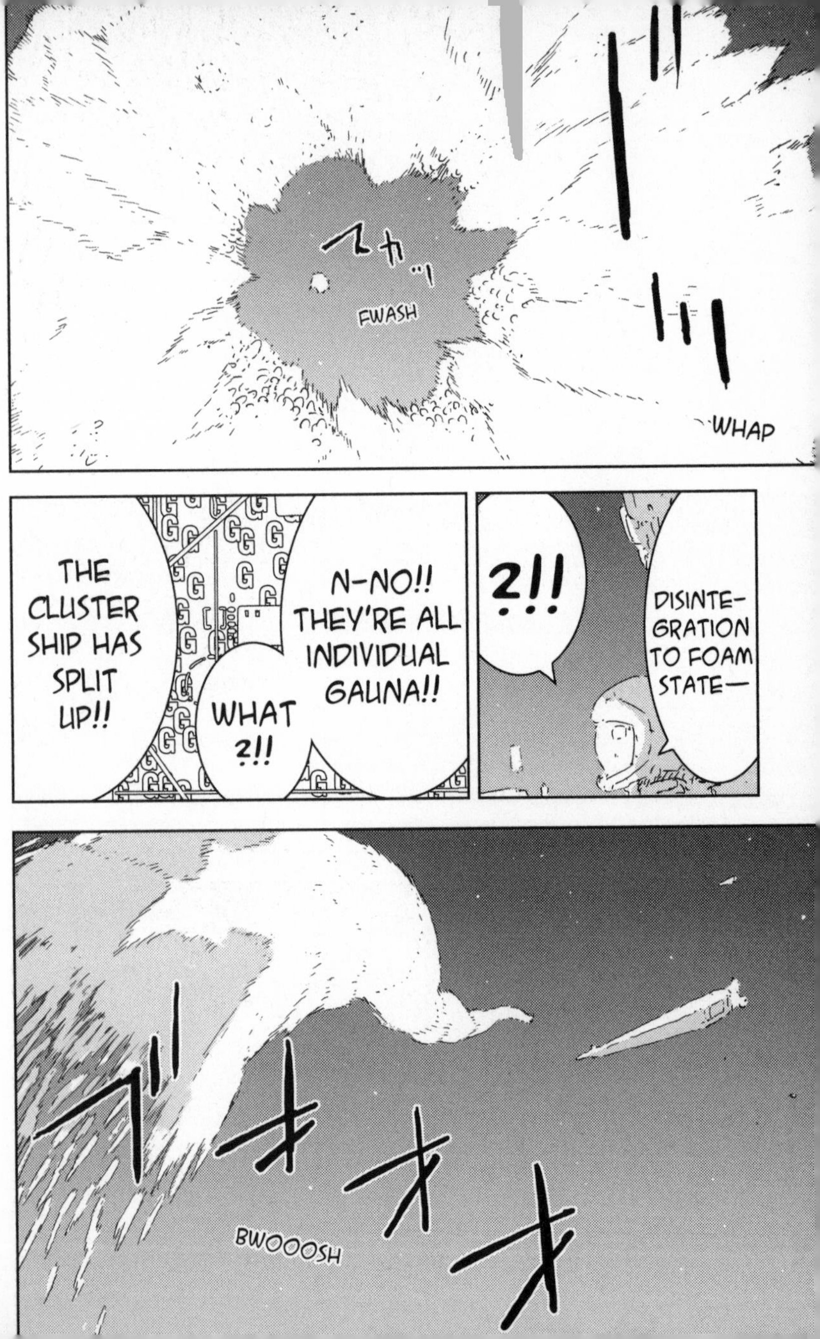
FWASH
WHAP
DISINTE-GRATION TO FOAM STATE—
?!!
THE CLUSTER SHIP HAS SPLIT UP!!
WHAT ?!!
N-NO!! THEY'RE ALL INDIVIDUAL GAUNA!!
BWOOOSH

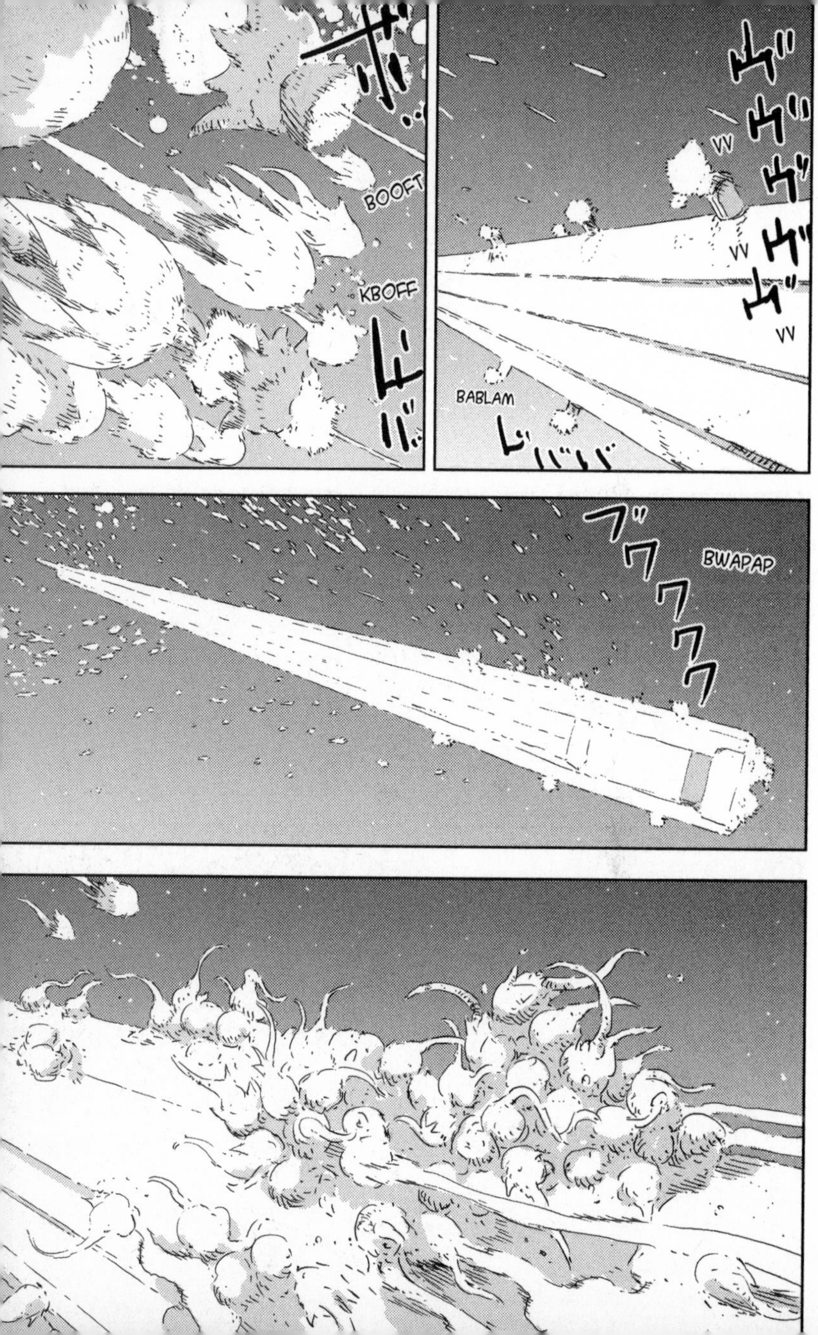
VV
VV
VV
BABLAM
BOOFT
KBOFF
BWAPAP

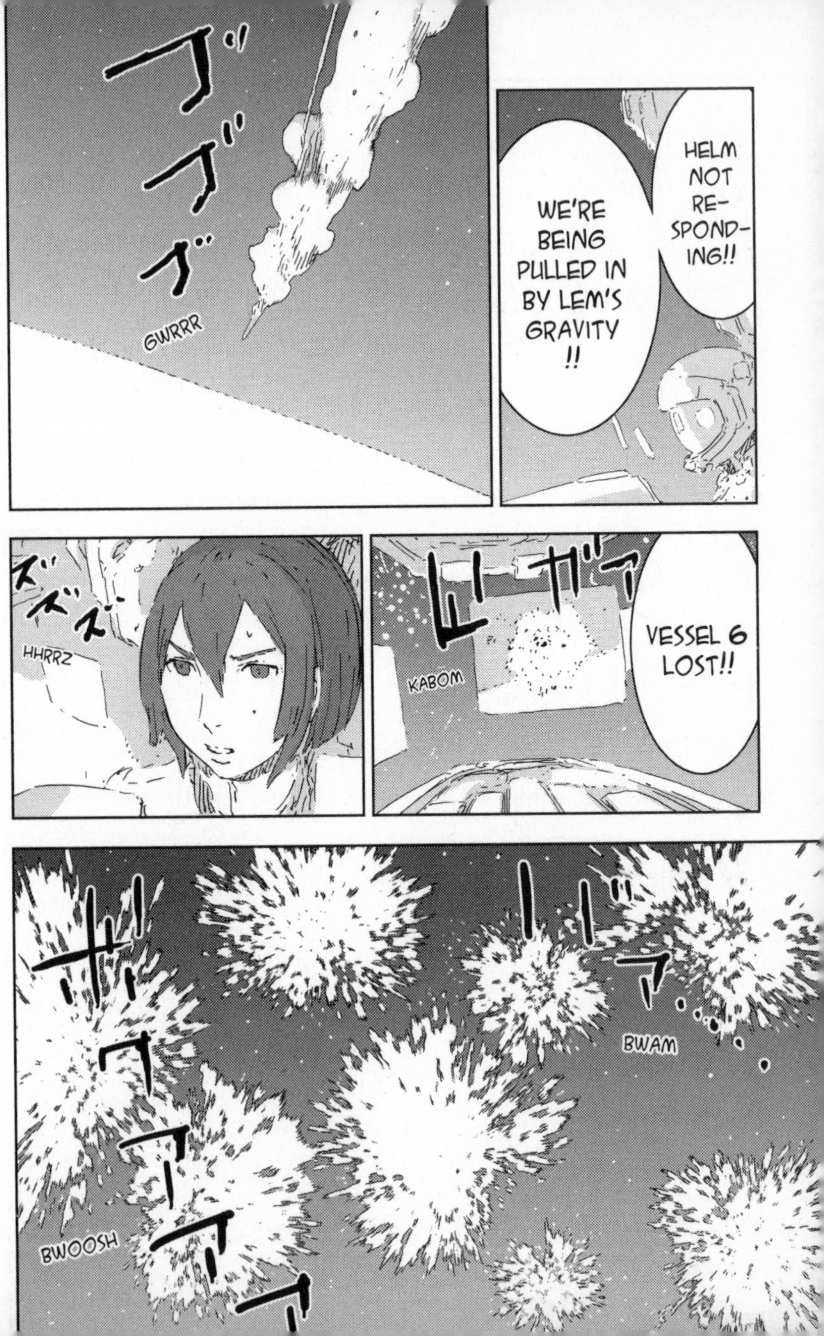
HELM NOT RE-SPOND-ING!!
WE'RE BEING PULLED IN BY LEM'S GRAVITY !!
GWRRR
VESSEL 6 LOST!!
KABOM
HHRRZ
BWAM
BWOOSH

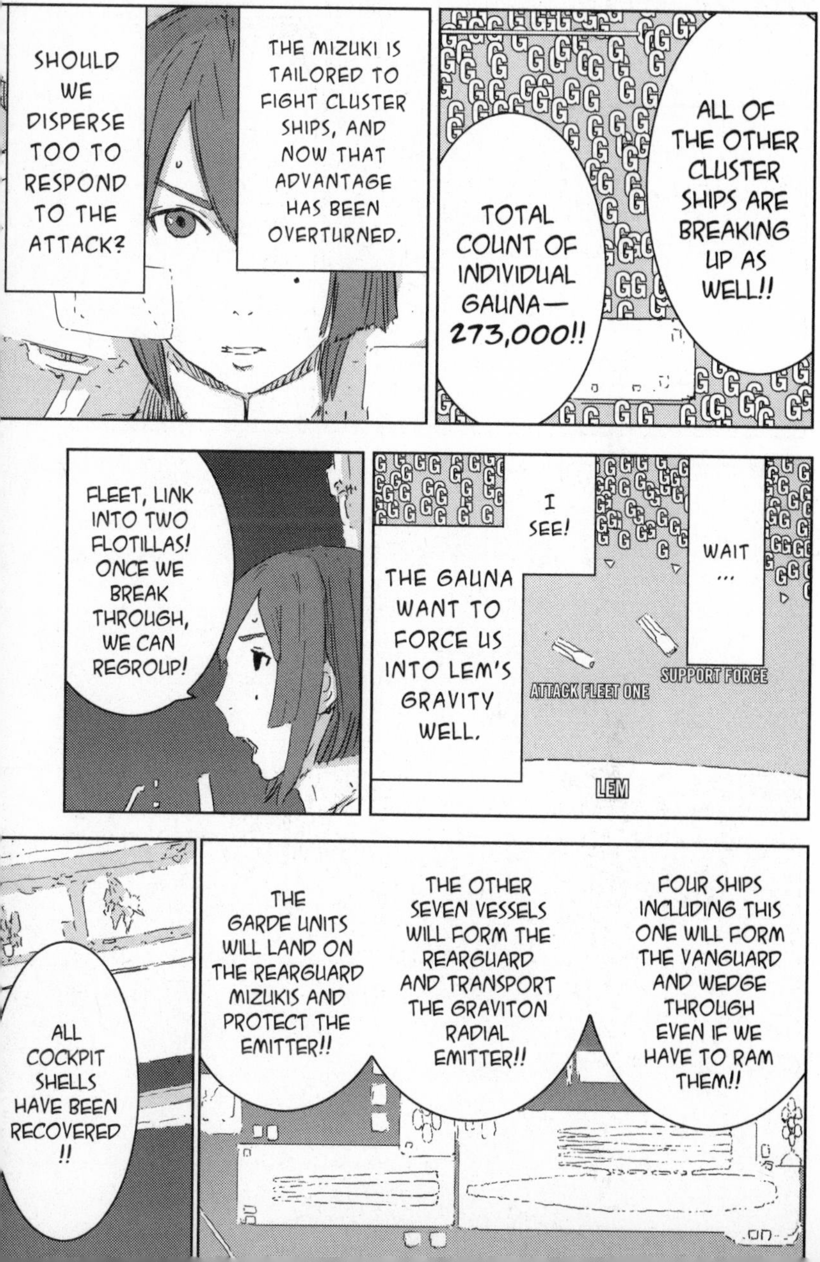
ALL OF THE OTHER CLUSTER SHIPS ARE BREAKING UP AS WELL!!
TOTAL COUNT OF INDIVIDUAL GAUNA—273,000!!
THE MIZUKI IS TAILORED TO FIGHT CLUSTER SHIPS, AND NOW THAT ADVANTAGE HAS BEEN OVERTURNED.
SHOULD WE DISPERSE TOO TO RESPOND TO THE ATTACK?
WAIT ...
I SEE!
THE GAUNA WANT TO FORCE US INTO LEM'S GRAVITY WELL.
SUPPORT FORCE
ATTACK FLEET ONE
LEM
FLEET, LINK INTO TWO FLOTILLAS! ONCE WE BREAK THROUGH, WE CAN REGROUP!
FOUR SHIPS INCLUDING THIS ONE WILL FORM THE VANGUARD AND WEDGE THROUGH EVEN IF WE HAVE TO RAM THEM!!
THE OTHER SEVEN VESSELS WILL FORM THE REARGUARD AND TRANSPORT THE GRAVITON RADIAL EMITTER!!
THE GARDE UNITS WILL LAND ON THE REARGUARD MIZUKIS AND PROTECT THE EMITTER!!
ALL COCKPIT SHELLS HAVE BEEN RECOVERED!!

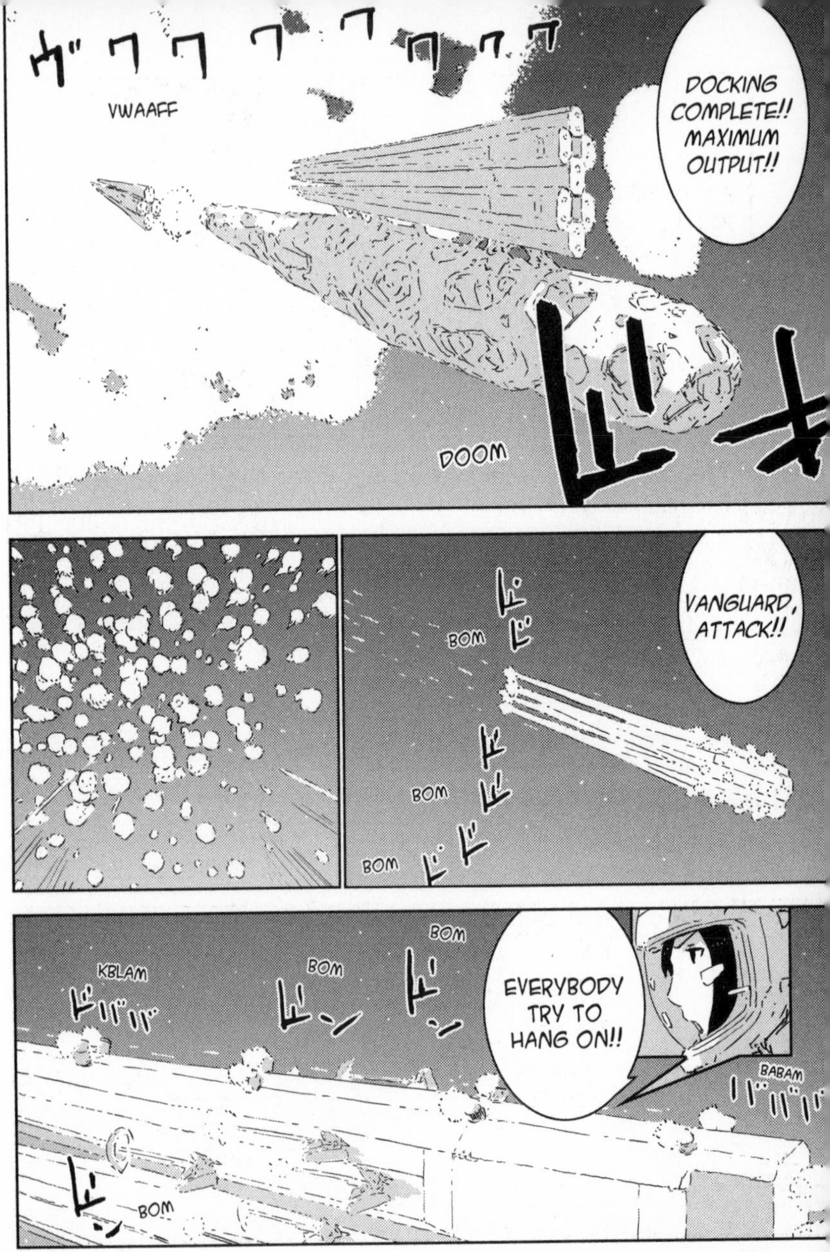
DOCKING COMPLETE!! MAXIMUM OUTPUT!!
VWAAFF
DOOM
VANGUARD, ATTACK!!
BOM
BOM
BOM
EVERYBODY TRY TO HANG ON!!
BABAM
BOM
BOM
KBLAM
BOM

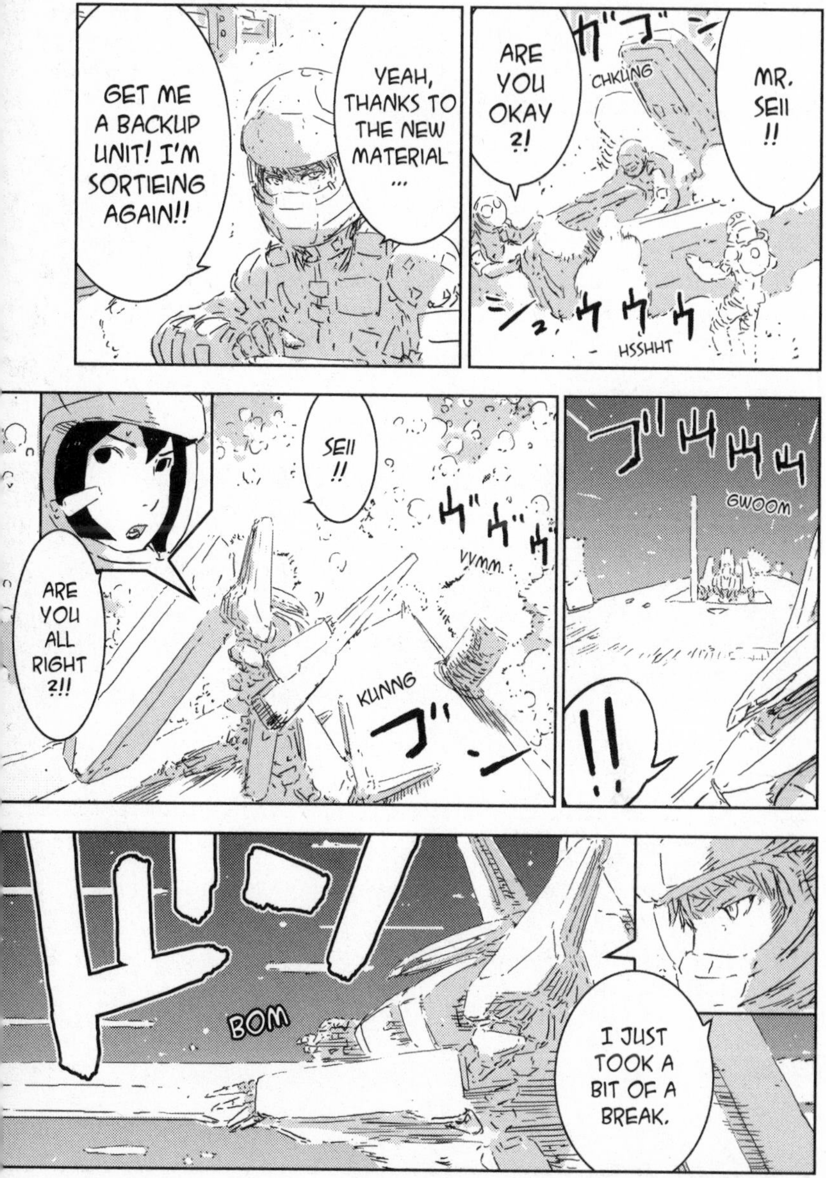
MR. SEII!!
ARE YOU OKAY?!
CHKUNG
HSSHHT
YEAH, THANKS TO THE NEW MATERIAL...
GET ME A BACKUP UNIT! I'M SORTIEING AGAIN!!
GWOOM
!!
SEII!!
VVMM.
KUNNG
ARE YOU ALL RIGHT?!!
BOM
I JUST TOOK A BIT OF A BREAK.

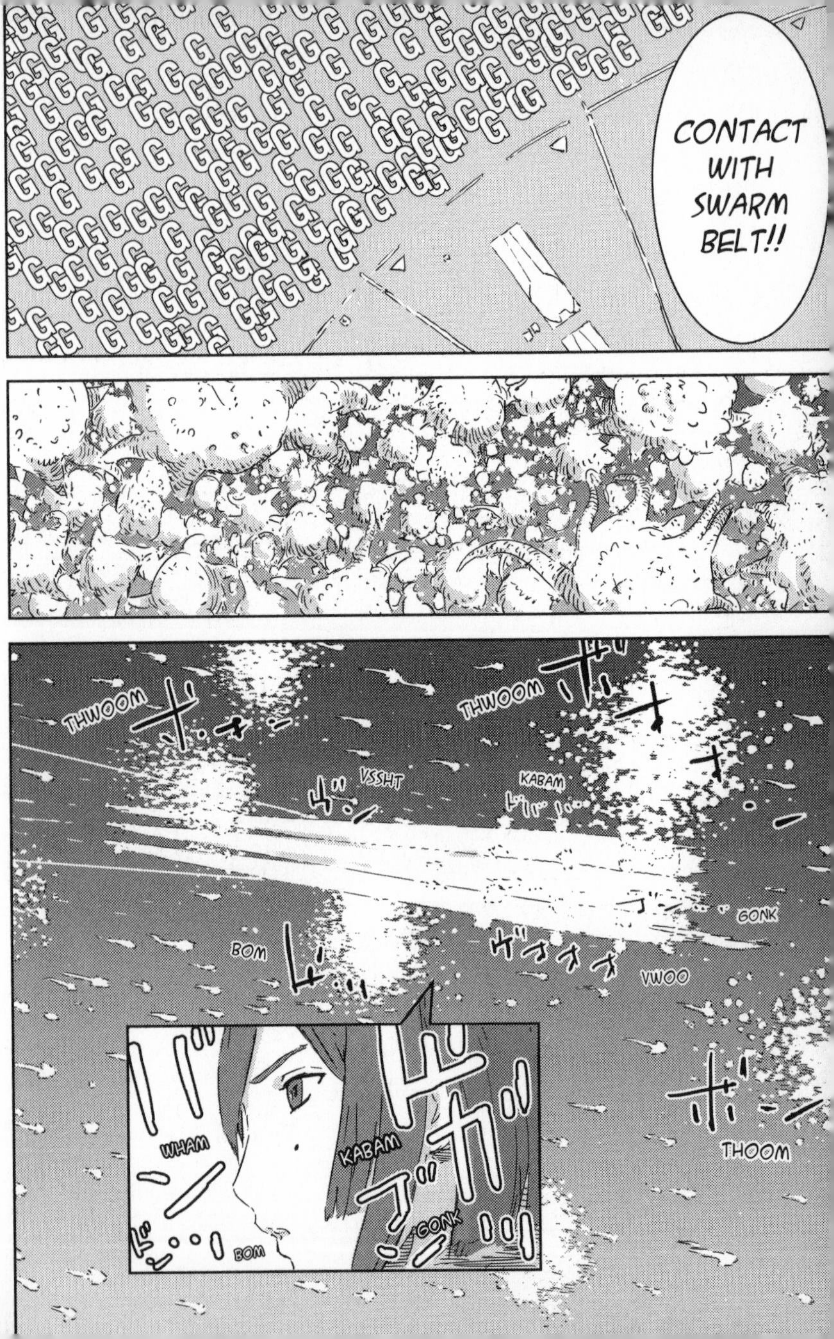
CONTACT WITH SWARM BELT!!
THWOOM
THWOOM
KABAM
VSSHT
GONK
VWOO
BOM
THOOM
KABAM
GONK
WHAM
BOM

DWOPP
BOM
VWMM
THWOOM
VVRRR
BOM
BOM
BOM
GONK
BOM
BLAAM
THOOM
DWOPP
PROTECT THE GRAVITON RADIAL EMITTER AT ALL COSTS!!
BOM
BOM
BOM
BOM
BOM
BOM
BOM
THWOOM
BOM
DWOPP

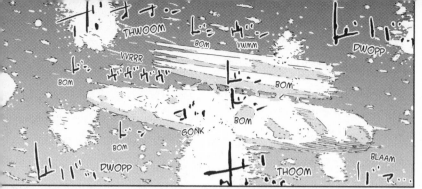

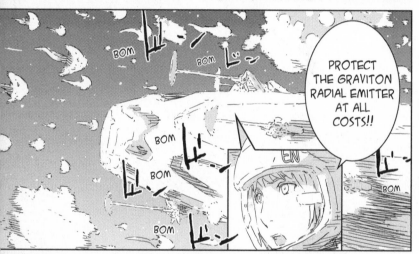

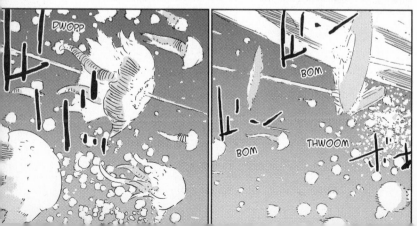

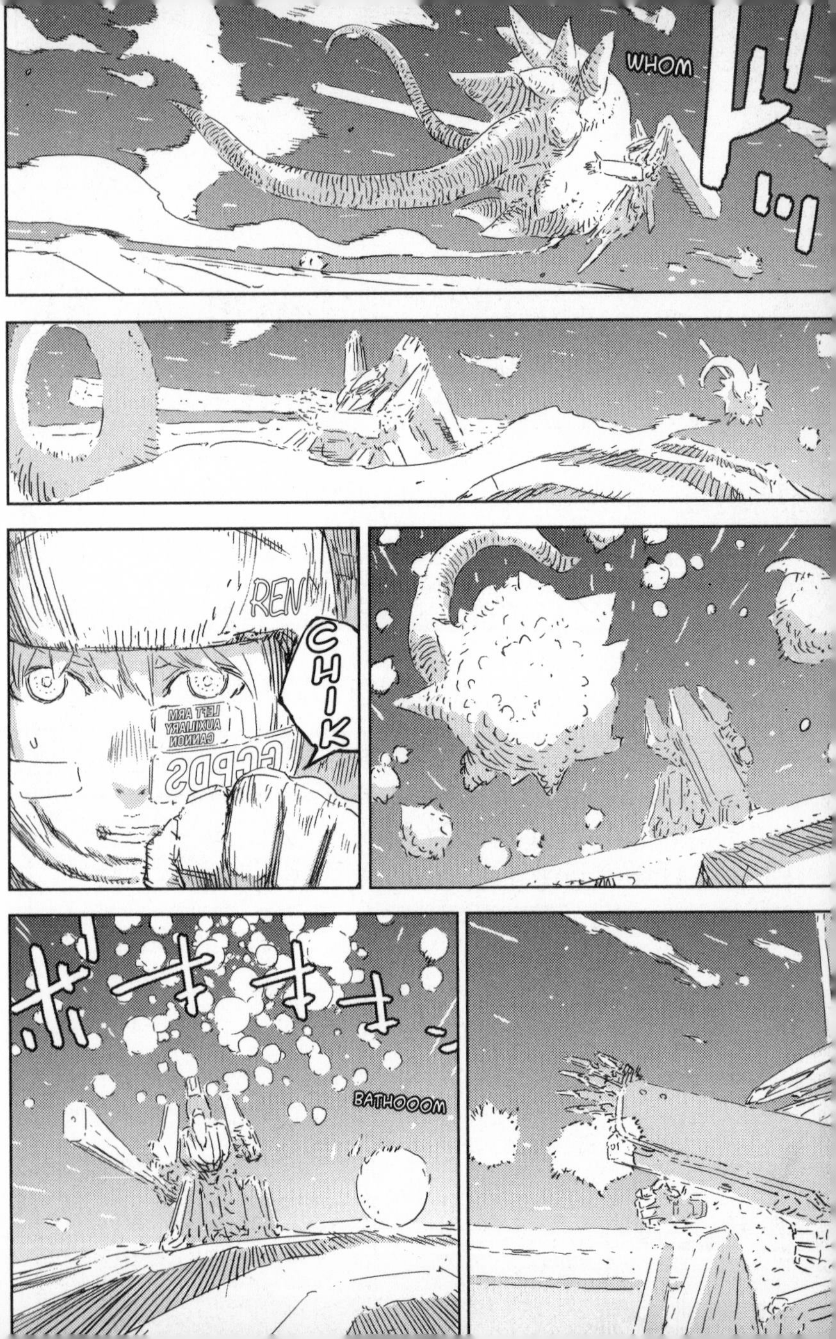
WHOM
REN
CHIK
LEFT ARM AUXILIARY CANNON
GCPDS
BATHOOOM

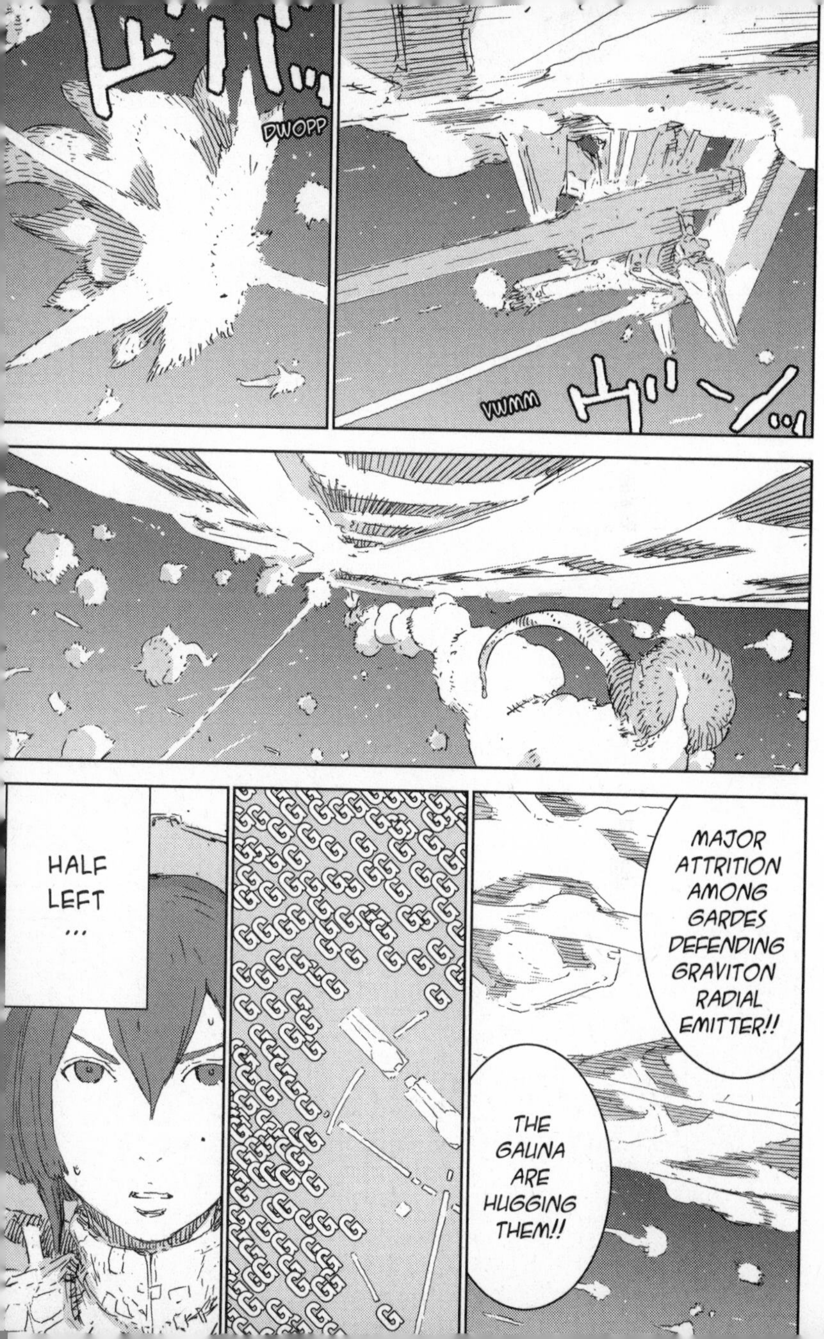
VWMM
DWOPP
MAJOR ATTRITION AMONG GARDES DEFENDING GRAVITON RADIAL EMITTER!!
THE GAUNA ARE HUGGING THEM!!
HALF LEFT ...

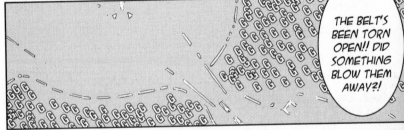

THE BELT'S BEEN TORN OPEN!! DID SOMETHING BLOW THEM AWAY?!

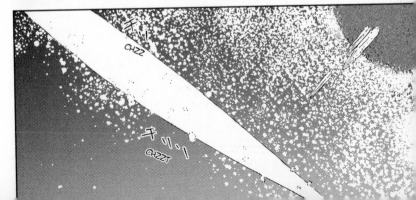

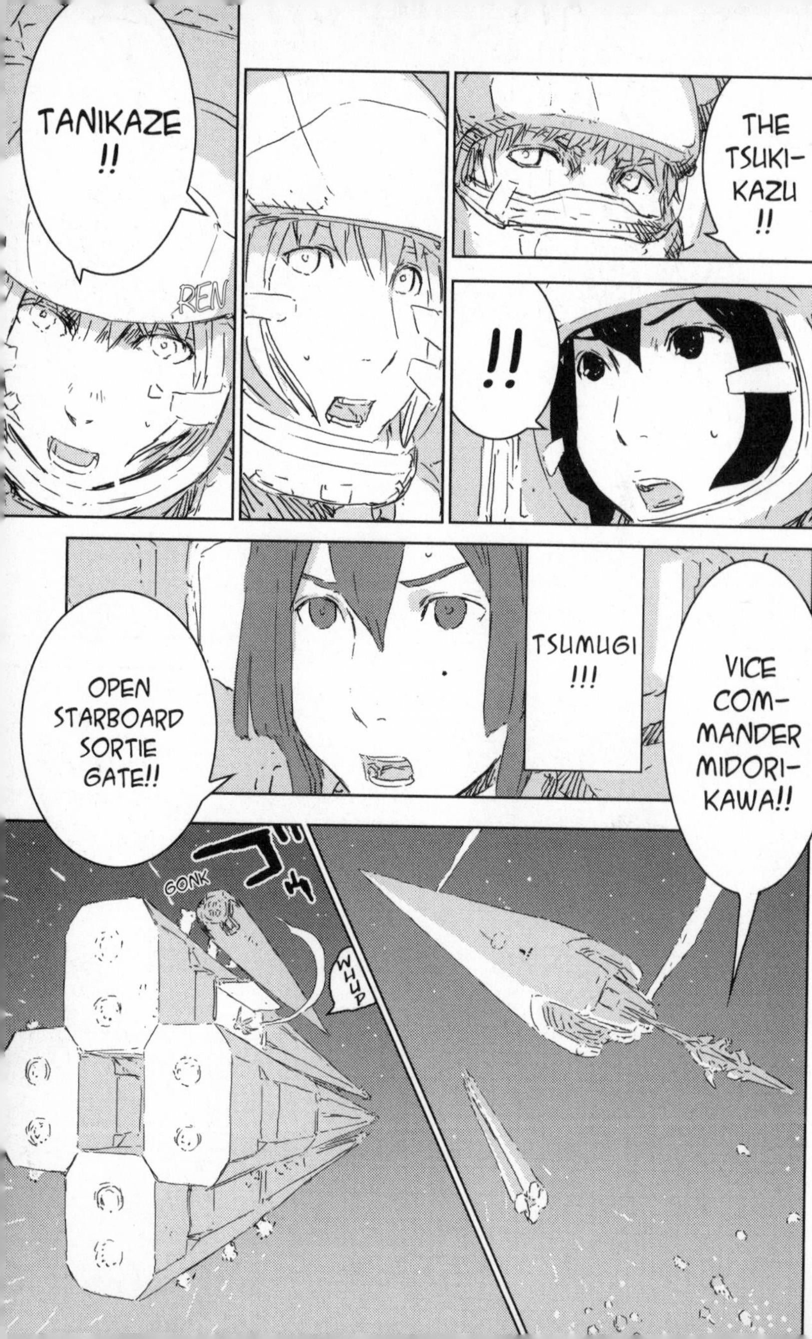
THE TSUKI-KAZU !!
!!
TANIKAZE !!
VICE COMMANDER MIDORI-KAWA!!
TSUMUGI !!!
OPEN STARBOARD SORTIE GATE!!
GONK
WHUP

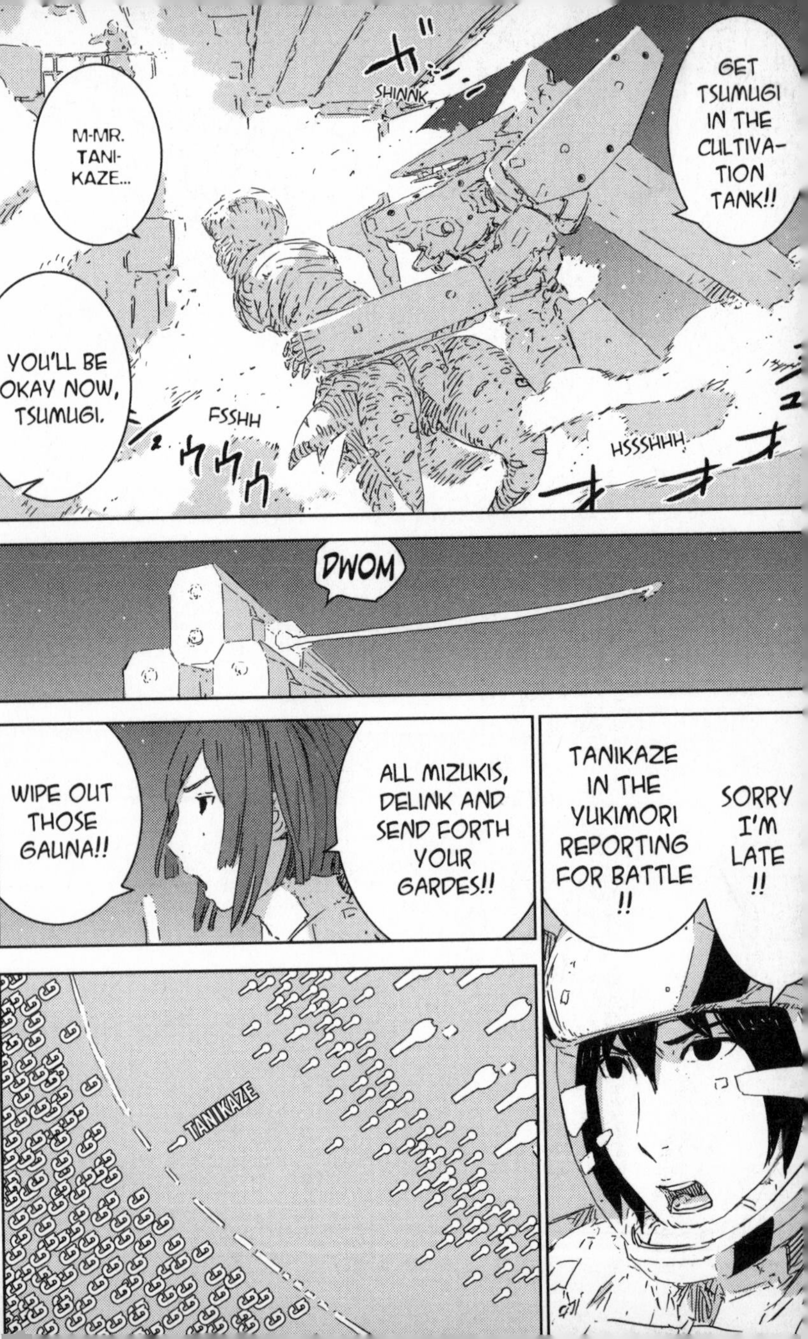
GET TSUMUGI IN THE CULTIVATION TANK!!
SHINNK
M-MR. TANIKAZE...
HSSSHHH
FSSHH
YOU'LL BE OKAY NOW, TSUMUGI.
DWOM
SORRY I'M LATE!!
TANIKAZE IN THE YUKIMORI REPORTING FOR BATTLE!!
ALL MIZUKIS, DELINK AND SEND FORTH YOUR GARDES!!
WIPE OUT THOSE GAUNA!!
TANIKAZE

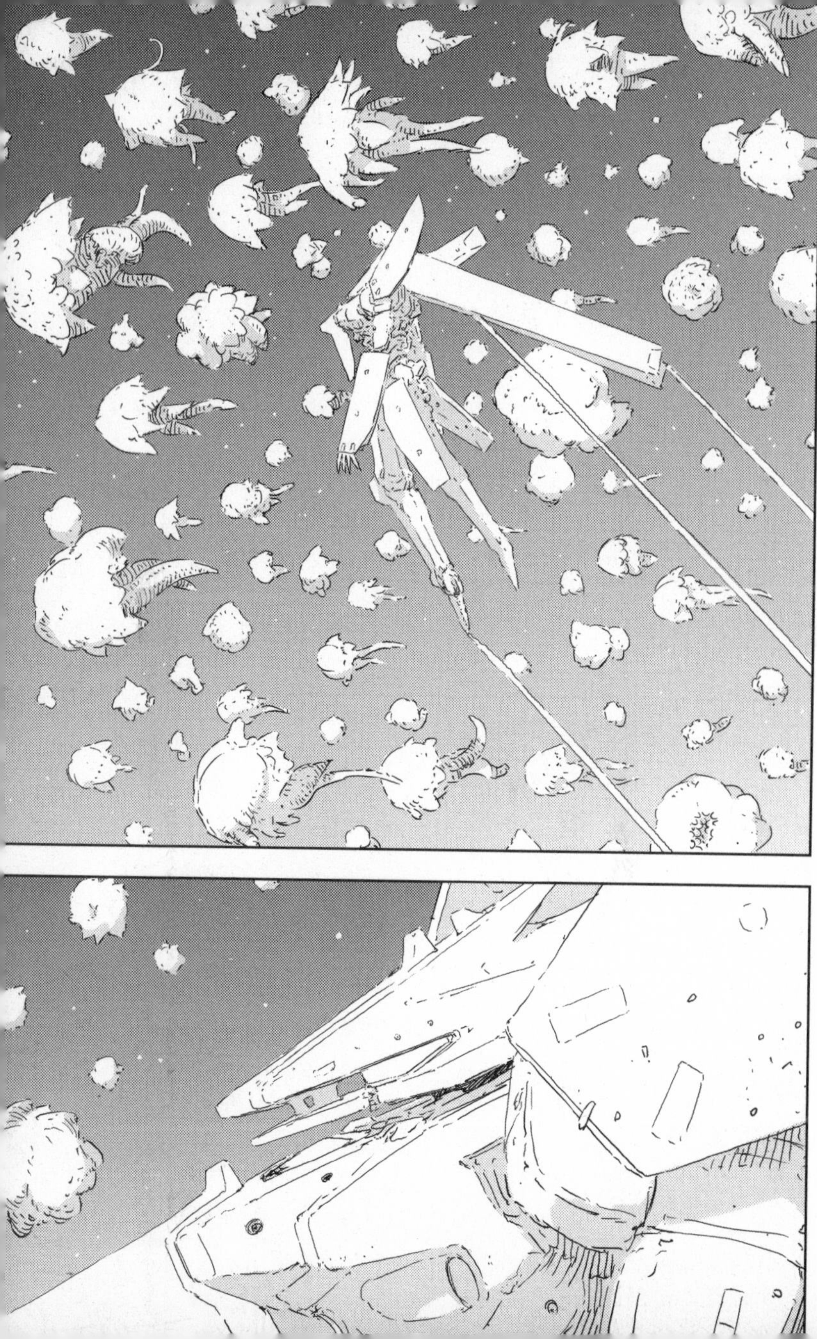

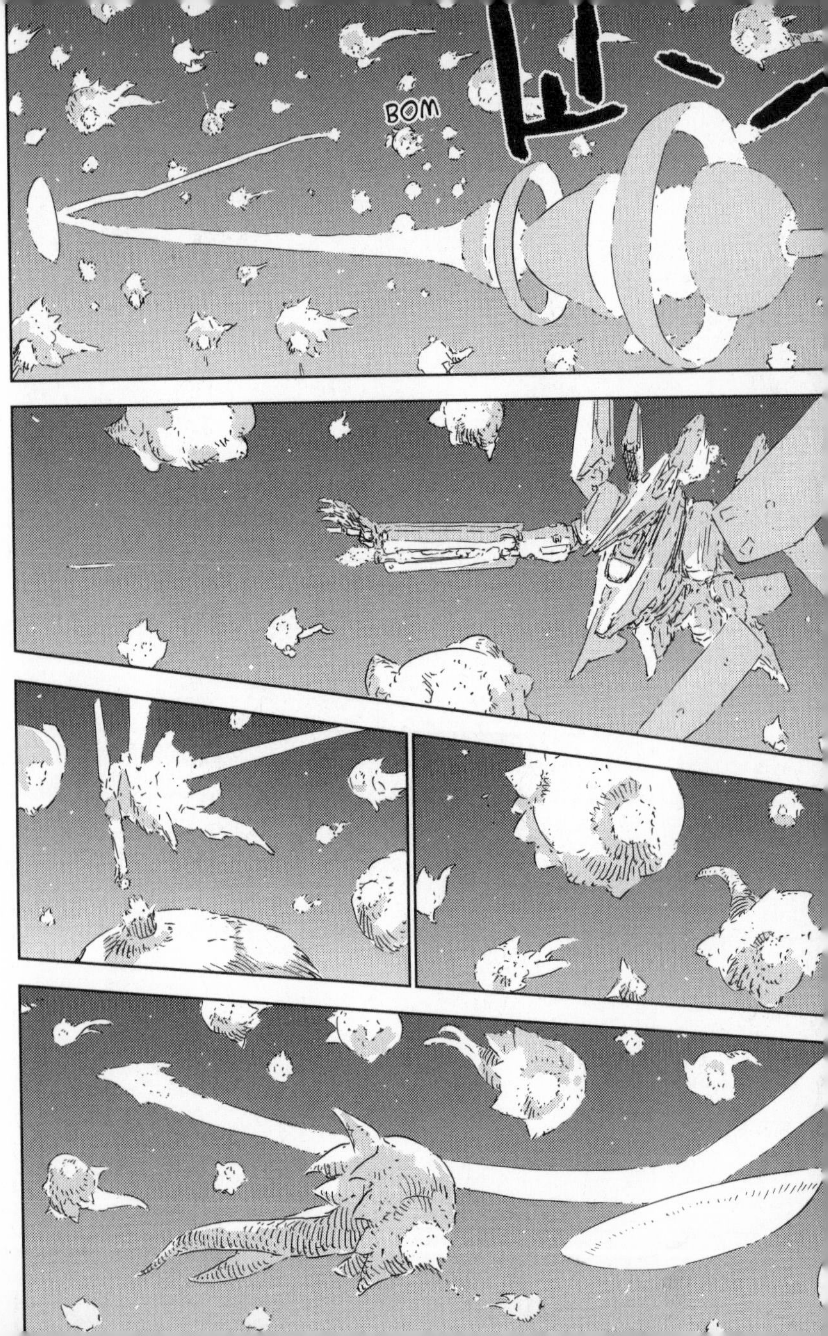
BOM

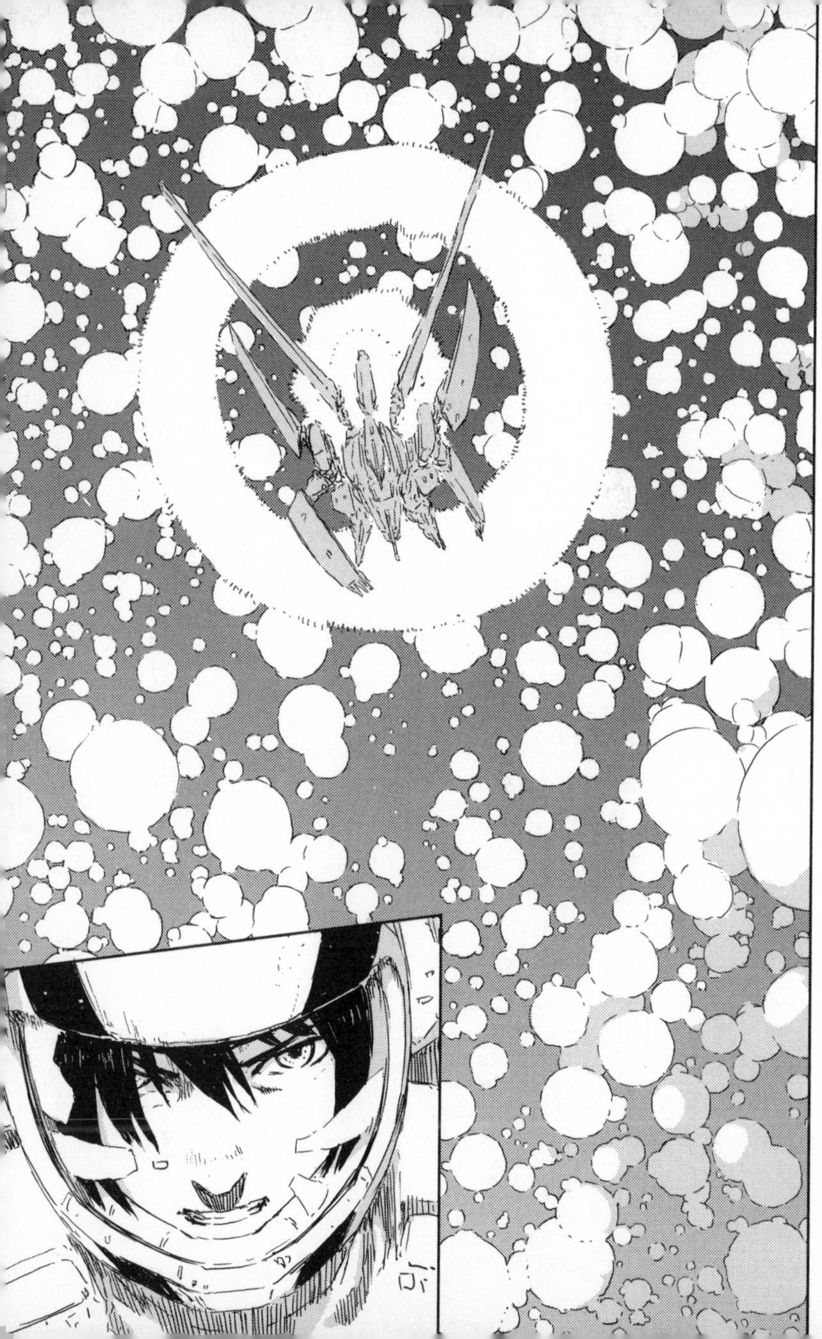

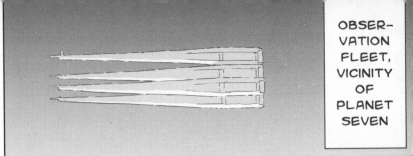

OBSER-
VATION
FLEET,
VICINITY
OF
PLANET
SEVEN

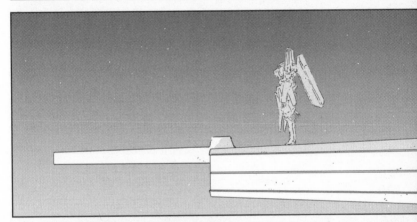

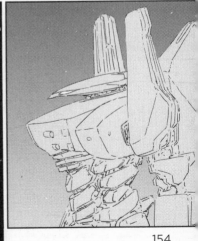

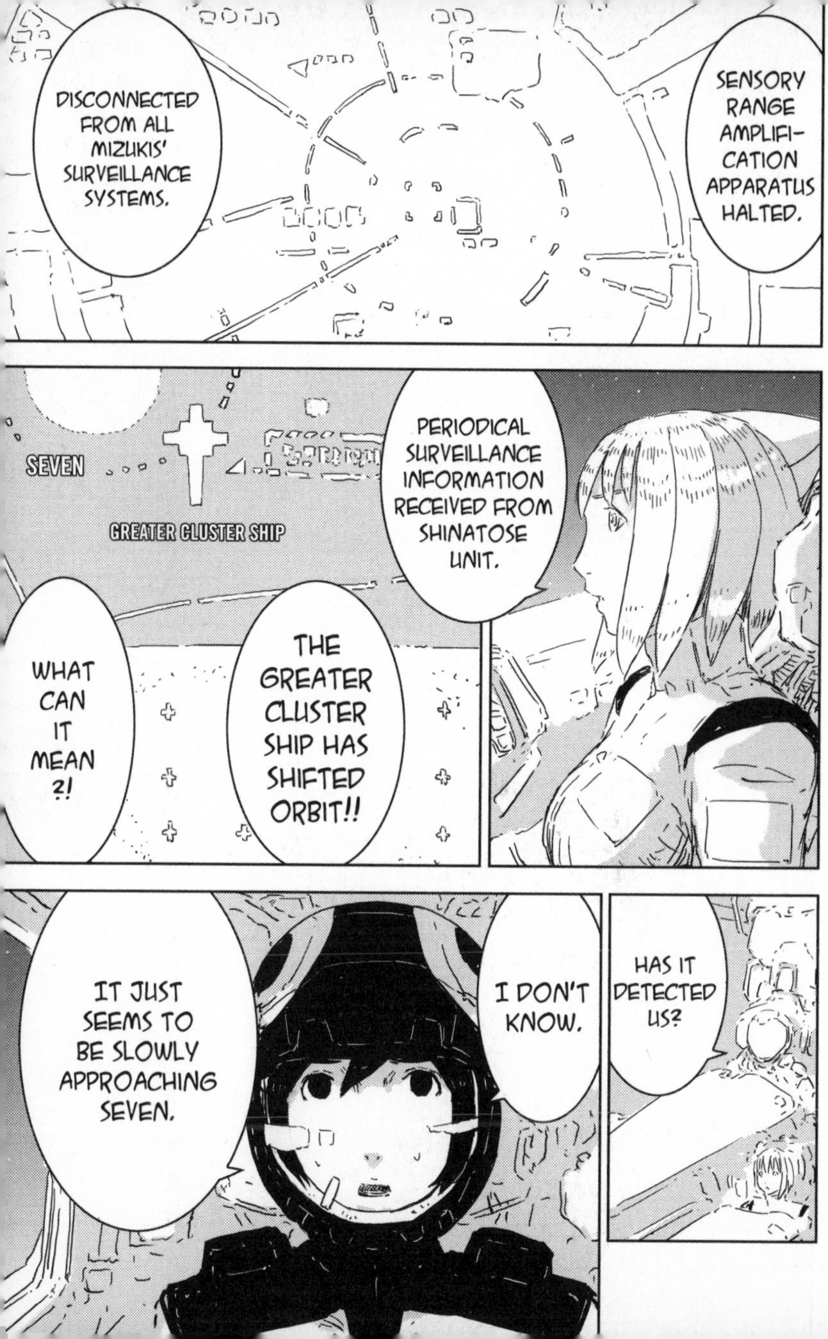
SENSORY RANGE AMPLIFICATION APPARATUS HALTED.
DISCONNECTED FROM ALL MIZUKIS' SURVEILLANCE SYSTEMS.
PERIODICAL SURVEILLANCE INFORMATION RECEIVED FROM SHINATOSE UNIT.
SEVEN
GREATER CLUSTER SHIP
THE GREATER CLUSTER SHIP HAS SHIFTED ORBIT!!
WHAT CAN IT MEAN?!
HAS IT DETECTED US?
I DON'T KNOW.
IT JUST SEEMS TO BE SLOWLY APPROACHING SEVEN.

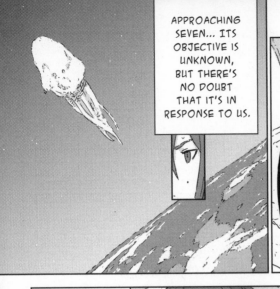

TRANS-MISSION FROM OBSER-VATION FLEET!
GREATER CLUSTER SHIP ON THE MOVE!!
APPROACHING SEVEN... ITS OBJECTIVE IS UNKNOWN, BUT THERE'S NO DOUBT THAT IT'S IN RESPONSE TO US.
WE NEED TO DESTROY IT ASAP!!
WE'LL SECURE A CONVERSION ORGAN AND USE THE GRAVITON RADIAL EMITTER!!
OBSERVATION FLEET, BEGIN SCANNING FOR THE GREATER CLUSTER SHIP'S MAIN CORE!!
CONFIRMING EXACT LOCATION OF CONVERSION ORGAN NO. 3!
!!
HIGH HIGGS PARTICLE ACTIVITY FROM TUBE NO. 3!!
LEM
C.O. TUBE NO. 3
HIGH HIGGS REACTION

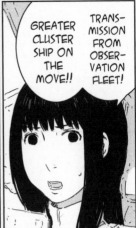

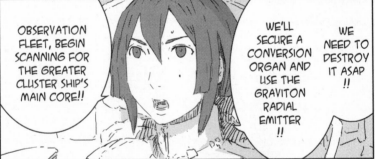

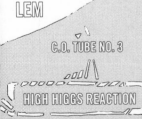

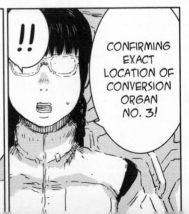

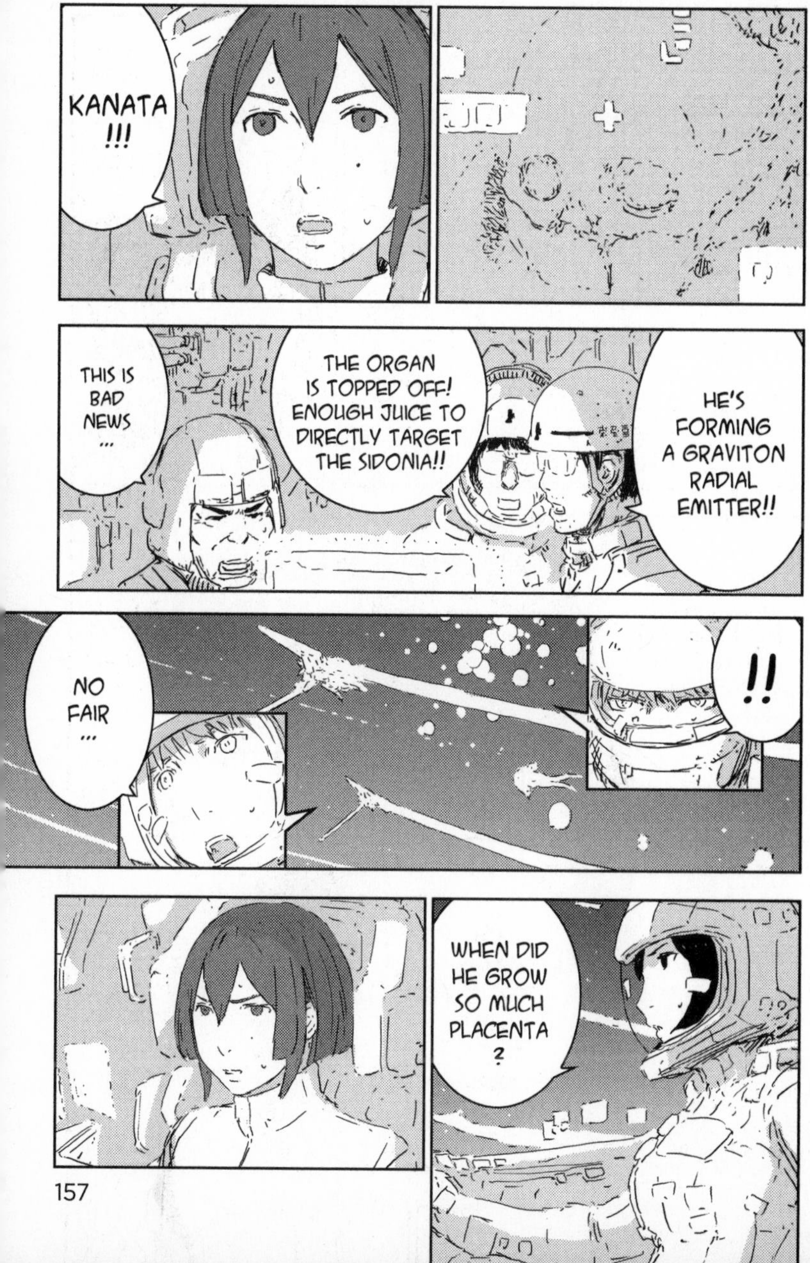
KANATA !!!
HE'S FORMING A GRAVITON RADIAL EMITTER!!
THE ORGAN IS TOPPED OFF! ENOUGH JUICE TO DIRECTLY TARGET THE SIDONIA!!
THIS IS BAD NEWS ...
!!
NO FAIR ...
WHEN DID HE GROW SO MUCH PLACENTA ?

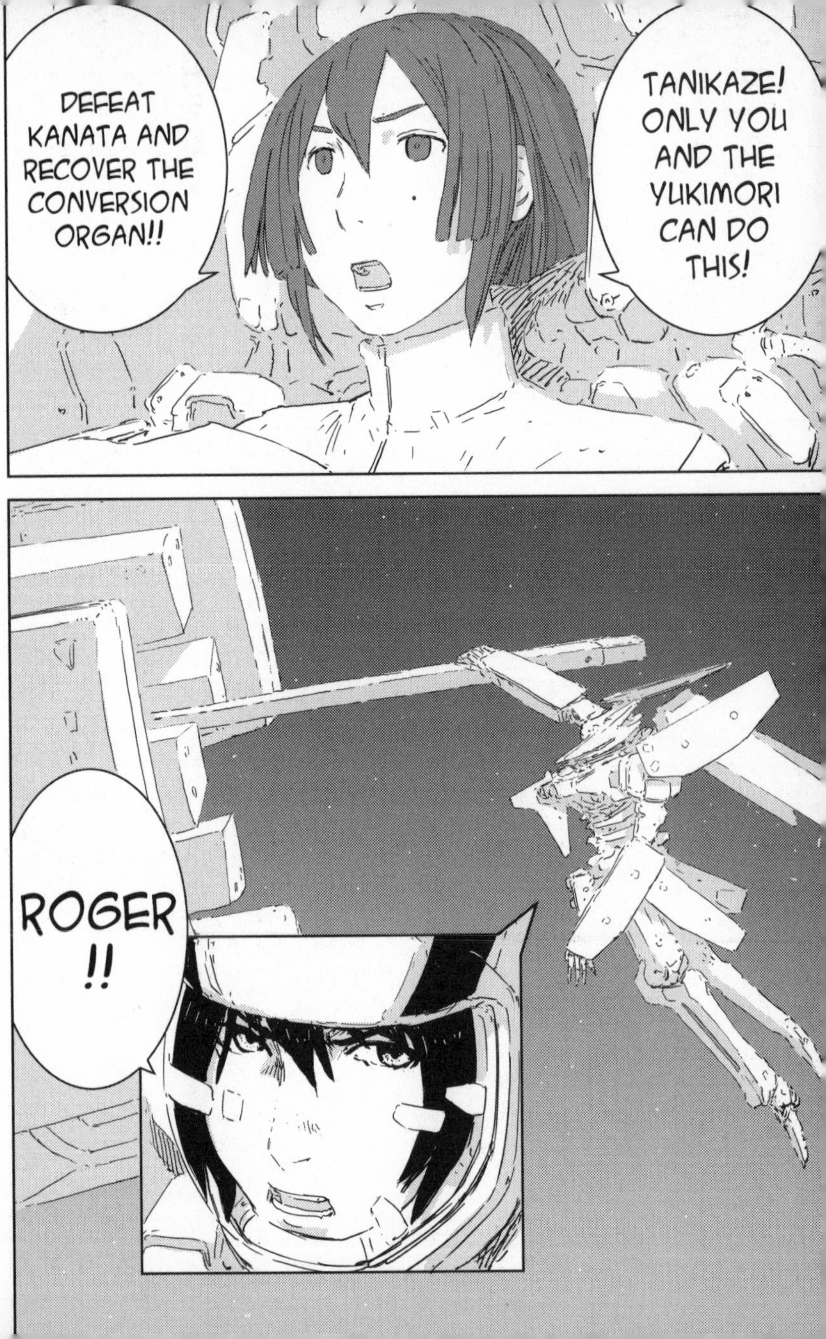
TANIKAZE! ONLY YOU AND THE YUKIMORI CAN DO THIS!
DEFEAT KANATA AND RECOVER THE CONVERSION ORGAN!!
ROGER!!

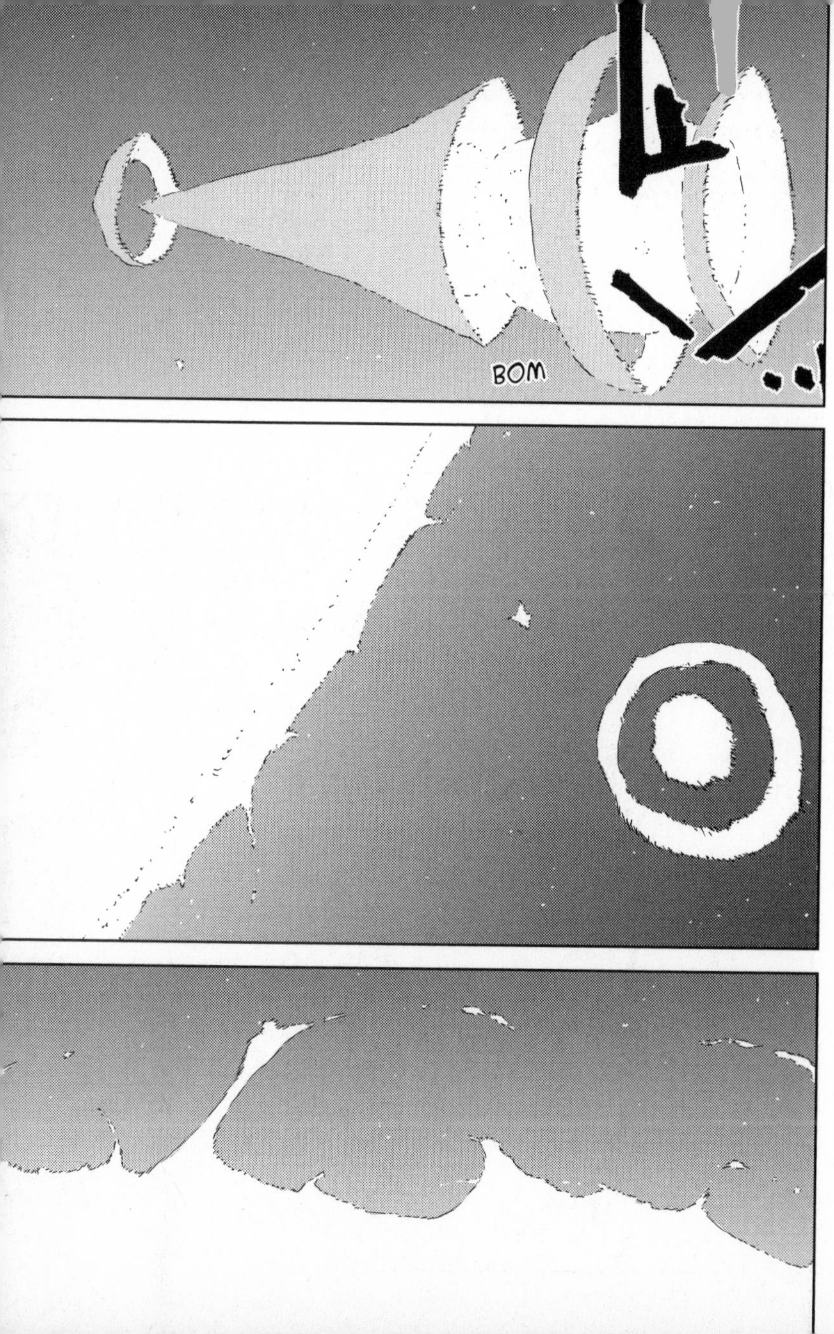
BOM

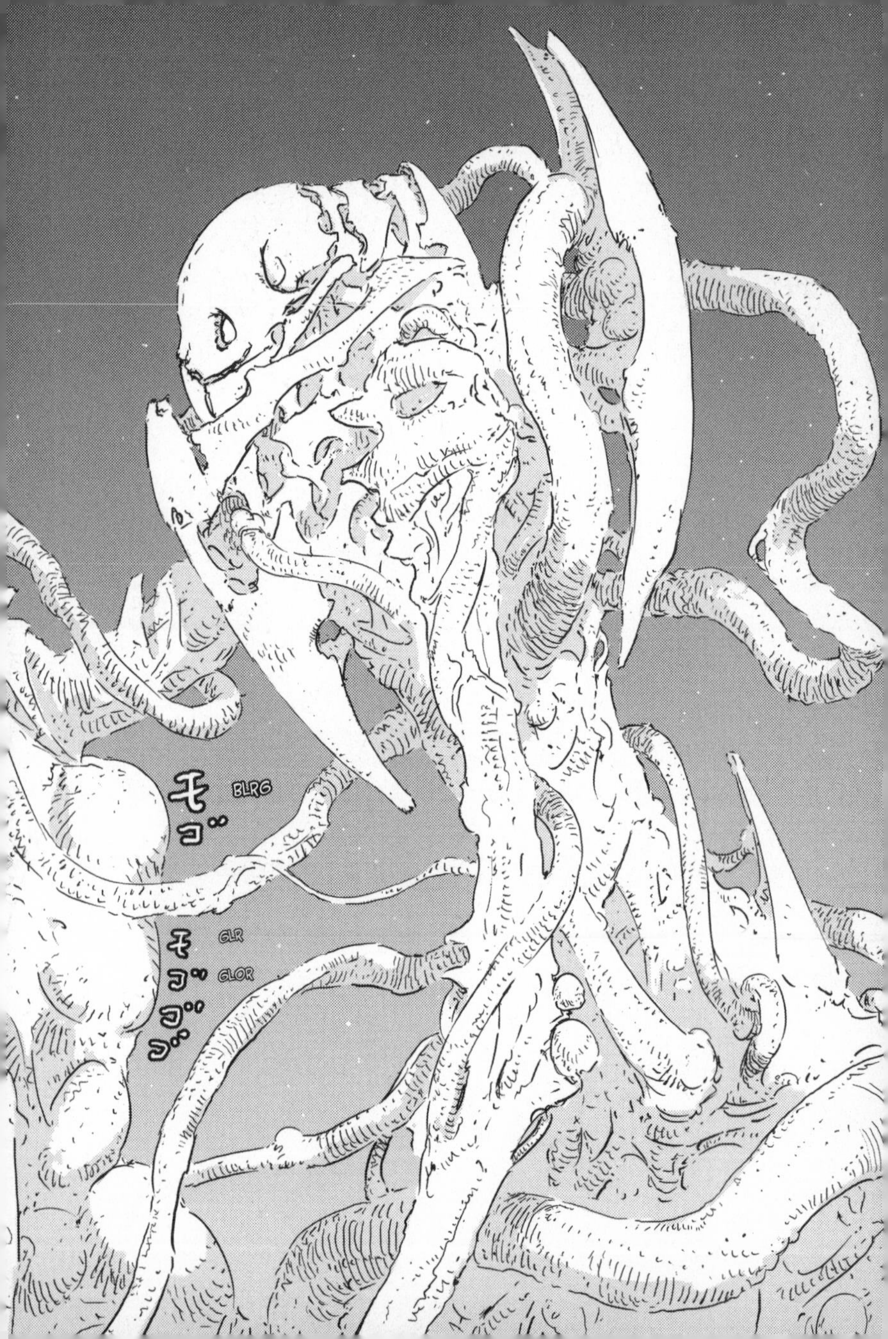
モゴ
BLRG
モゴゴゴ
GLR
GLOR

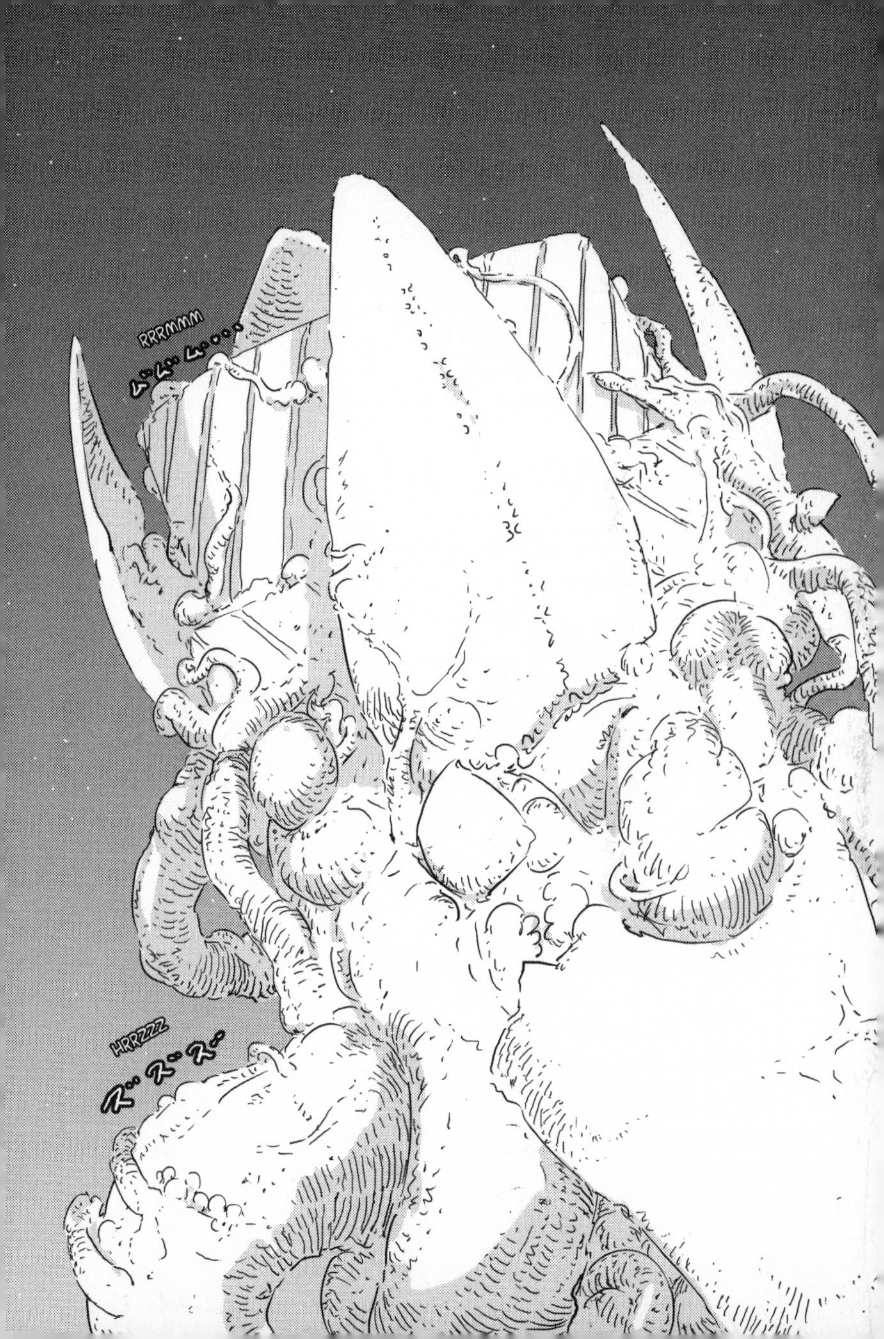
RRRMMM
ムームー・・・
HRRZZZ
ズーズー

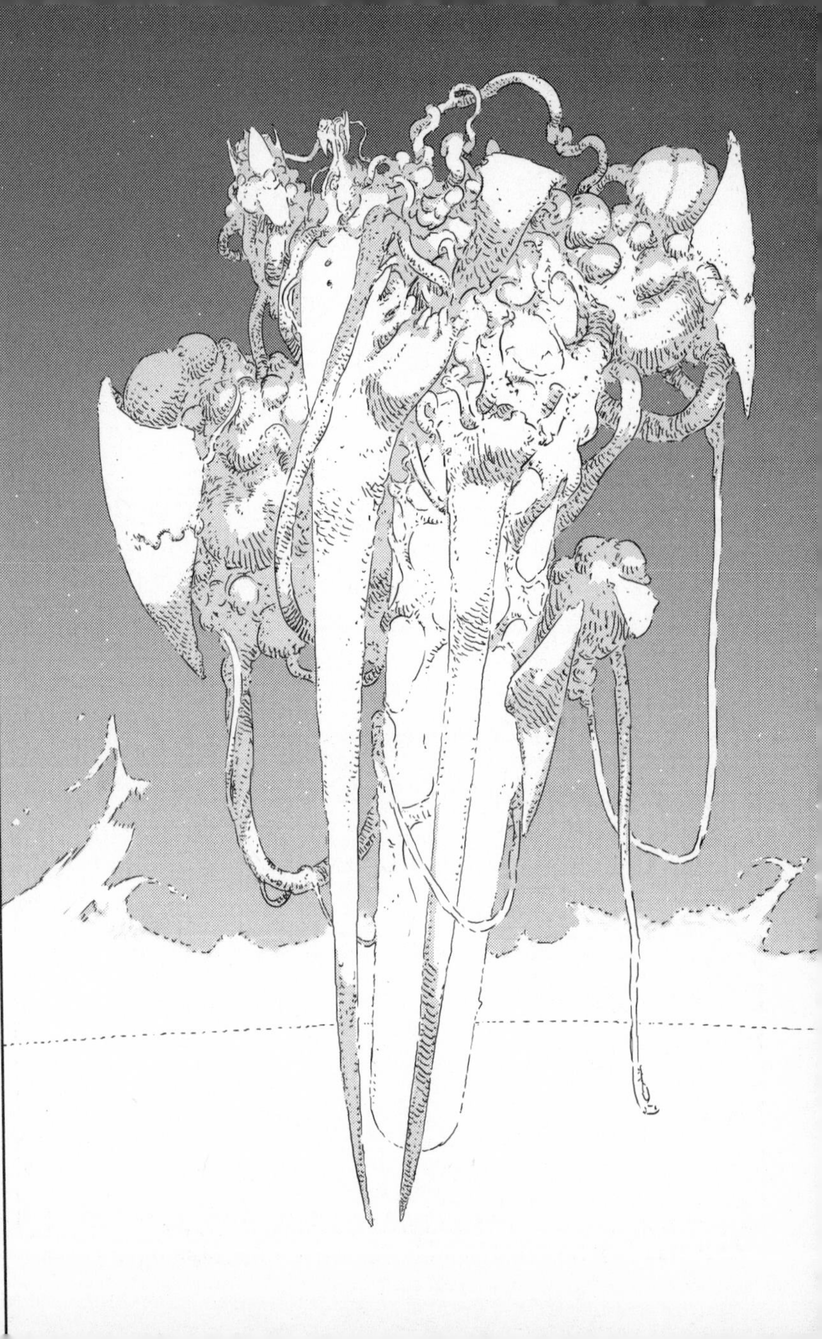

Chapter 76: END

Chapter 77: Sidonia's Knight

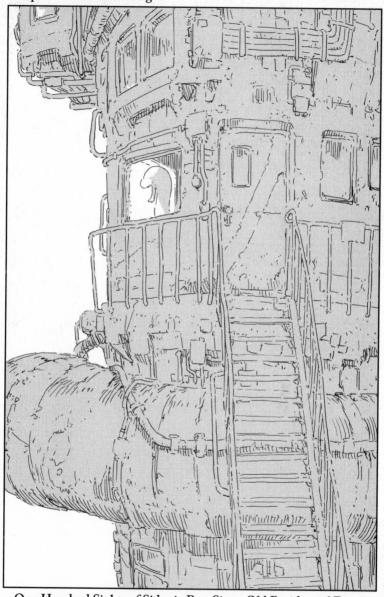

One Hundred Sights of Sidonia Part Sixty: Old Residential District

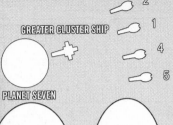

NEAR SEVEN
2
1
4
5
GREATER CLUSTER SHIP
PLANET SEVEN
ALL SHIPS ARE IN POSITION!
GOOD! SHINATOSE, YOU CAN START!
GOT IT!
COMMENCING SCANNING OF GREATER CLUSTER SHIP'S MAIN CORE POSITION!!
GWRR
GWRRR

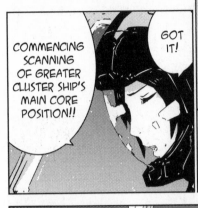

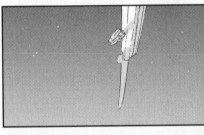

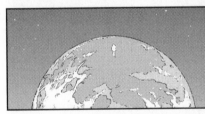

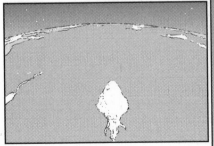

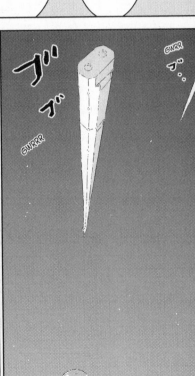

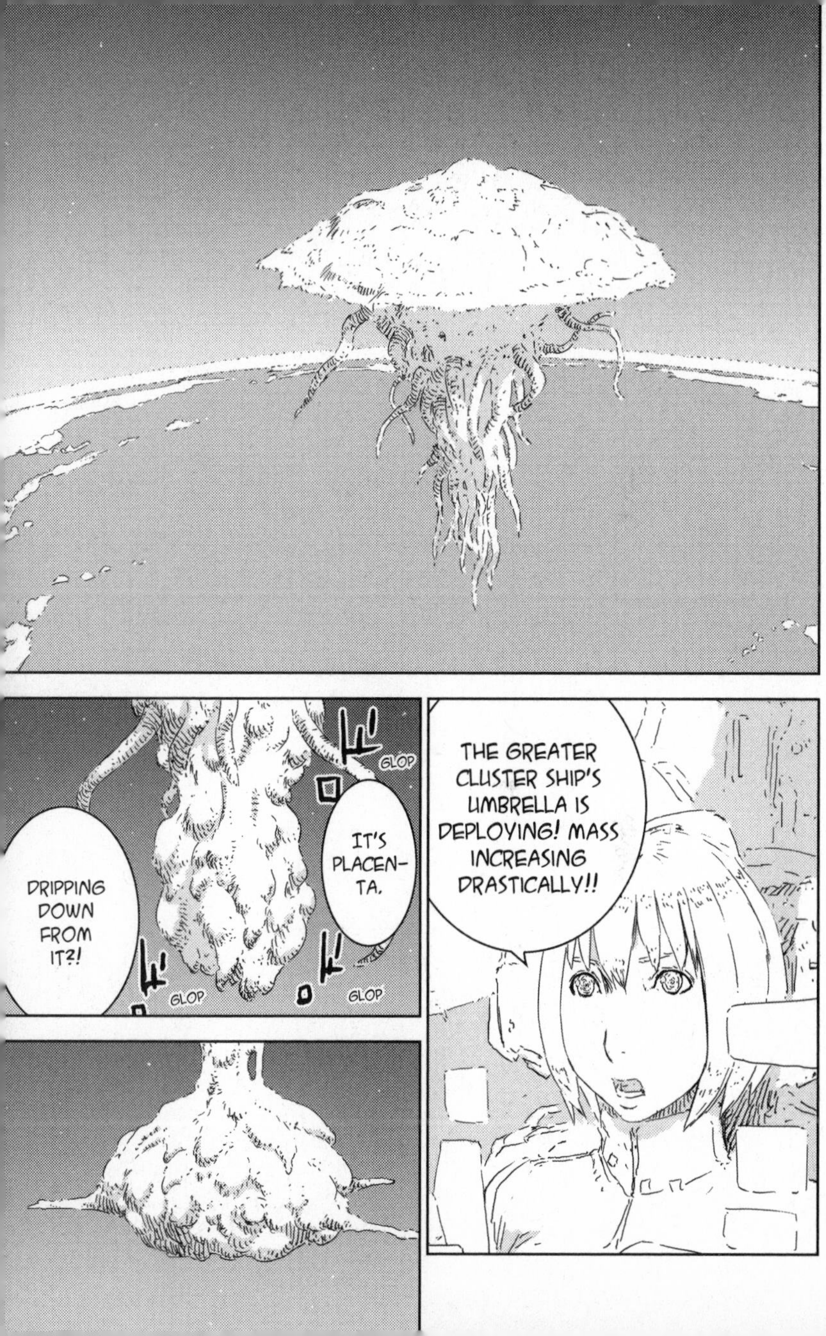
THE GREATER CLUSTER SHIP'S UMBRELLA IS DEPLOYING! MASS INCREASING DRASTICALLY!!
GLOP
IT'S PLACENTA.
DRIPPING DOWN FROM IT?!
GLOP
GLOP

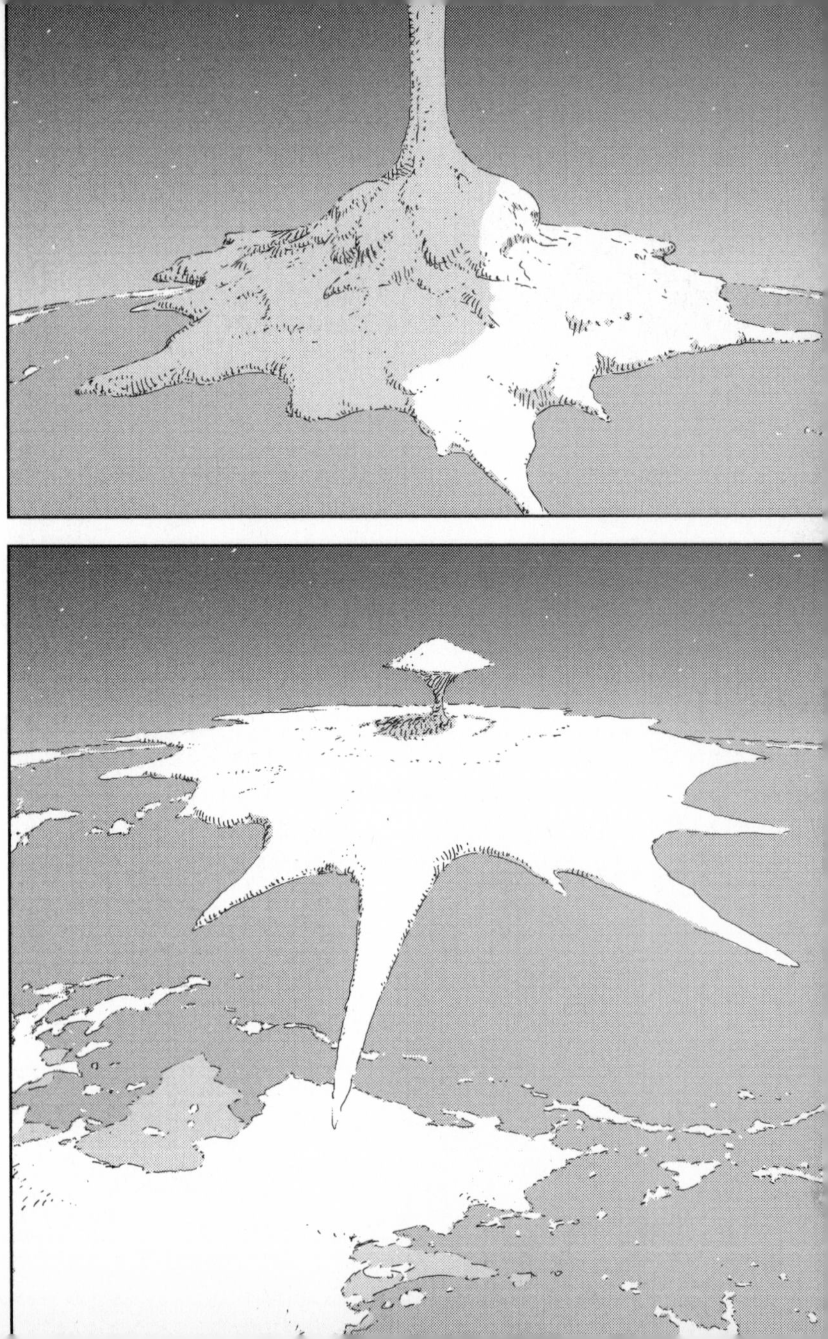

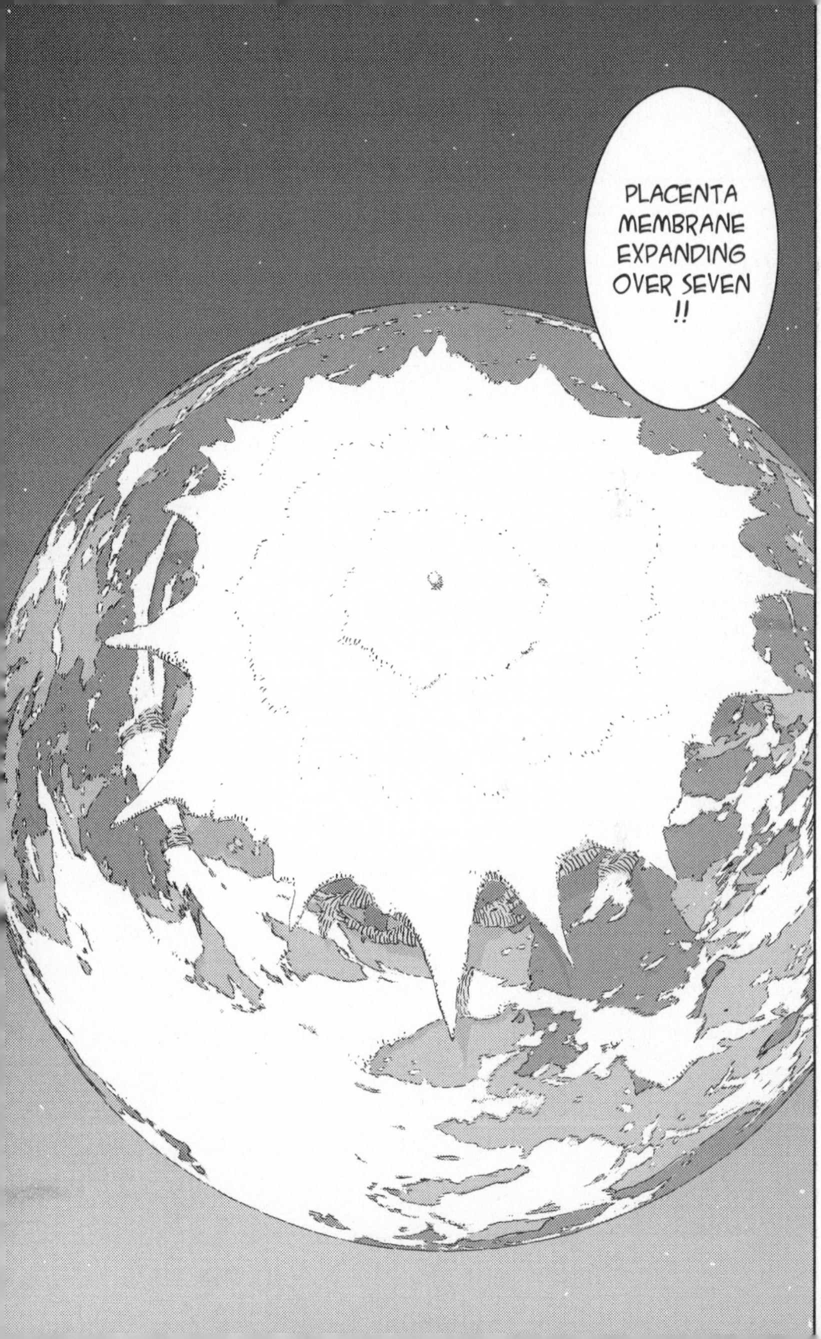
PLACENTA MEMBRANE EXPANDING OVER SEVEN !!

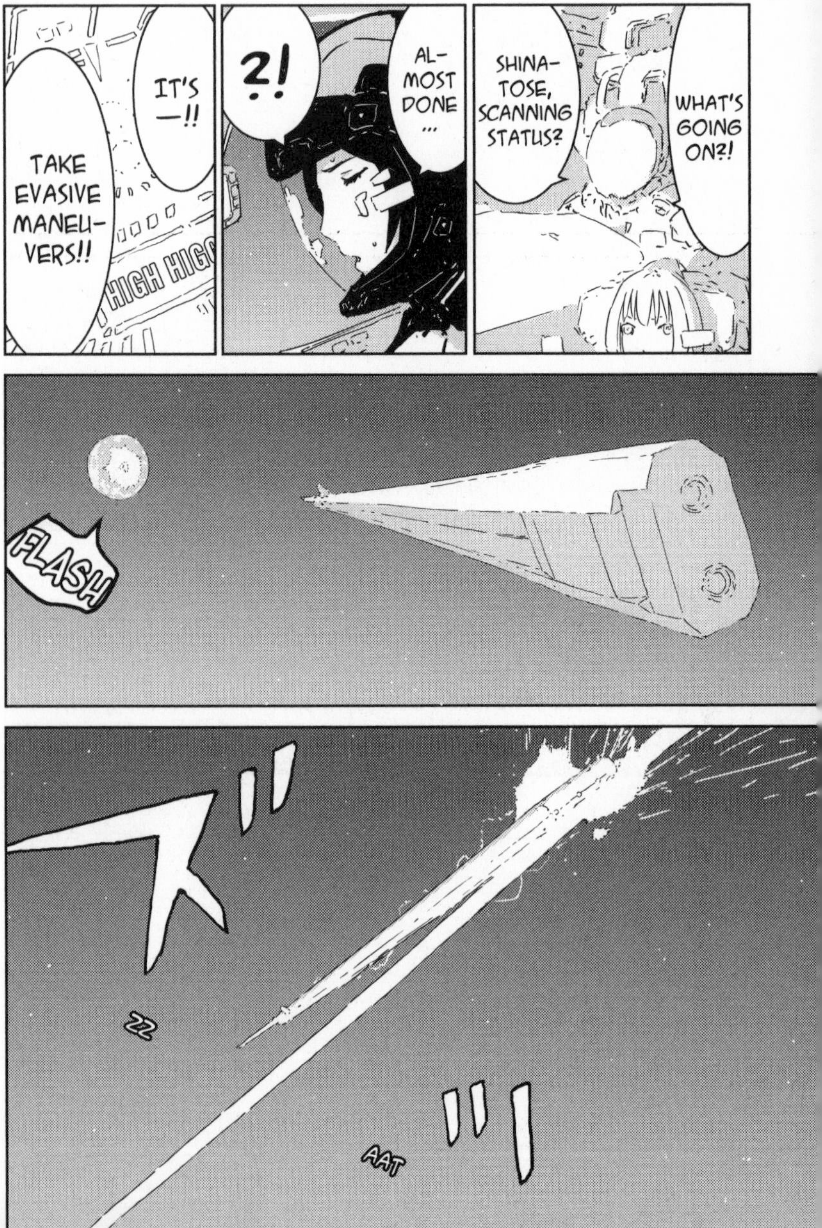
WHAT'S GOING ON?!
SHINA-TOSE, SCANNING STATUS?
AL-MOST DONE ...
?!
IT'S —!!
TAKE EVASIVE MANEU-VERS!!
FLASH
ZZ
AAT

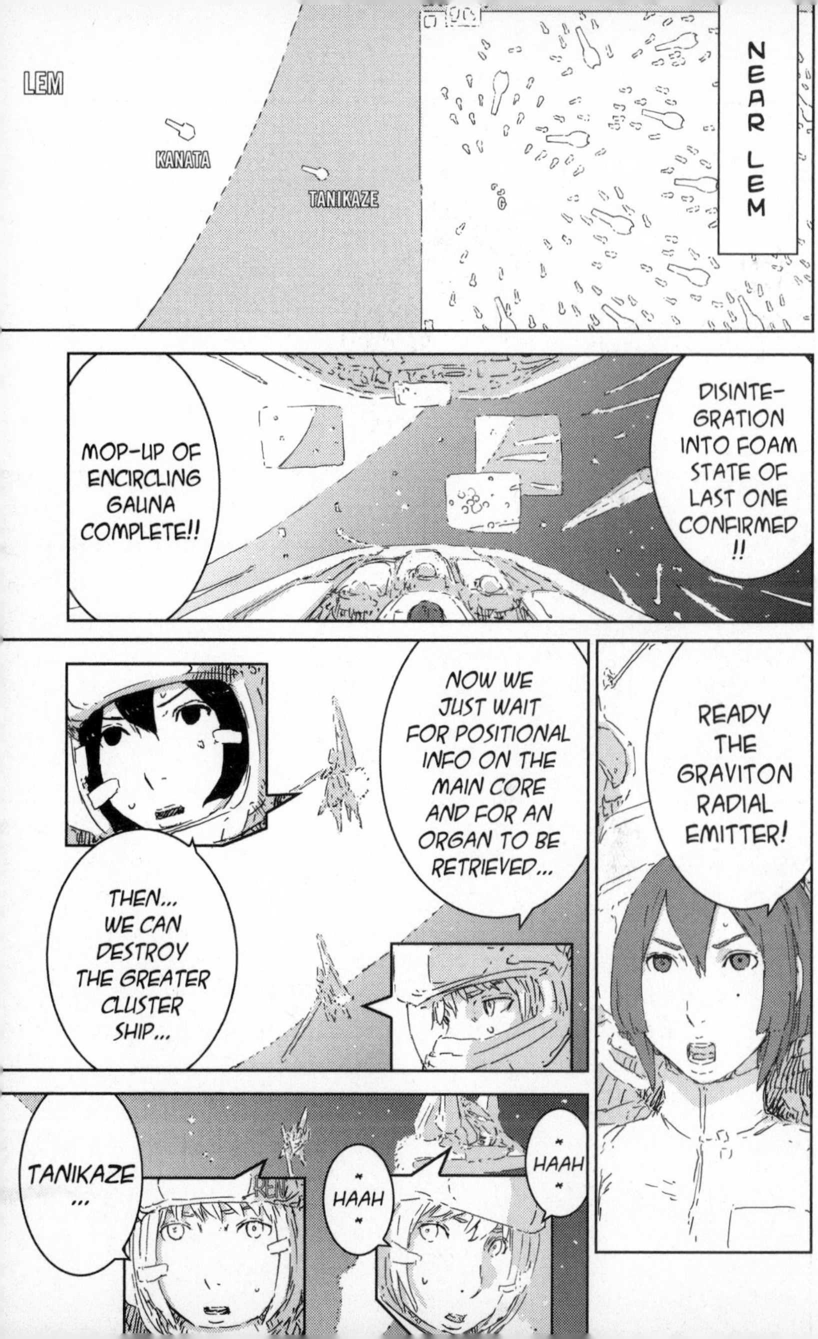

NEAR LEM
LEM
KANATA
TANIKAZE
DISINTE-GRATION INTO FOAM STATE OF LAST ONE CONFIRMED!!
MOP-UP OF ENCIRCLING GAUNA COMPLETE!!
READY THE GRAVITON RADIAL EMITTER!
NOW WE JUST WAIT FOR POSITIONAL INFO ON THE MAIN CORE AND FOR AN ORGAN TO BE RETRIEVED...
THEN... WE CAN DESTROY THE GREATER CLUSTER SHIP...
HAAH
HAAH
TANIKAZE...

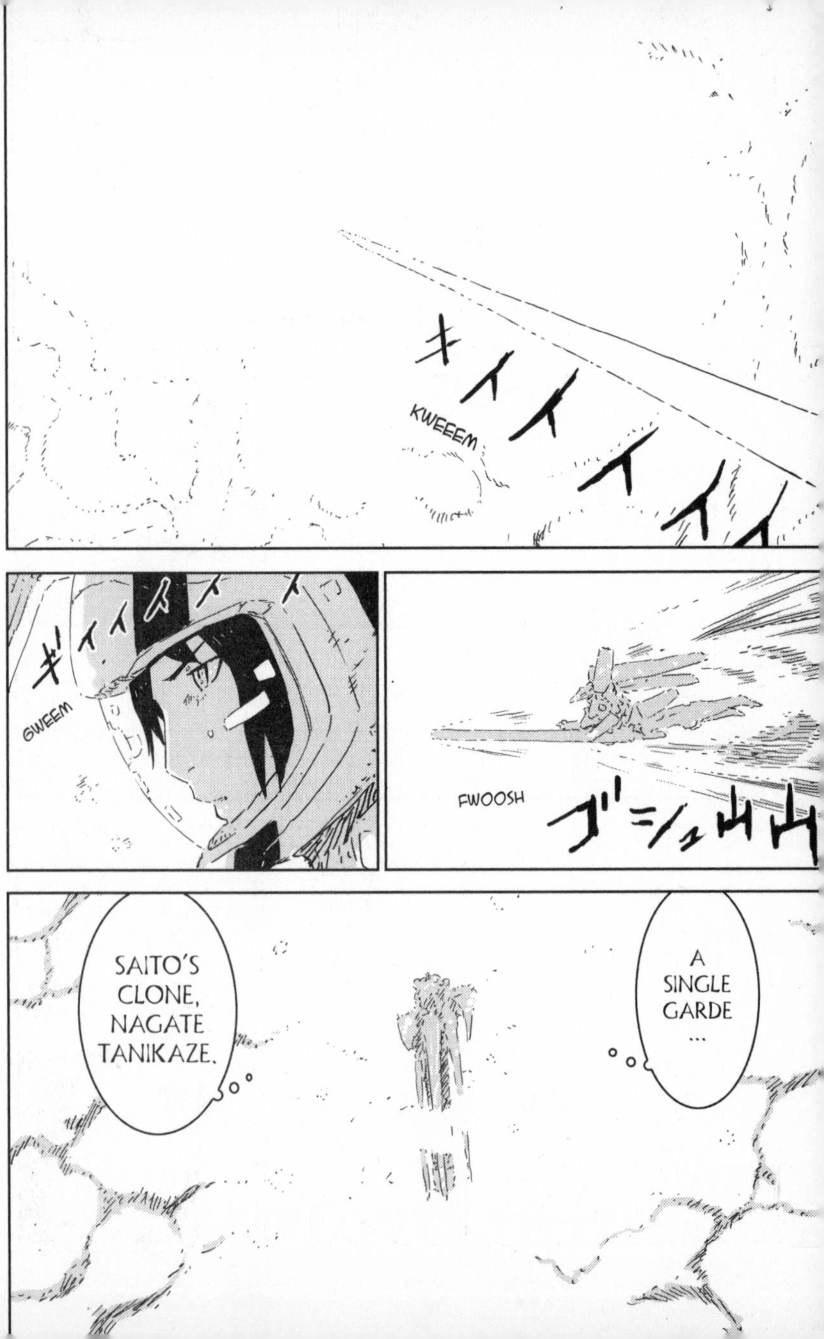

KWEEEM
FWOOSH
GWEEM
A SINGLE GARDE ...
SAITO'S CLONE, NAGATE TANIKAZE.

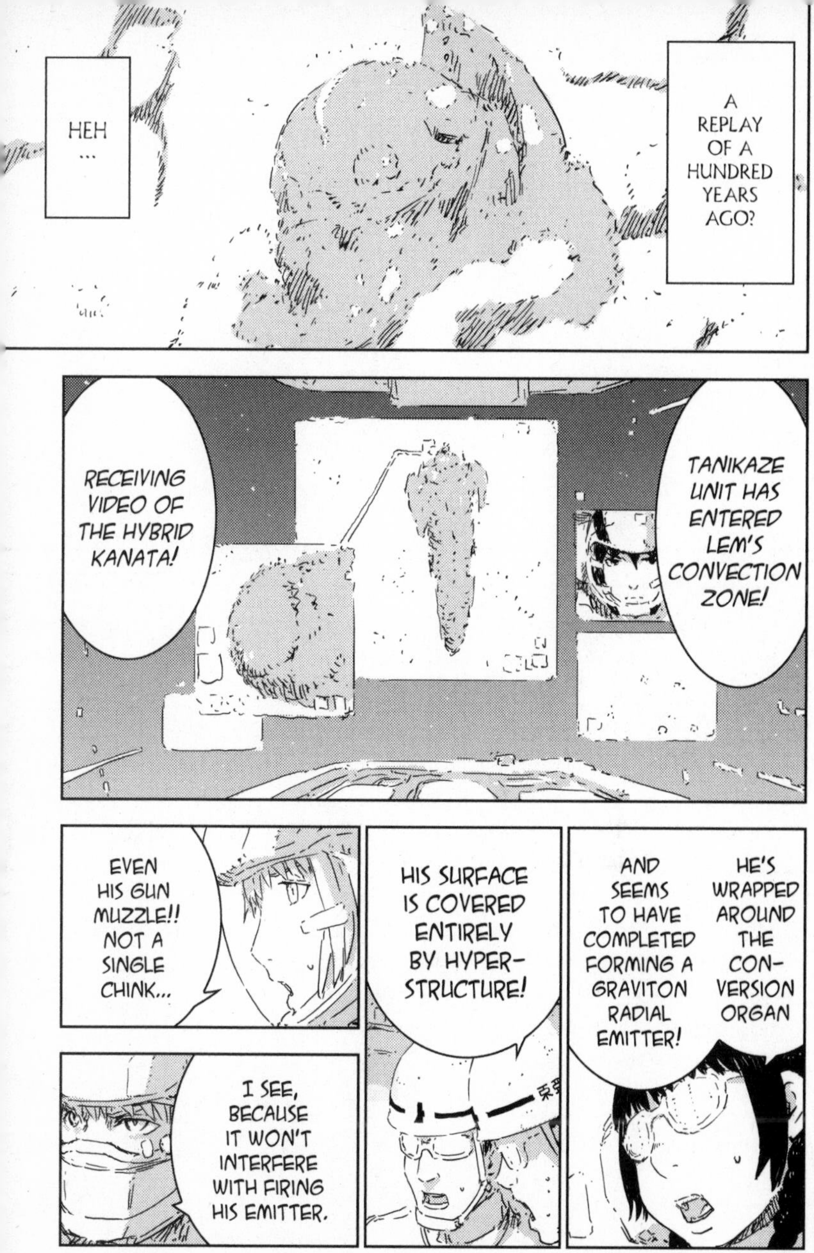
A REPLAY OF A HUNDRED YEARS AGO?
HEH ...
TANIKAZE UNIT HAS ENTERED LEM'S CONVECTION ZONE!
RECEIVING VIDEO OF THE HYBRID KANATA!
HE'S WRAPPED AROUND THE CON-VERSION ORGAN
AND SEEMS TO HAVE COMPLETED FORMING A GRAVITON RADIAL EMITTER!
HIS SURFACE IS COVERED ENTIRELY BY HYPER-STRUCTURE!
EVEN HIS GUN MUZZLE!! NOT A SINGLE CHINK...
I SEE, BECAUSE IT WON'T INTERFERE WITH FIRING HIS EMITTER.

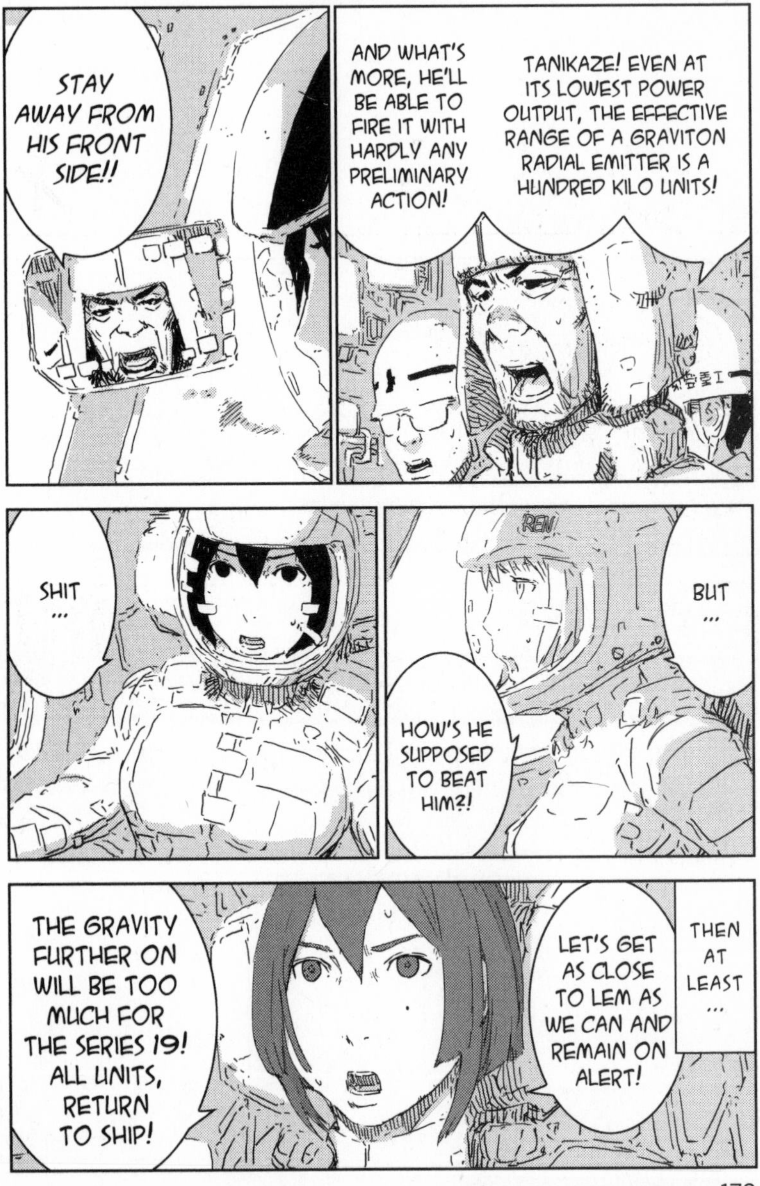
TANIKAZE! EVEN AT ITS LOWEST POWER OUTPUT, THE EFFECTIVE RANGE OF A GRAVITON RADIAL EMITTER IS A HUNDRED KILO UNITS!
AND WHAT'S MORE, HE'LL BE ABLE TO FIRE IT WITH HARDLY ANY PRELIMINARY ACTION!
STAY AWAY FROM HIS FRONT SIDE!!
REN
BUT ...
HOW'S HE SUPPOSED TO BEAT HIM?!
SHIT ...
THEN AT LEAST ...
LET'S GET AS CLOSE TO LEM AS WE CAN AND REMAIN ON ALERT!
THE GRAVITY FURTHER ON WILL BE TOO MUCH FOR THE SERIES 19! ALL UNITS, RETURN TO SHIP!

GWOOOSH

ゴリ＊＊＊＊＊

KWEEM

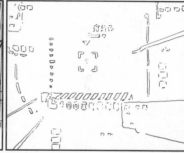

TANIKAZE UNIT AT 100 KILO UNITS FROM KANATA!!

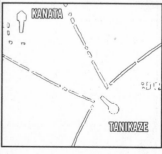

KANATA

TANIKAZE

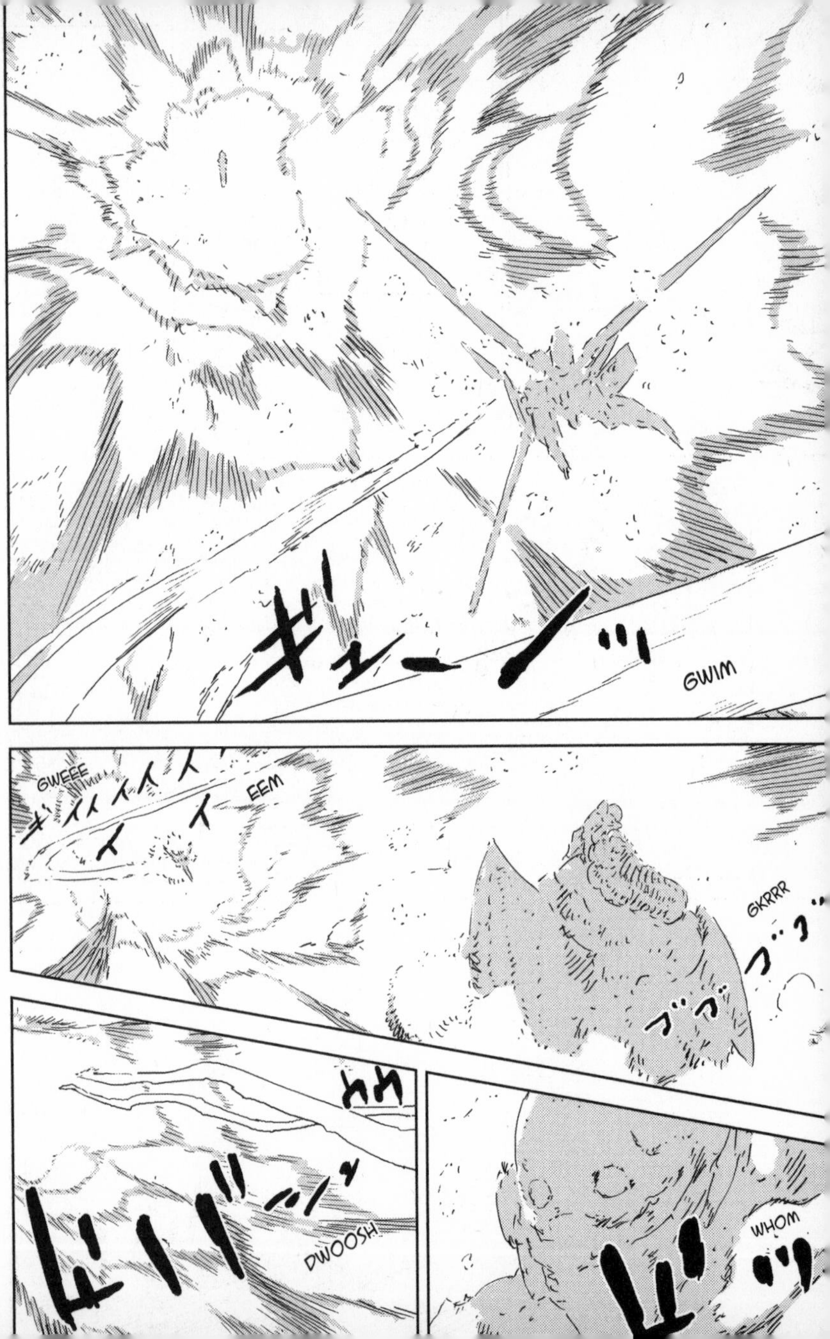
GWIM
GKRRR
GWEEE
EEM
WHOM
DWOOSH

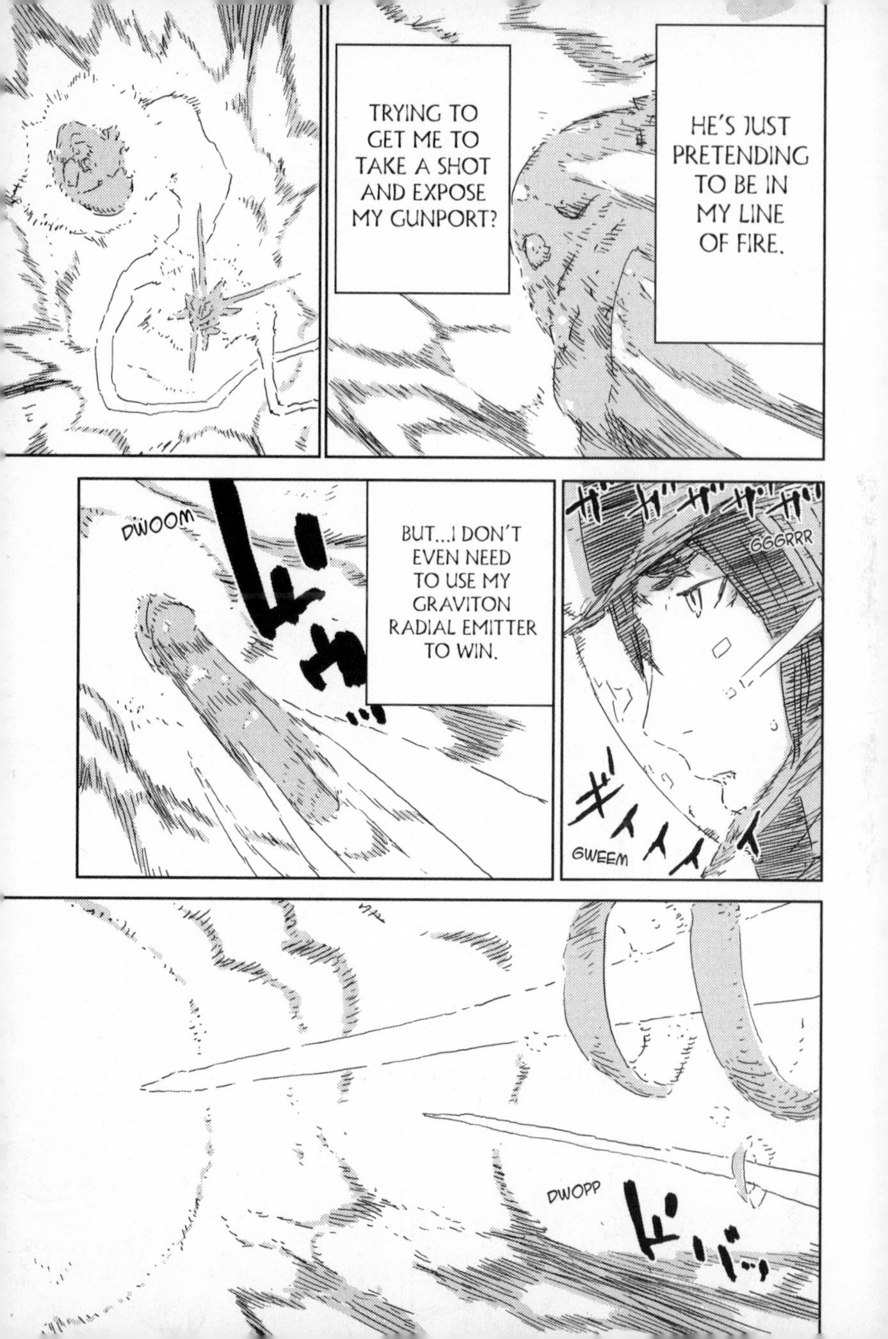
HE'S JUST PRETENDING TO BE IN MY LINE OF FIRE.
TRYING TO GET ME TO TAKE A SHOT AND EXPOSE MY GUNPORT?
GGGRRR
GWEEM
DWOOM
BUT...I DON'T EVEN NEED TO USE MY GRAVITON RADIAL EMITTER TO WIN.
DWOPP

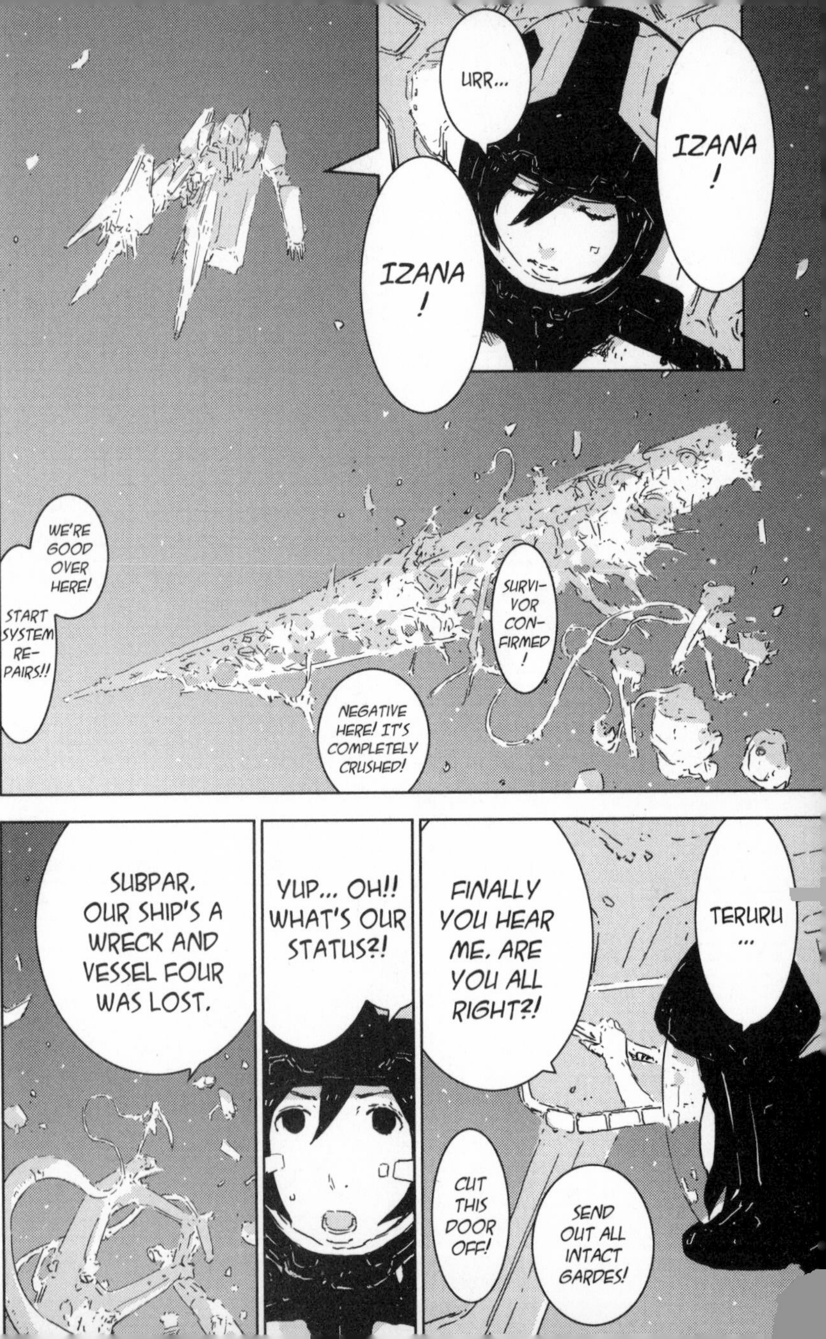
IZANA!
IZANA!
URR...
SURVIVOR CONFIRMED!
NEGATIVE HERE! IT'S COMPLETELY CRUSHED!
WE'RE GOOD OVER HERE!
START SYSTEM REPAIRS!!
TERURU...
FINALLY YOU HEAR ME. ARE YOU ALL RIGHT?!
SEND OUT ALL INTACT GARDES!
CUT THIS DOOR OFF!
YUP... OH!! WHAT'S OUR STATUS?!
SUBPAR. OUR SHIP'S A WRECK AND VESSEL FOUR WAS LOST.

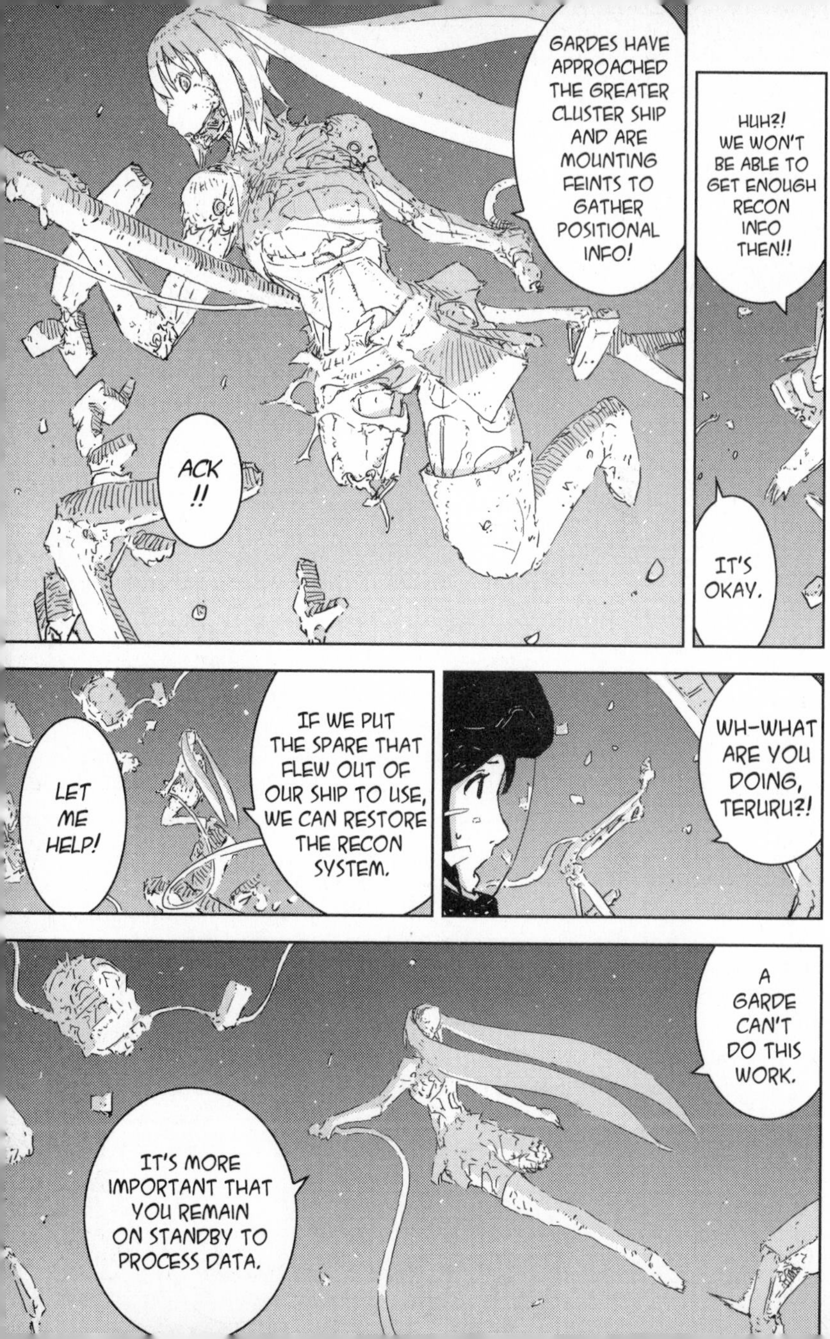
HUH?! WE WON'T BE ABLE TO GET ENOUGH RECON INFO THEN!!
IT'S OKAY.
GARDES HAVE APPROACHED THE GREATER CLUSTER SHIP AND ARE MOUNTING FEINTS TO GATHER POSITIONAL INFO!
ACK !!
WH-WHAT ARE YOU DOING, TERURU?!
IF WE PUT THE SPARE THAT FLEW OUT OF OUR SHIP TO USE, WE CAN RESTORE THE RECON SYSTEM.
LET ME HELP!
A GARDE CAN'T DO THIS WORK.
IT'S MORE IMPORTANT THAT YOU REMAIN ON STANDBY TO PROCESS DATA.

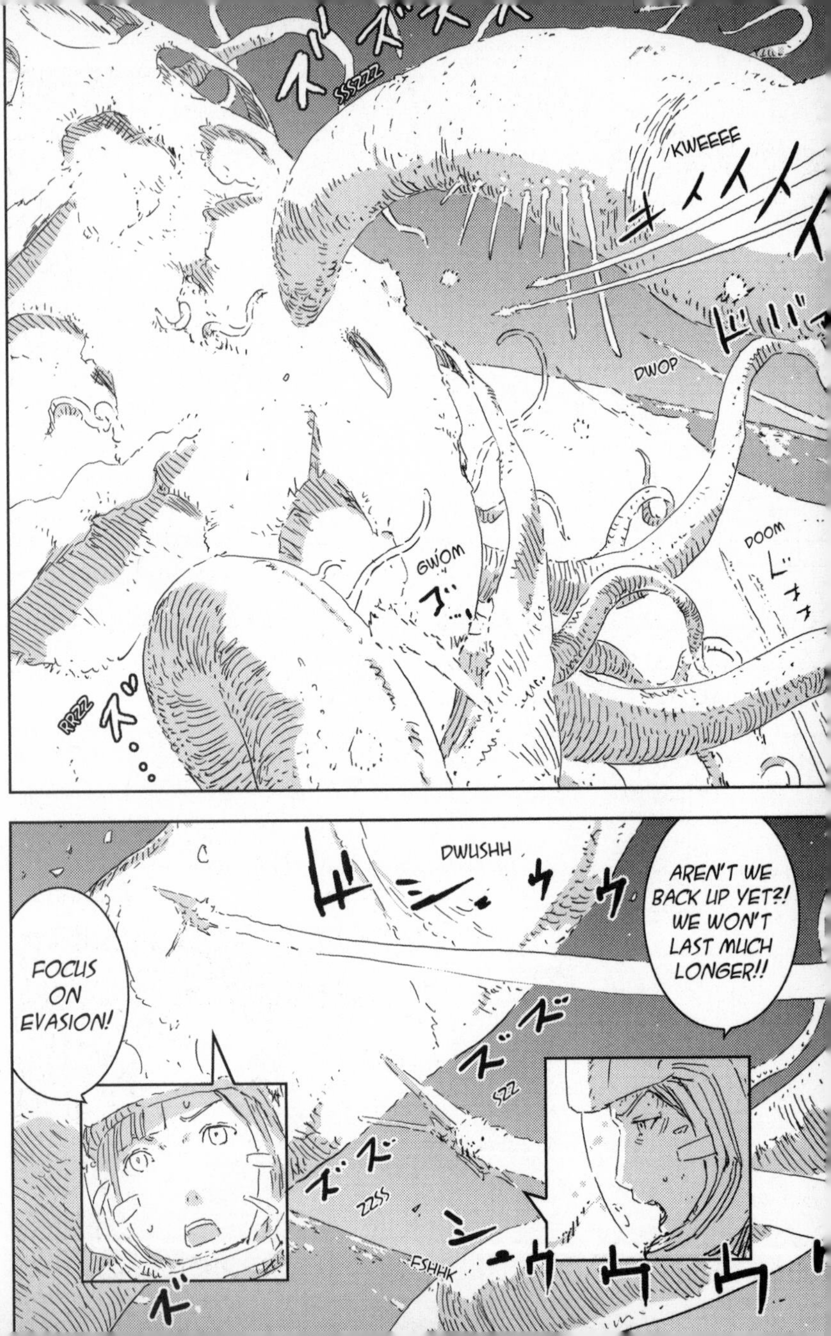

KWEEEE
DWOP
SSSZZZ
DOOM
GWOM
RRZZZ
DWUSHH
AREN'T WE BACK UP YET?! WE WON'T LAST MUCH LONGER!!
FOCUS ON EVASION!
SZZ
ZZSS
FSHHK

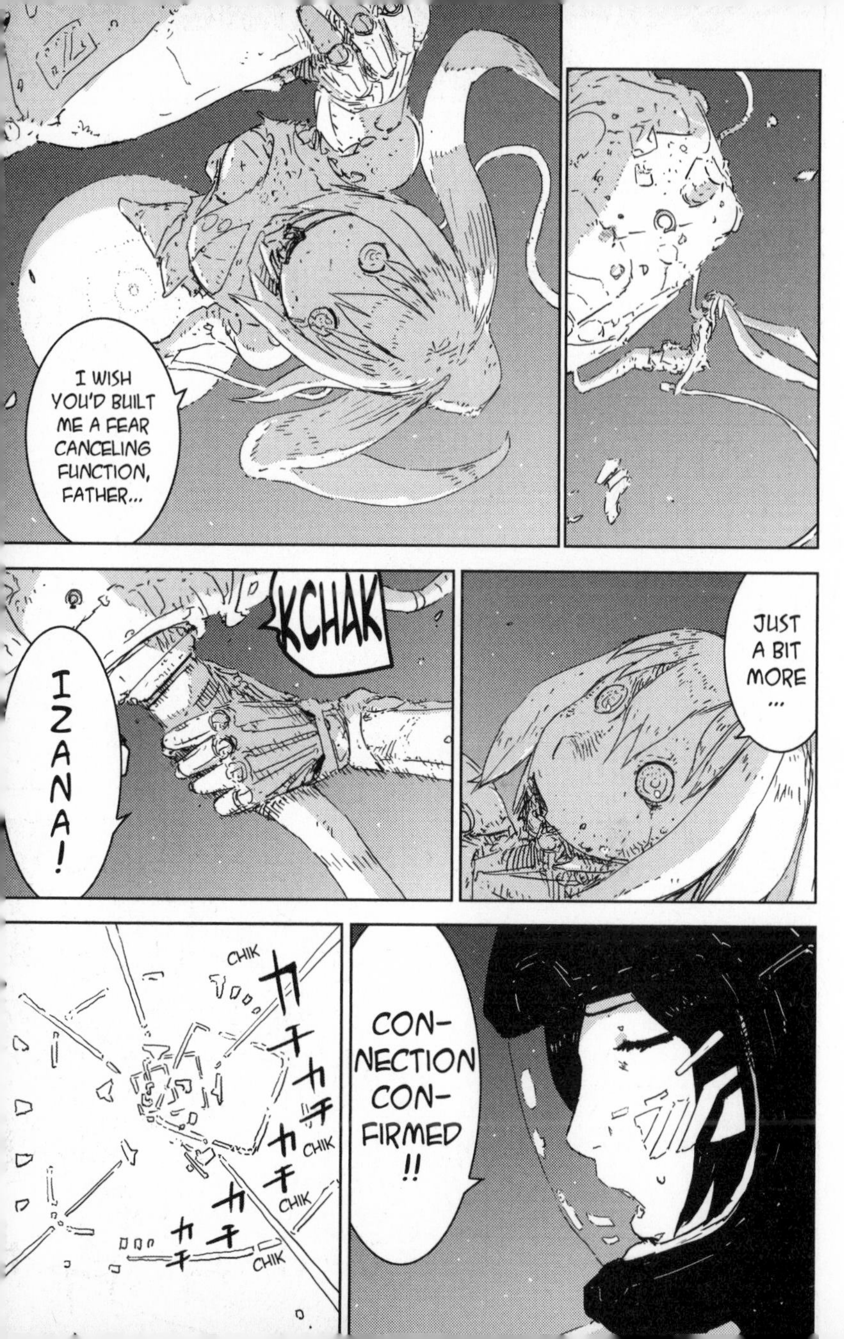
I WISH YOU'D BUILT ME A FEAR CANCELING FUNCTION, FATHER...
JUST A BIT MORE ...
KCHAK
IZANA!
CON-NECTION CON-FIRMED !!
CHIK
CHIK
CHIK
CHIK

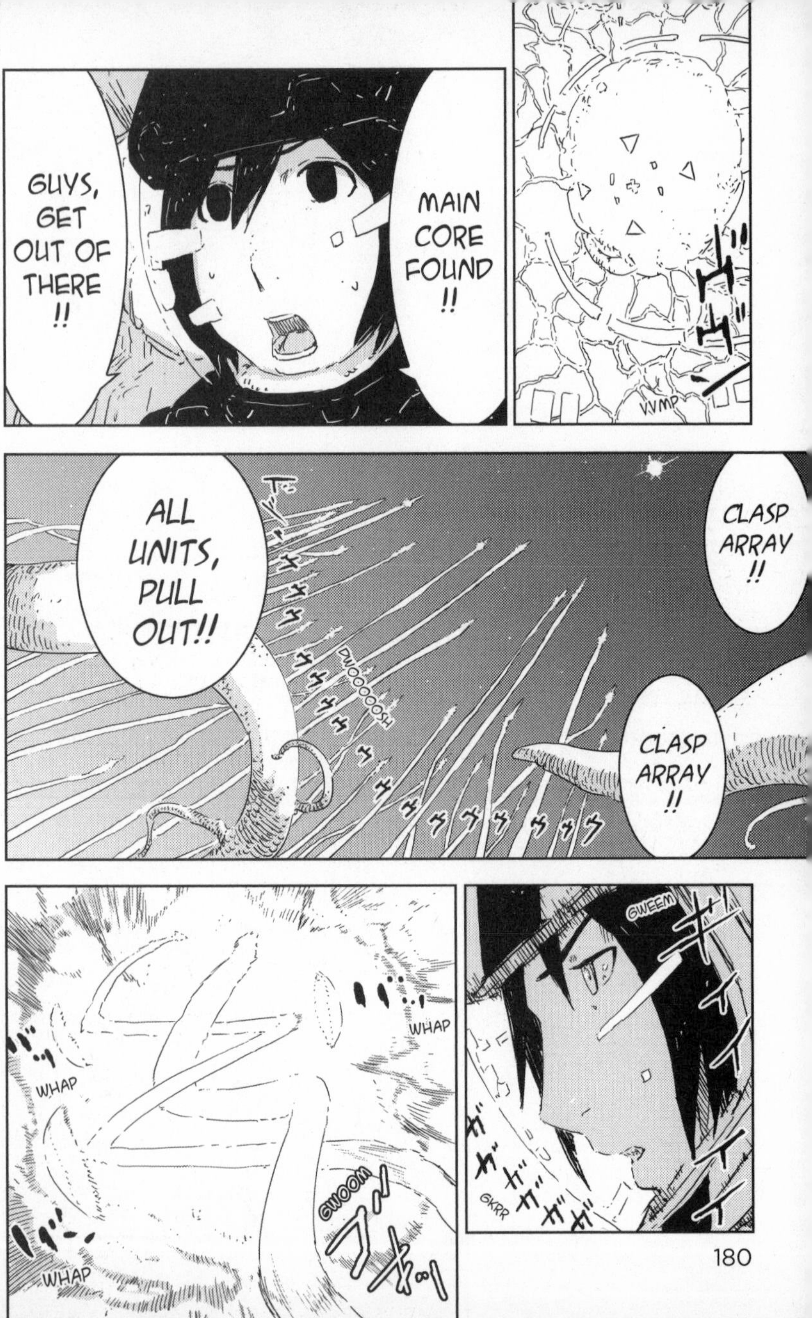
VVMP
MAIN CORE FOUND!!
GUYS, GET OUT OF THERE!!
CLASP ARRAY!!
CLASP ARRAY!!
ALL UNITS, PULL OUT!!
DWOOOOOSH
GWEEM
GKRR
WHAP
WHAP
WHAP
GWOOM

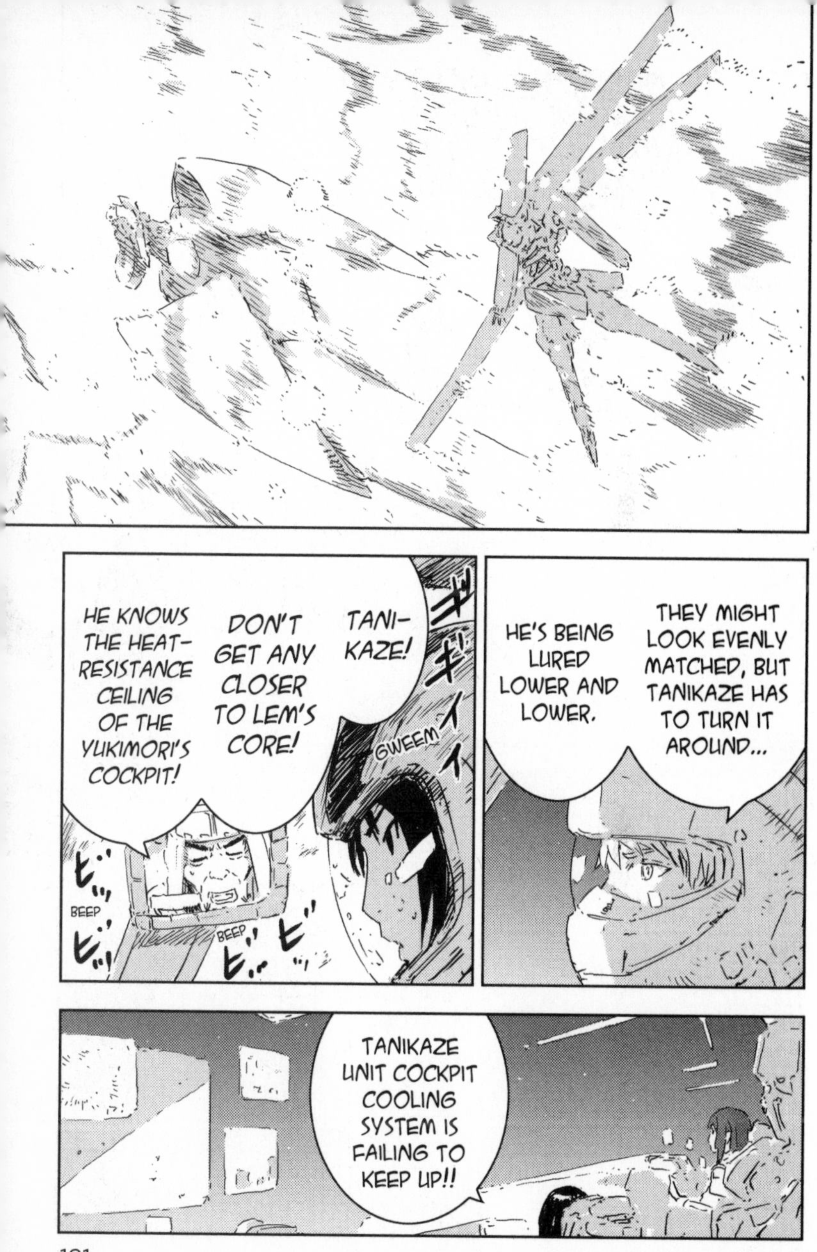
THEY MIGHT LOOK EVENLY MATCHED, BUT TANIKAZE HAS TO TURN IT AROUND...
HE'S BEING LURED LOWER AND LOWER.
TANI-KAZE!
GWEEM
DON'T GET ANY CLOSER TO LEM'S CORE!
HE KNOWS THE HEAT-RESISTANCE CEILING OF THE YUKIMORI'S COCKPIT!
BEEP
BEEP
TANIKAZE UNIT COCKPIT COOLING SYSTEM IS FAILING TO KEEP UP!!

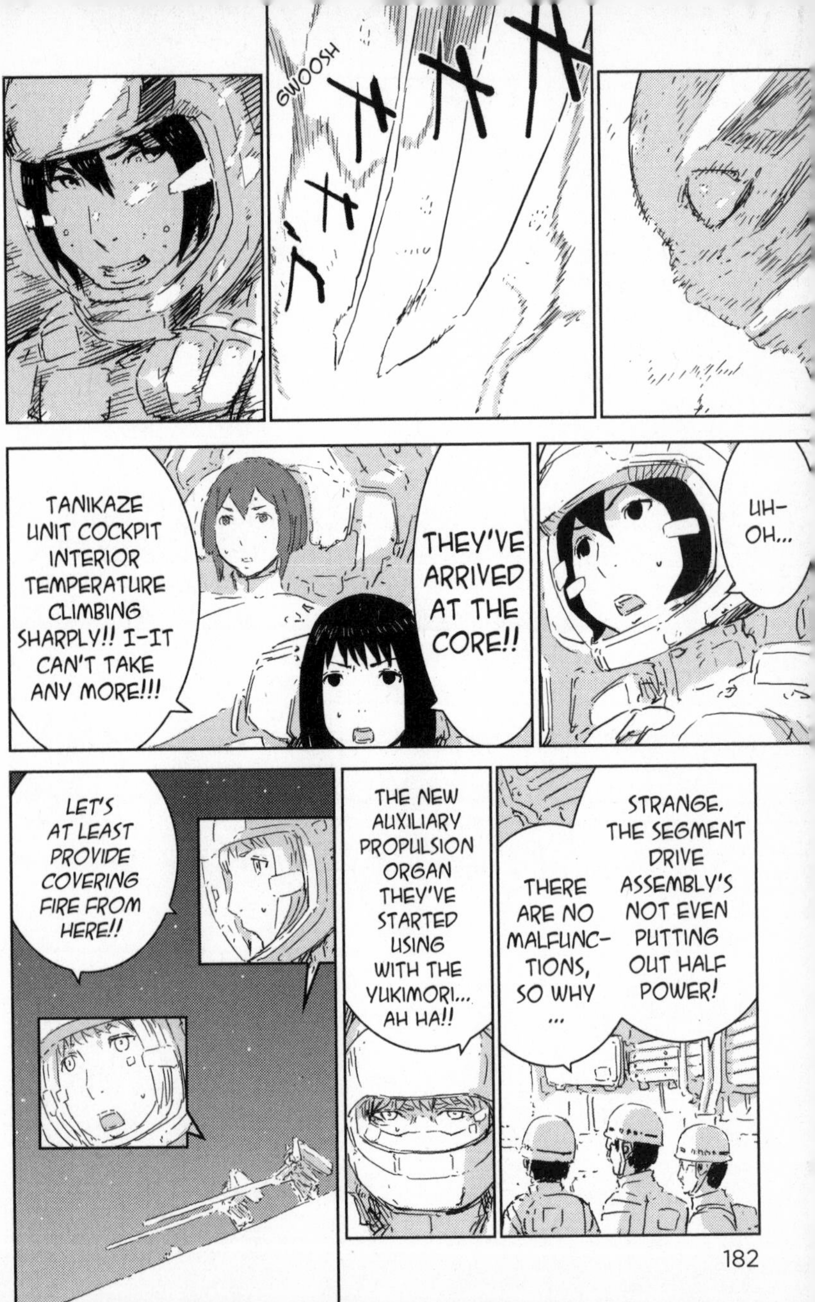
GWOOSH
UH-OH...
THEY'VE ARRIVED AT THE CORE!!
TANIKAZE UNIT COCKPIT INTERIOR TEMPERATURE CLIMBING SHARPLY!! I-IT CAN'T TAKE ANY MORE!!!
STRANGE. THE SEGMENT DRIVE ASSEMBLY'S NOT EVEN PUTTING OUT HALF POWER!
THERE ARE NO MALFUNC-TIONS, SO WHY ...
THE NEW AUXILIARY PROPULSION ORGAN THEY'VE STARTED USING WITH THE YUKIMORI... AH HA!!
LET'S AT LEAST PROVIDE COVERING FIRE FROM HERE!!

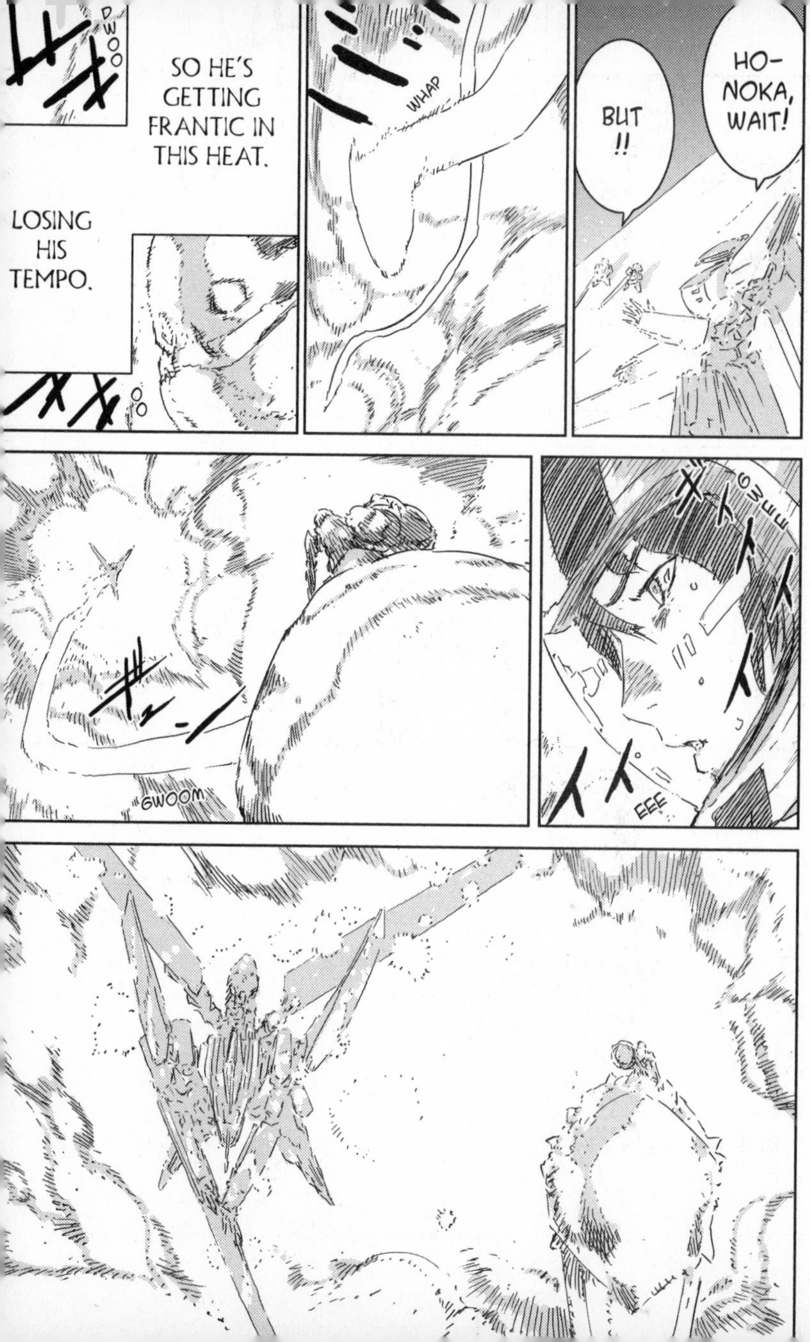
HO-NOKA, WAIT!
BUT !!
WHAP
DWOO
SO HE'S GETTING FRANTIC IN THIS HEAT.
LOSING HIS TEMPO.
OO
GWEE
EEE
GWOOM

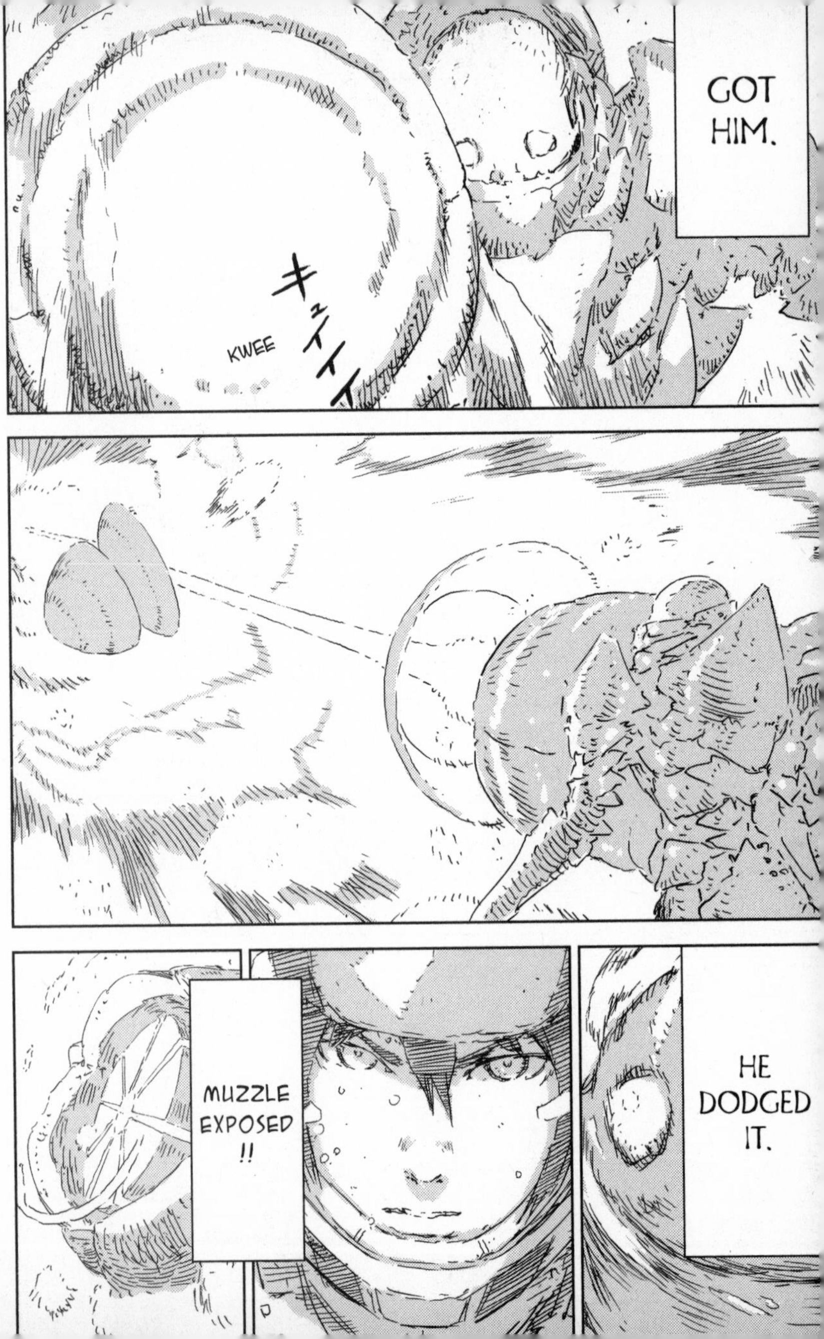
GOT HIM.
KWEE
HE DODGED IT.
MUZZLE EXPOSED !!

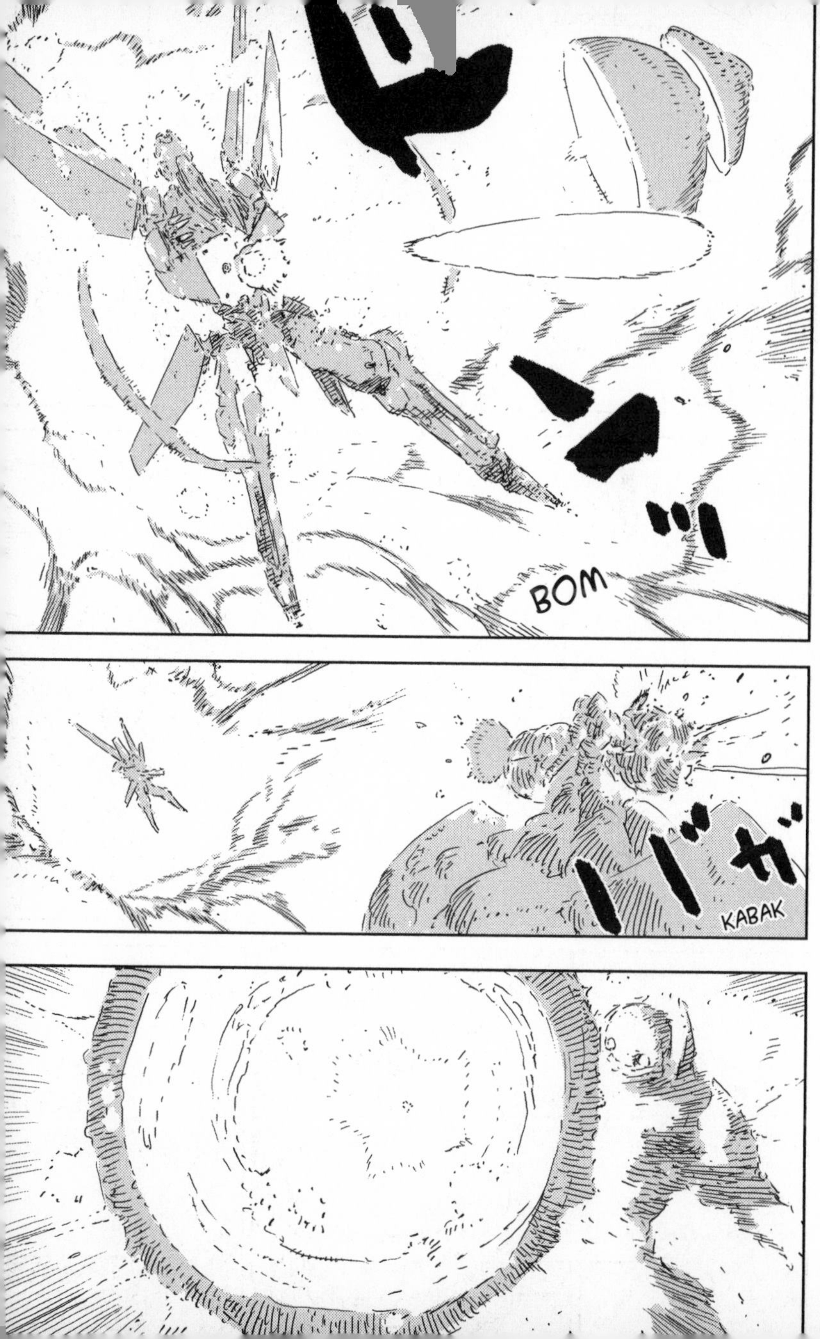
BOM
KABAK

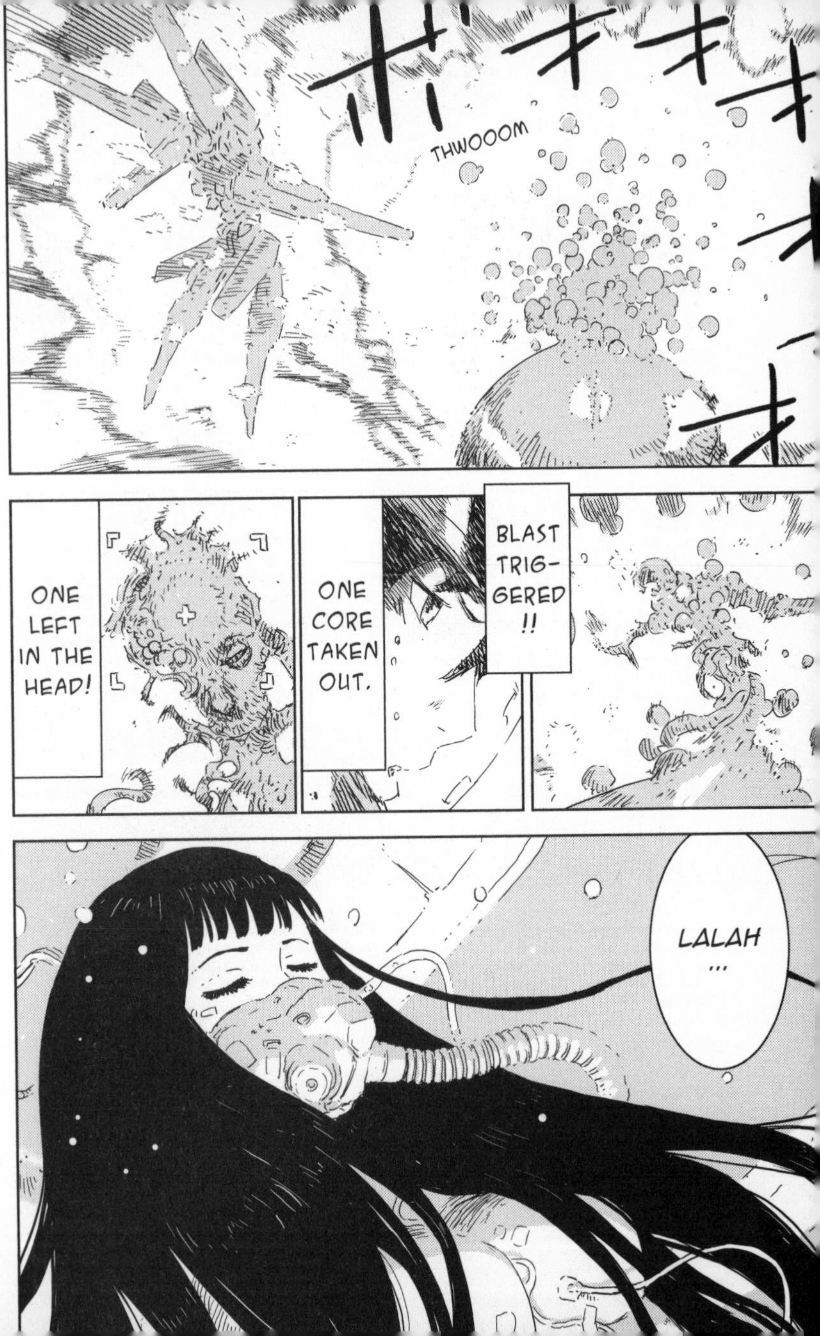
THWOOOM
BLAST TRIG-GERED!!
ONE CORE TAKEN OUT.
ONE LEFT IN THE HEAD!
LALAH ...

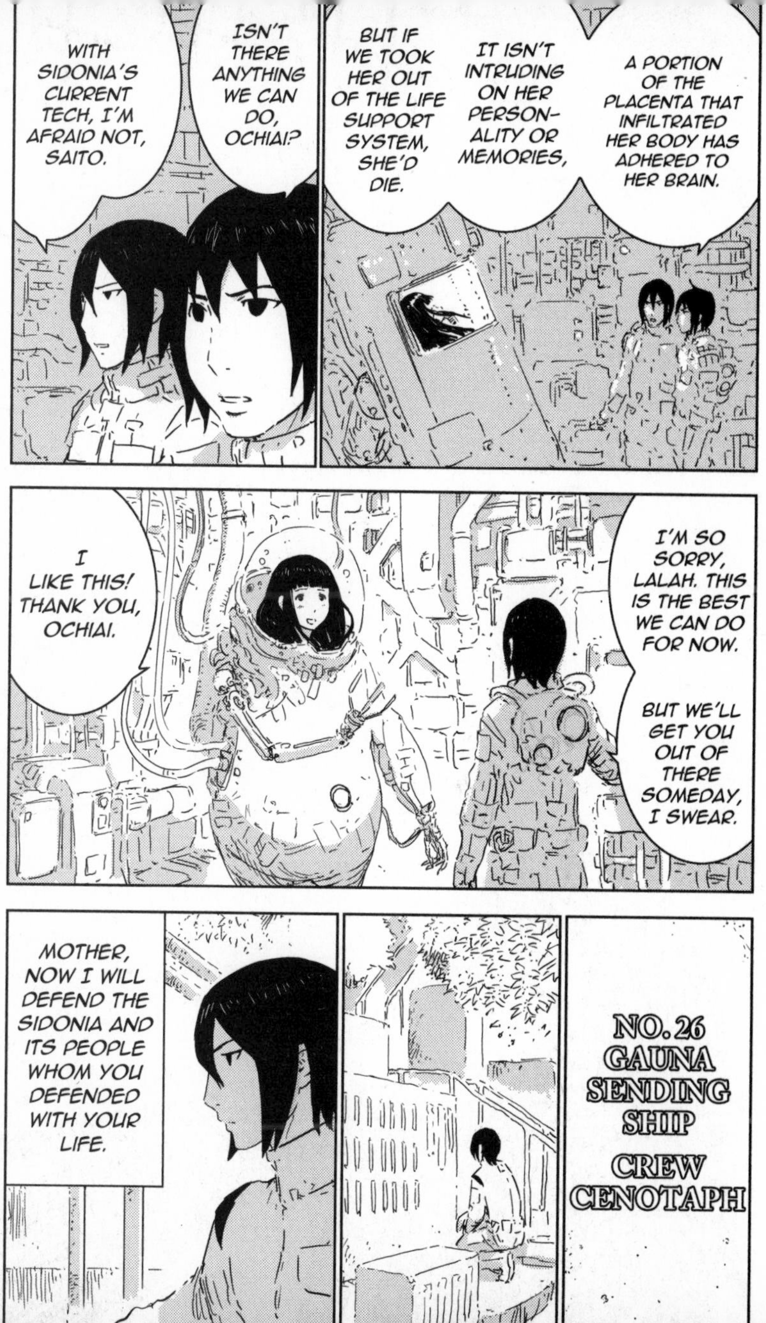
A PORTION OF THE PLACENTA THAT INFILTRATED HER BODY HAS ADHERED TO HER BRAIN.
IT ISN'T INTRUDING ON HER PERSON-ALITY OR MEMORIES,
BUT IF WE TOOK HER OUT OF THE LIFE SUPPORT SYSTEM, SHE'D DIE.
ISN'T THERE ANYTHING WE CAN DO, OCHIAI?
WITH SIDONIA'S CURRENT TECH, I'M AFRAID NOT, SAITO.
I'M SO SORRY, LALAH. THIS IS THE BEST WE CAN DO FOR NOW.
BUT WE'LL GET YOU OUT OF THERE SOMEDAY, I SWEAR.
I LIKE THIS! THANK YOU, OCHIAI.
NO. 26 GAUNA SENDING SHIP
CREW CENOTAPH
MOTHER, NOW I WILL DEFEND THE SIDONIA AND ITS PEOPLE WHOM YOU DEFENDED WITH YOUR LIFE.

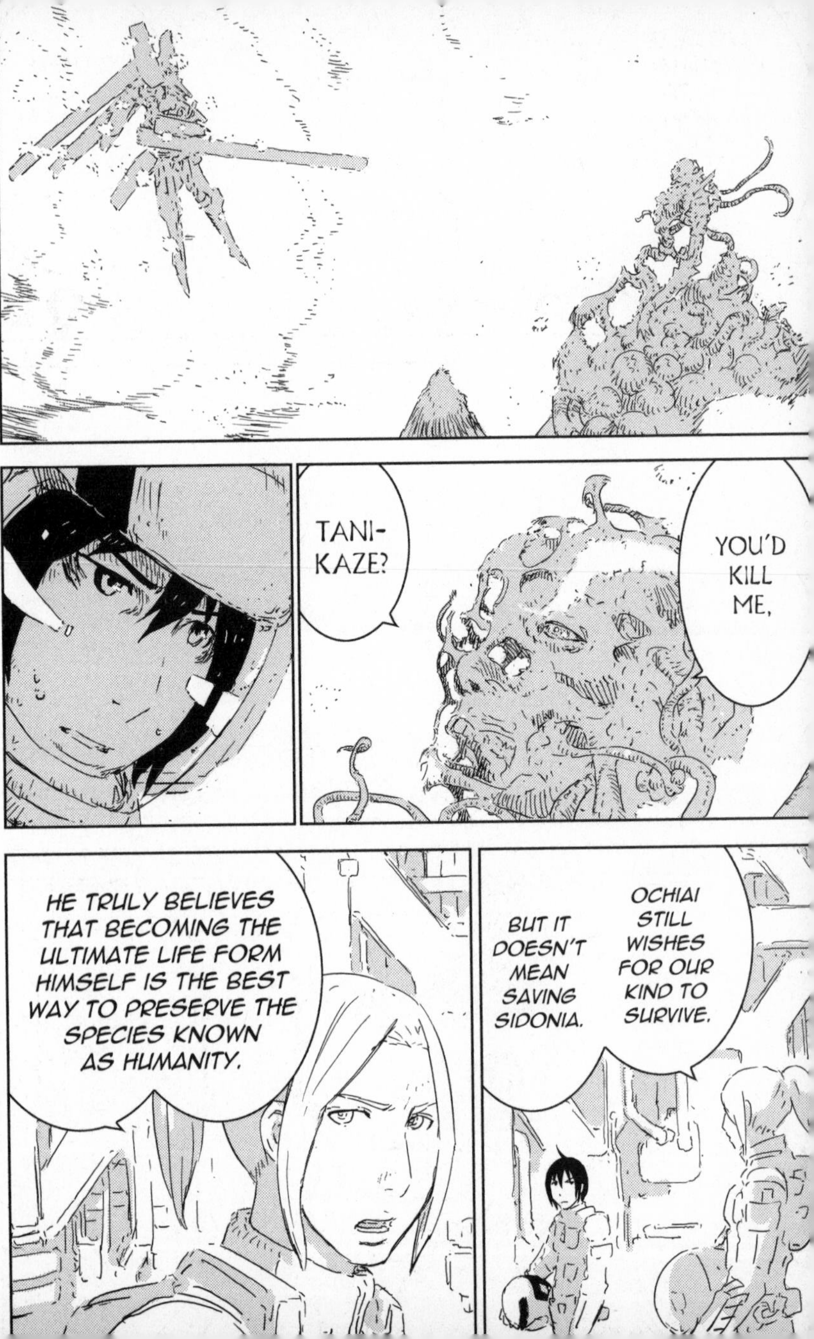
YOU'D KILL ME,
TANI-KAZE?
OCHIAI STILL WISHES FOR OUR KIND TO SURVIVE.
BUT IT DOESN'T MEAN SAVING SIDONIA.
HE TRULY BELIEVES THAT BECOMING THE ULTIMATE LIFE FORM HIMSELF IS THE BEST WAY TO PRESERVE THE SPECIES KNOWN AS HUMANITY.

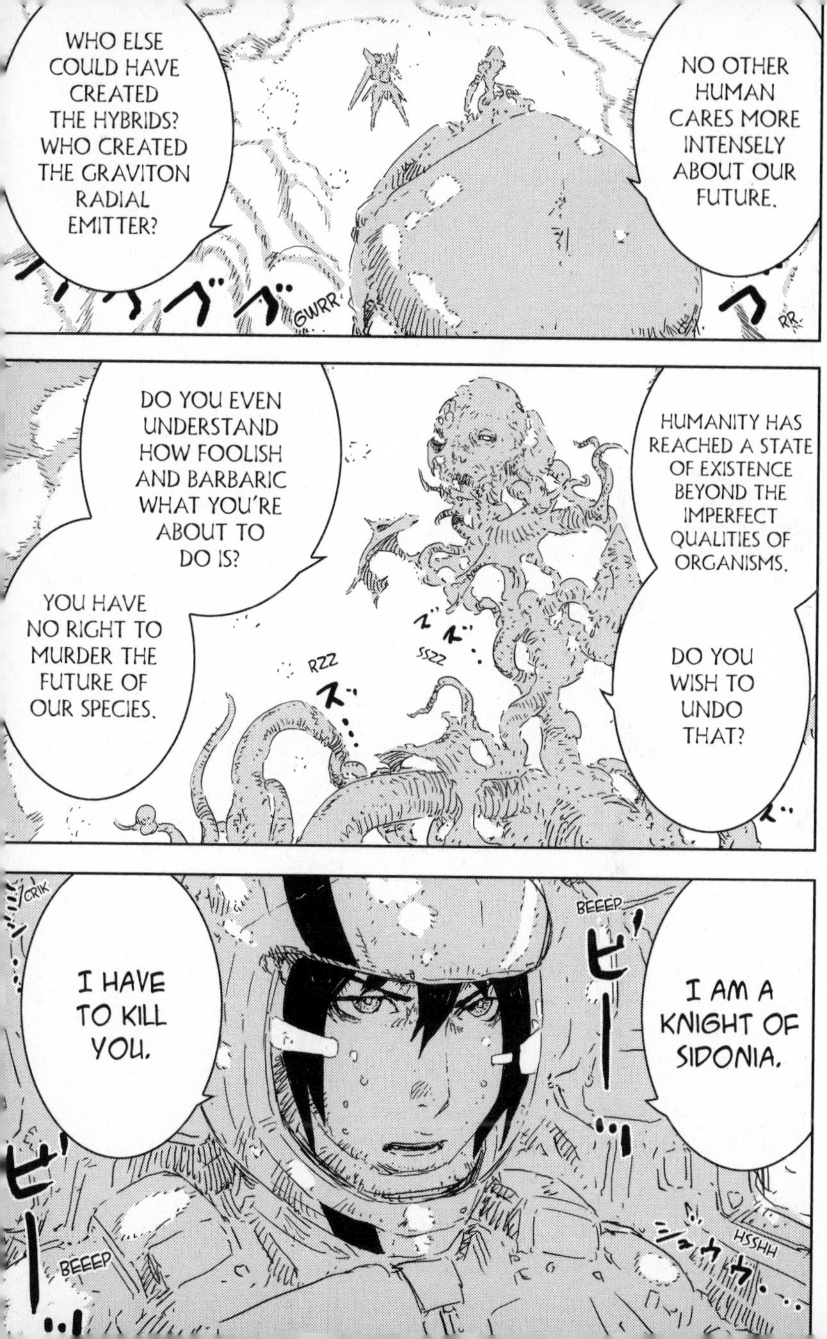
NO OTHER HUMAN CARES MORE INTENSELY ABOUT OUR FUTURE.
RR
WHO ELSE COULD HAVE CREATED THE HYBRIDS? WHO CREATED THE GRAVITON RADIAL EMITTER?
GWRR
HUMANITY HAS REACHED A STATE OF EXISTENCE BEYOND THE IMPERFECT QUALITIES OF ORGANISMS.
DO YOU WISH TO UNDO THAT?
DO YOU EVEN UNDERSTAND HOW FOOLISH AND BARBARIC WHAT YOU'RE ABOUT TO DO IS?
SSZZ
RZZ
YOU HAVE NO RIGHT TO MURDER THE FUTURE OF OUR SPECIES.
BEEEP
I AM A KNIGHT OF SIDONIA.
CRIK
I HAVE TO KILL YOU.
HSSHH
BEEEP

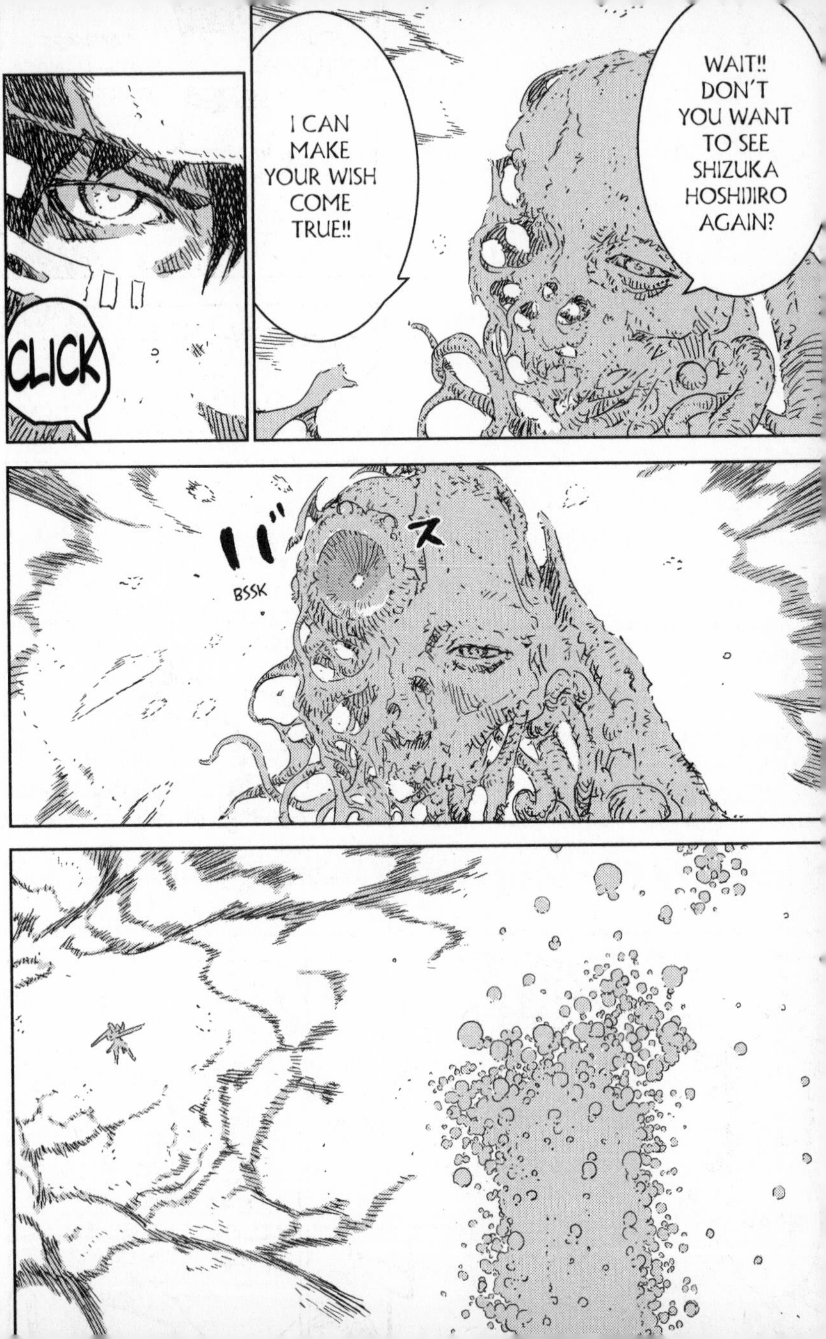
WAIT!! DON'T YOU WANT TO SEE SHIZUKA HOSHIJIRO AGAIN?
I CAN MAKE YOUR WISH COME TRUE!!
CLICK
バス
BSSK

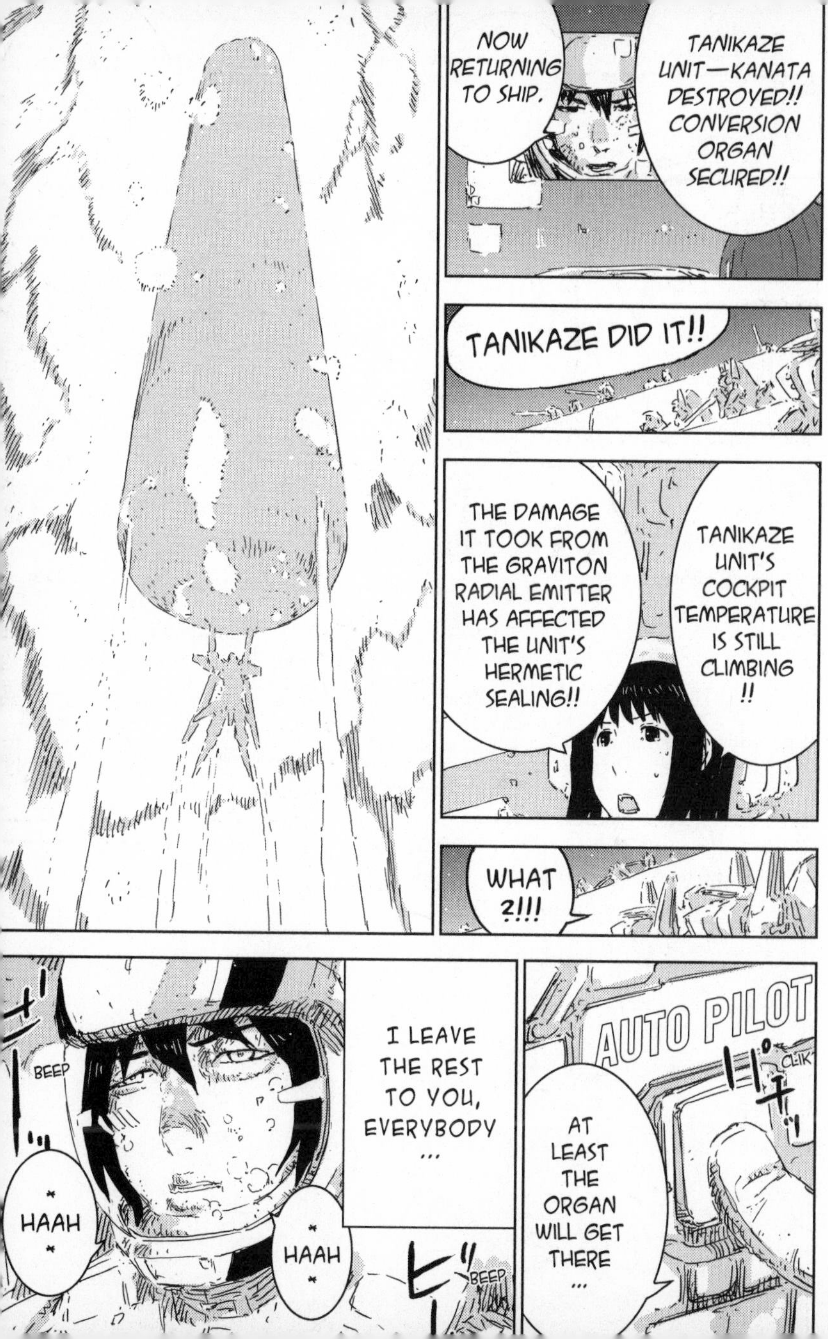
TANIKAZE UNIT—KANATA DESTROYED!! CONVERSION ORGAN SECURED!!
NOW RETURNING TO SHIP.
TANIKAZE DID IT!!
TANIKAZE UNIT'S COCKPIT TEMPERATURE IS STILL CLIMBING !!
THE DAMAGE IT TOOK FROM THE GRAVITON RADIAL EMITTER HAS AFFECTED THE UNIT'S HERMETIC SEALING!!
WHAT ?!!!
AUTO PILOT
CLIK
AT LEAST THE ORGAN WILL GET THERE ...
I LEAVE THE REST TO YOU, EVERYBODY ...
BEEP
* HAAH *
* HAAH *
BEEP

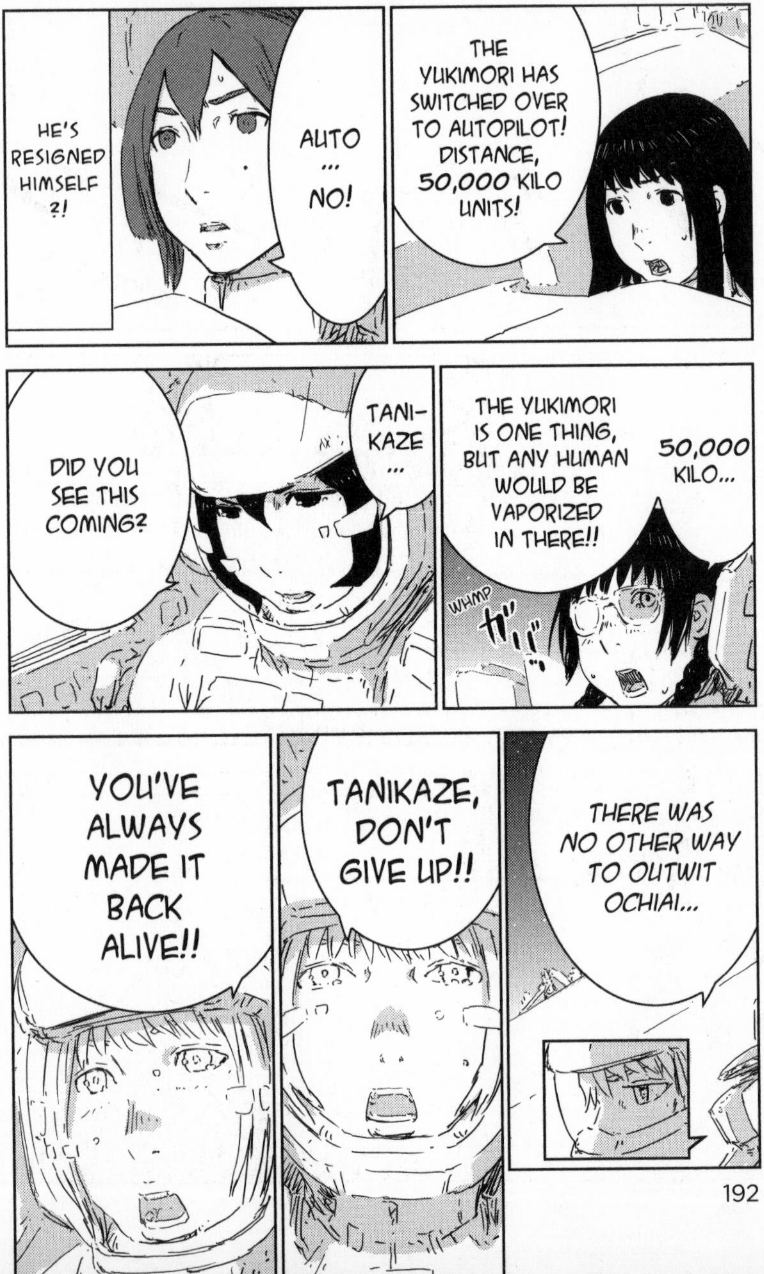
THE YUKIMORI HAS SWITCHED OVER TO AUTOPILOT! DISTANCE, 50,000 KILO UNITS!
AUTO... NO!
HE'S RESIGNED HIMSELF ?!
50,000 KILO...
THE YUKIMORI IS ONE THING, BUT ANY HUMAN WOULD BE VAPORIZED IN THERE!!
WHMP
TANI-KAZE...
DID YOU SEE THIS COMING?
THERE WAS NO OTHER WAY TO OUTWIT OCHIAI...
TANIKAZE, DON'T GIVE UP!!
YOU'VE ALWAYS MADE IT BACK ALIVE!!

GWOOOM

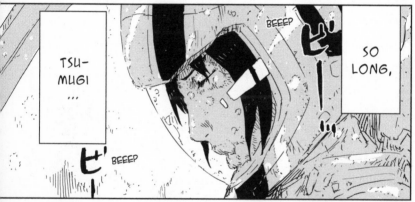

TSU-MUGI...

BEEEP

SO LONG,

BEEEP

BEEEP

VITAL SIGNS

TANI-KAZE!!

BEEEP

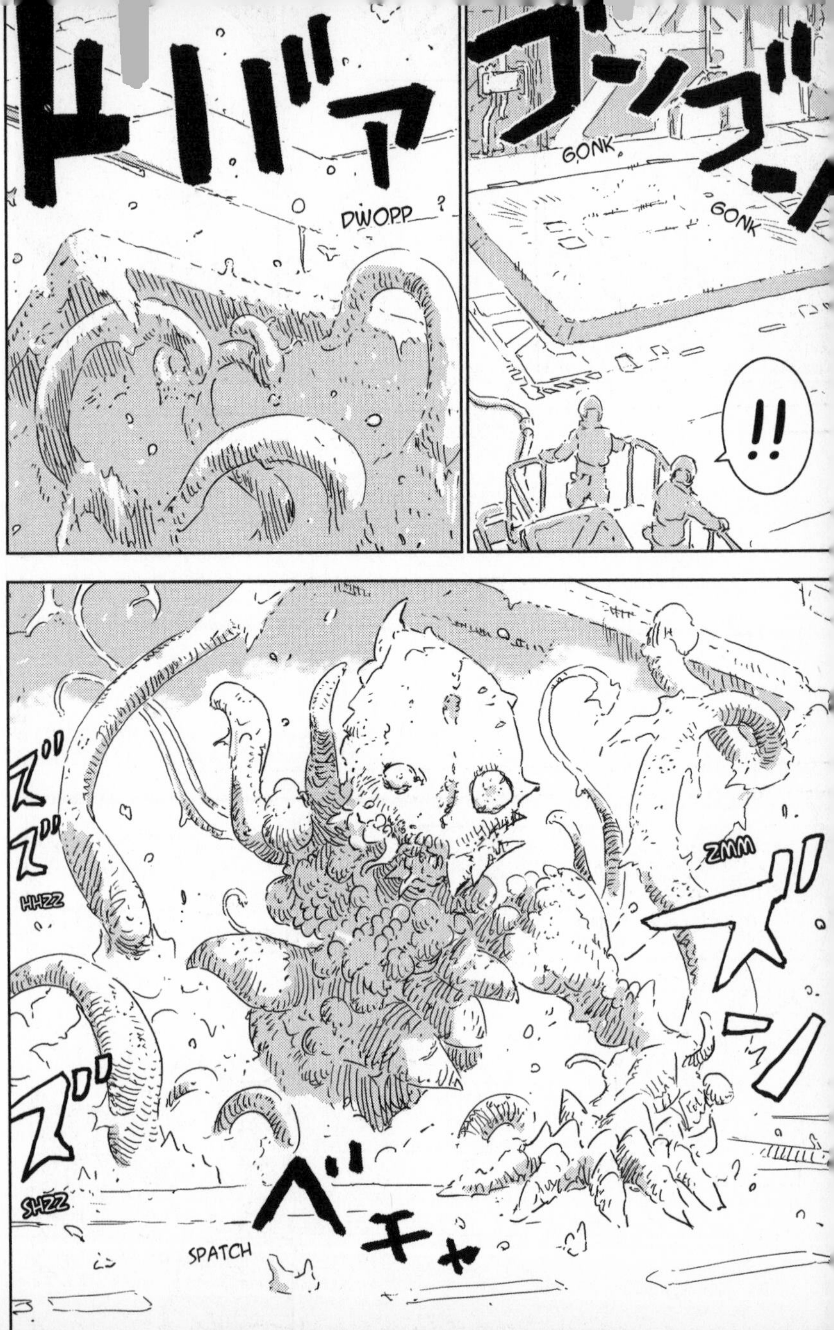
ゴンゴン
GONK
GONK
!!
ドバァ
DWOPP
ズン
ZMM
ズズズ
HHZZ
SHZZ
ベキャ
SPATCH

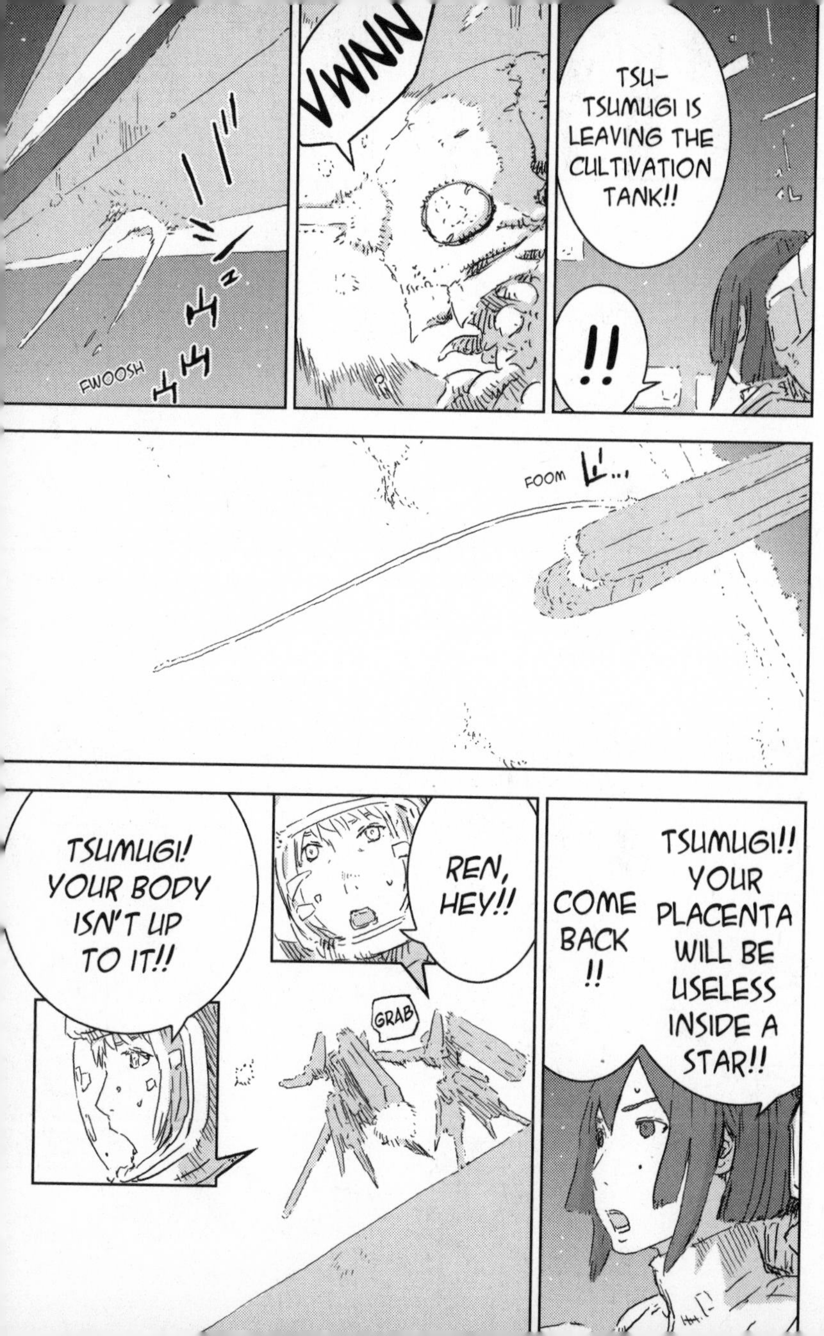
TSU-TSUMUGI IS LEAVING THE CULTIVATION TANK!!
!!
VWNN
FWOOSH
FOOM
TSUMUGI!! YOUR PLACENTA WILL BE USELESS INSIDE A STAR!!
COME BACK!!
REN, HEY!!
TSUMUGI! YOUR BODY ISN'T UP TO IT!!
GRAB

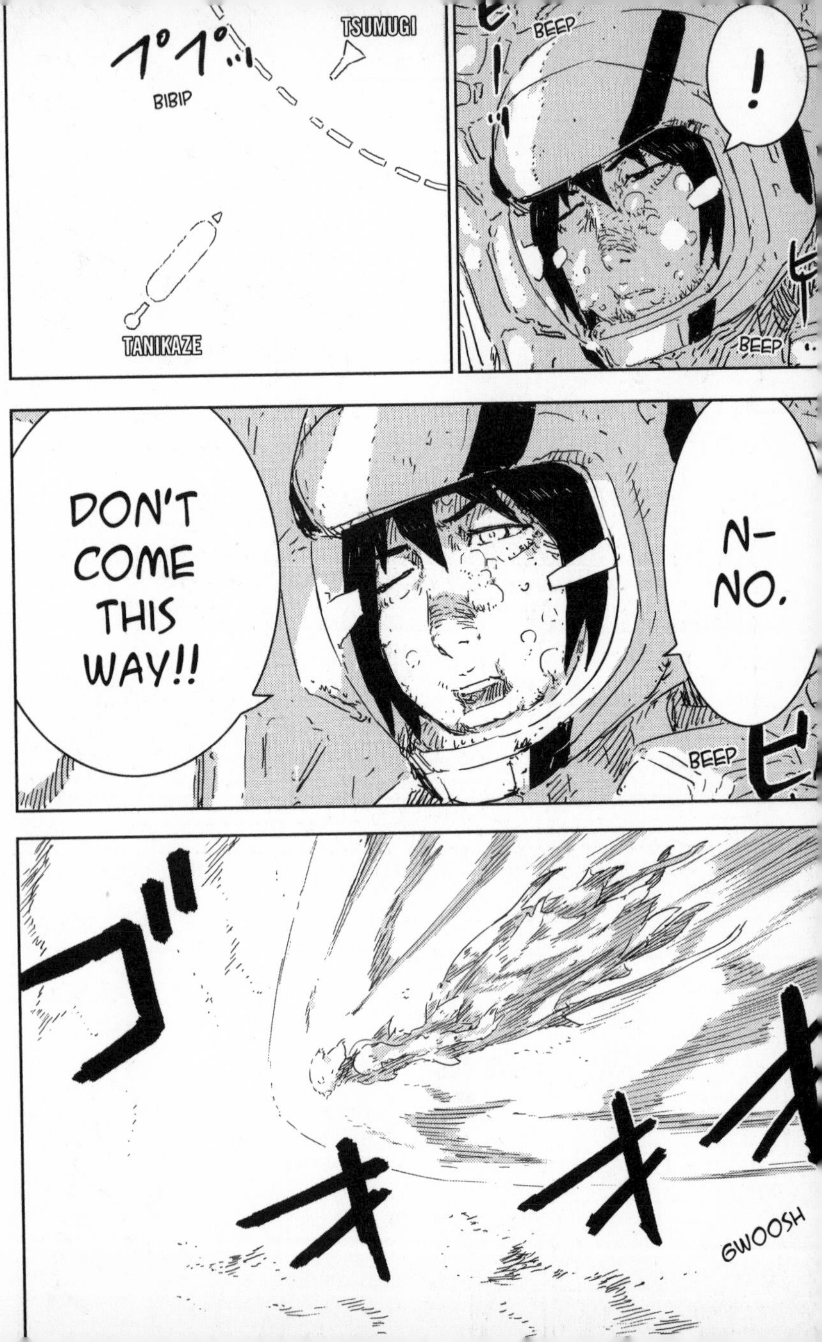

BEEP
!
BEEP
BIBIP
TSUMUGI
TANIKAZE
N- NO.
DON'T COME THIS WAY!!
BEEP
GWOOSH

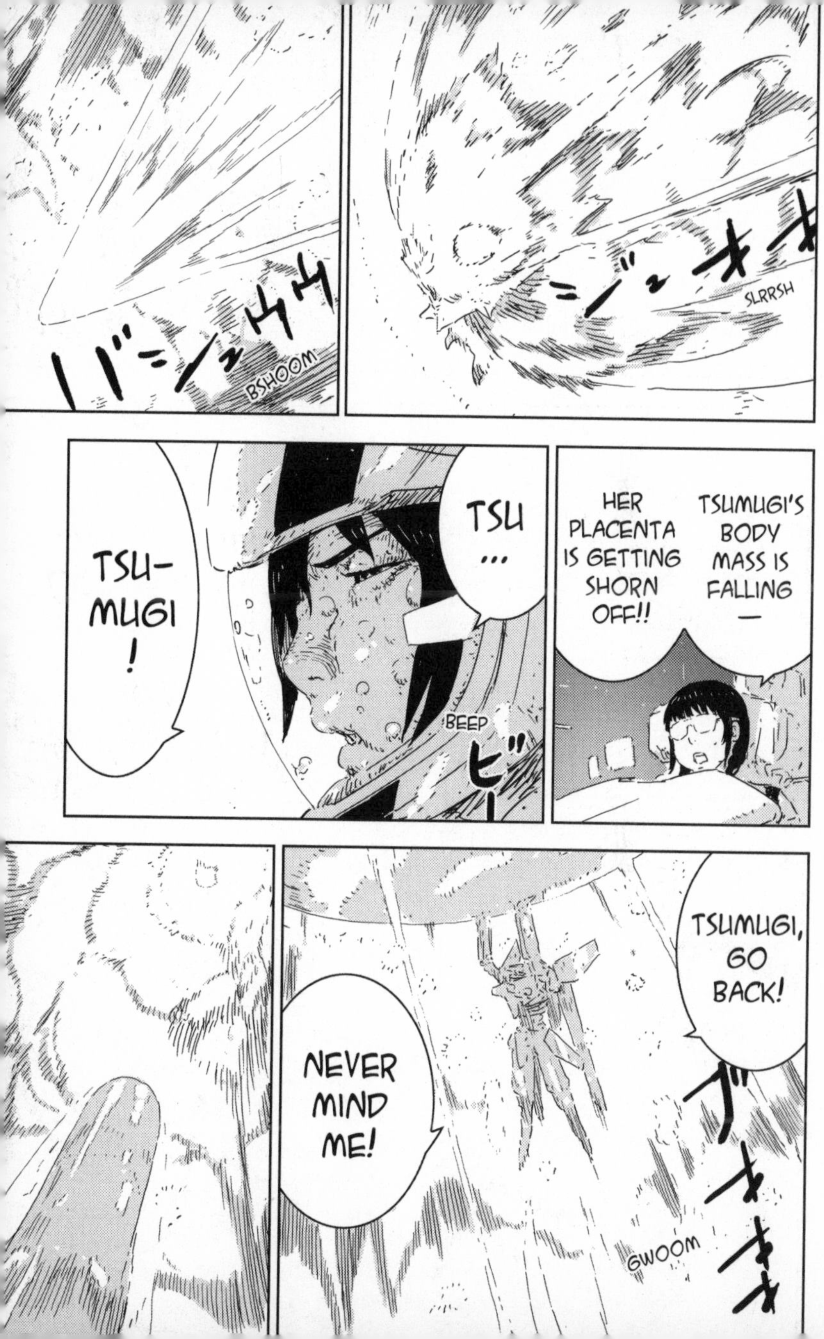
SLRRSH
BSHOOM
TSUMUGI'S BODY MASS IS FALLING —
HER PLACENTA IS GETTING SHORN OFF!!
TSU ...
TSU-MUGI !
BEEP
TSUMUGI, GO BACK!
NEVER MIND ME!
GWOOM

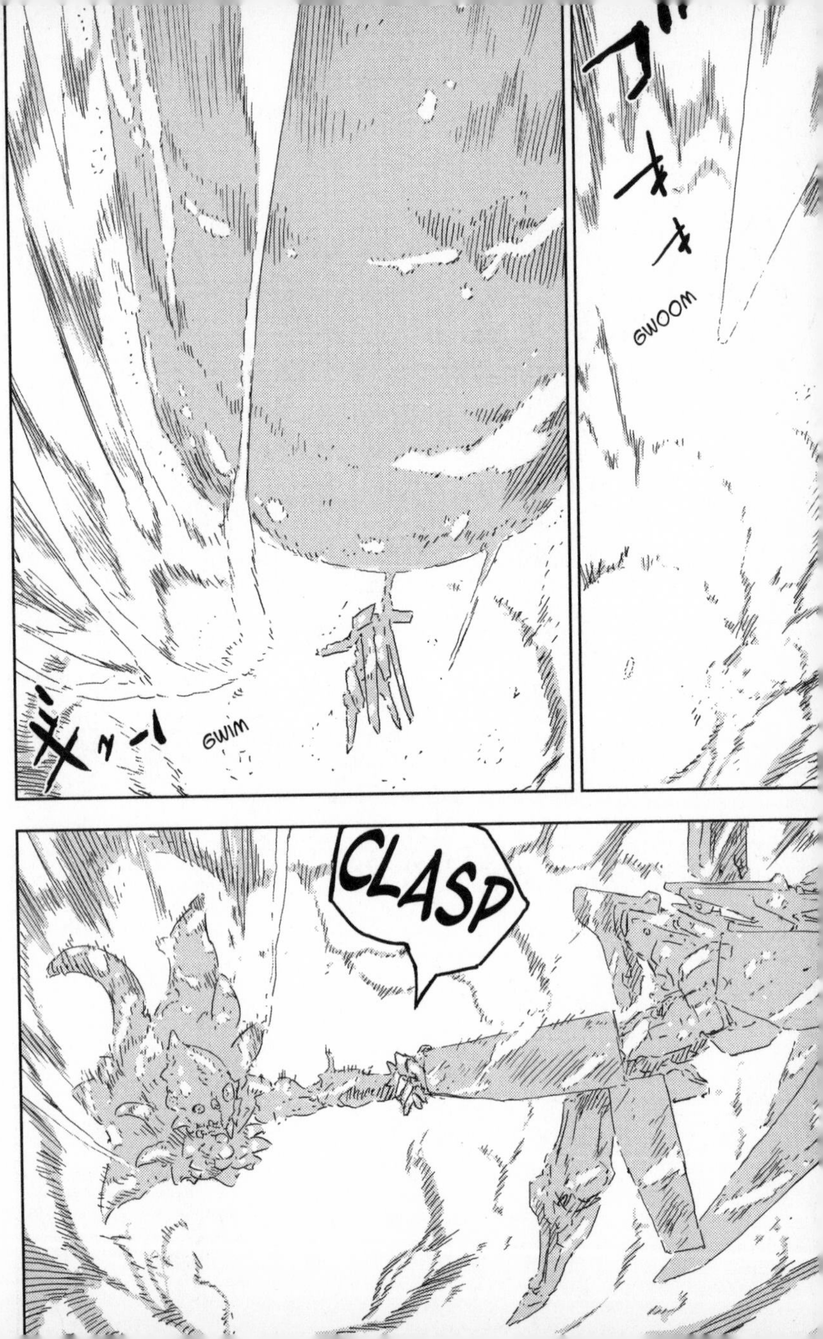
ゴキキ
GWOOM
GWIM
CLASP

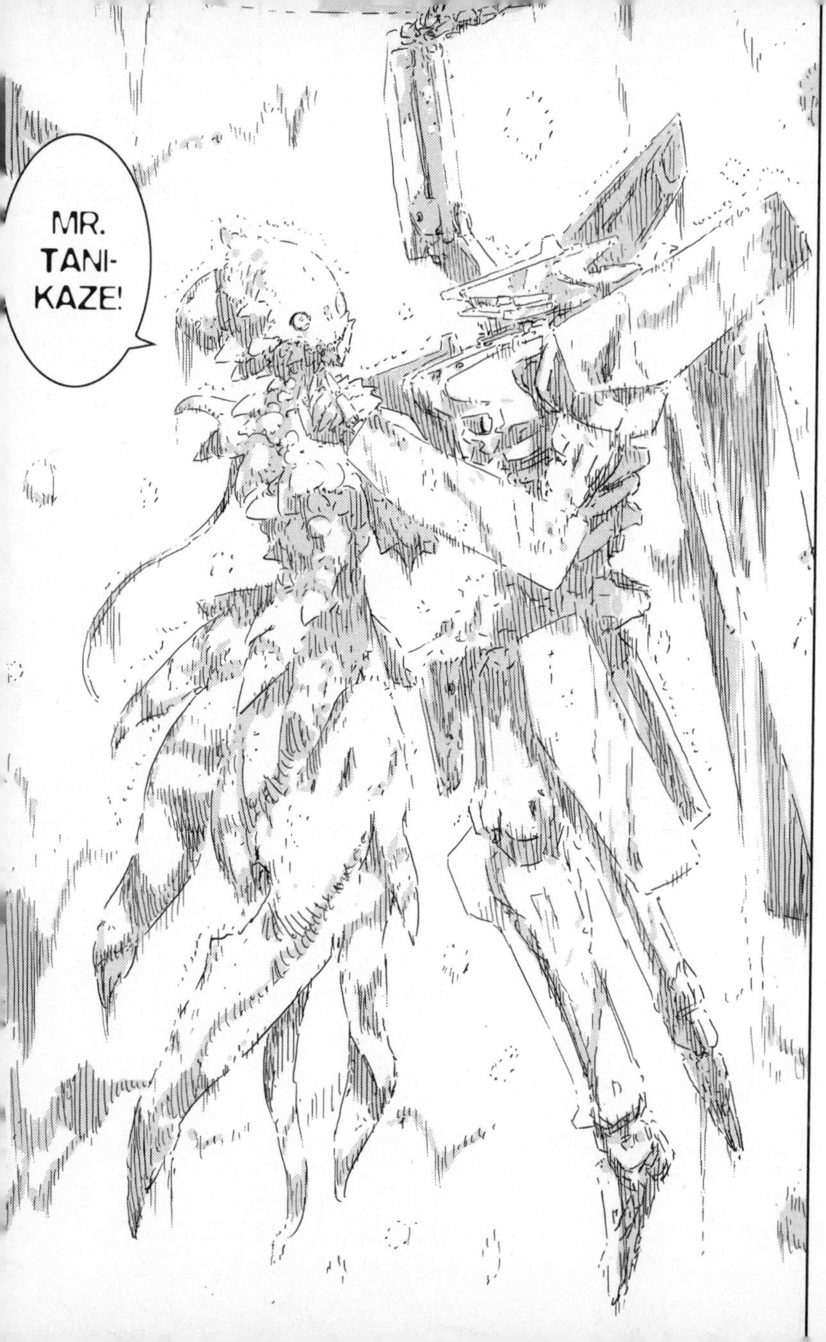
MR. TANI-KAZE!

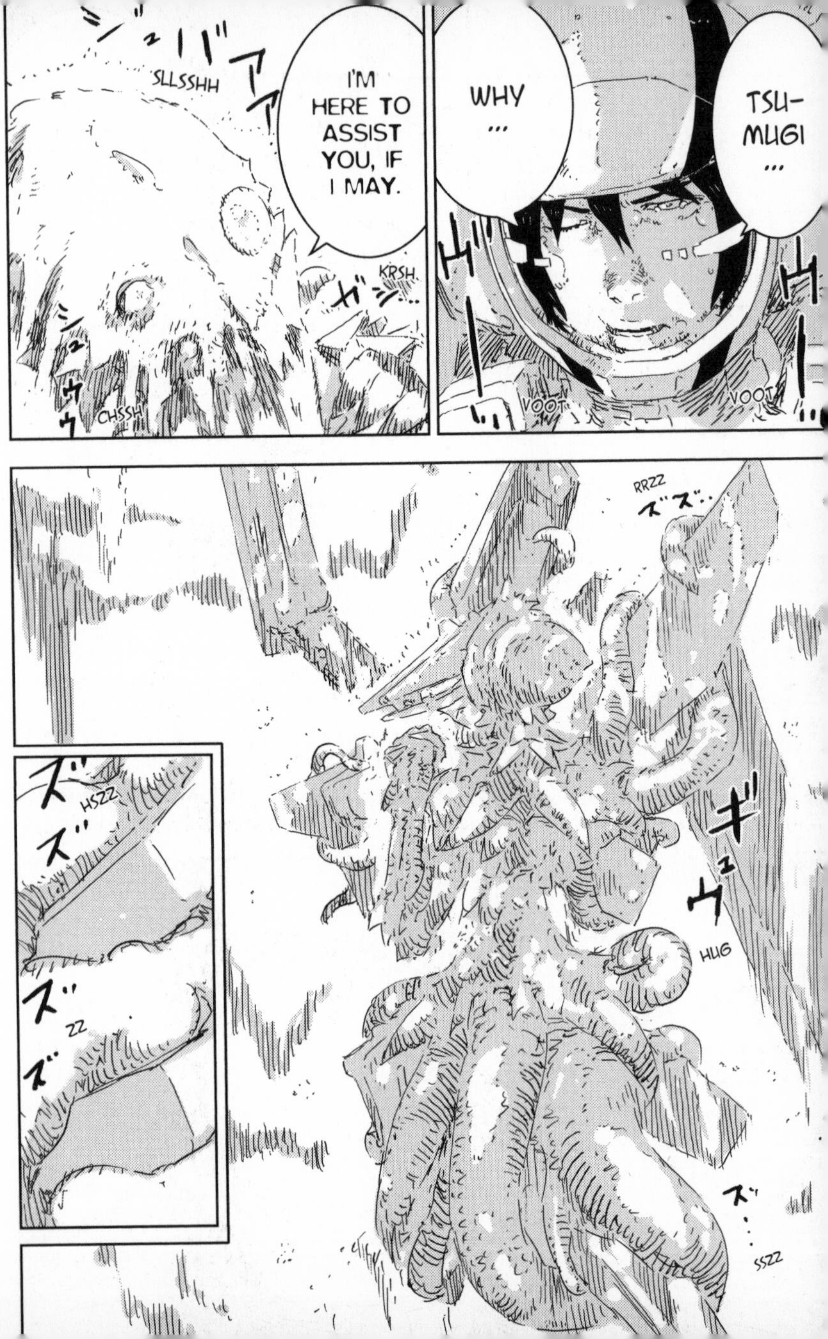
TSU-MUGI ...
WHY ...
VOOT
VOOT
I'M HERE TO ASSIST YOU, IF I MAY.
SLLSSHH
KRSH
CHSSH
RRZZ
HUG
SSZZ
HSZZ
ZZ

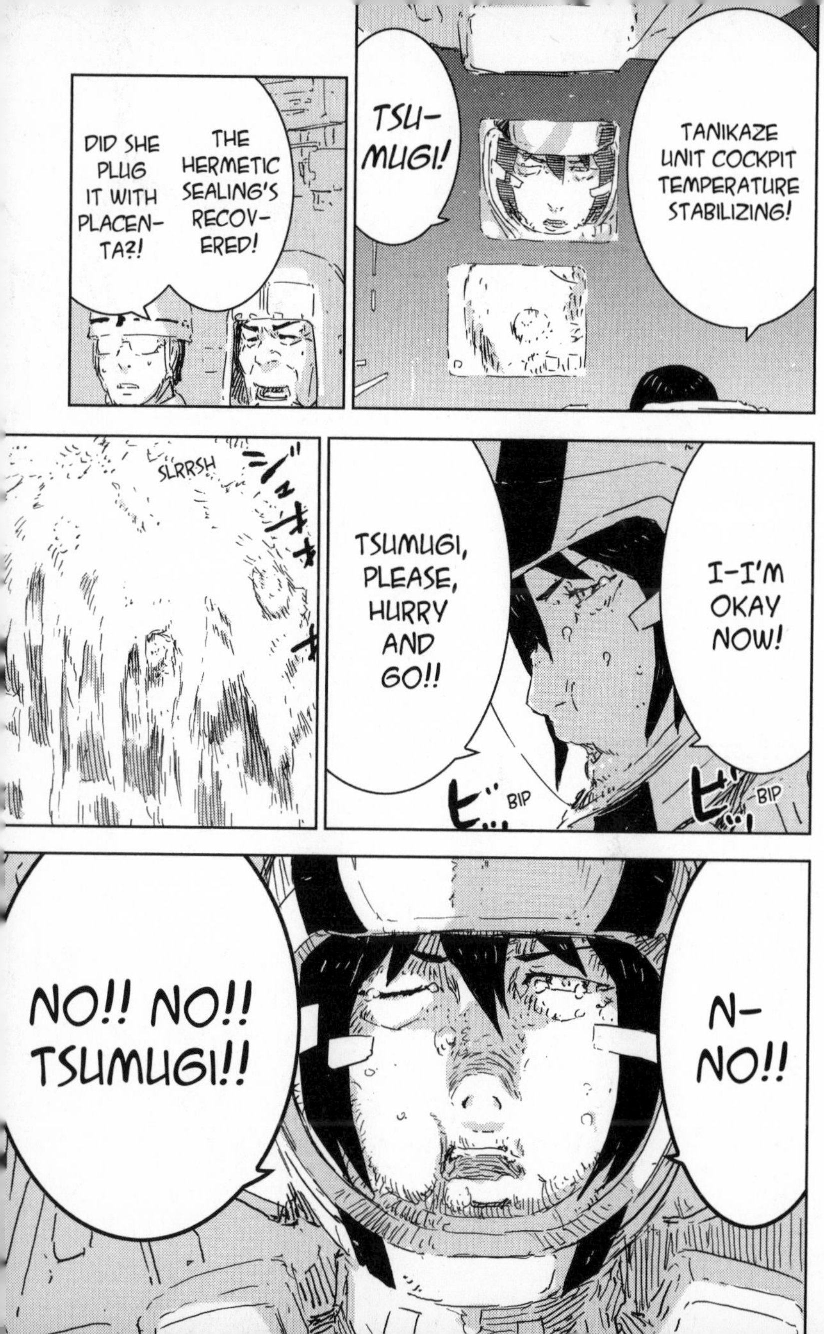
TANIKAZE UNIT COCKPIT TEMPERATURE STABILIZING!
TSU-MUGI!
THE HERMETIC SEALING'S RECOV-ERED!
DID SHE PLUG IT WITH PLACEN-TA?!
I-I'M OKAY NOW!
ピッ BIP
TSUMUGI, PLEASE, HURRY AND GO!!
ピッ BIP
SLRRSH
N-NO!!
NO!! NO!! TSUMUGI!!

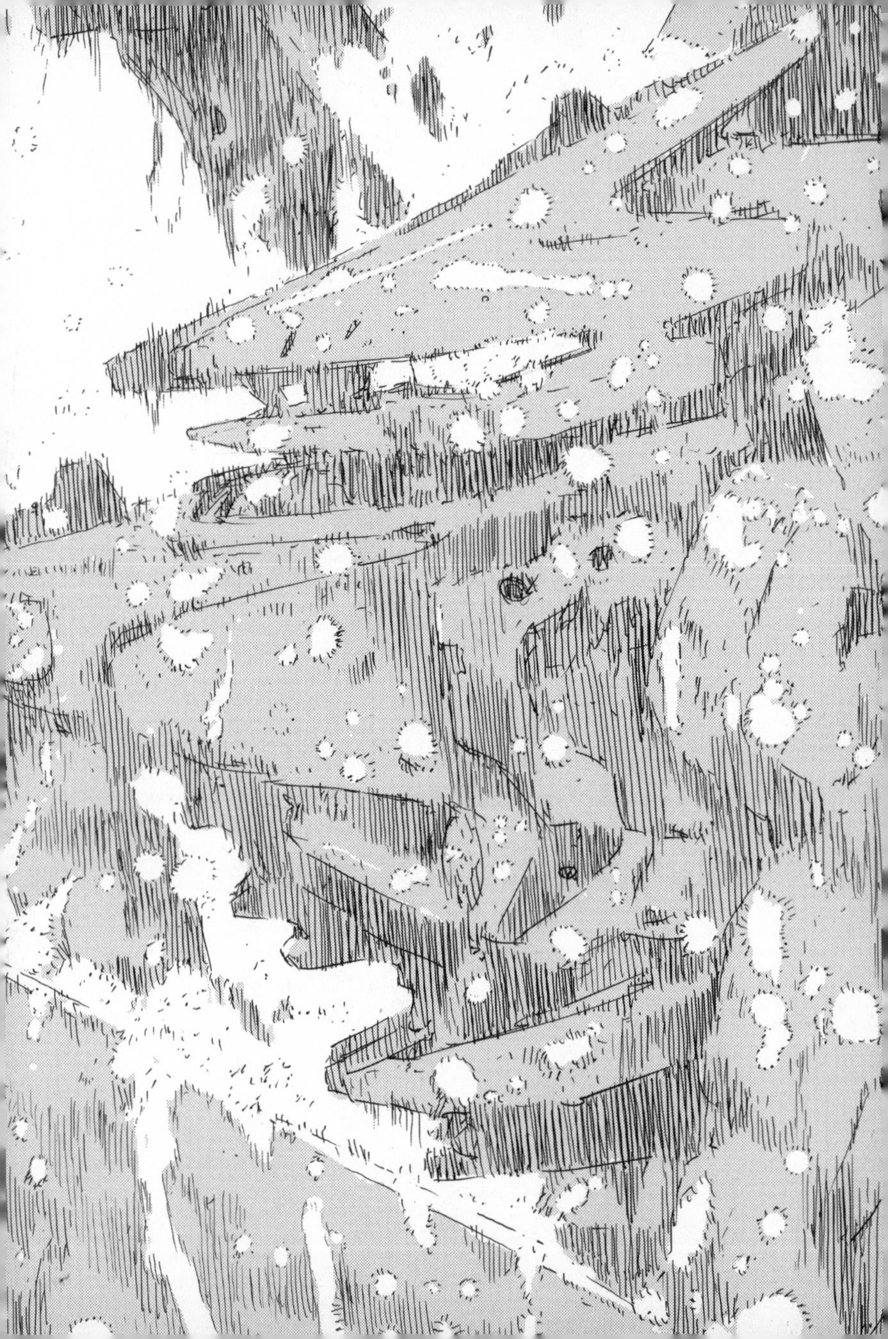

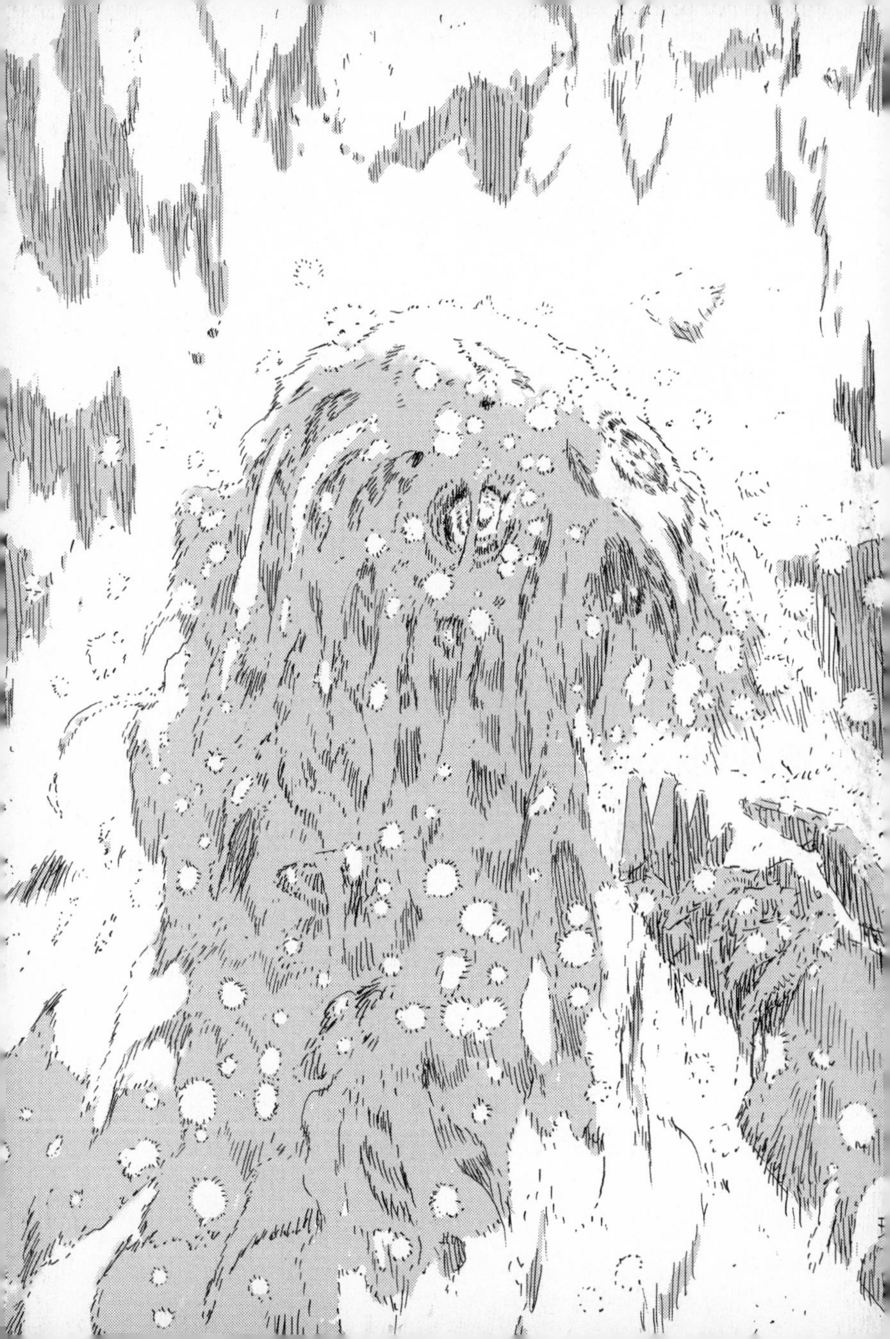

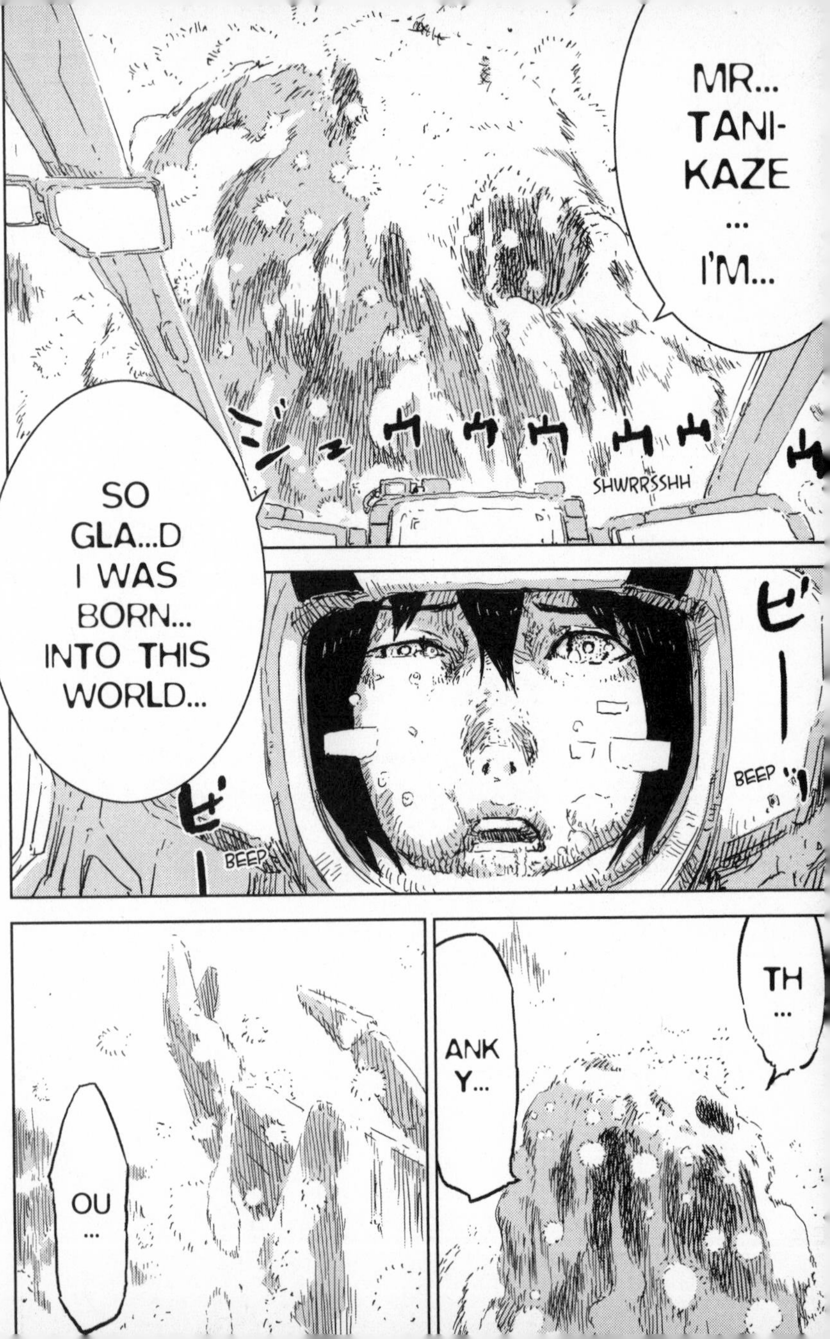
MR... TANI-KAZE ... I'M...
SO GLA...D I WAS BORN... INTO THIS WORLD...
SHWRRSSHH
ビー
BEEP
ビー
BEEP
TH ...
ANK Y...
OU ...

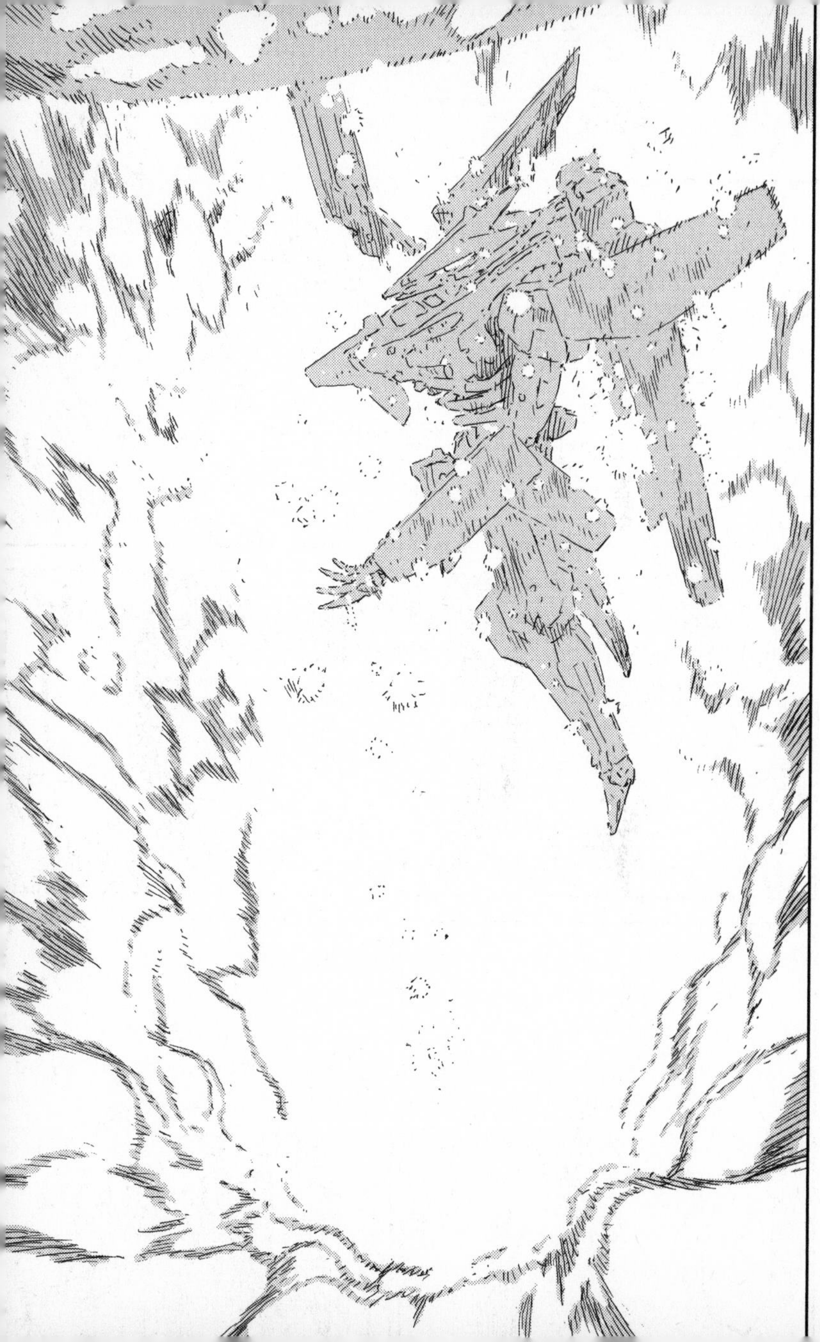

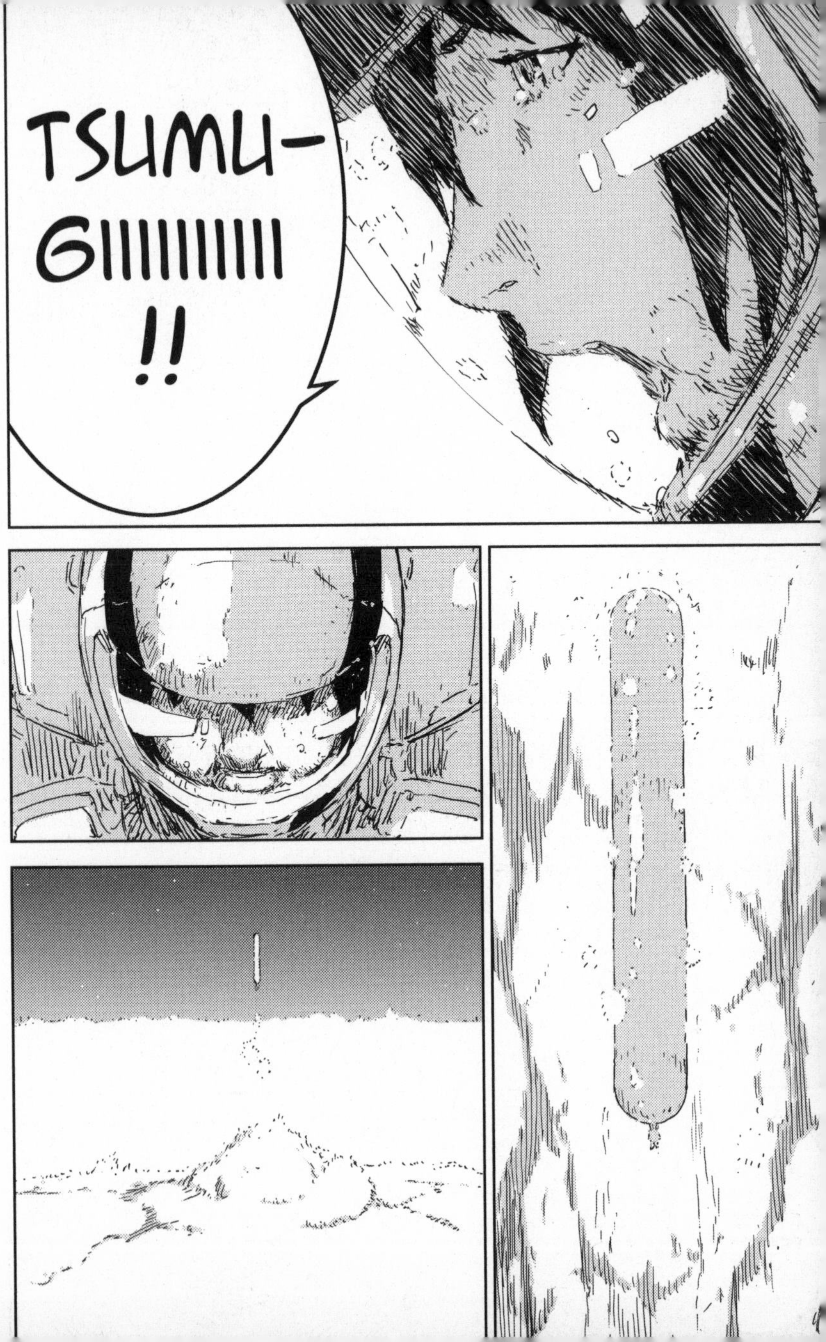
TSUMU-GIIIIIIIIIII!!

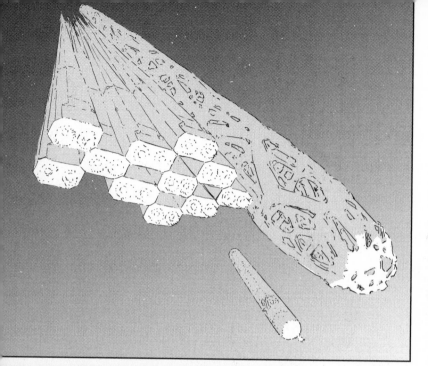

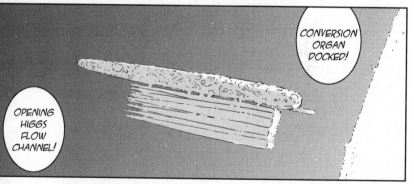

CONVERSION ORGAN DOCKED!

OPENING HIGGS FLOW CHANNEL!

GRAVITON RADIAL EMITTER IS READY TO FIRE!!

KWEEM

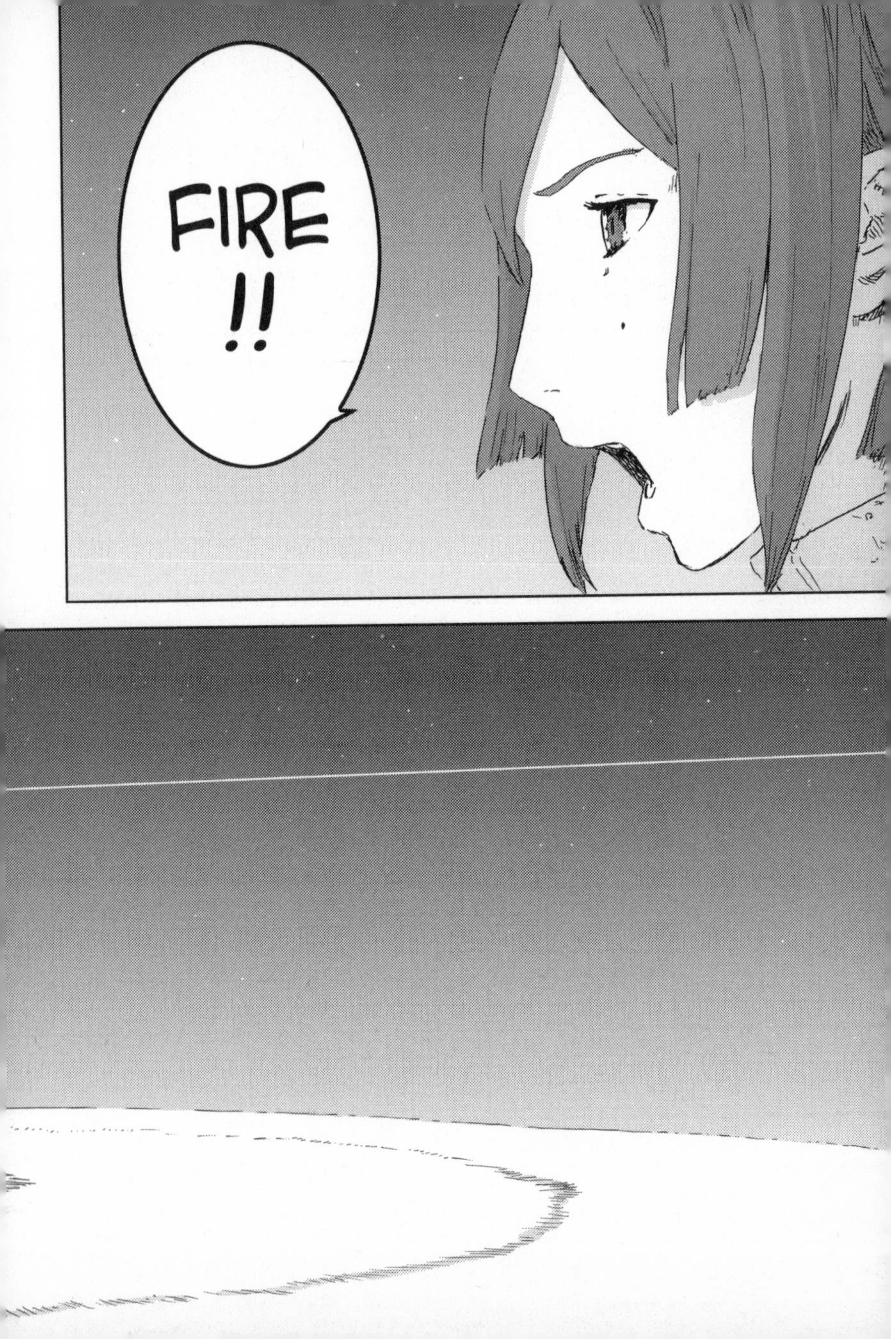
FIRE !!

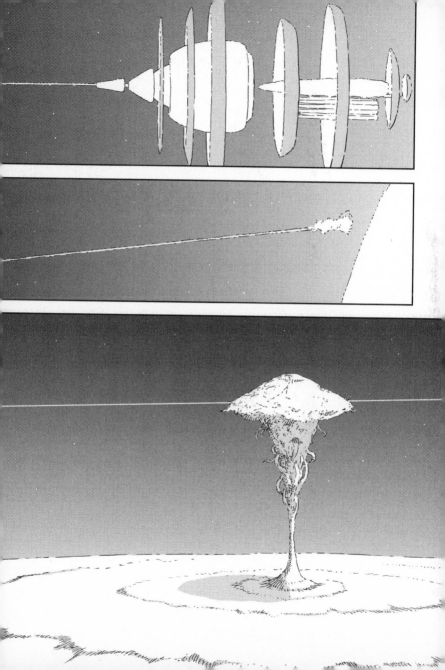

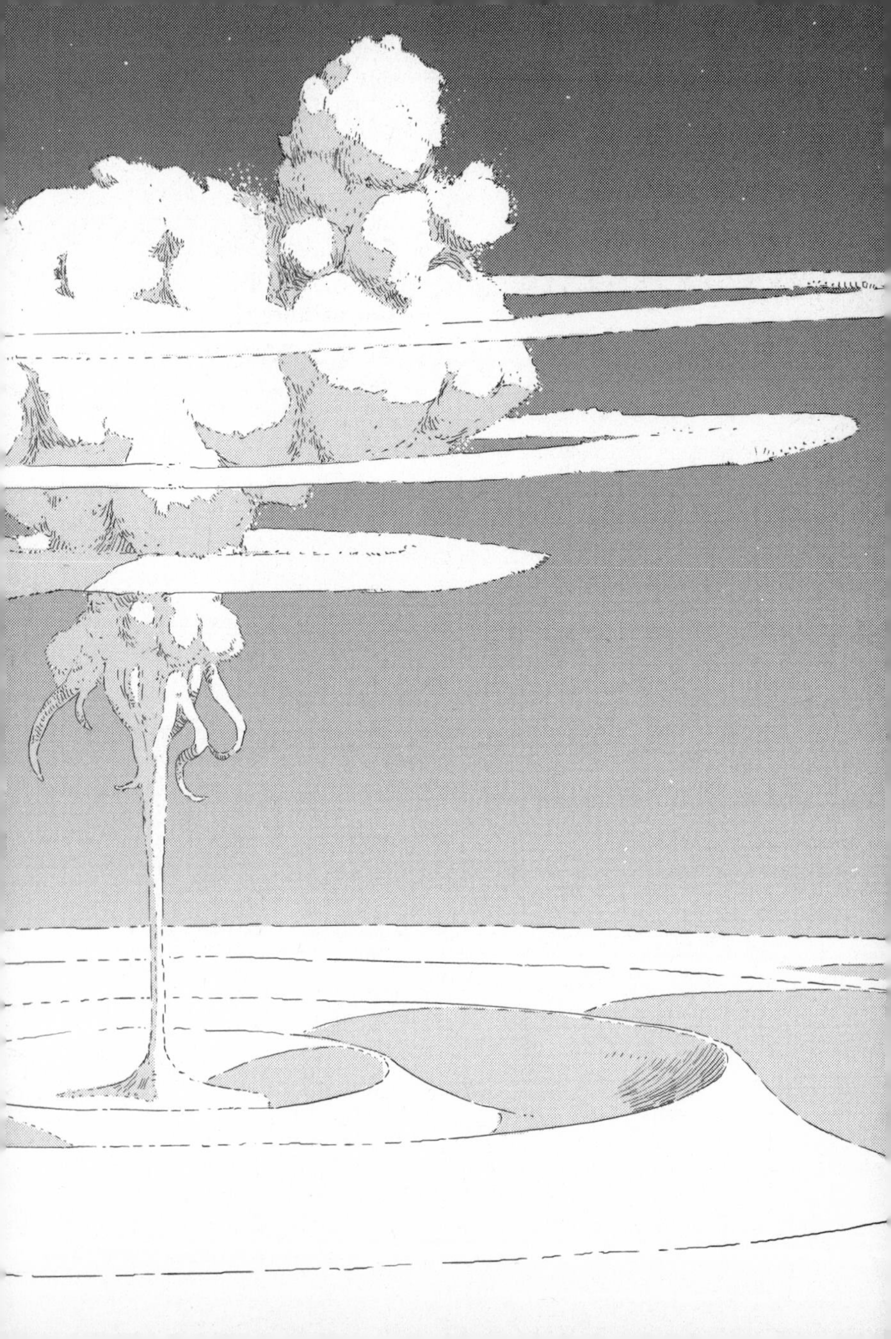

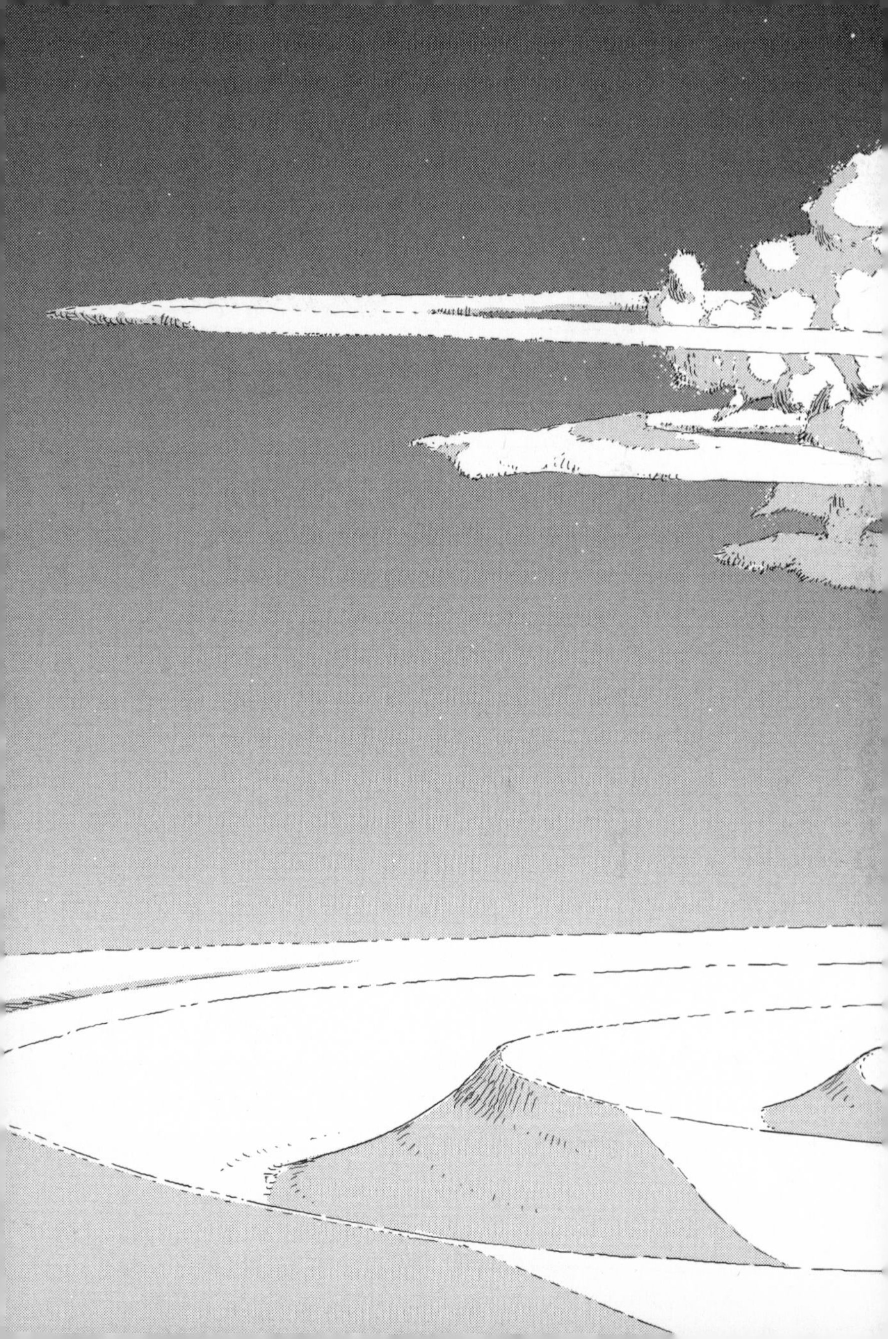

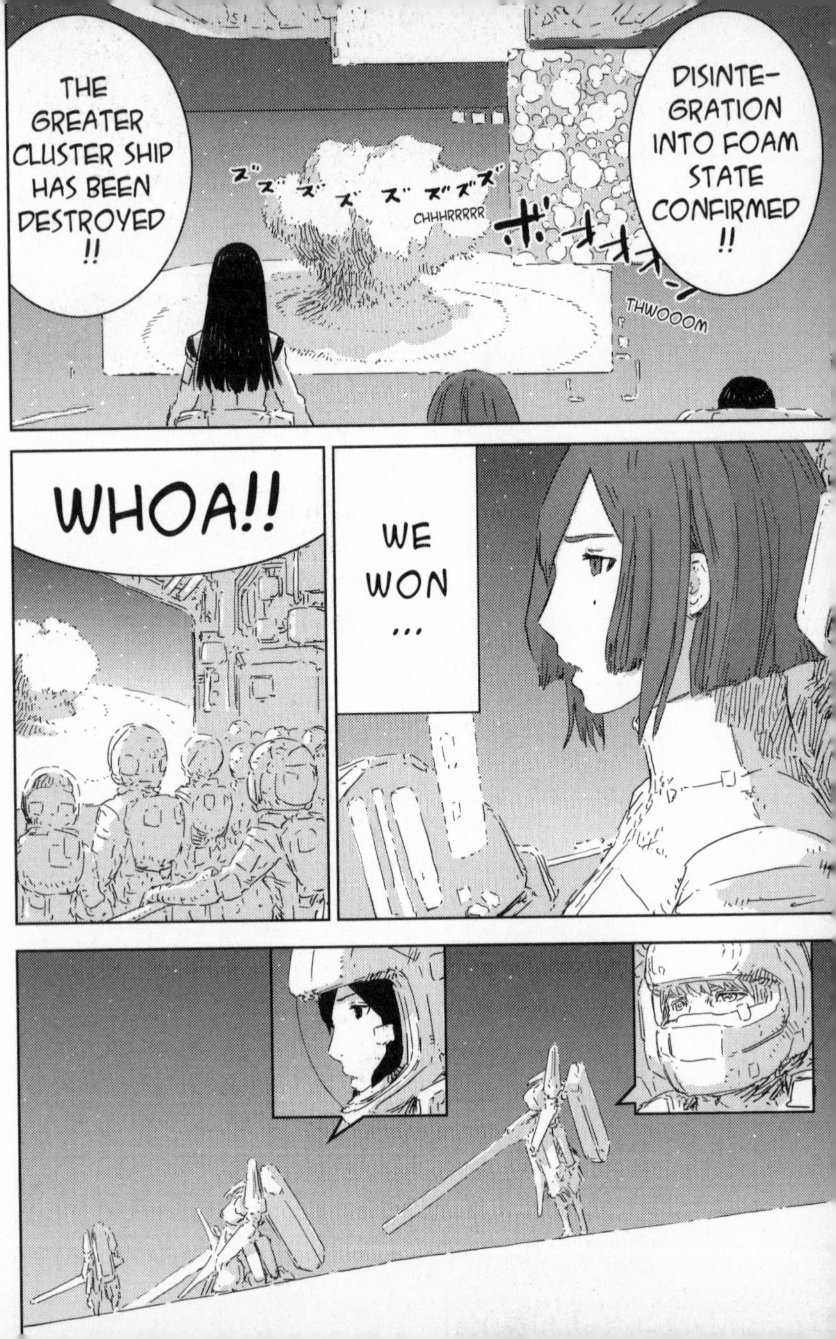
DISINTE-GRATION INTO FOAM STATE CONFIRMED !!
THWOOOM
CHHHRRRR
THE GREATER CLUSTER SHIP HAS BEEN DESTROYED !!
WE WON ...
WHOA!!

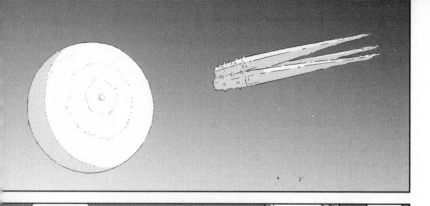

THE GREATER CLUSTER SHIP IS VANISHING ...

AWE-SOME !!

YEAH !

IZANA, WE DID IT!

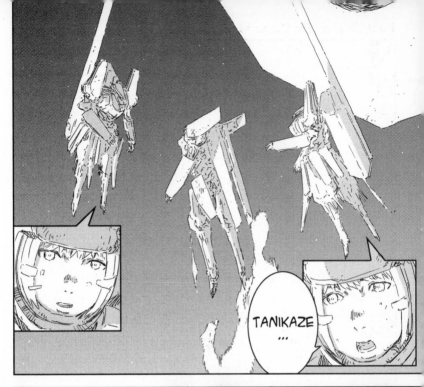

TANIKAZE
...

I COULDN'T PROTECT TSUMUGI !!

Final Chapter: The Gauna War's Conclusion

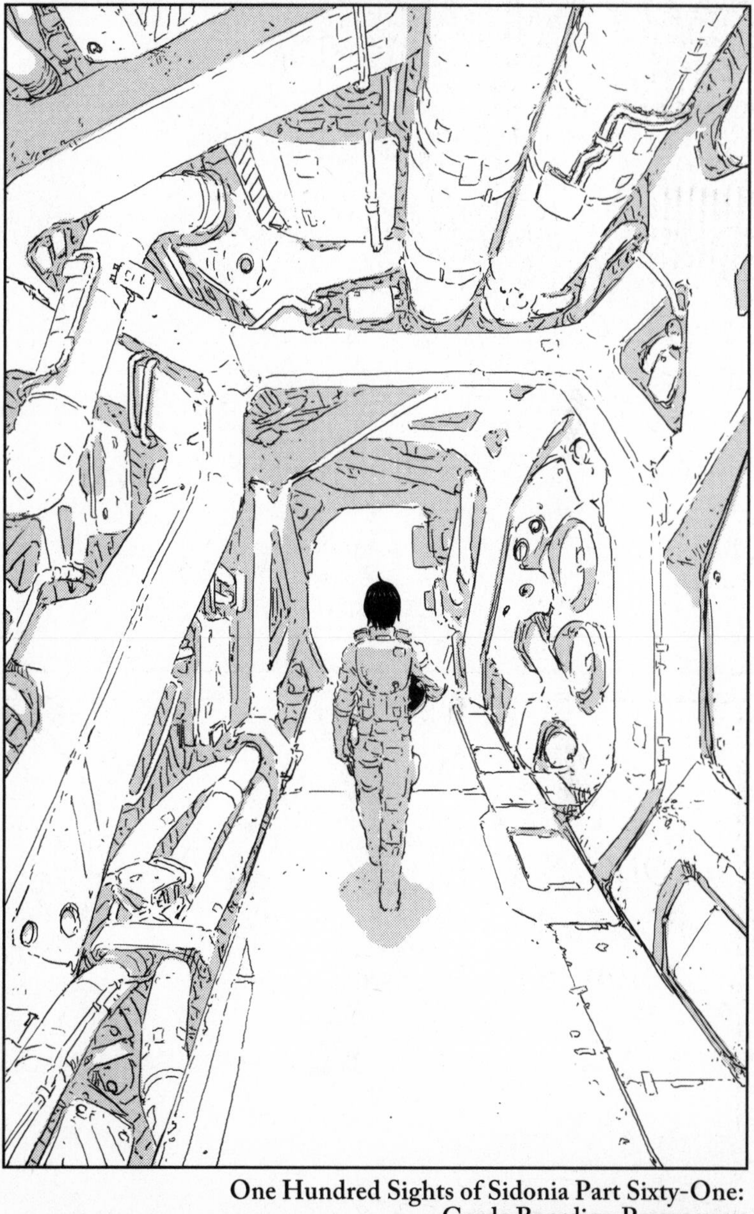

One Hundred Sights of Sidonia Part Sixty-One:
Garde Boarding Passageway

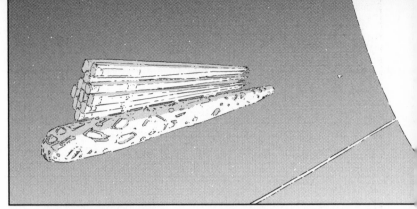

SIDONIA
...

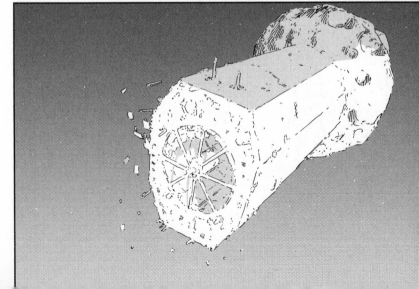

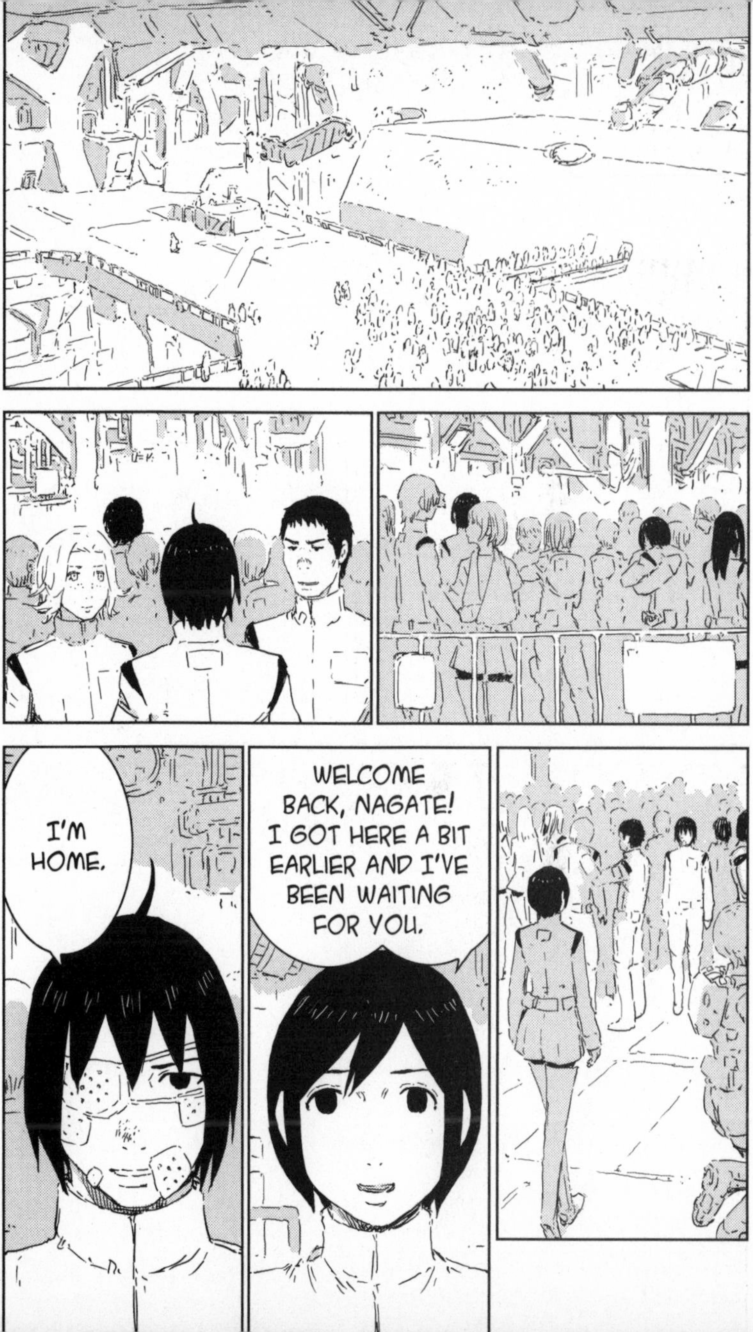
WELCOME BACK, NAGATE! I GOT HERE A BIT EARLIER AND I'VE BEEN WAITING FOR YOU.
I'M HOME.

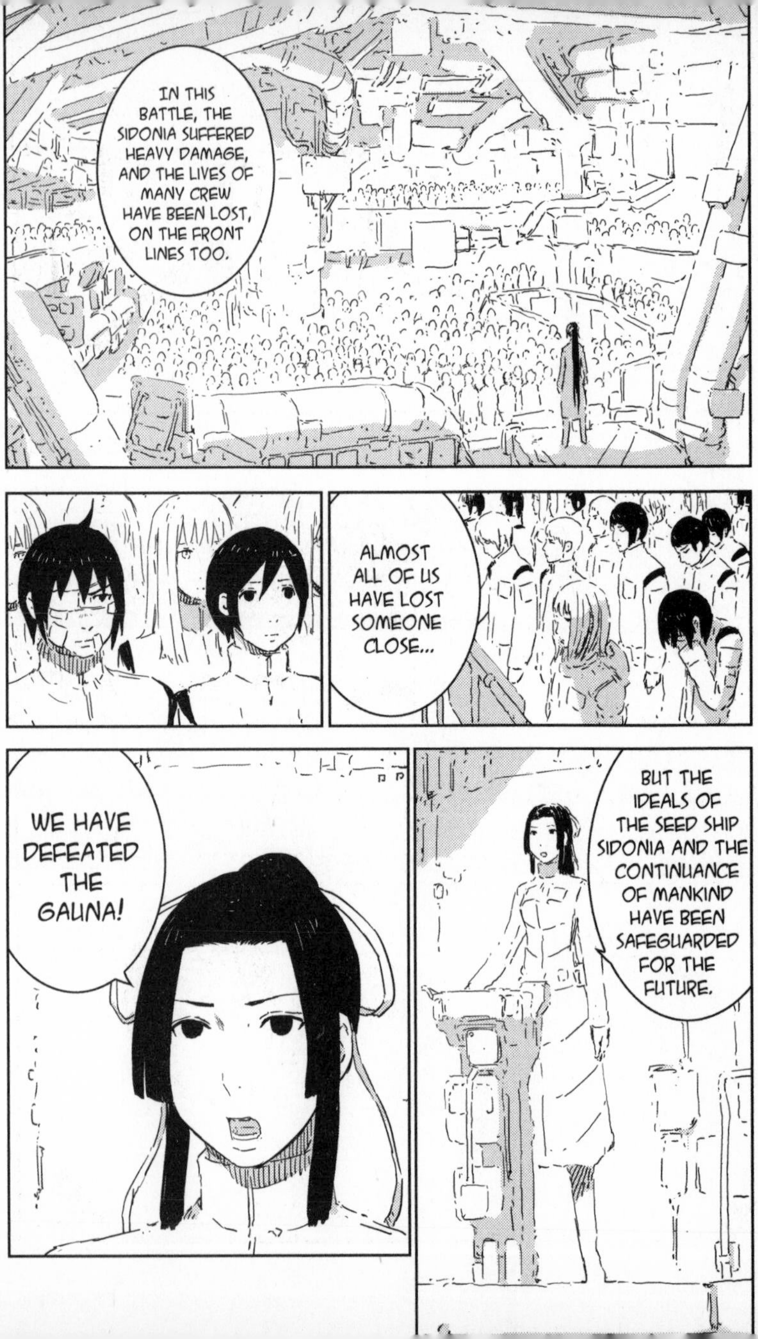
IN THIS BATTLE, THE SIDONIA SUFFERED HEAVY DAMAGE, AND THE LIVES OF MANY CREW HAVE BEEN LOST, ON THE FRONT LINES TOO.
ALMOST ALL OF US HAVE LOST SOMEONE CLOSE...
BUT THE IDEALS OF THE SEED SHIP SIDONIA AND THE CONTINUANCE OF MANKIND HAVE BEEN SAFEGUARDED FOR THE FUTURE.
WE HAVE DEFEATED THE GAUNA!

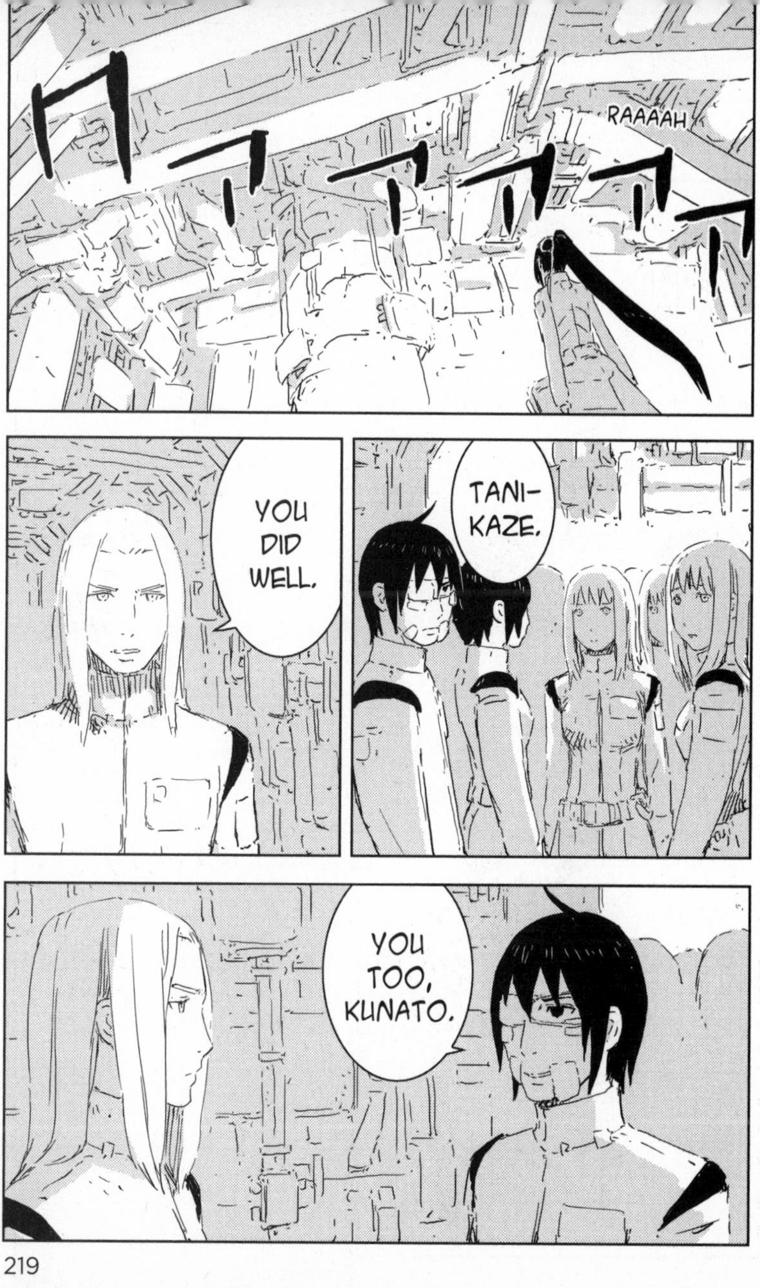
RAAAAH
TANI-KAZE.
YOU DID WELL.
YOU TOO, KUNATO.

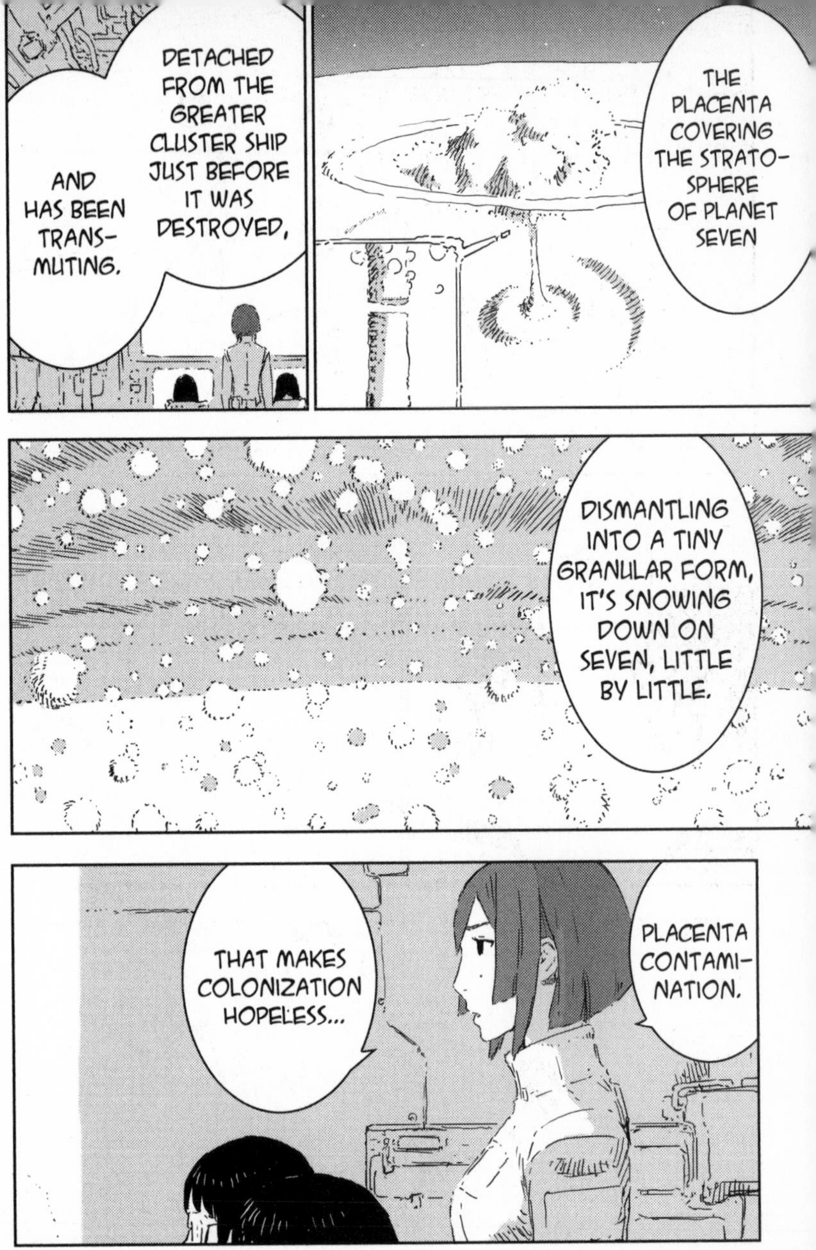

THE PLACENTA COVERING THE STRATO-SPHERE OF PLANET SEVEN
DETACHED FROM THE GREATER CLUSTER SHIP JUST BEFORE IT WAS DESTROYED,
AND HAS BEEN TRANS-MUTING.
DISMANTLING INTO A TINY GRANULAR FORM, IT'S SNOWING DOWN ON SEVEN, LITTLE BY LITTLE.
PLACENTA CONTAMI-NATION.
THAT MAKES COLONIZATION HOPELESS...

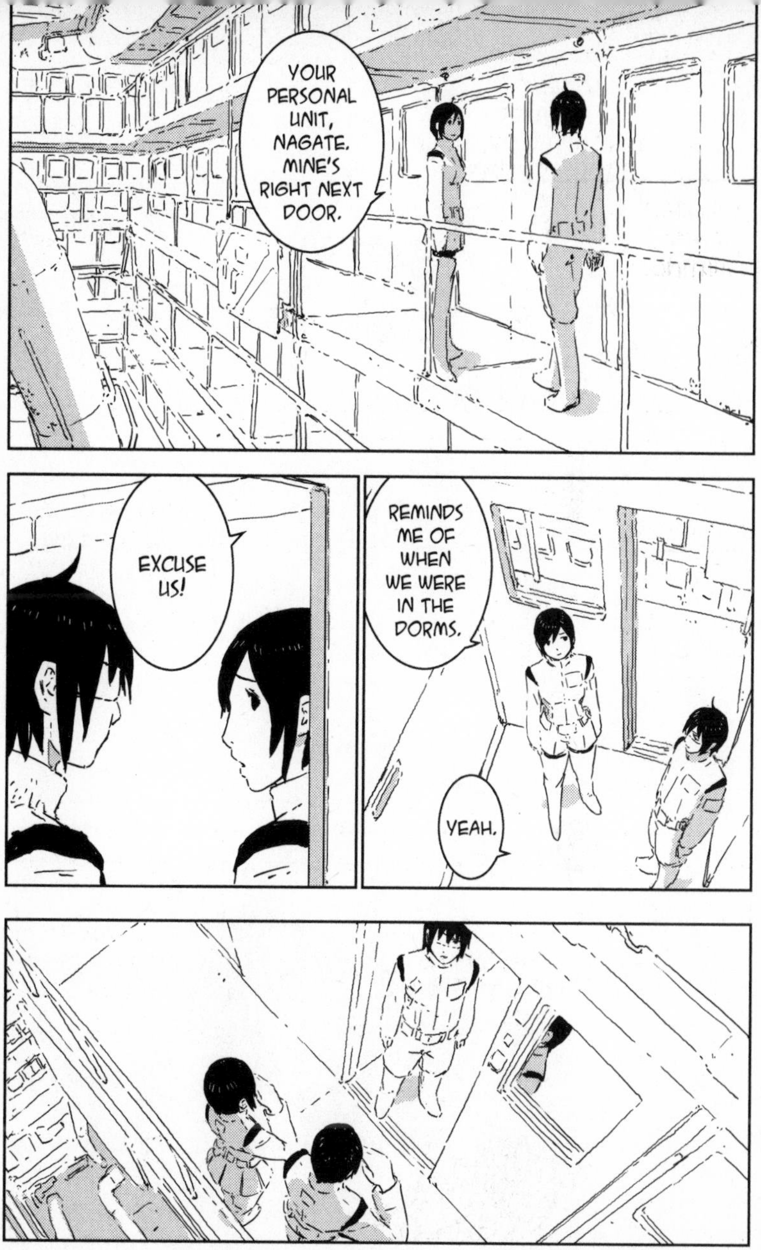
YOUR PERSONAL UNIT, NAGATE. MINE'S RIGHT NEXT DOOR.
REMINDS ME OF WHEN WE WERE IN THE DORMS.
YEAH.
EXCUSE US!

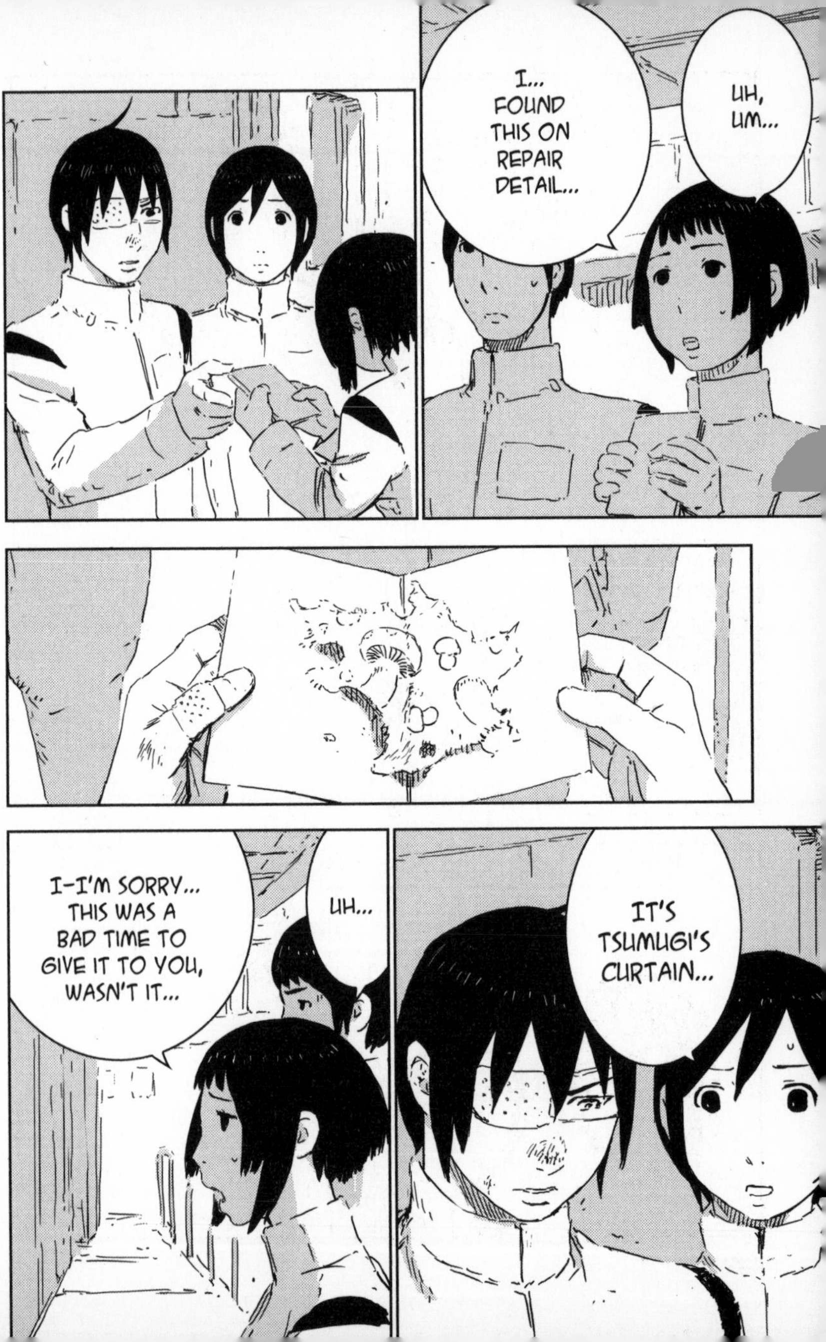
UH, UM...
I... FOUND THIS ON REPAIR DETAIL...
IT'S TSUMUGI'S CURTAIN...
UH...
I-I'M SORRY... THIS WAS A BAD TIME TO GIVE IT TO YOU, WASN'T IT...

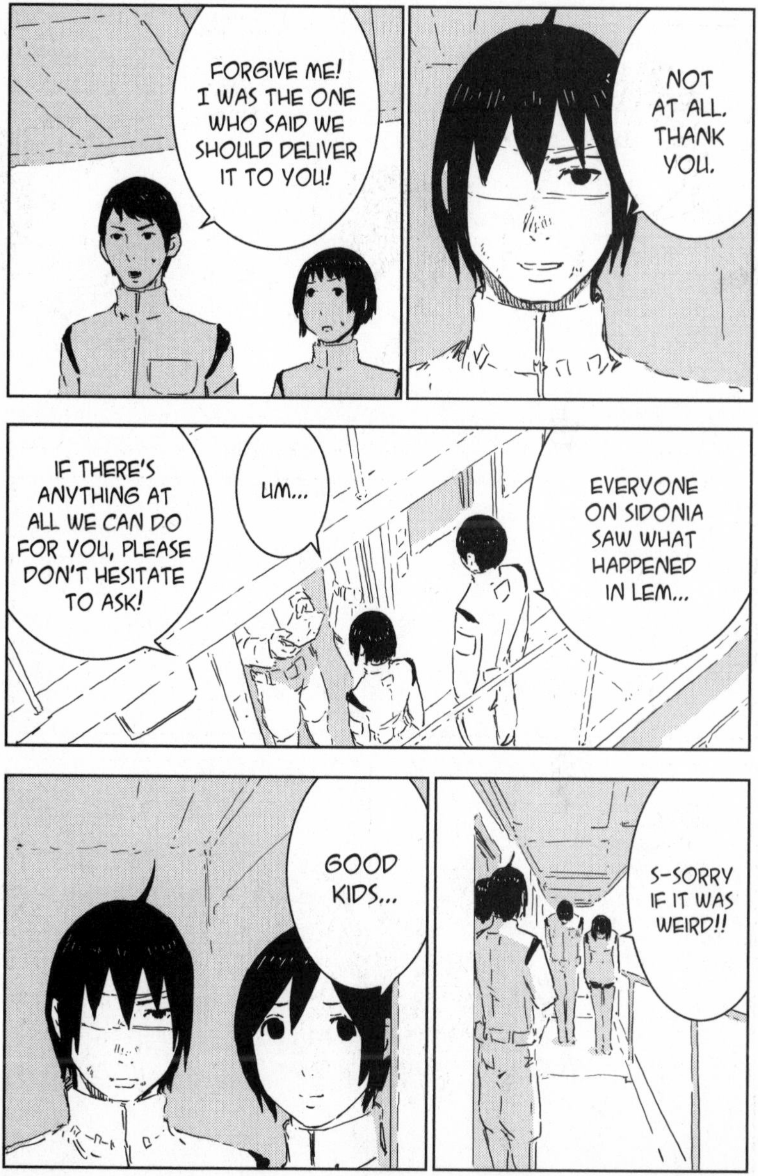
NOT AT ALL. THANK YOU.
FORGIVE ME! I WAS THE ONE WHO SAID WE SHOULD DELIVER IT TO YOU!
EVERYONE ON SIDONIA SAW WHAT HAPPENED IN LEM...
UM...
IF THERE'S ANYTHING AT ALL WE CAN DO FOR YOU, PLEASE DON'T HESITATE TO ASK!
S-SORRY IF IT WAS WEIRD!!
GOOD KIDS...

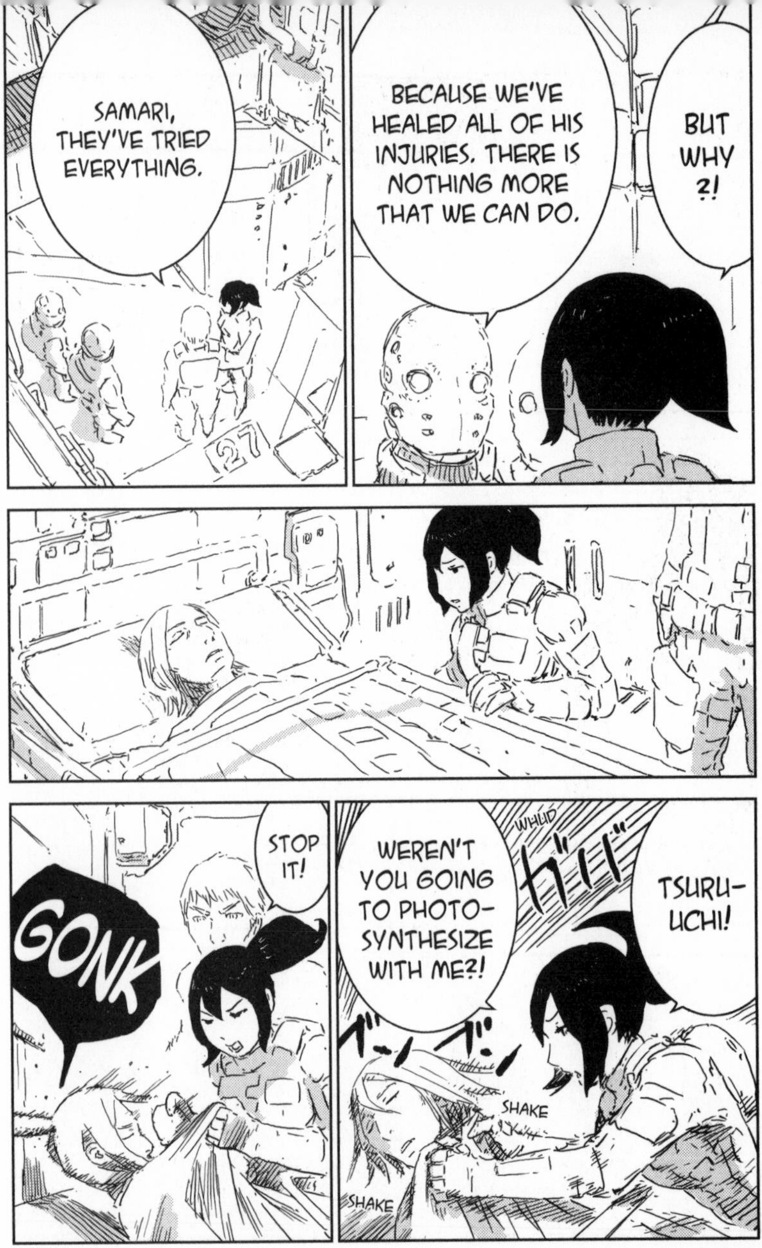
BUT WHY ?!
BECAUSE WE'VE HEALED ALL OF HIS INJURIES. THERE IS NOTHING MORE THAT WE CAN DO.
SAMARI, THEY'VE TRIED EVERYTHING.
TSURU-UCHI!
WHUD
WEREN'T YOU GOING TO PHOTO-SYNTHESIZE WITH ME?!
SHAKE
SHAKE
STOP IT!
GONK

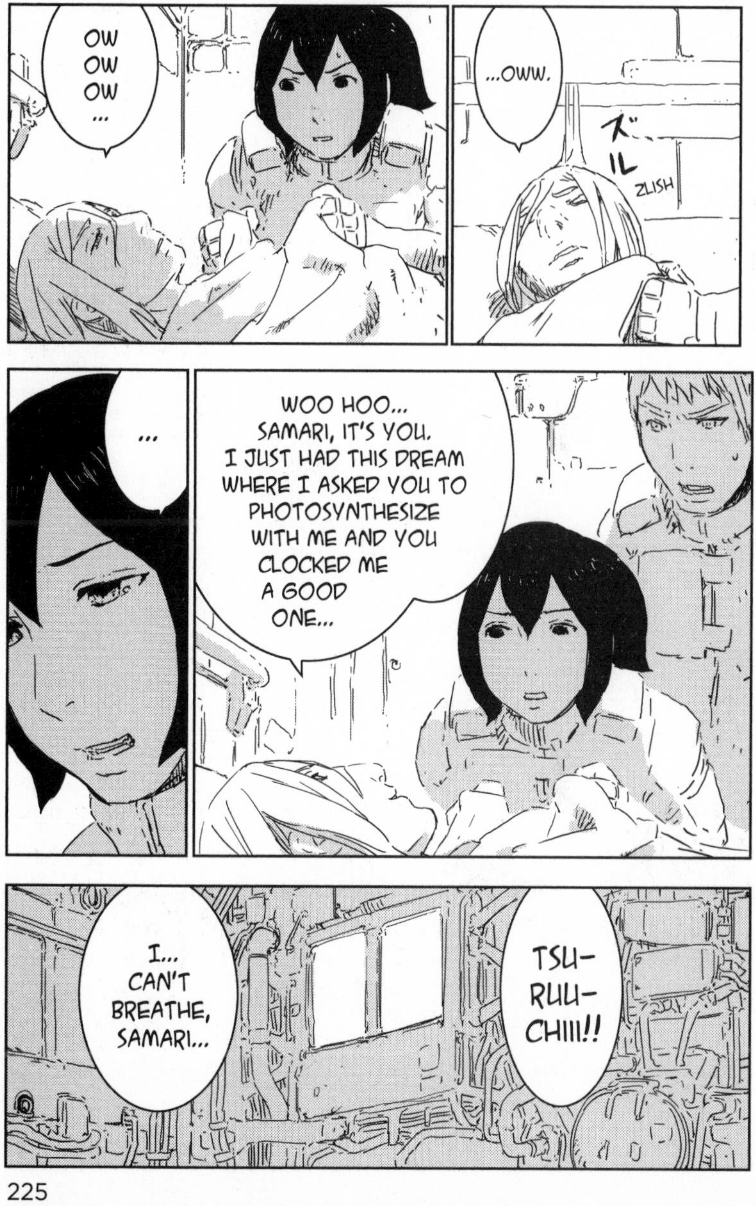
...OWW.
ズル
ZLISH
OW OW OW ...
WOO HOO... SAMARI, IT'S YOU. I JUST HAD THIS DREAM WHERE I ASKED YOU TO PHOTOSYNTHESIZE WITH ME AND YOU CLOCKED ME A GOOD ONE...
...
TSU-RUU-CHIII!!
I... CAN'T BREATHE, SAMARI...

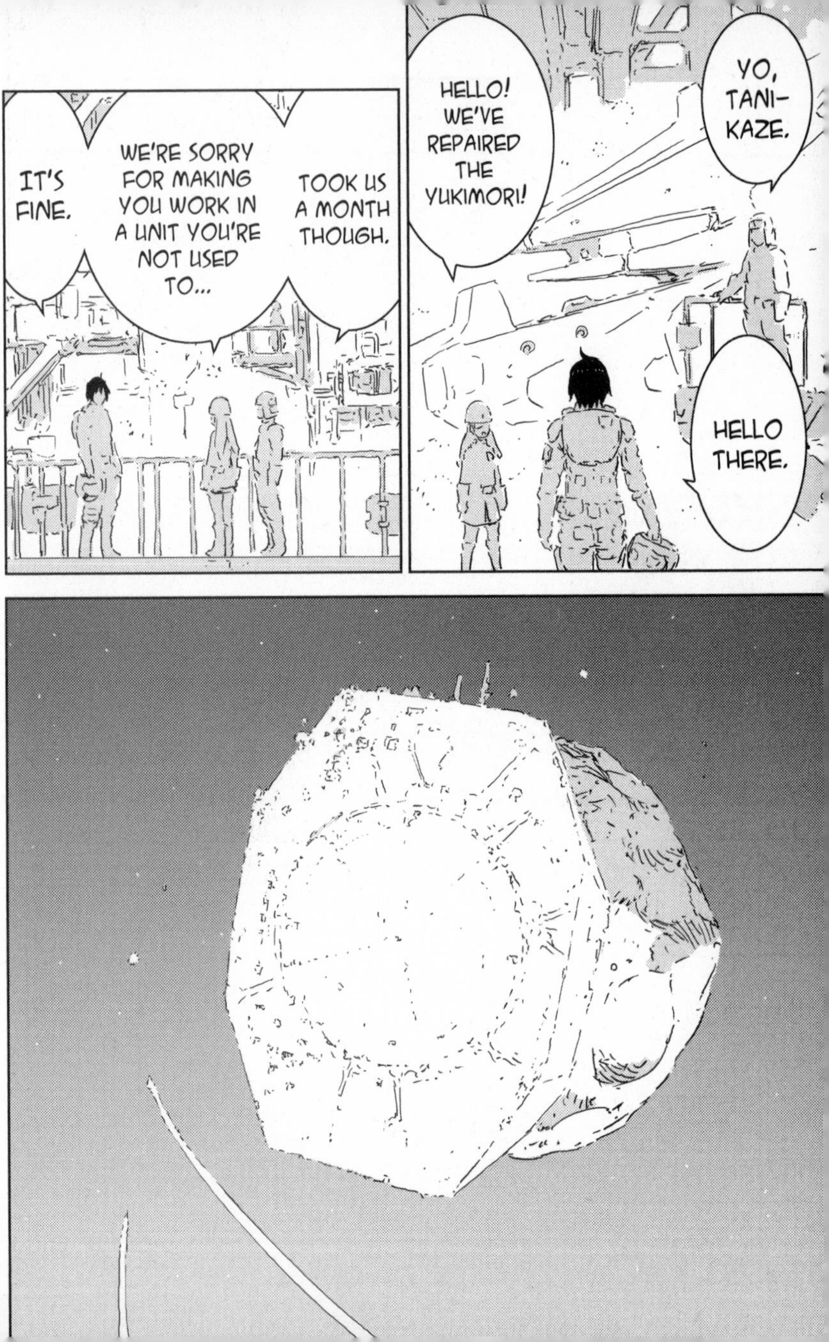
YO, TANI-KAZE.
HELLO! WE'VE REPAIRED THE YUKIMORI!
HELLO THERE.
TOOK US A MONTH THOUGH.
WE'RE SORRY FOR MAKING YOU WORK IN A UNIT YOU'RE NOT USED TO...
IT'S FINE.

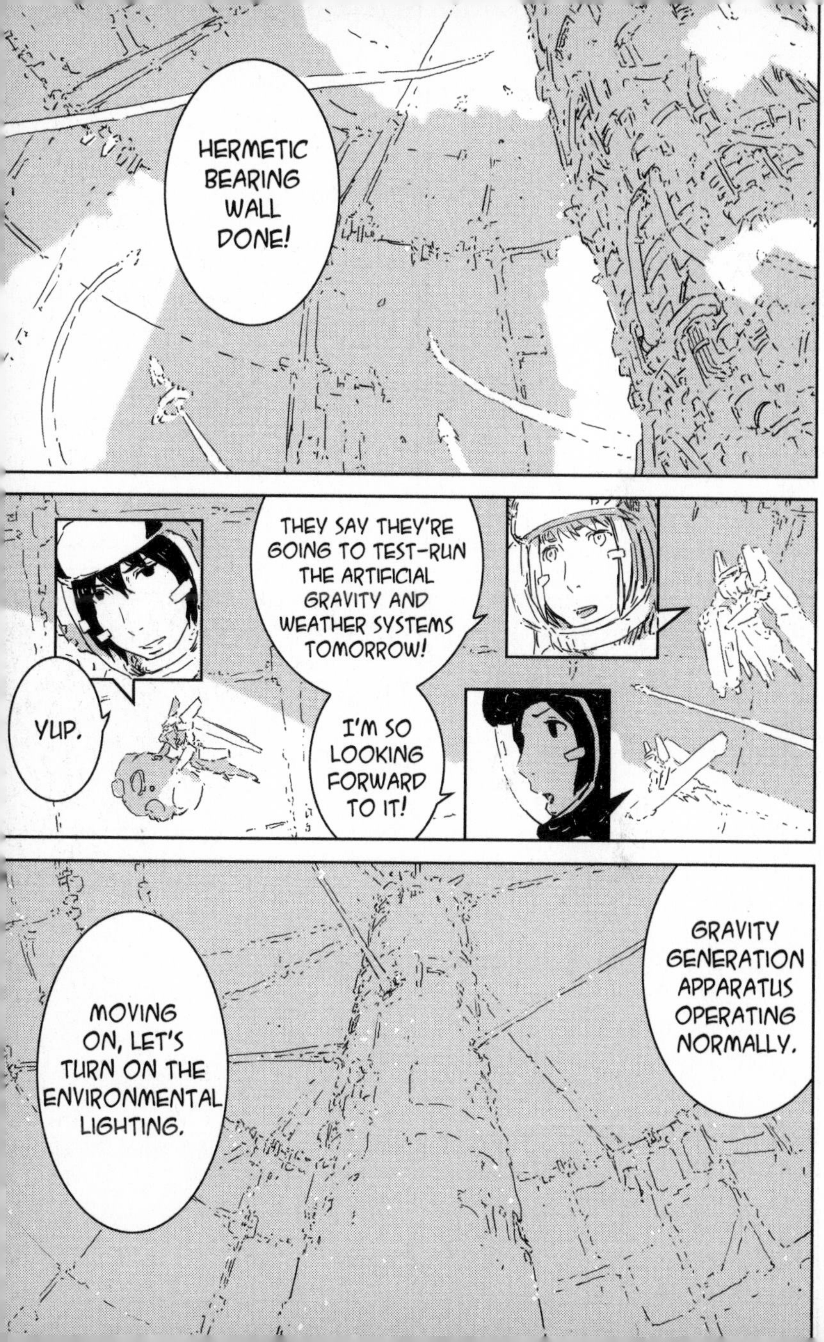
HERMETIC BEARING WALL DONE!
THEY SAY THEY'RE GOING TO TEST-RUN THE ARTIFICIAL GRAVITY AND WEATHER SYSTEMS TOMORROW!
I'M SO LOOKING FORWARD TO IT!
YUP.
GRAVITY GENERATION APPARATUS OPERATING NORMALLY.
MOVING ON, LET'S TURN ON THE ENVIRONMENTAL LIGHTING.

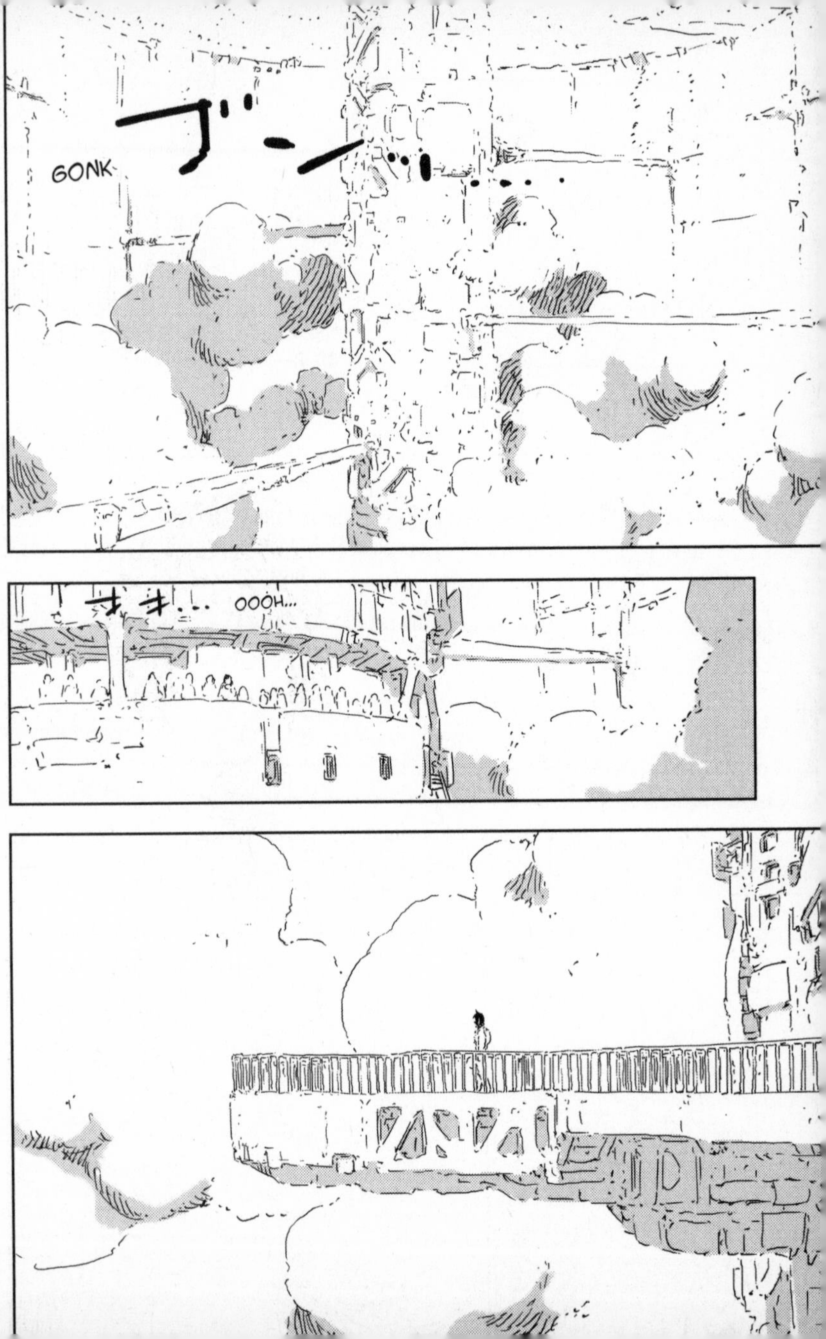
GONK
OOOH...

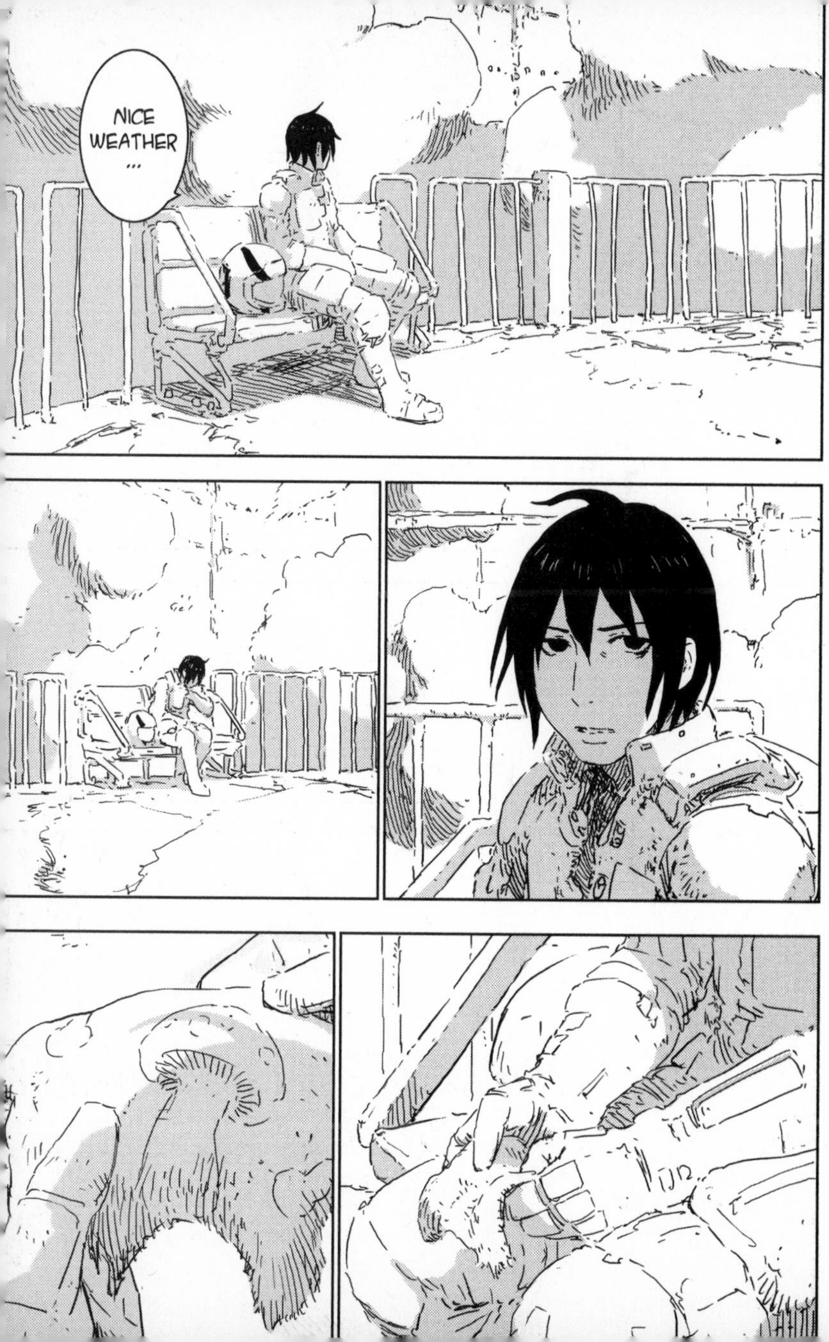
NICE WEATHER ...

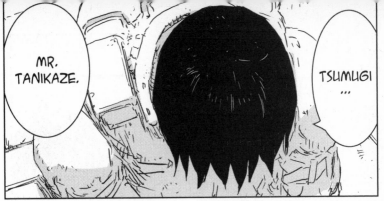

MR. TANIKAZE.

TSUMUGI...

ARE YOU OKAY?

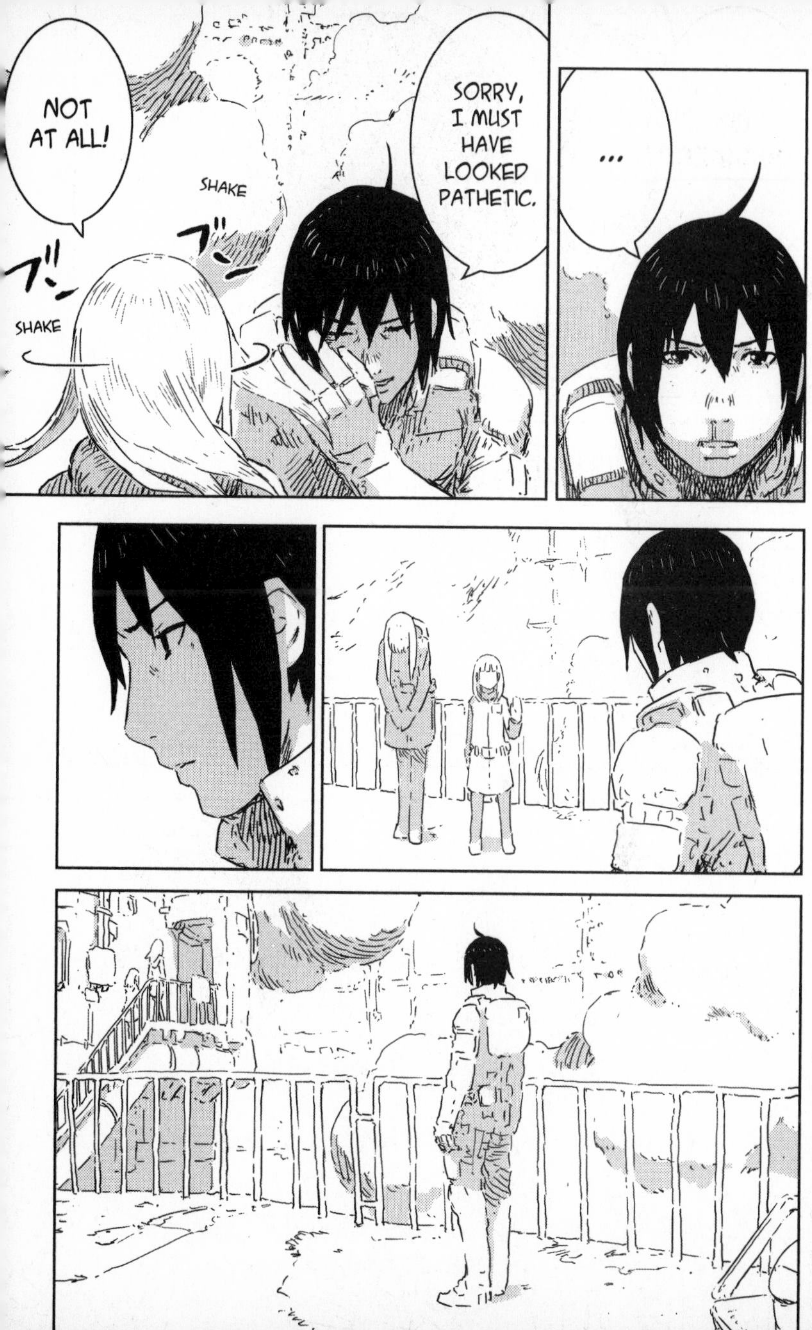
...
SORRY, I MUST HAVE LOOKED PATHETIC.
NOT AT ALL!
SHAKE
SHAKE

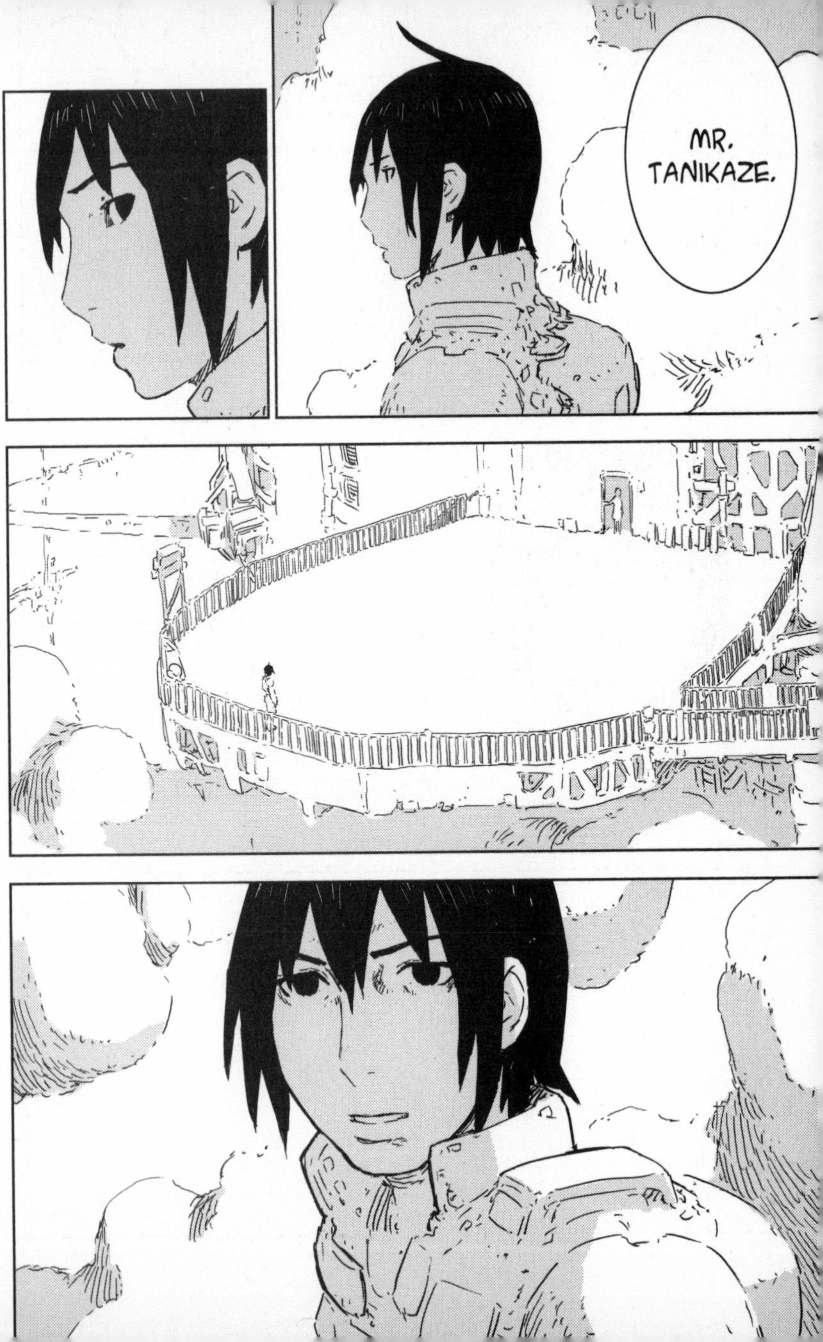
MR. TANIKAZE.

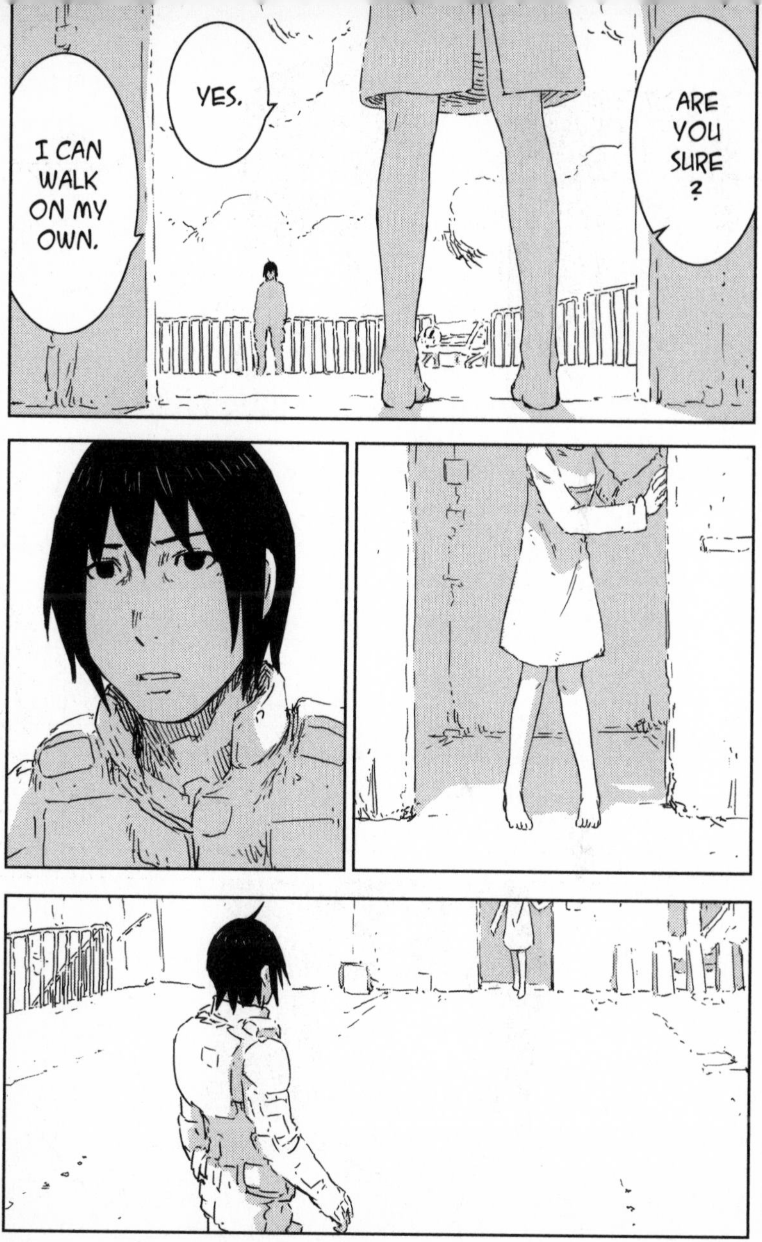
ARE YOU SURE?
YES.
I CAN WALK ON MY OWN.

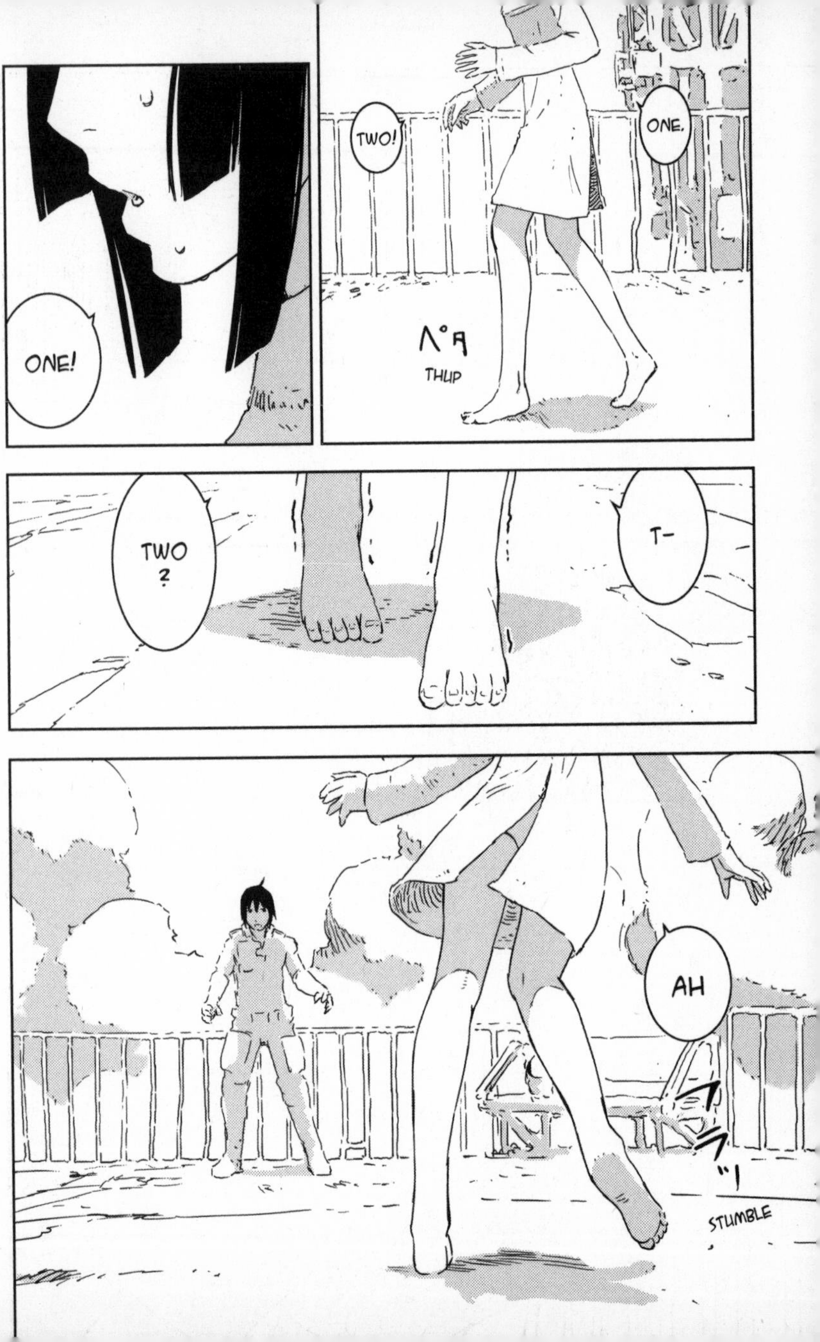
ONE.
TWO!
ペタ
THUP
ONE!
T-
TWO ?
AH
STUMBLE

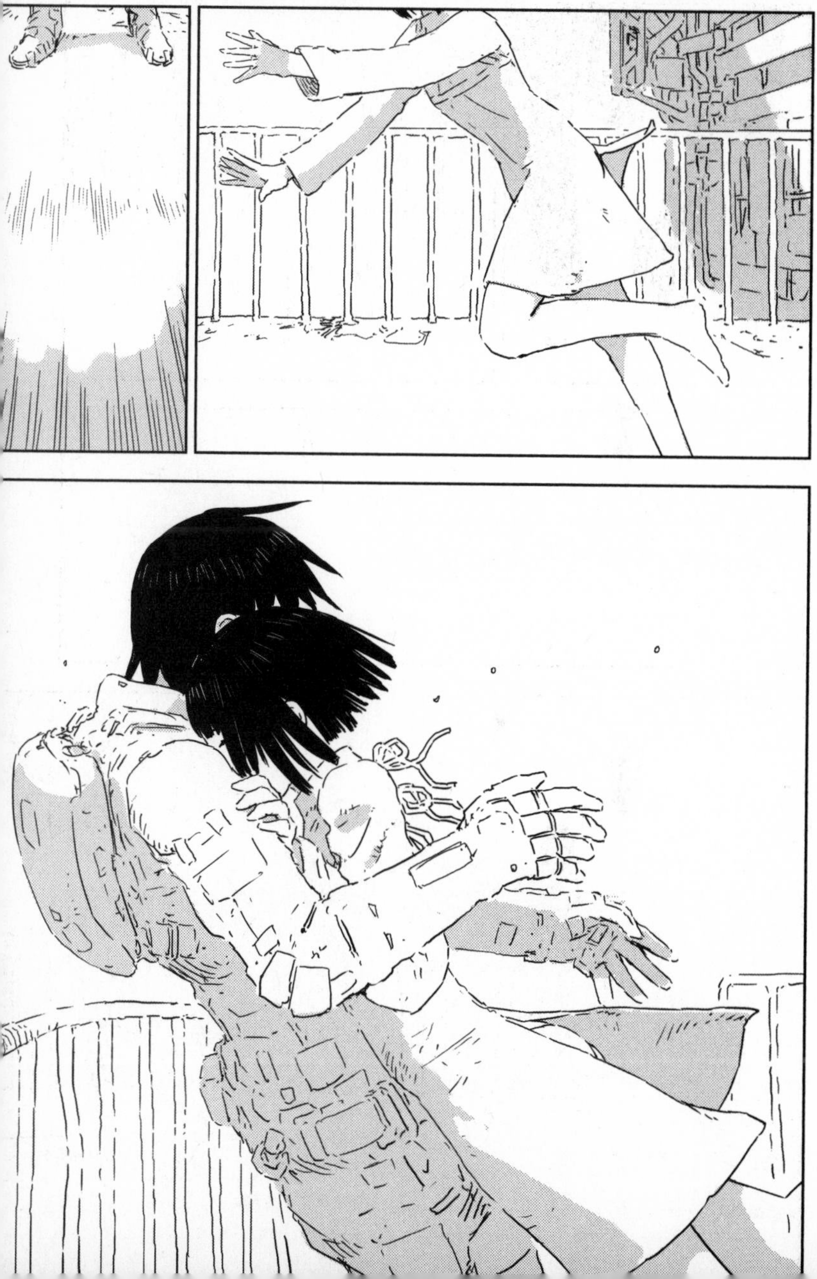

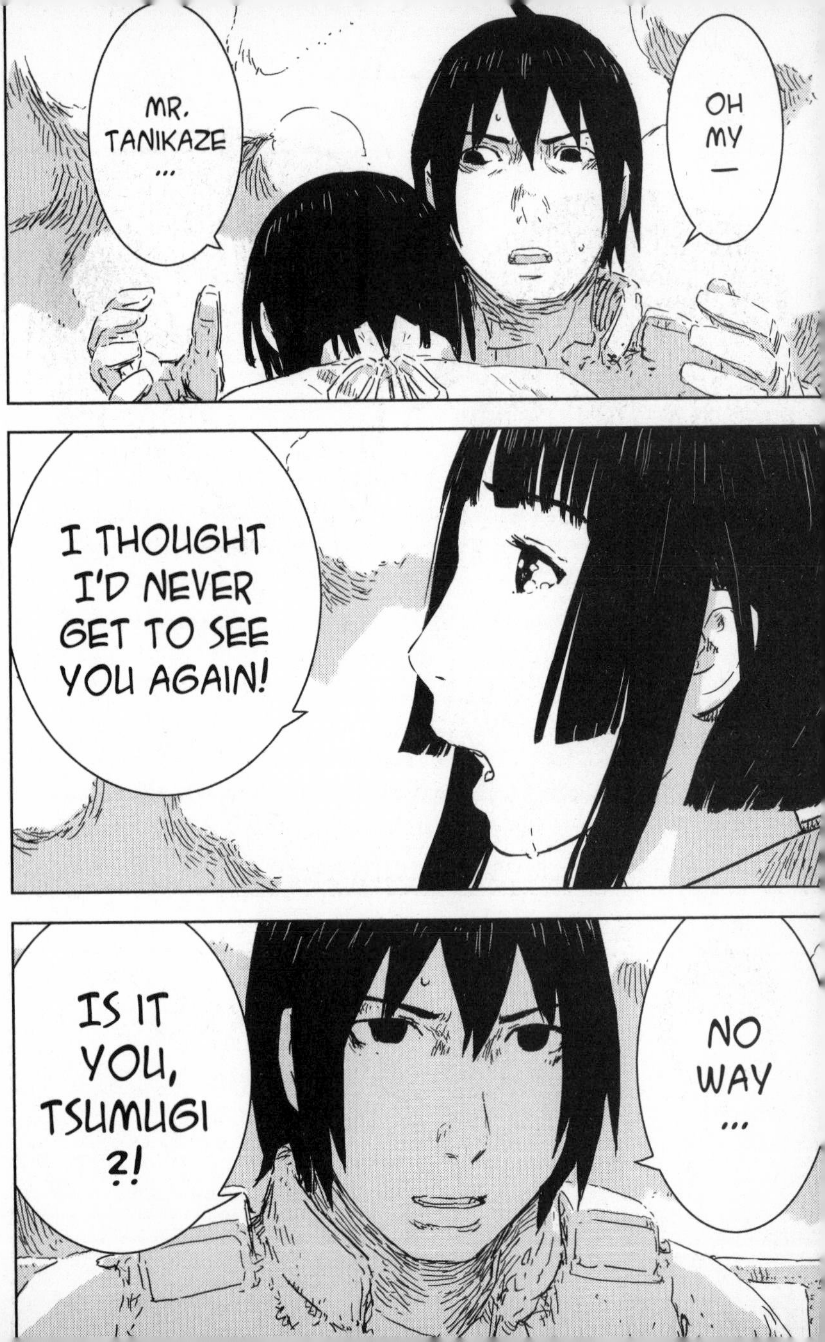
OH MY —
MR. TANIKAZE ...
I THOUGHT I'D NEVER GET TO SEE YOU AGAIN!
NO WAY ...
IS IT YOU, TSUMUGI ?!

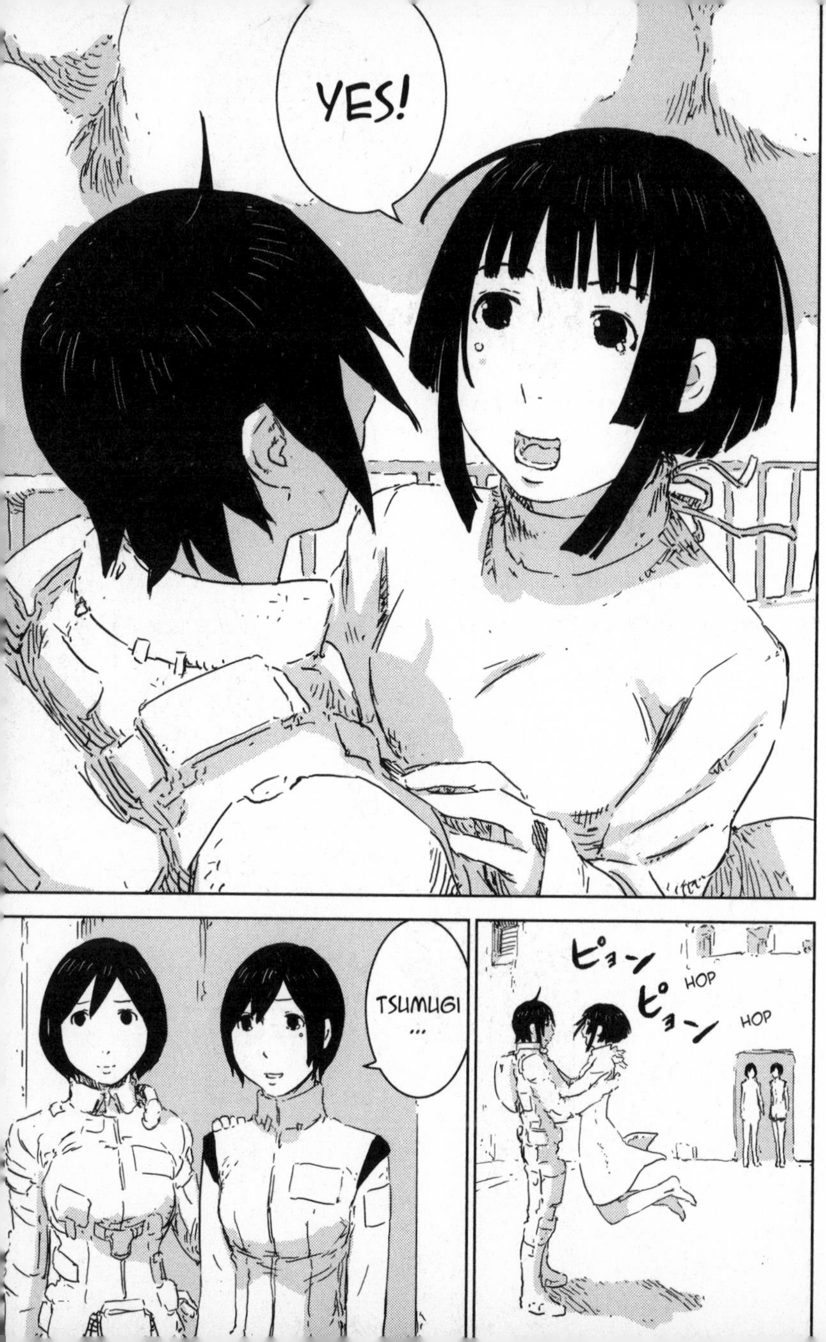
YES!
ピョン
HOP
ピョン
HOP
TSUMUGI
...

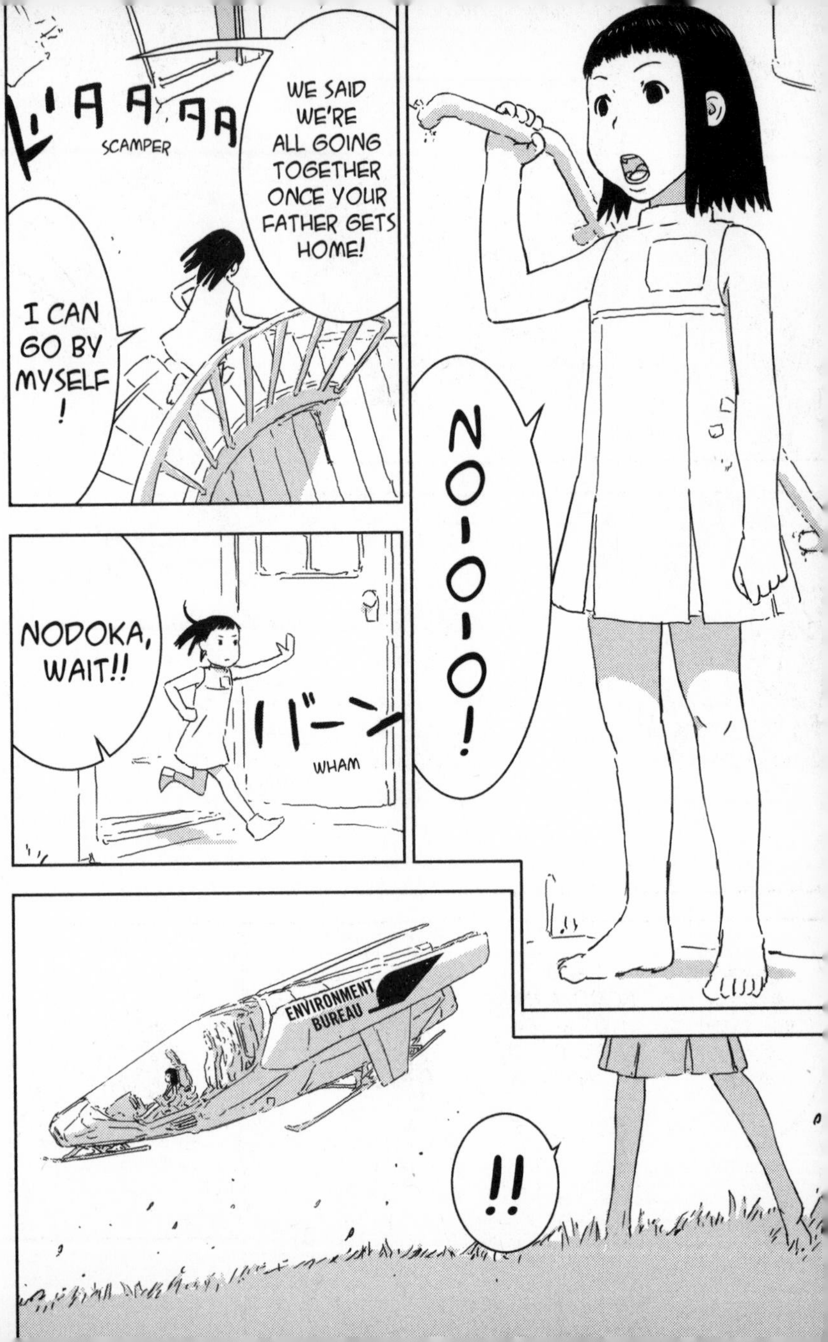
NO-O-O-O!
WE SAID WE'RE ALL GOING TOGETHER ONCE YOUR FATHER GETS HOME!
SCAMPER
I CAN GO BY MYSELF!
NODOKA, WAIT!!
バーン
WHAM
ENVIRONMENT BUREAU
!!

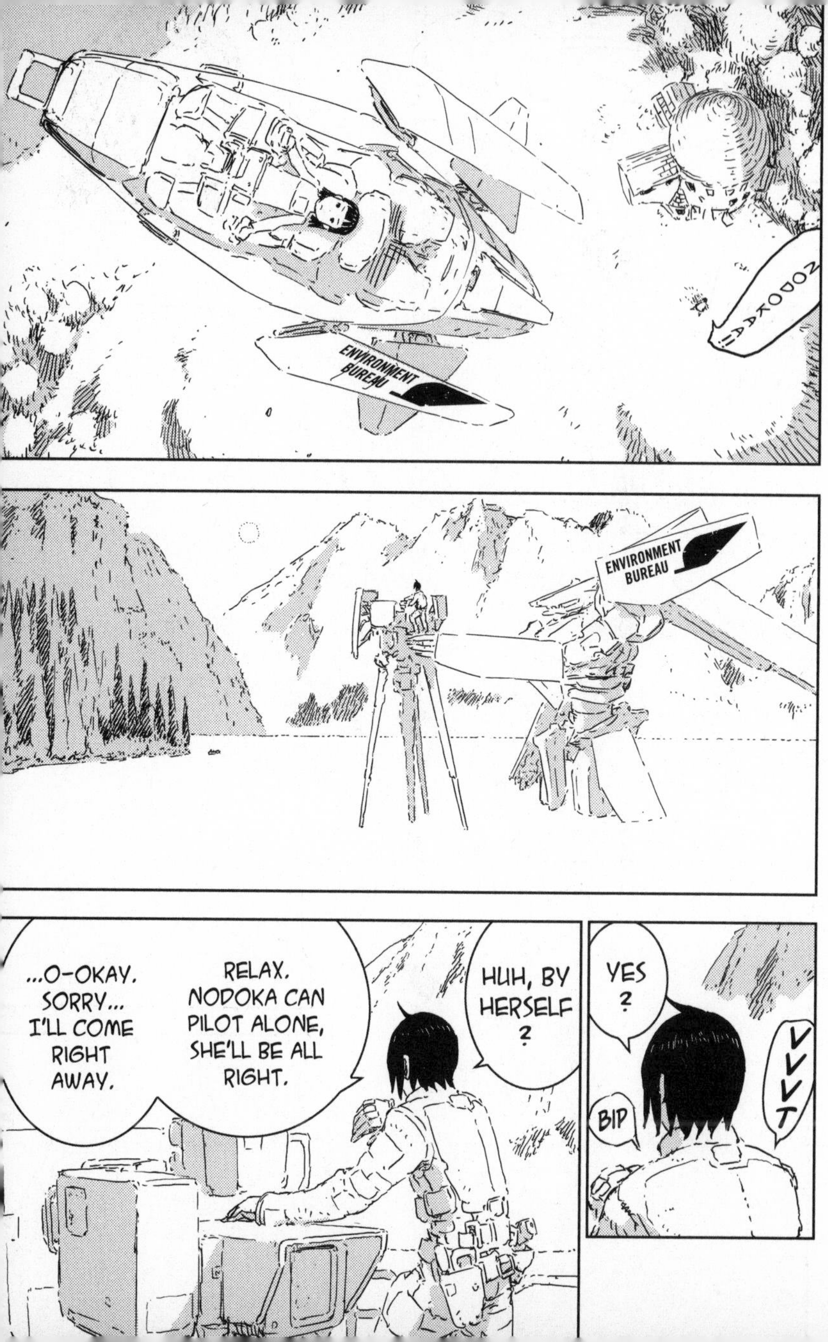
NODOKA!!
ENVIRONMENT BUREAU
ENVIRONMENT BUREAU
VVVT
BIP
YES?
HUH, BY HERSELF?
RELAX. NODOKA CAN PILOT ALONE, SHE'LL BE ALL RIGHT.
...O-OKAY. SORRY... I'LL COME RIGHT AWAY.

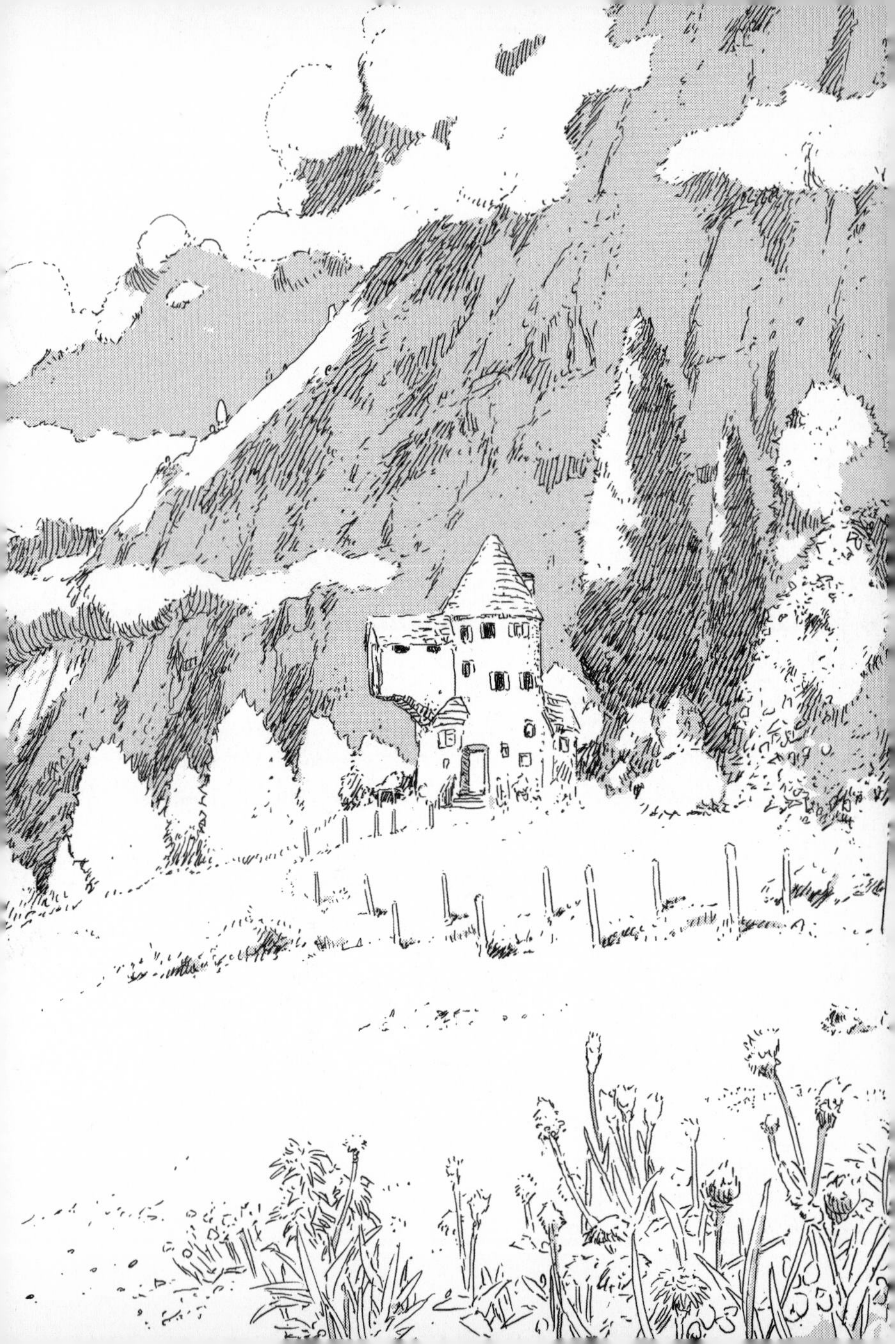

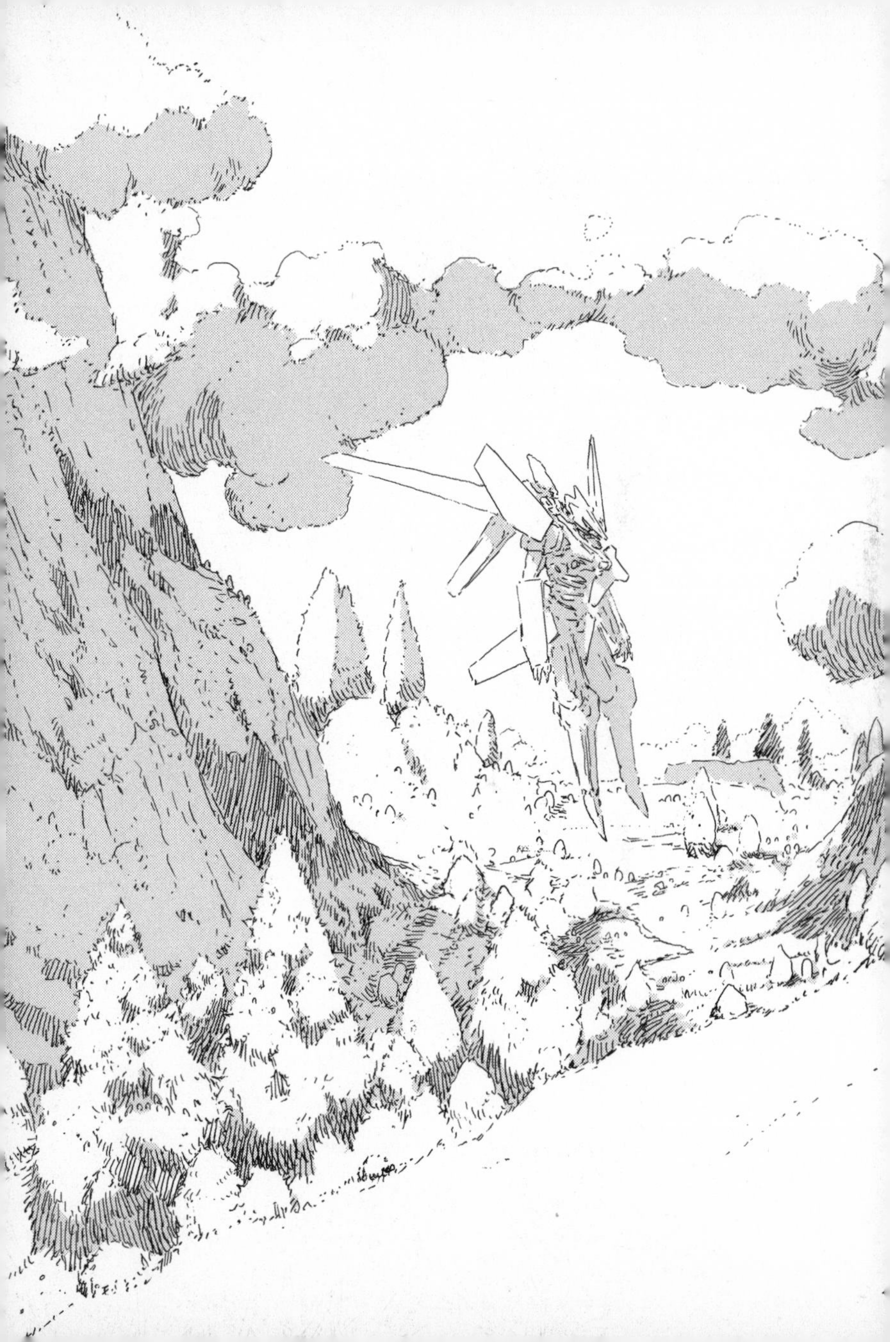

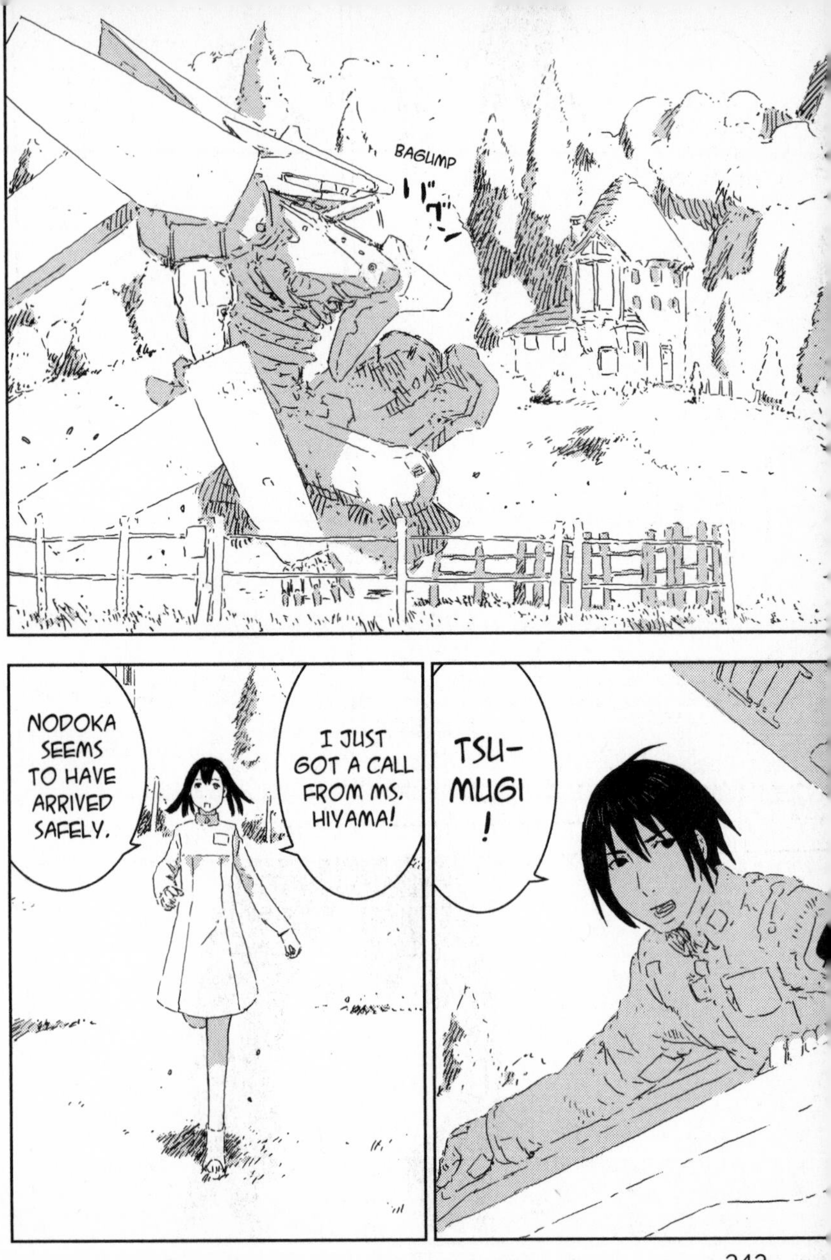
BAGUMP
TSU-MUGI!
I JUST GOT A CALL FROM MS. HIYAMA!
NODOKA SEEMS TO HAVE ARRIVED SAFELY.

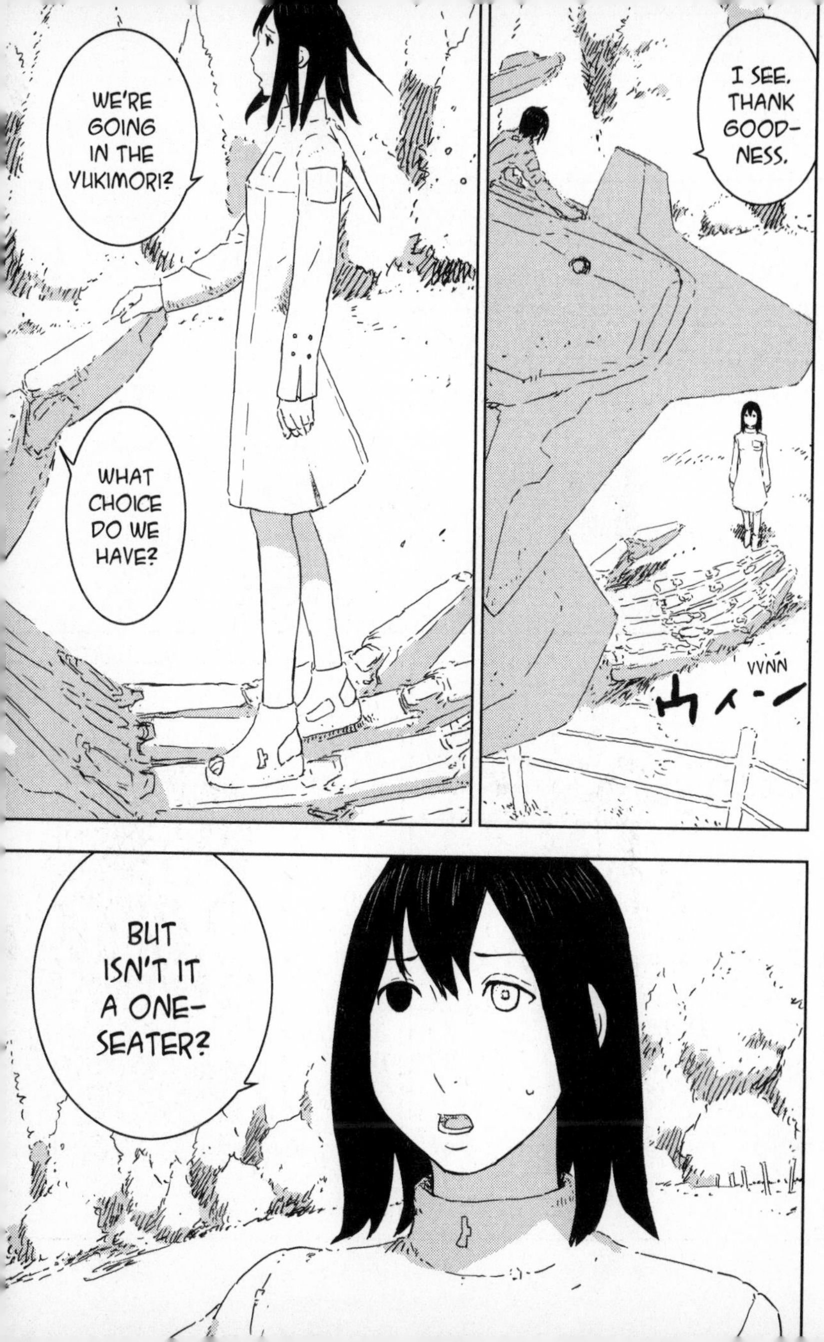
I SEE. THANK GOODNESS.
VVNN
ウィーン
WE'RE GOING IN THE YUKIMORI?
WHAT CHOICE DO WE HAVE?
BUT ISN'T IT A ONE-SEATER?

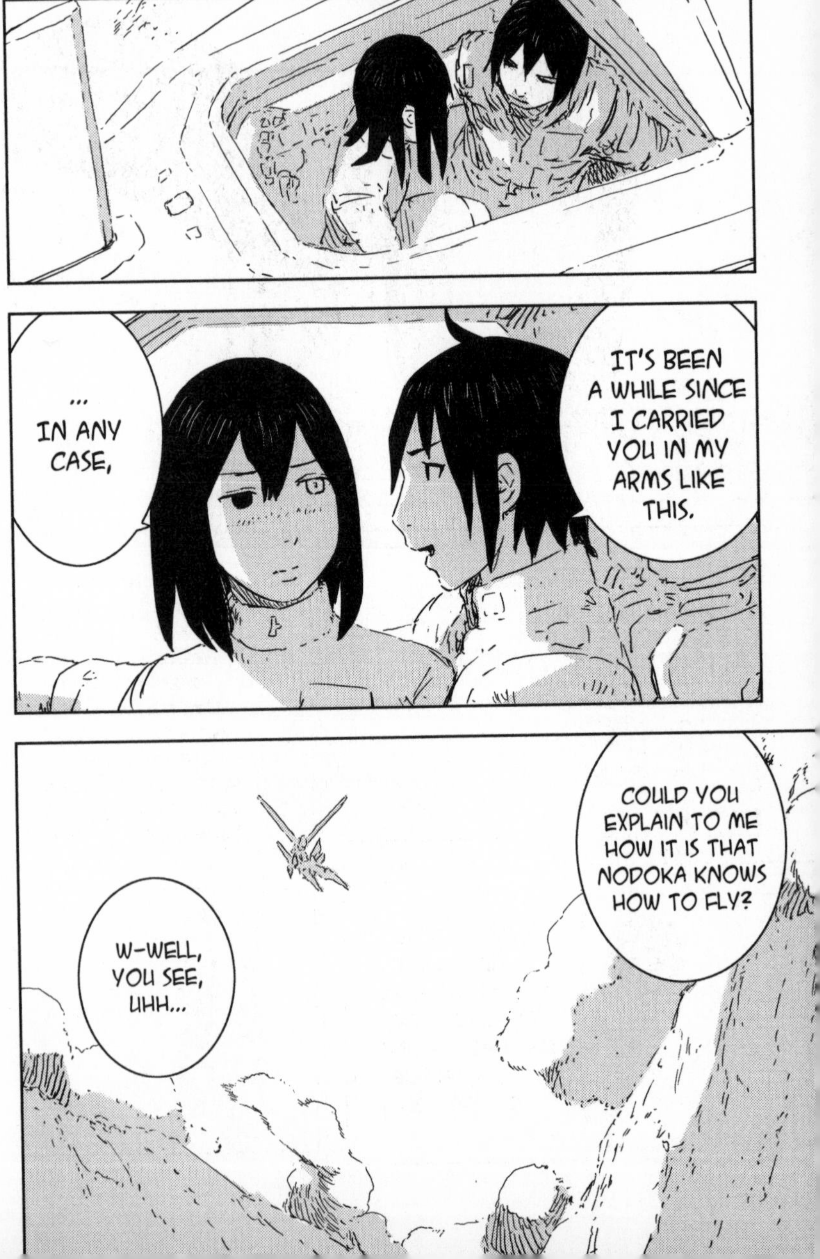
IT'S BEEN A WHILE SINCE I CARRIED YOU IN MY ARMS LIKE THIS.
... IN ANY CASE,
COULD YOU EXPLAIN TO ME HOW IT IS THAT NODOKA KNOWS HOW TO FLY?
W-WELL, YOU SEE, UHH...

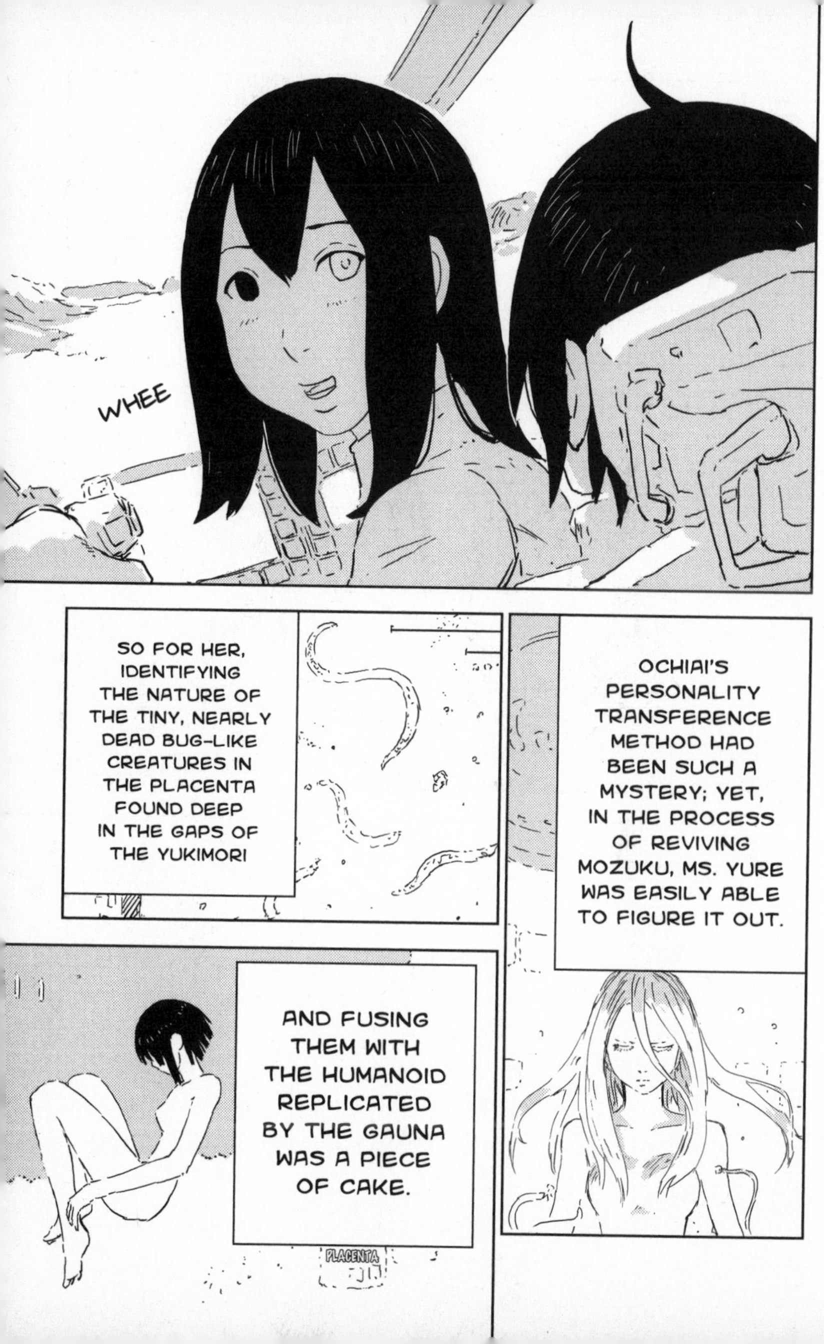
WHEE
OCHIAI'S PERSONALITY TRANSFERENCE METHOD HAD BEEN SUCH A MYSTERY; YET, IN THE PROCESS OF REVIVING MOZUKU, MS. YURE WAS EASILY ABLE TO FIGURE IT OUT.
SO FOR HER, IDENTIFYING THE NATURE OF THE TINY, NEARLY DEAD BUG-LIKE CREATURES IN THE PLACENTA FOUND DEEP IN THE GAPS OF THE YUKIMORI
AND FUSING THEM WITH THE HUMANOID REPLICATED BY THE GAUNA WAS A PIECE OF CAKE.
PLACENTA

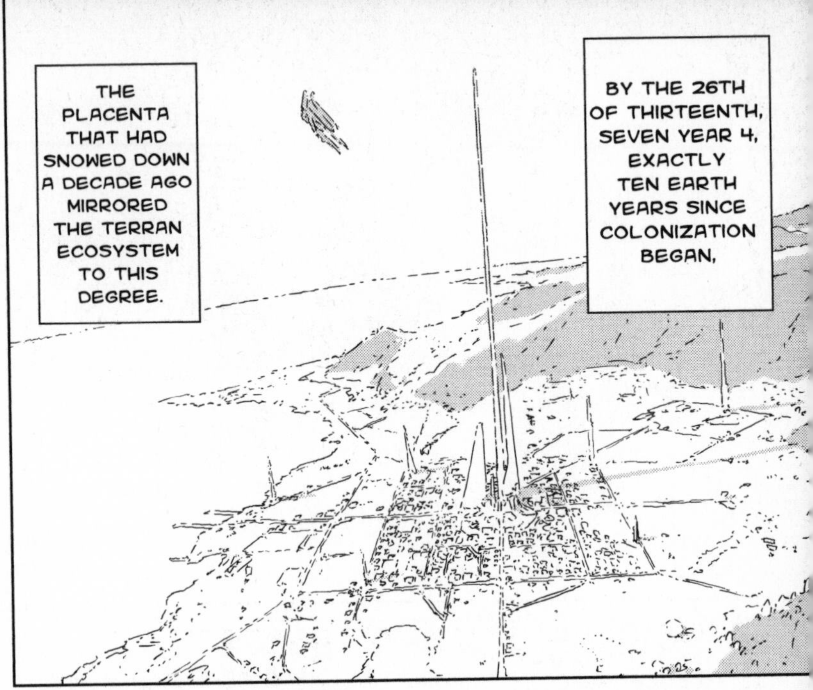
BY THE 26TH OF THIRTEENTH, SEVEN YEAR 4, EXACTLY TEN EARTH YEARS SINCE COLONIZATION BEGAN,
THE PLACENTA THAT HAD SNOWED DOWN A DECADE AGO MIRRORED THE TERRAN ECOSYSTEM TO THIS DEGREE.
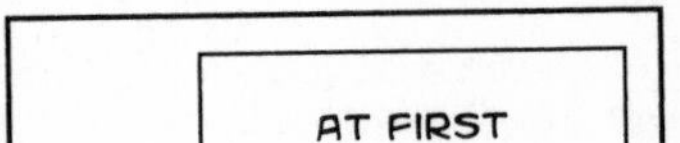
AT FIRST EVERYONE WAS A BIT CREEPED OUT, BUT TSUMUGI'S INPUT THAT "IT SHOULD BE FINE" CLINCHED IT.
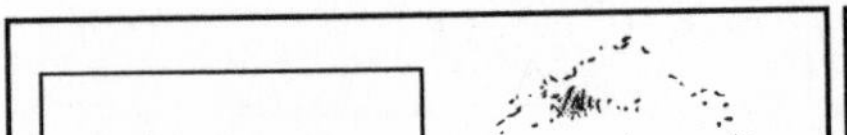
ABOUT HALF OF SIDONIA'S POPULATION DECIDED TO SETTLE PERMANENTLY ON SEVEN.

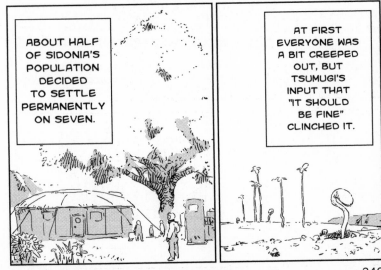

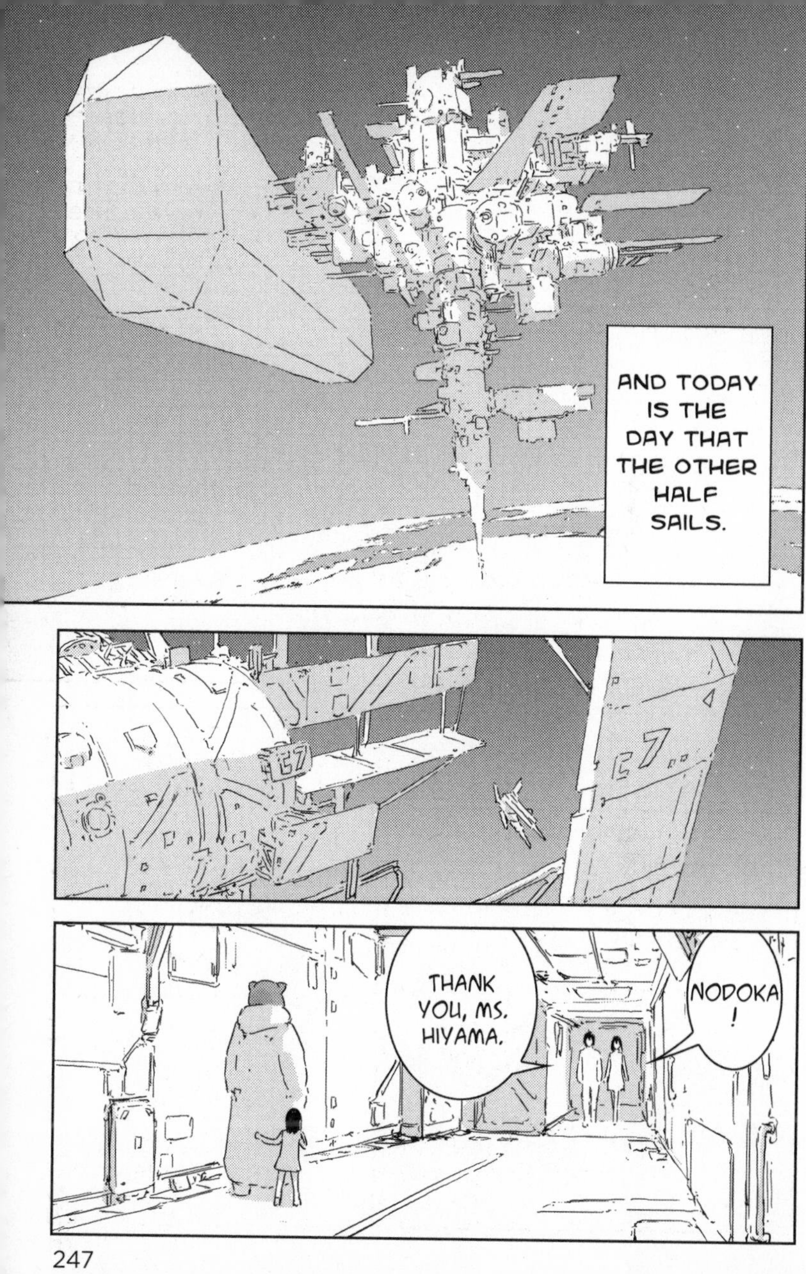
AND TODAY IS THE DAY THAT THE OTHER HALF SAILS.
NODOKA!
THANK YOU, MS. HIYAMA.

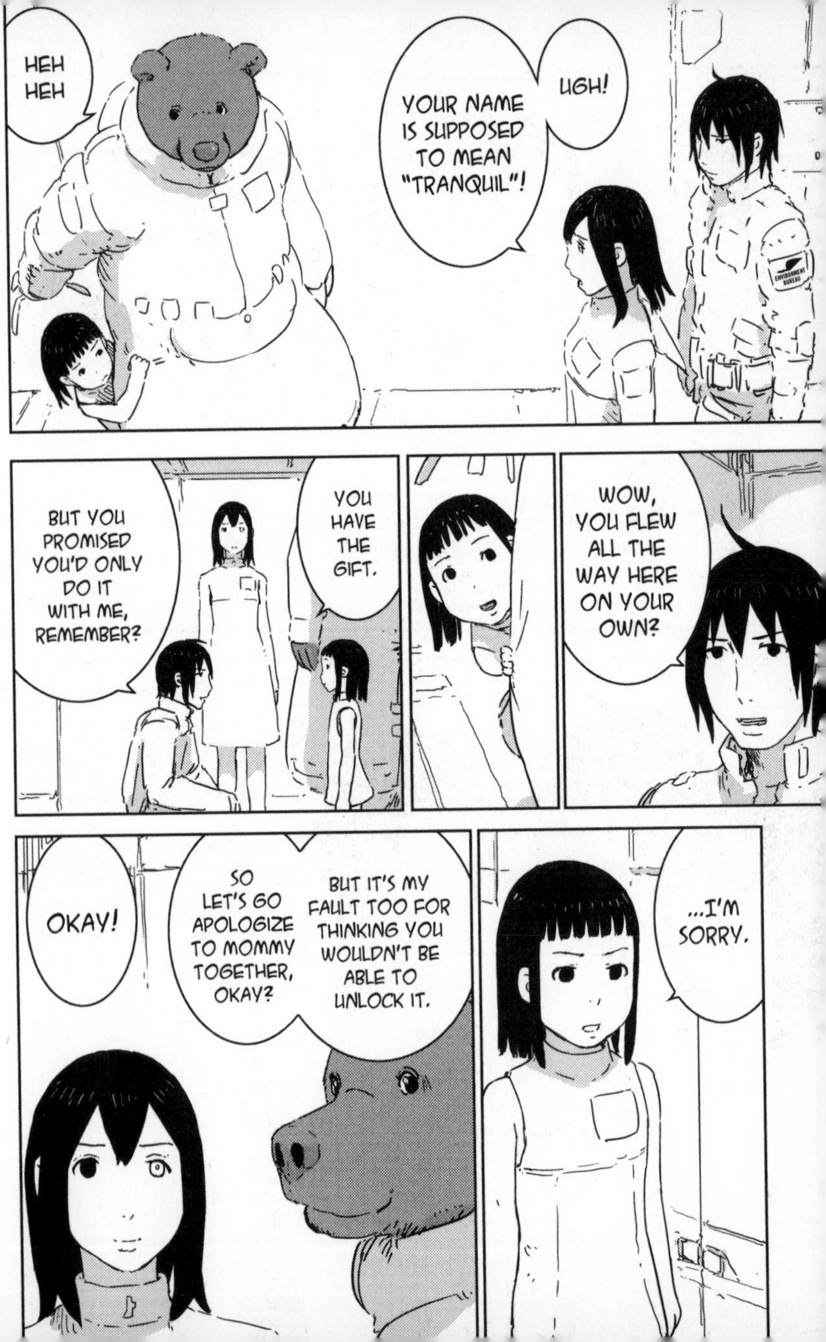
UGH!
YOUR NAME IS SUPPOSED TO MEAN "TRANQUIL"!
ENVIRONMENT BUREAU
HEH HEH
WOW, YOU FLEW ALL THE WAY HERE ON YOUR OWN?
YOU HAVE THE GIFT.
BUT YOU PROMISED YOU'D ONLY DO IT WITH ME, REMEMBER?
...I'M SORRY.
BUT IT'S MY FAULT TOO FOR THINKING YOU WOULDN'T BE ABLE TO UNLOCK IT.
SO LET'S GO APOLOGIZE TO MOMMY TOGETHER, OKAY?
OKAY!

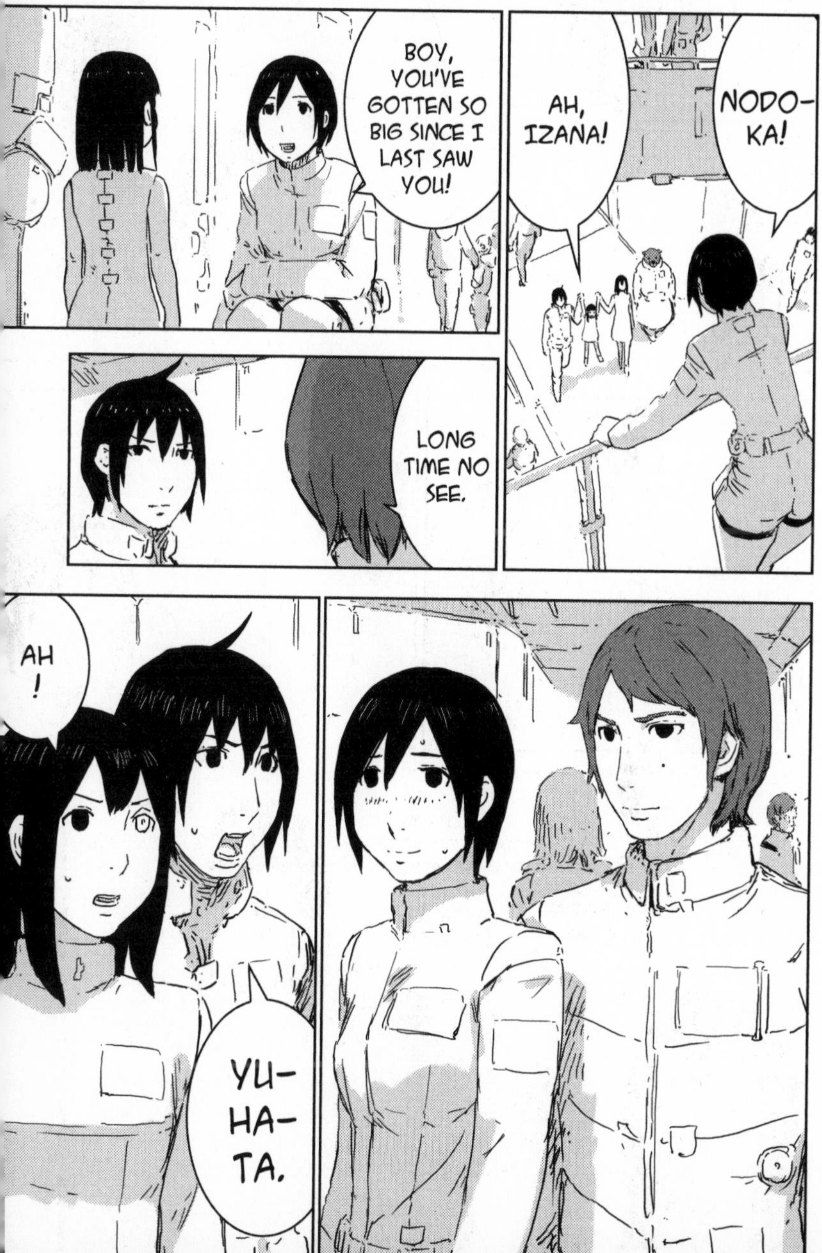
NODO-KA!
AH, IZANA!
BOY, YOU'VE GOTTEN SO BIG SINCE I LAST SAW YOU!
LONG TIME NO SEE.
AH!
YU-HA-TA.

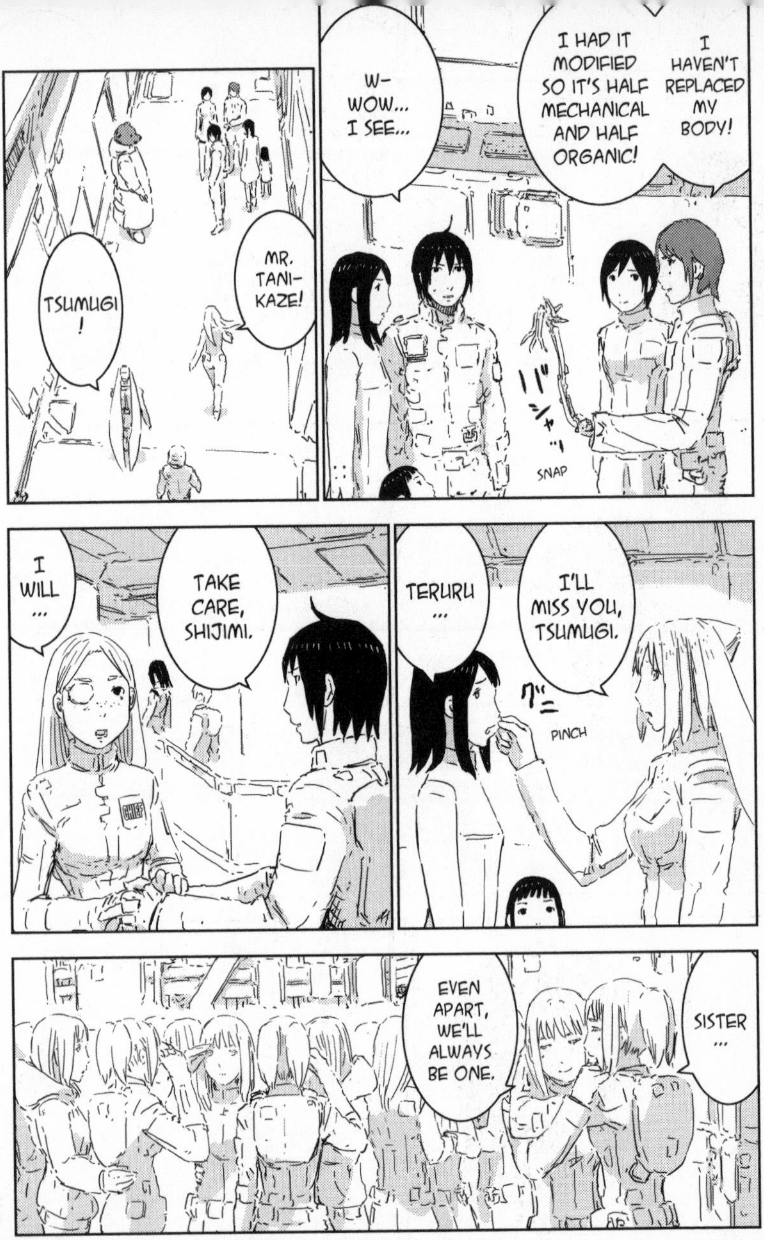

I HAVEN'T REPLACED MY BODY!
I HAD IT MODIFIED SO IT'S HALF MECHANICAL AND HALF ORGANIC!
W-WOW... I SEE...
バシャッ
SNAP
MR. TANI-KAZE!
TSUMUGI!
I'LL MISS YOU, TSUMUGI.
TERURU...
グニ
PINCH
TAKE CARE, SHIJIMI.
I WILL...
SISTER...
EVEN APART, WE'LL ALWAYS BE ONE.

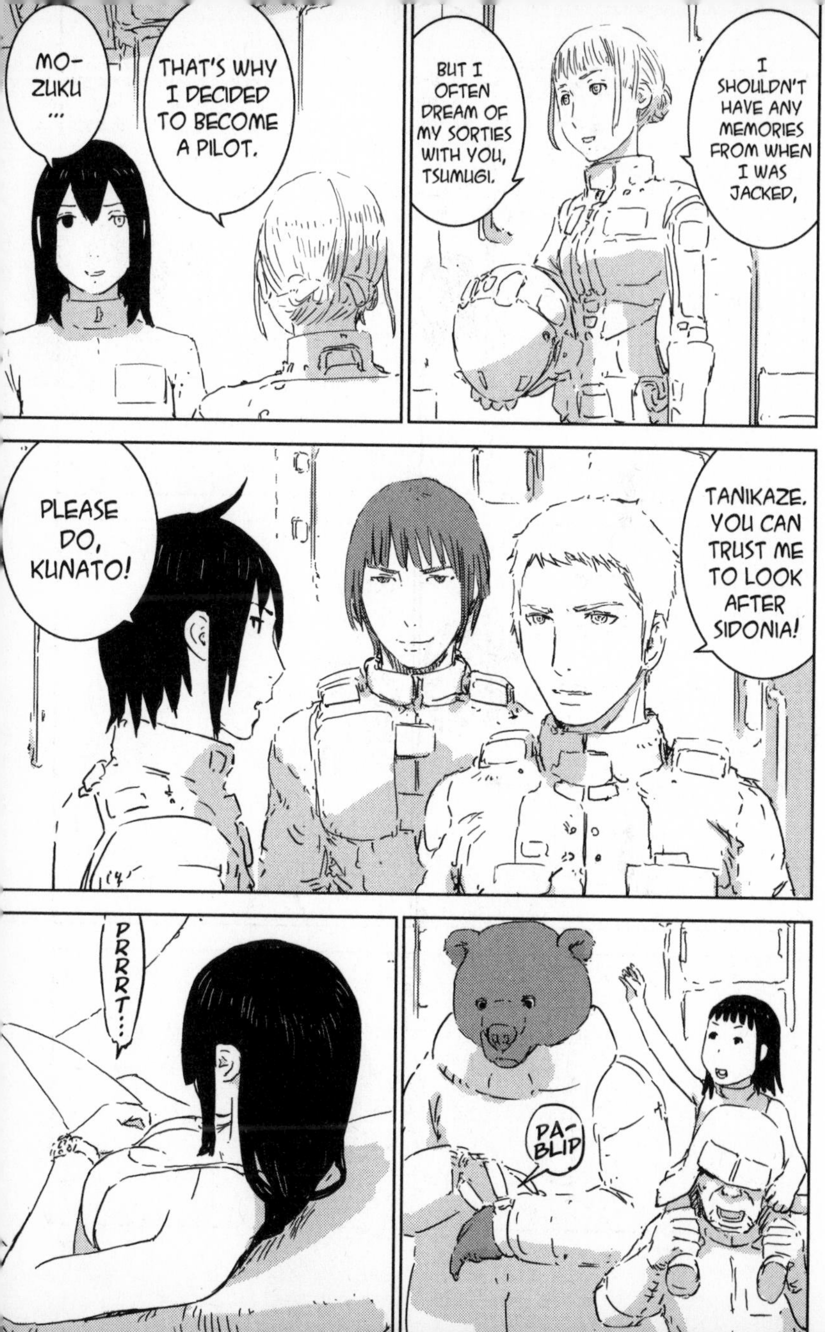
I SHOULDN'T HAVE ANY MEMORIES FROM WHEN I WAS JACKED,
BUT I OFTEN DREAM OF MY SORTIES WITH YOU, TSUMUGI.
THAT'S WHY I DECIDED TO BECOME A PILOT.
MO-ZUKU ...
TANIKAZE. YOU CAN TRUST ME TO LOOK AFTER SIDONIA!
PLEASE DO, KUNATO!
PA-BLIP
PRRRT...

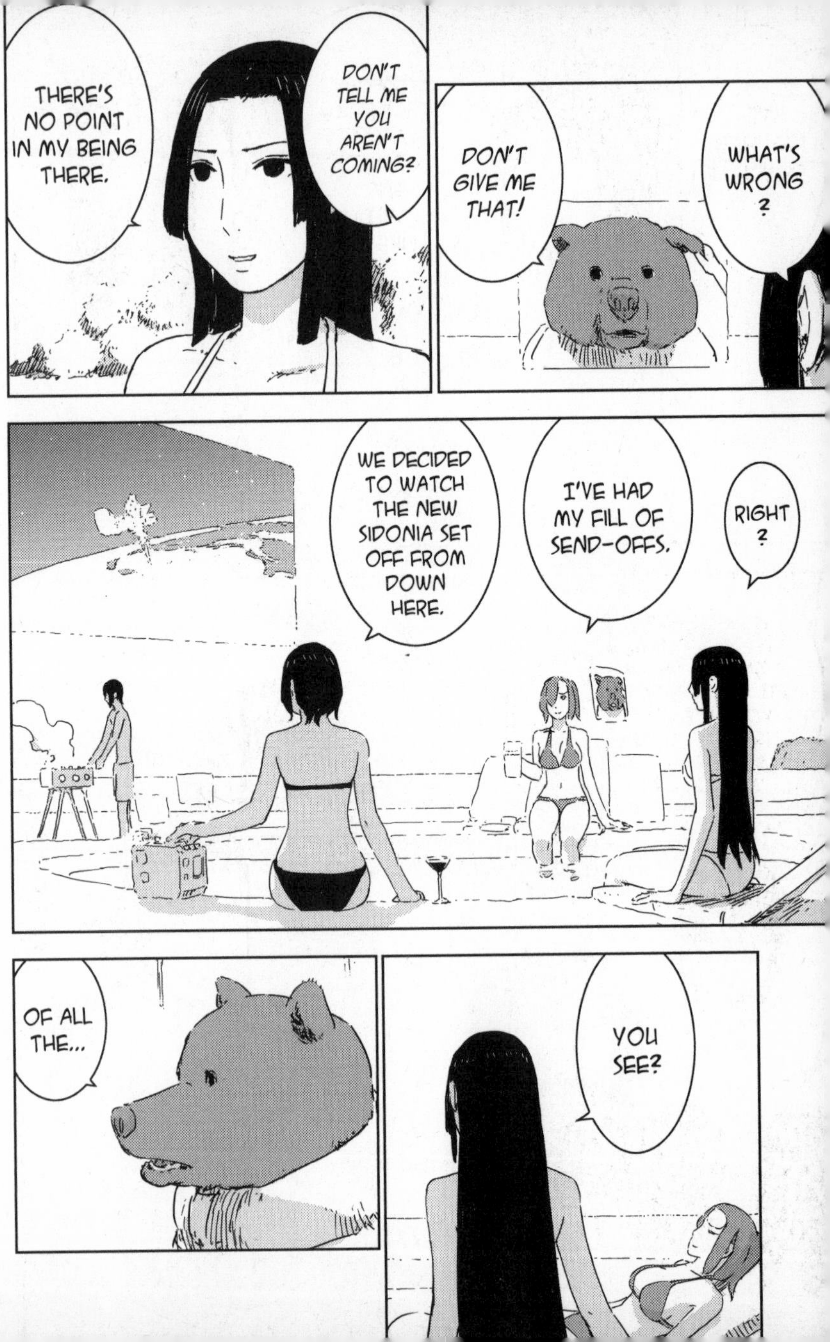
WHAT'S WRONG?
DON'T GIVE ME THAT!
DON'T TELL ME YOU AREN'T COMING?
THERE'S NO POINT IN MY BEING THERE.
RIGHT?
I'VE HAD MY FILL OF SEND-OFFS.
WE DECIDED TO WATCH THE NEW SIDONIA SET OFF FROM DOWN HERE.
YOU SEE?
OF ALL THE...

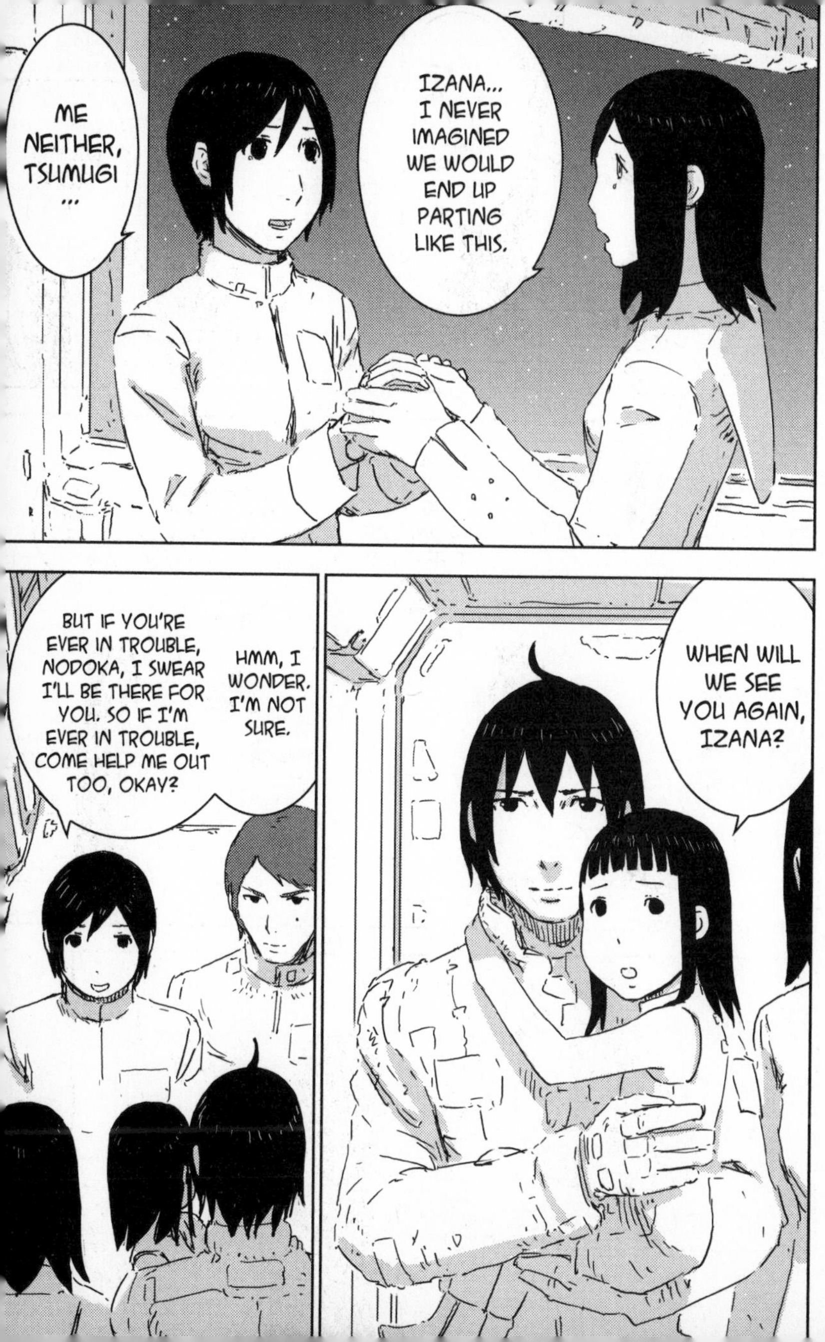
IZANA... I NEVER IMAGINED WE WOULD END UP PARTING LIKE THIS.
ME NEITHER, TSUMUGI...
WHEN WILL WE SEE YOU AGAIN, IZANA?
HMM, I WONDER. I'M NOT SURE.
BUT IF YOU'RE EVER IN TROUBLE, NODOKA, I SWEAR I'LL BE THERE FOR YOU. SO IF I'M EVER IN TROUBLE, COME HELP ME OUT TOO, OKAY?

BELIEVE IT OR NOT, NODOKA AND IZANA'S PROMISE THAT DAY COMES TO BE FULFILLED...

OKAY!

COMMANDER MIDORIKAWA! THE DEPARTURE CEREMONY IS BEGINNING!

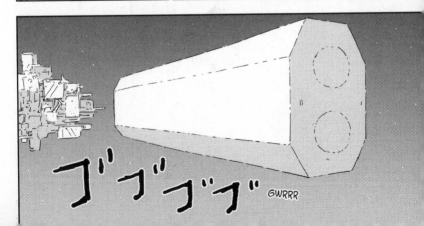

ゴブゴブ GWRRR

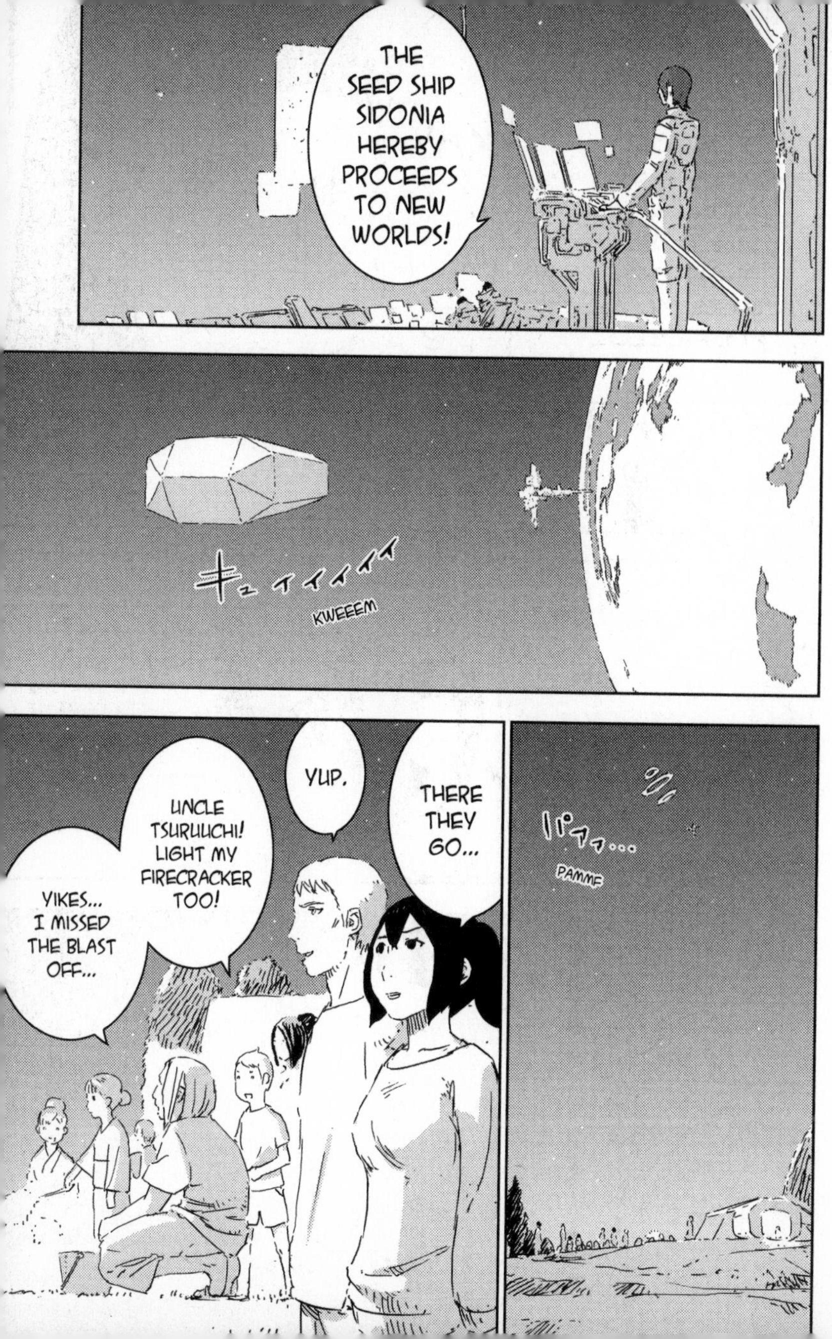
THE SEED SHIP SIDONIA HEREBY PROCEEDS TO NEW WORLDS!
キュイイイイイ
KWEEEM
パァァ...
PAMMF
THERE THEY GO...
YUP.
UNCLE TSURUUCHI! LIGHT MY FIRECRACKER TOO!
YIKES... I MISSED THE BLAST OFF...

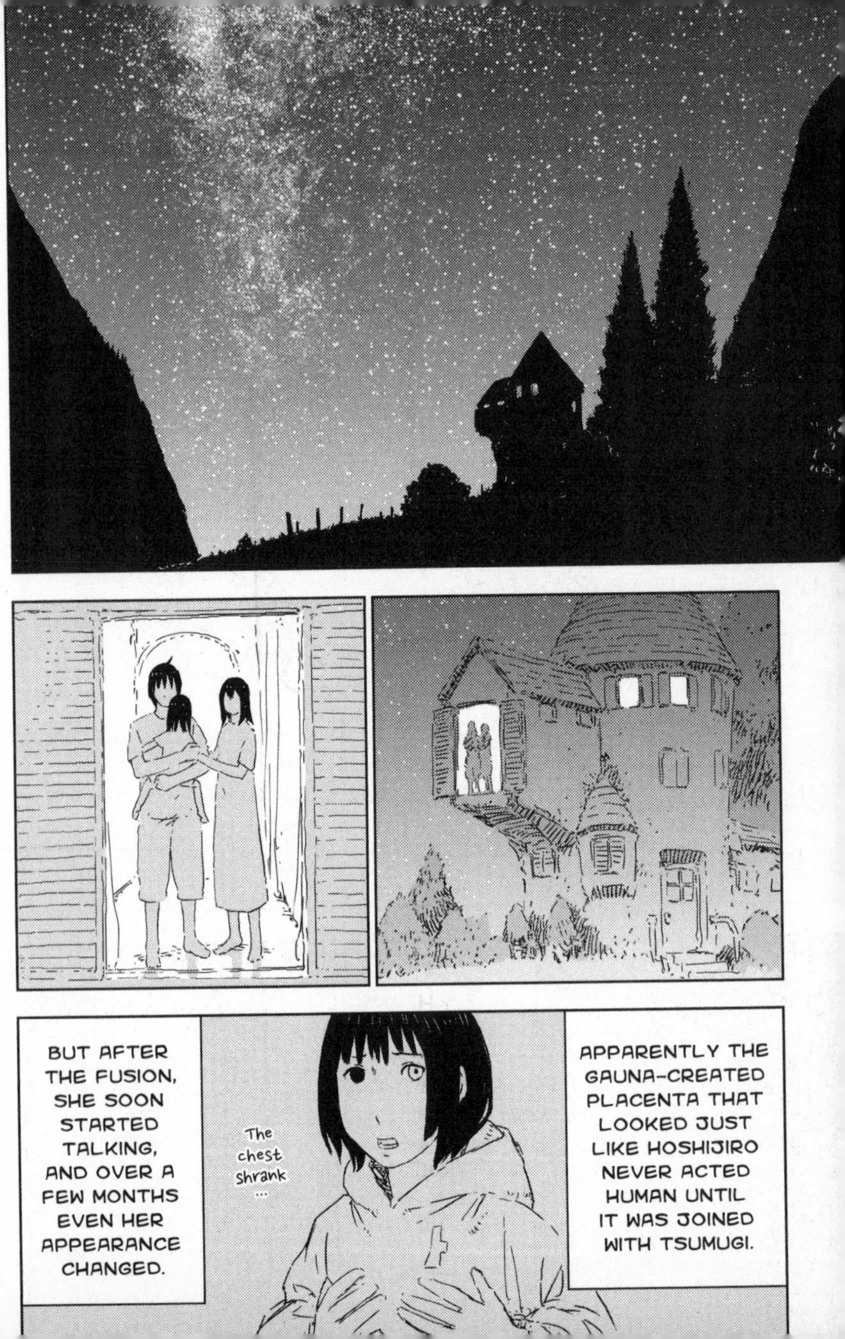
APPARENTLY THE GAUNA-CREATED PLACENTA THAT LOOKED JUST LIKE HOSHIJIRO NEVER ACTED HUMAN UNTIL IT WAS JOINED WITH TSUMUGI.
The chest shrank …
BUT AFTER THE FUSION, SHE SOON STARTED TALKING, AND OVER A FEW MONTHS EVEN HER APPEARANCE CHANGED.

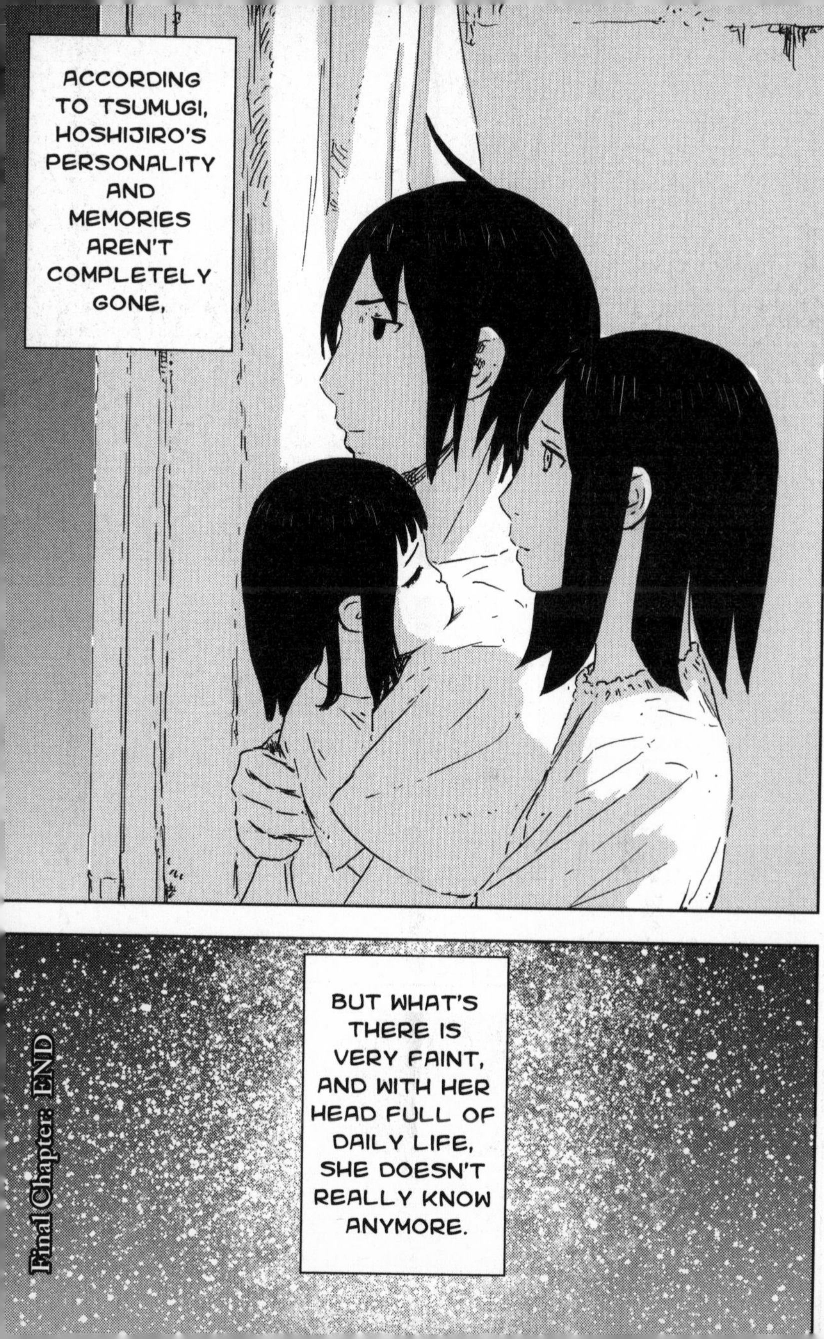
ACCORDING TO TSUMUGI, HOSHIJIRO'S PERSONALITY AND MEMORIES AREN'T COMPLETELY GONE,
BUT WHAT'S THERE IS VERY FAINT, AND WITH HER HEAD FULL OF DAILY LIFE, SHE DOESN'T REALLY KNOW ANYMORE.
Final Chapter: END

Bound Format Extra: "Nodoka Tanikaze's Battle"

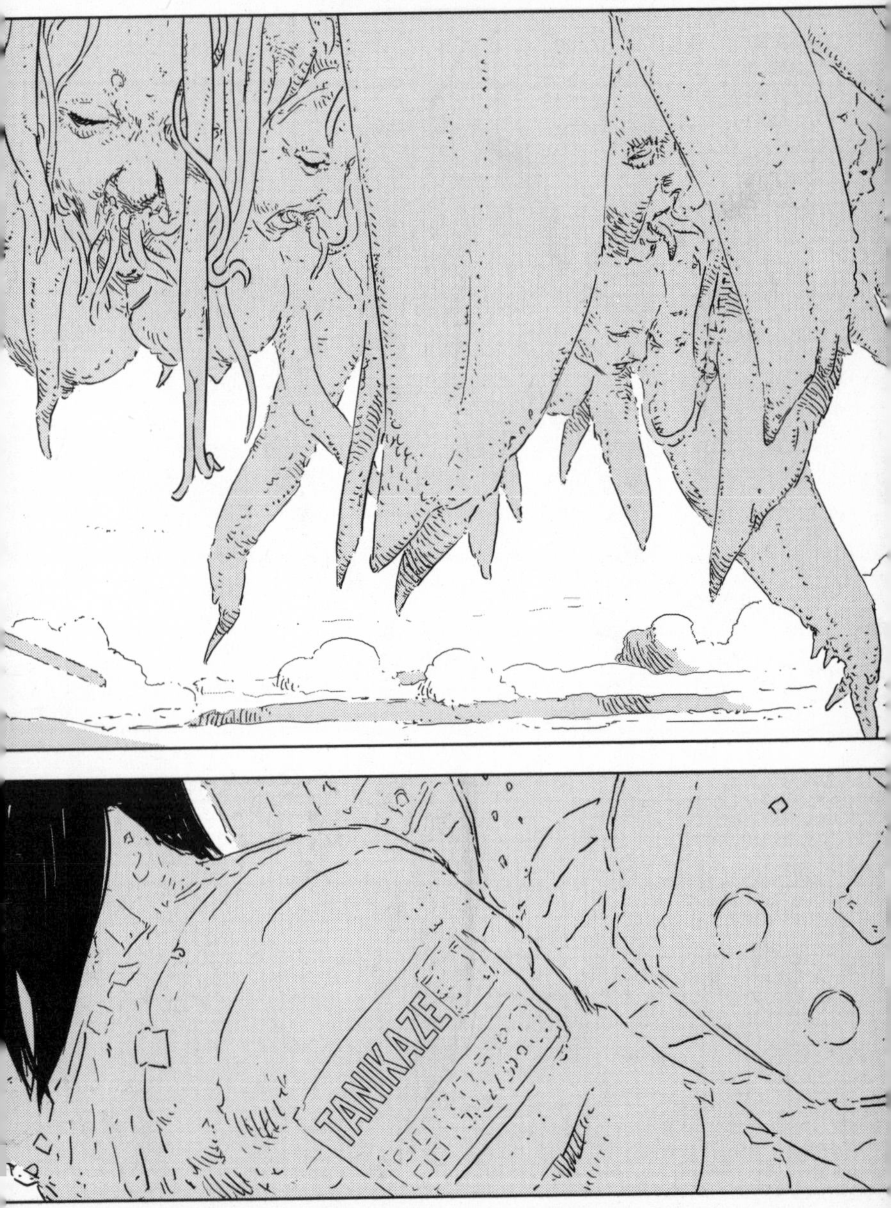
TANIKAZE